The

Modern Encyclopedia

of

Russian *and* Soviet

History

CONTRIBUTORS

Gustave Alef
University of Oregon

Audrey L. Altstadt
University of Massachusetts at Amherst

Milka T. Bliznakov
Virginia Polytechnic Institute and State University

William C. Brumfield
Tulane University

Julia Brun-Zeijmis
Lincoln University

Loren D. Calder
Wilfred Laurier University

Otto Preston Chaney
United States Army War College

William J. Chase
University of Pittsburgh

William R. Copeland
University of Helsinki

Richard D.G. Crockatt
University of East Anglia

Alexander Dallin
Stanford University

Terence Emmons
Stanford University

Robert O. Freedman
Baltimore Hebrew University

Theodore H. Friedgut
Hebrew University of Jerusalem

Anna Geifman
Boston University

Musya M. Glants
Harvard University

Hugh F. Graham
California State College at Bakersfield

David M. Griffiths
University of North Carolina at Chapel Hill

Irina Gutkin
University of California at Los Angeles

Richard Hellie
University of Chicago

Linda J. Ivanits
Pennsylvania State University

Gerald J. Janecek
University of Kentucky

Stephen F. Jones
Mount Holyoke College

Mark N. Katz
George Mason University

Valerie A. Kivelson
University of Michigan

Phillip E. Koerper
Jacksonville State University

Edward J. Lazzerini
University of New Orleans

Therese M. Malhame
State University of New York

Alfred G. Meyer
University of Michigan

Michael M. Naydan
Pennsylvania State College

Barbara A. Niemczyk
Dickinson College

Joseph L. Nogee
University of Houston

Norma C. Noonan
Augsburg College

John O. Norman
Western Michigan University

Samuel A. Oppenheim
California State University

Alexander Orbach
University of Pittsburgh

Rakhmiel Peltz
Columbia University

George N. Rhyne
Dickinson College

Joshua Rubinstein
Amnesty International

Steven O. Sabol
Georgia State University

Alfred E. Senn
University of Wisconsin

Michael Share
University of Hong Kong

continued on page vi...

The Modern Encyclopedia

of

Russian and Soviet

History

➤➤➤-➤➤➤-➤➤➤-➤➤➤-➤➤➤-➤➤➤⦀⦀-⦀⦀-⦀⦀-⦀⦀-⦀⦀-⦀⦀

Edited by
George N. Rhyne

➤➤➤-➤➤➤-➤➤➤-➤➤➤-➤➤➤-➤➤➤⦀⦀-⦀⦀-⦀⦀-⦀⦀-⦀⦀-⦀⦀

Vol. 55

SUPPLEMENT

WITCHCRAFT IN RUSSIA –

ZVENIGOROD

Academic International Press

1993

ACKNOWLEDGEMENTS

I would like to thank the Charles A. Dana Student Intern Program and especially my Dana Interns John Hope, Jennifer Simpson, and Christine Bombaro. I would be remiss if I did not also recognize Gladys Cashman, secretary of the Dickinson College History Department, for her frequent help; Peter von Wahlde of Academic International Press for his advice and encouragement; and my wife Gloria for her infinite patience.

George N. Rhyne

THE MODERN ENCYCLOPEDIA OF RUSSIAN AND SOVIET HISTORY
Volume 55

Copyright 1993 by Academic International Press
Library of Congress Catalog Card Number: 75-11091
ISBN: 0-87569-064-5

Title page by King & Queen Press
Composition by Janice Frye

Printed in the United States of America
By direct subscription with the publisher.

*A list of Academic International Press publications
is found at the end of this volume.*

ACADEMIC INTERNATIONAL PRESS
Box 1111 Gulf Breeze FL 32562 USA

Preparation of this volume

was greatly facilitated by the

support of

Dickinson College

CONTRIBUTORS (continued)

Lewis H. Siegelbaum
Michigan State University

Wallace H. Spaulding
Central Intelligence Agency, ret.

Margaret K. Stolee
State University of New York at Geneseo

Patrick R. Taylor
University of Tennessee at Martin

Leon I. Twarog
Ohio State University

Jeanette E. Tuve
Cleveland State University

Robert B. Valliant
University of Hawaii at Manoa

Lynne Viola
University of Toronto

Mark L. von Hagen
Columbia University

Rex A. Wade
George Mason University

Allen S. Whiting
University of Arizona

Seth L. Wolitz
University of Texas at Austin

Richard S. Wortman
Harriman Institute

Natalia Zitzelsberger
New York Public Library

W

WITCHCRAFT IN RUSSIA. Meddling in human affairs or inflicting harm through supernatural means. Witchcraft accusations appear in Russia from earliest times through at least the early twentieth century.

The English term "witchcraft" subsumes a wide variety of Russian words indicating various forms of magic practiced or suspected among the population throughout most of Russia's history. Whereas the English word generally connotes the practice of evil or black magic, the Russian variants—koldovstvo, vedovstvo, charodeistvo, and others—imply a far more ambiguous magical practice. Like the prototypical witch of Russian folk lore, Baba Yaga, Russian witches generally were capable of using their powers for either good or evil, depending on the circumstances and on the merits of the individuals involved. Practitioners likewise were known by a variety of terms, most frequently koldun for male and ved'ma for female witches.

Medieval Russian chronicles record episodic outbreaks of witchcraft hysteria through the early centuries of Rus' development. The Primary Chronicle relates that in pre-Christian times Kievan princes consulted pagan sorcerers and fortune-tellers, who continued to appear in chronicle entries into early Christian times. The thirteenth-century Bishop Serapion of Vladimir condemned witchcraft belief as a pagan superstition, and later churchmen also attempted to discredit the power of witches. The ecclesiastical campaign to invalidate the entire basis of magical powers did not succeed in eliminating popular belief in the efficacy of witchcraft. The linkage between paganism and witchcraft endured, although in time the explicitly pagan practices associated with sorcery in the Kievan period faded. By Muscovite times practicing witches relied more on a combination of naturalistic folk practices and explicitly satanic permutations of Christian rites than on the assistance of pagan deities, although official decrees still linked them with paganism.

Ivan IV, the Terrible, was the first Muscovite ruler to take concrete measures to confront the problem of witchcraft in the realm. After the Stoglav Church Council of 1551 voiced concern over lingering paganism in the realm, an official decree transferred witchcraft cases from ecclesiastical to secular courts. During the seventeenth century this trend continued, witchcraft receiving increasing attention from secular and church authorities. Penitentials and sermons of the seventeenth century often turned to problems of witchcraft. A series of decrees issued by Tsar Alexis Mikhailovich outlawed all practices associated with witchcraft, including pagan worship, fortune-telling, and herbal healing. These decrees mandated increasingly harsh punishments for the practitioners. In 1648 a decree prescribed that witches be beaten with a knout and repeat offenders be exiled. In 1653 a new decree escalated the punishment to burning, a harsh resolve which was repeated in 1682 during the reign of Tsar

Fedor Alekseevich. Peter the Great issued more comprehensive legislation in 1716, specifying execution for practicing witches. Only during the reign of Catherine II did Russia join the general trend of the Enlightenment in demoting witchcraft from a dangerous capital offense to a misdemeanor involving attempted fraud.

In spite of this mandate from the empress, witches retained their menacing power in the popular eye. Ethnographic studies of the nineteenth century indicate that lynchings of witches who had invoked the community's ire were not uncommon. Peasant communities continued to consult local witches at least into the early twentieth century.

Witchcraft was suspected not only among the common people but also in the highest political circles. In Muscovite times rumors of witchcraft quite frequently surrounded prominent women of the grand princely and later the tsarist court. Generally these charges surfaced during periods of change or competition within the inner circles at court. This was particularly the case when one set of royal in-laws, customarily the closest advisers to the tsar or grand prince, replaced another. Evidently practices and charges of witchcraft were considered effective weapons in the struggles of marriage politics at court. In the late fifteenth century during a prolonged struggle over the succession rumors circulated that Ivan III's second wife, Grand Princess Sofia Paleologue, practiced sorcery. Again in the early sixteenth century, when Vasily III banished his first wife, Solomonida Saburova, to a convent, rumors asserted that she had resorted to magic to try to keep her husband's love. During the sixteenth century interest in witchcraft rose. The chronicles report that in 1547 rioting Muscovites hostile to the powerful Glinsky clan blamed their problems on Anna Glinskaia, grandmother of young Ivan IV. They claimed that Glinskaia had scattered ground-up human hearts in the waters of the Moscow River, with accompanying incantations, presumably to further her clans' prospects.

The same association between witchcraft and high politics at times of uncertainty and dynastic change continued into the seventeenth and eighteenth centuries. Charges of sorcery were lodged both by and against Boris Godunov, and then against his successor, the first False Dmitry. Throughout the century the tsars' brides were thought to suffer from magical efforts to curse their success, through incantations and poisonous potions. As depicted in a well-known print of the early eighteenth century, rumors credited Catherine I's hold over her husband, Peter the Great, to her sorcery.

Beyond occasional brief chronicle entries and a few sermons, little evidence survives to document the actual practice or prosecution of witches until the beginning of the seventeenth century. From the reign of Boris Godunov on through the mid-eighteenth century transcripts of secular trials of witches survive, documenting the particular charges lodged against suspected witches, the circumstances under which such charges were made, and the social profiles of both accusers and accused. The most intriguing finding emerging from analyses of court records is that at the latest count 68 percent of those accused of witchcraft in Muscovite courts were male. This gender distribution contrasts strikingly with the familiar profile of witches in the West and even more surprisingly contradicts the Russian ecclesiastical and folkloric image of the female witch.

A significant number of magical spells survived and were recorded from the seventeenth through nineteenth centuries. Together with ethnographic evidence from the nineteenth century, the numerous spells indicate that witchcraft accusations had some basis in reality. Self-styled practitioners of magic did exist in the Russian countryside. A large number of works have appeared on the subject of Russian spells and incantation. Much of the discussion concentrated on the literary and folkloric value of this category of folk production, but some works addressed the question of the basis of magical power as expressed in the surviving spells. Debate has taken place in the literature about whether folk magic relied on a Christian, pagan, or folkloric principles. The most sophisticated recent work, such as that of N.N. Pokrovskii, acknowledges that all of these forces could coexist without any sense of contradiction in the peasant practitioner of magic. Some spells invoked the assistance of the Christian God, the Virgin Mary, or saints and angels, but the majority relied on a more animistic base. The force of analogy was employed often, so that a love potion might suggest that a passion should burn as intensely as a fire or a curse might suggest that an enemy wither like a leaf. Satanism or demonism played a less central role in Russian sorcery than in much of the West, and many of the classic elements of witchcraft lore in the West, such as night-flying and black sabbaths, were absent. Satanic spells did occur in the records of the seventeenth and eighteenth century, including renunciation of God, church, and family and explicit oaths of loyalty to Satan and his minions.

Most charges of witchcraft in Russia involved hexes rather than any more involved demonism. Much of the historical research on Russian witchcraft emerged in connection with the history of traditional folk medicine. Legal records from the seventeenth through nineteenth centuries show that Russians turned to folk healers when they were ill, all the more so in the Muscovite period when no other alternative medicine existed in the countryside. Witchcraft charges were brought against healers, indicating that suspicion accompanied faith in them. The mystical power to heal implied a kind of unknowable power that could be turned toward any ends, so healers often were both respected and feared. Nearly one-third of witchcraft trials from the seventeenth century involved sorcery charges against healers. Particularly when a healer failed to cure a patient, the would-be healer was prone to charges of sorcery. Another high risk category was the healer who attempted to cure a fit of spirit possession, an affliction affecting mainly women. A healer capable of exorcising dark spirits could be suspected of causing the possession in the first place.

Porcha, or "spoiling," was the common charge against witches from Muscovite times through the late nineteenth century. Victims of spoiling manifested a variety of symptoms, ranging from indeterminate "withering" and wasting diseases to the most dramatic manifestation of what is known in the West as possession and in Russian as klikushestvo or "shrieking." Shriekers, who were most commonly married women, writhed in agony, called out in animal voices, "hiccupped," and "said things not pleasing to man or to God" (TsGADA [M.], fond. 210, Prikaznyi stol, no. 300, fols. 1-89v., passim). The hysterical symptoms of possession remained remarkably unchanged from the seventeenth through the twentieth century. Ethnographers and historians generally agree that spirit possession provided an outlet for the tensions and oppression of a severely oppressed group in society, married women, although the particularly burdensome conditions and aspects of their subordinate position that most likely produced their outbreaks changed over the centuries.

Historians of Muscovite witchcraft have attempted to set the problem in comparative perspective by asking whether Russia's witchcraft persecution ever reached the scale or intensity of the hysteria experienced in much of Western Europe in the sixteenth and seventeenth centuries. The surviving records indicate that few cases reached trial. Only a few hundred seventeenth-century court cases have been catalogued. Particularly in light of the evidence that witchcraft practice was actually extremely widespread in the Russian countryside, these numbers of trials suggest that few practitioners of magic ended up in court. Furthermore, in spite of its harsh edicts against sorcerers, the Muscovite state did not actually adhere to the intensity of its decrees. Tsar Alexis Mikhailovich's mid-seventeenth-century legislation prescribed death by burning for witches, but throughout the century exile to the borderlands and registration in infantry regiments remained the punishment most commonly dealt to convicted male witches. Although concerned with the moral welfare of the Orthodox realm, the responses of the tsarist authorities to witchcraft focused on the more pressing need to staff their armies and protect their borders.

The evidence of the early modern and modern periods suggests that magic of all varieties commonly was practiced in the Russian countryside, and was viewed with some degree of distrust and unease by the population and the state alike. For a variety of reasons, including faith in magical powers, the absence of any alternative mode of healing, a need to man the military frontiers, and perhaps a historical tolerance of the traditional dvoeverie or dual belief in an admixture of paganism and Christianity, practicing or suspected witches never suffered the same degree of persecution as their counterparts in Western Europe.

Bibliography: The best historical survey in English is by Russell Zguta, "Witchcraft Trials in Seventeenth-Century Russia," *American Historical Review*, 82 (1977), 1187-1207. A.A. Turilov and A.V. Chernetsov, "O pis'mennykh istochnikakh izucheniia vostochnoslavianskikh narodnykh verovanii i obriadov," *Sovetskaia etnografiia*, No. 1 (1986), 95-103 is very useful in describing sources for studying early modern witchcraft. The most complete source publication of witchcraft trials is N. Novombergskii, *Koldovstvo v Moskovskoi Rusi XVII st.* (SPb., 1906). The classic work in Russian is S.V. Maksimov, *Nechistaia, nevedomaia i krestnaia sila* (SPb., 1903). See also N. N. Pokrovskii, "Tetrad' zagovorov 1734 goda," Aleksei Trofimovich Moskalenko, ed., *Nauchnyi ateizm, religiia i sovremennost'* (Novosibirsk, 1987); Linda Ivanits, *Russian Folk Belief* (Armonk, N.Y., 1989); Samuel C. Ramer, "Traditional Healers and Peasant Culture in Russia, 1861-1917," Esther Kingston-Mann and Timothy Mixter, eds., *Peasant Economy, Culture, and Politics of European Russia, 1800-1921* (Princeton, 1991); Valerie A. Kivelson, "Through the Prism of Witchcraft. Gender and Social Change in Seventeenth-Century Muscovy," Barbara Evans Clements, et. al., eds., *Russia's Women. Accommodation, Resistance, Transformation* (Berkeley, 1991).

Valerie A. Kivelson

WOJNAROWSKA, CEZARYNA WANDA (1864-1911). Polish revolutionary, political journalist, feminist. One of the founders and leaders of the Association of the Workers Social-Democrats Abroad. Led opposition in Poland's Social Democratic parties to Rosa Luxemburg's dominant views on the question of national independence.

Wojnarowska was born on 1 May 1864 (1861 and 1862 also cited) in Kamieniec Podolski, Ukraine, to an impoverished Polish gentry family. In 1878, after graduation from the female gymnasium in Kishinev, she began to study medicine in St. Petersburg's Medical School for Women at the Military Medical Academy. As a student she became involved in the revolutionary activities of Polish and Russian youth. In 1879 Wojnarowska arrived in Warsaw and became one of the pioneers of the socialist movement in the Kingdom of Poland together with such revolutionaries as Ludwik Warynski, the founder of the first Polish Marxist party, Proletariat (1882). As a result she was arrested and imprisoned in the infamous X Pavilion of the Warsaw Citadel (1879-1881). In 1881 she was arrested briefly in Odessa for helping Russian revolutionaries and in 1883 imprisoned in Cracow for her involvement in Proletariat.

By the end of 1883 Wojnarowska was forced to settle in Geneva where she met such other Polish political exiles as Szymon Diksztajn, Kazimierz Dluski, and Stanislaw Mendelson as well as the Russian revolutionaries, Georgy Valentinovich Plekhanov, Vera Ivanovna Zasulich, and Lev Grigorievich Deutsch. In Switzerland Wojnarowska distinguished herself as a well-read and highly educated young woman. She was one of the few who actually studied Marx's *Capital* in its entirety. She also studied history and political science at Geneva University. In addition Wojnarowska worked as an editor of the emigré socialist journals Przedswit (Daybreak) and Walka Klas (The Class Struggle). She often published articles on philosophy and social history in Warsaw's Przeglad Tygodniowy (Weekly Review) and literary weekly Glos (The Voice).

In 1889 Wojnarowska was expelled from Switzerland for her ties with Polish revolutionaries involved in terroristic activities. She moved to Paris where she was introduced to the Polish socialist circle of Boleslaw Limanowski and Stanislaw Mendelson. In their homes she became acquainted with Friedrich Engels and Wilhelm Liebknecht. She continued her studies in history and literature at the University of Paris.

The political division in the Polish socialist movement between the Polish Socialist Party (PPS, founded in 1892) and the Social Democracy of the Kingdom of Poland (SDKP, founded in 1893) was a traumatic experience for Wojnarowska. Faithful to her social democratic ideas, she had to abandon her previous friends. Like many Polish socialist internationalists she considered PPS's patriotic agitation to be threatening to the class solidarity between Polish and Russian workers, and joined SDKP.

As an SDKP member Wojnarowska was most active in her remarkable effort to help political prisoners and exiles. She established a social democratic chapter of Red Cross and organized several fund-raisers for Polish prisoners. In 1896 she became a leader of the Association of Workers Social Democrats Abroad. During massive arrests of SDKP members in 1895-1896 Wojnarowska helped to rebuild SDKP illegal circles in the Kingdom of Poland. She trained new emissaries and supported their revolutionary work with money and literature. In 1900 SDKP and Social Democracy of Lithuania joined to form SDKPiL; shortly thereafter Wojnarowska became its official representative in the International Socialist Bureau in Brussels.

Wojnarowska was most famous for her political disagreement with Rosa Luxemburg, the chief theoretician of SDKPiL, on the question of Poland's independence. In particular, Wojnarowska opposed Luxemburg's theory about the process of "organic incorporation" of the Polish economy into the Russian state. In Luxemburg's view striving for Polish independence would jeopardize the integrative tendencies of capitalism and slow both Polish and Russian workers' common struggle for a socialist society. Wojnarowska criticized such views as theoretically weak and harmful to the SDKPiL. She insisted on addressing Polish national self-determination in the party's program. She worried about the party's antipatriotic image which alienated many workers and young members of the Polish intelligentsia from SDKPiL's international ideology.

Wojnarowska's opposition to Luxemburg's views was manifested first at the SDKPiL Congress in Leipzig (25 February 1900). Wojnarowska was supported by Stanislaw Trusiewicz-Zalewski, Stanislaw Guttmayer, Tadeusz Warynski and Wladyslaw Olszewski, while Leon Jogiches-Tyszka, Adolf Warszawski-Warski and Feliks Edmundovich Dzerzhinski supported Luxemburg's ideas. Julian Marchlewski to a large extent shared Wojnarowska's reservations about the concept of "organic incorporation". He believed that SDKPiL should defend both the social and national interests of the Polish workers and tried to mediate between the two opposing factions.

Wojnarowska openly expressed her concerns at the SDKPiL's Fourth Congress in Berlin (25-29 July 1903). She was accused of opportunism and was dropped from SDKPiL's delegation to the Second Congress of the Russian Social Democratic Labor Party (RSDLP) in Berlin (24 July 1903) despite her expertise and longtime personal relations with the Russian revolutionaries. Wojnarowska bitterly criticized SDKPiL for breaking the negotiations between both parties. In her view, the Polish party should accept Lenin's principle on the right of every nation of the Russian Empire to national self-determination. Finally Wojnarowska left her position of SDKPiL representative at the International Socialist Bureau (4 February 1904), citing political disagreement with the party's leadership as the cause for her resignation.

During the 1905 revolution in Russia Wojnarowska was unable to travel to Poland due to severe health problems. While in Paris she concentrated her efforts on organizing monetary help for all Polish revolutionaries regardless of party affiliation. After twenty-three years of political exile Wojnarowska arrived in Zakopane, Poland, where she was greeted as the honorary guest at the Fifth Congress of SDKPiL (1906).

During the last years of her life Wojnarowska devoted herself to the Polish political exiles in Paris. She was active in the Red Cross and the Society for Helping Political Victims Abroad.

Wojnarowska died in Paris on 15 April 1911 of a heart ailment. Her funeral the next day at the cemetery Père Lachaise became a great socialist demonstration. Among the notable speakers was V.I. Lenin; no one from SKDPiL attended in an official capacity. Wojnarowska, next to Luxemburg, was the most distinguished woman in the Polish social democratic movement. She emphasized the importance of the Polish national question in Marxist ideology and fought for the democratic right to form opposition within the revolutionary party.

Bibliography: Bozena Krzywoblocka, *Cezarna Wojnarowska* (Warsaw, 1979); Janina Kasprzakowa, *Cezaryna Wojnarowska* (Warszawa, 1978); Janina Dioniza Wawrzykowska-Wierciochowa, "Cezaryna Wanda Wojnarowska," *Z pola walki*, No. 4 (1964), 180-208; Julian Marchlewski, "Bojowniczka (Cezaryna Wanda Wojnarowska)," *Z pola walki*, No. 1 (Moskwa, 1926); Feliks Tych, "Cezaryna Wojnarowska w oczach policji francuskiej," *Z pola walki*, No. 3 (1964), 189-191; Zanna Kormanowa, "Wlodzimierz Lenin na pogrzebie Cezaryny Wojnarowskiej," *Z pola walki*, No. 2 (1965), 208-209; Jan Krz (Cynarski), "Wanda Cezaryna Wojnarowska," *Z pola walki*, No. 4 (1963), 180-208. About Wojnarowska's political activities: L. Baumgarten, *Dzieje Wielkiego Proletariatu* (Warszawa, 1966); L. Baumgarten, ed. *Kolka socjalistyczne Gminy i Wielki Proletariat. Procesy polityczne 1878-1888* (Warszawa, 1966); Feliks Tych, ed. *SDKPiL. Matrialy i dokumenty*, Vols. 1-2 (Warszawa, 1962); L. Dejcz, "Pionierzy ruchu socjalistycznego w Krolestwie Polskim," *Z pola walki*, Nos. 9-10 (Moskwa, 1930); Feliks Tych, "Listy Rozy Luksemburg do Cezaryny Wojnarowskiej," *Z pola walki*, No. 1 (1971), 197-239; R. Luksemburg, *Lisy do Leona Jogichesa-Tyszki*, Vols. 1-2, ed. Feliks Tych, Vols. 1-2 (Warszawa, 1968); "Korespondencja Juliana Marchlewskiego (Listy do Cezaryny Wandy Wojnarowskiej)," *Z pola walki*, No. 3 (1968), 171-193; Bronislaw Radlak, "Odbudowa i dzialalnosc SDKPiL 1899-1901," *Z pola walki*, No. 2 (1971), 20-26; Walentyna Najdus, "Z historii ksztaltowania sie pogladow SDKPiL w kwestii narodowej," *Z pola walki*, No. 3 (1962), 3-25; Adolf Warski, "Materialy o IV Zjezdzie SDKPiL," *Z pola walki*, Nos. 7-8 (Moskwa, 1929). Archives: Archiwum Lewicy Polskiej (Archiwum Akt Nowych) Cezaryna Wanda Wojnarowska, teczka osobowa no. 6443; ZG (Zarzad Glowny) SDKPiL, 9/II.

Julia Brun-Zeijmis

WOLFE, BERTRAM DAVID (1896-1977). Successively, a prominent American and Mexican communist official, and prolific anticommunist historian and activist.

Wolfe was born in 1896 in Brooklyn, New York to a family of German-Jewish immigrants. A bright boy, good at writing and speaking, he went to City College of New York and soon displayed an activist streak and a social conscience that led him, during World War I, to join pacifist organizations opposed to US entry into the war. He later claimed that this landed him in the socialist movement and after the Russian Revolution in its left wing, which was to become the Communist Party of America. In 1919 he joined with John

Reed and Louis Raina in drafting a manifesto calling for revolutionary action in the United States and support of Soviet Russia. The United States authorities considered this document, which contained some modifications Wolfe did not support, to be subversive. Under indictment Wolfe changed identities to escape arrest in the "Palmer Raids" organized by US Attorney General A. Mitchell Palmer to arrest "Reds." For Wolfe, this was only the first of several changes of name, residence, and passport. He surfaced in San Francisco, where he founded a modest labor college and became editor of a radical union paper. He was chosen to represent California at a clandestine Michigan convention of American communists in 1922, as a result of which once again he was obliged to go underground.

After a stint in the Boston area he and his wife set off for Mexico, which was to become—after communism—his great fascination. After several years as teacher, editor, and organizer Wolfe was chosen in 1924 to represent the Mexican Communist Party at the Fourth Congress of the Comintern (Communist International) and at the Third Congress of the Profintern (Trade-Union International). Upon his return from Moscow in 1925 he was deported from Mexico, ostensibly for dealing in narcotics, but in fact for his political activities. He returned to the United States to become educational director—that is, he was placed in charge of agitation and propaganda—of the Workers Party of America, one of several communist organizations. In the intense in-fighting among communists he emerged in effect as lieutenant to Jay Lovestone, the leader of the "rightist" but Moscow-oriented faction, which for the following several years controlled the American Communist party. Not surprisingly, the accounts of Wolfe's and Lovestone's principles and tactics by their factional opponents are less charitable than those of these "City College boys."

Wolfe was a delegate to the Sixth Comintern Congress in 1928 and to a special meeting of the Comintern's Executive Committee in January 1929. By then Soviet leader Joseph Vissarionovich Stalin evidently had decided to replace the Lovestoneites as leaders of the American party with another faction and thus embarked on a tug-of-war in the American Commission of the Comintern. This led Wolfe and his comrades to a confrontation with Stalin in May, a showdown they were bound to lose. In addition to Wolfe's autobiographical account the crisis is analyzed in Theodore Draper's *American Communism and Soviet Russia*.

Other than Stalin's quest for total control the principal issues in the dispute were first, an unstated identification of Wolfe and Lovestone with the arguments and supporters of Nikolai Ivanovich Bukharin; second, some resistance on the part of the Americans to accepting total direction from Moscow; and third, the argument of Lovestone, Wolfe, and others on behalf of American "exceptionalism." Essentially they argued that for a number of reasons political and economic conditions in the United States were different from those of other developed capitalist countries and therefore called for different political strategy and tactics. In this they foreshadowed national communism.

Upon his refusal to endorse the Comintern's position, Wolfe was expelled from the official Communist movement, as was the entire Lovestone group.

Thereupon he helped Lovestone organize a communist opposition party, later renamed the Independent Labor League of America. This group bitterly opposed the Stalinists in New York and Moscow but remained committed to the principles of Leninism and the goals of a proletarian revolution.

Wolfe spent most of the 1930s as an educator, organizer, and journalist—an opposition communist outwardly loyal to Moscow until 1938. Some of his observations in Spain during the civil war, more generally the Soviet purges, and especially the execution of Bukharin, forced him to reconsider his position, as did the Nazi-Soviet pact of 1939. Gradually, slowly, and painfully Wolfe shed his commitment to the Soviet Union, to Leninism, and ultimately to Marxism. And as he observed Soviet behavior during the second World War and the first years of the Cold War that followed, he swung over to a vigorous public condemnation of Stalinism and of Soviet policy at home and abroad. In this sense his evolution was emblematic of a larger class of former communists who later became ardent and committed anticommunists.

It had been a difficult change of positions for him. In the process of emancipation he had stumbled more than once. He had broken with the Lovestoneites and in 1939 co-authored with socialist leader Norman Thomas a booklet indicative of his position, Keep America Out of War. But while continuing with some journalism and lecturing, he concentrated on writing a major book that finally appeared in 1948 under the title, *Three Who Made a Revolution*, a skillful and at the time pioneering political history of Vladimir Ilich Lenin, Leon Davidovich Trotsky, and Stalin prior to their capture of power. Here and later Wolfe's experience of many years as an insider in the communist movement proved invaluable. Now he could join it to scholarly instincts that served him well. He established his credentials as a serious, articulate, often uncompromising, and sometimes brilliant anti-Stalinist and was offered a variety of fellowships and lectureships that enabled him to continue his research and writing.

Meanwhile, after the start of the Korean War in 1950, he was encouraged to apply for the position of chief of the Ideological Advisory Board of the Voice of America, a new position whose cause Wolfe found to his liking. After a fight—predictable given his past—to get a security clearance, he was made a US government official, an ironic twist of fortune. Until 1954 it enabled him to write broadcast scripts and to make his mark in shaping the arguments that guided American propaganda aimed at the communist world. Both in those years and later he proved to be a prolific writer, producing a number of books and essays marked by their sharp and direct approach and by a combination of ideological intransigence and thorough factual knowledge. Best known among his other writings were *Six Keys to the Soviet System* (1956), *Strange Communists I Have Known* (1965), and *An Ideology in Power* (1969), which includes an essay, "The Durability of Despotism in the Soviet System." The latter was perhaps the most characteristic summation of Wolfe's outlook as of 1957, essentially denying both the reality and the prospect of any improvement, mellowing, or increasing legitimacy of the Soviet system. He never completed what was to have been the sequel to *Three Who Made a Revolution*, to be called *The Uses of Power*.

In the 1920s he had befriended the Mexican painter, Diego Rivera. They co-authored two books: *Portrait of America* (1934) and *Portrait of Mexico* (1937). In addition Wolfe wrote three books on Diego Rivera (1939, 1947, 1963). These writings are indicative of Wolfe's breadth of interests and skills.

He taught at various times at the University of Colorado, at the University of California, Davis, and elsewhere. During the last ten years of his life, until his death in 1977, he was a senior research fellow at the Hoover Institution at Stanford, California, to which he left his papers. His unfinished but readable autobiography and several collections of articles, letters, and scripts were published posthumously.

See Also: Theodore Draper, *American Communism and Soviet Russia* (New York, 1960); James P. Cannon, *The First Ten Years of American Communism* (New York, 1962); and Irving Howe and Lewis Coser, *The American Communist Party. A Critical History (1919-1957)*, (Boston, 1957).

Bibliography: For a comprehensive listing of Wolfe's writings, see his *Breaking with Communism*, 287-303. The following of his works are essential: *Three Who Made a Revolution* (New York, 1948; rev. ed., New York, 1964); *Six Keys to the Soviet System* (Boston, 1956); *Marxism. A Hundred Years in the Life of a Doctrine* (New York, 1965); *An Ideology in Power* (New York, 1969); *Strange Communists I Have Known* (New York, 1965); *Revolution and Reality. Essays on the Origin and Fate of the Soviet System* (Chapel Hill, N.C., 1981); *A Life in Two Centuries. An Autobiography* (New York, 1981); Robert Hessen, ed. *Breaking with Communism. The Intellectual Odyssey of Bertram D. Wolfe* (Stanford, 1990).

Important articles by Wolfe are: "The Influence of Early Military Decisions upon the National Structure of the Soviet Union," *American Slavic and East European Review*, 9 (October, 1950), 169-179; "Operation Rewrite: The Agony of Soviet Historians," *Foreign Affairs*, Vol. 31, No. 1 (October, 1952), 39-57; "Communist Ideology and Soviet Foreign Policy," *Foreign Affairs*, Vol. 41, No. 1 (October 1962), 152-170; "Backwardness and Industrialization in Russian History and Thought," *Slavic Review*, Vol. 26, No. 2 (June 1967), 177-203.

Alexander Dallin

WOMEN IN THE COMMUNIST PARTY OF THE SOVIET UNION. For one hundred years women made significant but often underrated contributions to the Communist Party of the Soviet Union (CPSU) and its prerevolutionary predecessor, the Russian Social Democratic Labor Party (RSDLP). During most of this time women, ethnic minorities, workers, and peasants were underrepresented in contrast to Russian male intellectuals and white collar personnel who tended to be overrepresented. Despite this fact women played important roles in the party, both before the revolution and during the Soviet period.

Marxism found a receptive audience in Russia in the late nineteenth century among intellectuals who sought radical solutions to the problems of the empire. Although they accounted for less than 10 percent of the membership, women were active in this movement and some of them played important roles. Vera

Ivanovna Zasulich, with Georgy Valentinovich Plekhanov, founded the Emancipation of Labor group in 1884, precursor of the RSDLP. The RSDLP, rooted in advocacy of Marxist revolution, provided a more rational option than the populist terrorism prevalent in the 1870s and 1880s. By the mid-1890s women such as Elena Dmitrievna Stasova, Aleksandra Mikhailovna Kollontai, and Nadezhda Konstantinovna Krupskaia were already committed to Marxism. In the years prior to 1917 women both in Russia and in exile abroad played prominent roles. Stasova, for example, was a secretary to Vladimir Ilich Lenin before the revolution and assisted Yakov Mikhailovich Sverdlov in party administration prior to the establishment of the party's Secretariat in 1919. Stasova later worked for the Communist International. In July 1917 shortly before the revolution, women constituted 9.7 percent of the Party's Central Committee, a figure never duplicated in the Soviet period.

When the Bolsheviks came to power in November 1917, Kollontai, a writer and revolutionary activist and a member of the party's Central Committee, became a minister (commissar) in the new government, the Council of People's Commissars (Sovnarkom). Later she headed the Women's Department (Zhenotdel) of the CPSU. Inessa Armand, another prominent revolutionary, became the first head of the party's newly created Zhenotdel in 1919, a position she held only briefly before succumbing to cholera.

Since women constituted only about 8 percent of overall party membership by 1920, the party's goal was to recruit women into the party through their involvement in Zhenotdel. By 1930 the number of women in the party increased to 13 percent, gradually reaching a plateau at 20 percent in 1950 and remaining at that level for approximately two decades. Party membership among women rose above 21 percent only in the 1970s and by the 1980s had risen to 27 percent. In the era of Soviet leader Mikhail Sergeevich Gorbachev (1985-1991) a major drive to recruit women and other underrepresented groups into the party was successful. By 1990, at the Twenty-eighth Party Congress, women constituted 33 percent of the party's membership.

Although they formed over half the Soviet population, women historically were underrepresented in the CPSU for several reasons. The heavy burden of work and domestic responsibilities and the fact that there were few opportunities to advance in the party discouraged participation. Whereas the Soviet Union began as a revolutionary society that sought to change fundamental values, many traditional attitudes survived. It was women's work to raise children and cook meals. Political issues were the purview of men. For party members working outside the apparatus (apparat), the cadre of party professionals, party activities might demand at least a day's volunteer work each week, precious time that women did not have. If political rhetoric emphasized the need for political consciousness among all citizens, in the post-Stalin Soviet Union the unstated reality was that women often could excuse themselves from political work because of family obligations. Society did not ask less of women than of men; it just asked different things. Women's burdens were heavy, and it was acceptable for women to avoid political involvement because of their domestic obligations. Women working within the party bureaucracy were likely to have less time than their male colleagues to devote to extra projects that might lead to promotion and advancement. A "glass ceiling" was lowered early in a woman's party career. Soviet society encouraged women to do a good job at the local level but not to aspire to higher positions.

Few women were promoted to the highest levels of the party and government. In the seventy-four-year history of the Soviet Union, only three women served on either the Politburo or the Secretariat: Ekaterina Alekseevna Furtseva (1957-1961), Aleksandra Pavlovna Biriukova (1986-1990), and Galina Vladimirovna Semenova (1990-1991). The Central Committee of the CPSU, in its latter years a body exceeding 300 full members, normally included fewer than 10 women. The percentage of women on the Central Committee rose under the leadership of Nikita Sergeevich Khrushchev (1955-1964) and then dropped slightly. Although Khrushchev and his successors, from Leonid Ilich Brezhnev onward, repeatedly urged the party to promote women, relatively little progress was made. The number of women on the Central Committee remained at or below 4 percent until 1990. In 1981, after the Twenty-sixth Party Congress, out of 470 members of the Central Committee (319 full and 151 candidate members), only 18 (3.8 percent) were women (8 full and 10 candidates). Thirteen women (4.2 percent) were among the 307 full members elected at the Twenty-seventh Party Congress in 1986.

Gorbachev's concerted effort to promote women succeeded. In 1990 at the Twenty-eighth Party Congress, the last Congress during the period of Communist party rule, the number of women elected to the Central Committee increased significantly. Thirty-one women (7.5 percent) were elected as full and candidate members of the 412 member Central Committee. It is ironic that in the twilight days of the party, the number of women on the Central Committee reached its highest level since the revolution. Another indicator of Gorbachev's concern for women was his appointment of Galina Semenova, editor of the journal Krestianka (The Peasant Woman), to the Politburo to take special responsibility for women's issues. Her predecessor on the Politburo, Biriukova, had been involved in general social and economic issues, especially consumer problems.

Women elected to the Central Committee and high party positions over the years did not always progress through the same career paths as their male colleagues. For men, the career path normally lay through regional party organizations, especially the position of First Secretary of a provincial party committee (obkom), which carried Central Committee status. Women elected to the Politburo or Central Committee often achieved success through other organizations. For example Biriukova rose through the labor unions; Semenova through journalism; and Valentina Vladimirovna Nikolaeva-Tereshkova because of her fame as a cosmonaut, and later, as head of the Committee on Soviet Women. Among the women who achieved Politburo membership, only Furtseva had been a local party secretary. Although women worked in the CPSU, they rarely became city or provincial first secretaries, positions that were stepping stones to higher posts. In elections to the Central Committee women often filled the "model worker" slots, which were limited to one term. Even women who could balance the difficult tasks of work and family or who remained single were unlikely to advance in the party hierarchy.

Within the party, women often were perceived as "helpers," a notion that can be traced to Zasulich's role in the establishment of the party. She was rarely perceived as anything other than Plekhanov's assistant. At the turn of the century, when editing Iskra, the RSDLP journal, her role was deprecated because editorial work was not as highly valued as contributions to theory. Stasova functioned as an aide to Lenin and subsequently to Sverdlov, but was not deemed an appropriate successor to Sverdlov.

At the same time, it must be noted that over the years Soviet authorities encouraged women's participation in the formal political process. Women responded and filled about 50 percent of the seats on the local councils (soviets) and even constituted one-third of the deputies in the pre-1989 Supreme Soviet convocations. Traditionally the Supreme Soviet met rarely as a full body—only about once or twice a year—although its standing committees met more often. Unless women lived near Moscow or were among the few in the party or government hierarchy, they were unlikely to play an active role in the committees, but their membership on the Supreme Soviet was a showcase to demonstrate to the world the emancipation of Soviet women. When in 1989, as part of the democratization policy introduced by Gorbachev, the Supreme Soviet was reconstituted as the Congress of People's Deputies, the number of women deputies, either popularly elected or selected by associations, fell to 15 percent.

In the Komsomol, the communist youth group, membership in which was normally a prerequisite to party membership, young women were equally active with young men. Their activism tended to carry over into the lower echelons of the party. In the early 1980s women constituted about 35 percent of the secretaries in primary party organizations and about 31 percent of the members of district (raion) and city (gorod) party committees. The gradual exclusion of women occurred as they attempted to rise up the party ladder. Only about 3 percent of obkom bureau members were women, and women rarely even became second secretary of an obkom.

Related to women's underrepresentation in party organizations was their underrepresentation in the nomenklatura, the highly rated jobs controlled by CPSU appointment. Soviet women, while well-educated, rarely held high-level nomenklatura positions. Although Khrushchev, Brezhnev, and other leaders called for the promotion of women to responsible positions, very little happened. In the decades in which the USSR was competing actively with the West to secure superpower status, the Soviet Union had a relatively favorable position relative to the West in respect to women's role in society. If women in the West had been more prominent in political roles in the 1960s and early 1970s, the Soviet leadership might possibly have paid more attention to this matter. So long as the USSR could demonstrate, with ample statistics, that Soviet women had a higher profile in society than their Western counterparts, there was little reason for concern. But by the 1980s women in the West had made progress in politics and society, whereas Soviet women had advanced comparatively little since the 1960s.

Gorbachev made a conscious effort to recruit and promote outstanding women, as reflected by the larger number of women in the party and its Central Committee and by the appointments of Biriukova and Semenova. As the 1980s progressed party membership became increasingly less attractive to young people. As citizens were encouraged to participate in the political process the CPSU, long the dominant force in Soviet politics, steadily lost prestige. The Twenty-eighth Party Congress in 1990 was marked by Boris Nikolaevich Yeltsin's dramatic resignation, a metaphor for the general exodus of party members disgusted with the slow pace of reform. A year later as president of the Russian Federation, Yeltsin abolished the activities of the CPSU in the Russian Republic with the acquiescence of Gorbachev, president of the rapidly disintegrating USSR. The leadership of other republics followed this move.

Bibliography: Dorothy Atkinson, Alexander Dallin, and Gail Warshovsky Lapidus, eds., *Women in Russia* (Stanford, 1977); Archie Brown, ed., *The Soviet Union. A Biographical Dictionary* (London, 1990); Genia Browning, *Women and Politics in the USSR* (New York, 1987); Mary Buckley, *Women and Ideology in the Soviet Union* (Ann Arbor, 1989); Barbara Evans Clements, *Bolshevik Feminist. The Life of Aleksandra Kollontai* (Bloomington, 1979); Barbara Clements, Barbara Engle, Christine Worobec, *Russia's Women* (Berkeley, 1991); Y.Z. Danilova, et al., eds., *Soviet Women* (M., 1975); Ronald J. Hill and Peter Frank, *The Soviet Communist Party* (London, 1981); Barbara Holland, ed., *Soviet Sisterhood* (Bloomington, 1985); Barbara Jancar, *Women Under Communism* (Baltimore, 1978); Gail Warshovsky Lapidus, *Women in Soviet Society* (Berkeley, 1978); Vladimir Ilich Lenin, *The Emancipation of Women* (New York, 1966); Alastair McCauley, *Women's Work and Wages in the Soviet Union* (London, 1981); Norma C. Noonan, "Zhenotdel," *Modern Encyclopedia of Russian and Soviet History*, ed. by Joseph L. Wieczynski, 55 vols., Vol. 46 (Gulf Breeze Fla., Academic International Press, 1976-), 39-43; Gordon B. Smith, *Soviet Politics. Struggling with Change*, 2nd ed. (New York, 1992); Phillippa Strum, "Conversations with Women Policy-makers in the USSR," *Women and Politics*, Vol. 1, No. 3 (1980), 21-33; *Zhenshchiny v SSSR, 1991. Statisticheskie materialy* (M., 1991) and preceding years.

Norma C. Noonan

WOMEN PHYSICIANS IN RUSSIA AND THE SOVIET UNION. Women have been prominent in Russian medicine since the latter third of the nineteenth century and have dominated Soviet health services from the 1930s.

Women's participation in the medical field began during the reign of Alexander II (1856-1881). His liberal reforms created new opportunities for employment in a variety of public services including medicine. Social movements occurring at the time provided incentives, especially for women, to fill them.

In the 1860s the imperial government turned over to the zemstvos (local councils) a small and inadequate network of medical installations for their administration. Zemstvo medicine established a pattern of rural dispensaries, delivering free public health care and including curative as well as preventive medicine. This created a great demand for physicians and other medical personnel. It also encouraged a new social and professional type: the salaried physician, who combined traditional medical ethics with the humanitarian and missionary zeal of the young populist generation that appeared after the Crimean War.

The government severely limited the zemstvo's taxation rights. This meant that doctors and other professionals received salaries so low that women were more likely than men to accept them. Idealistic young people liked the zemstvo goals in health care. Although the positions were neither prestigious nor profitable, they satisfied the urge to do something for the peasantry.

Alexander II also reformed city government. City councils, called dumas, took over city hospitals and dispensaries and opened new opportunities for medical personnel.

This era of reform was an age of imperial expansion as well, particularly into the Moslem lands in Central Asia. Moslem women could not be treated by male doctors. Humanitarian interest in sending women doctors to Moslem women in the southern borderlands was an important impetus for providing medical education for Russian women.

Individual women were motivated to become physicians by a variety of social movements that accompanied the reforms of Alexander II. The feminist movement took root in Russia in mid-nineteenth century. Nikolai Gavrilovich Chernyshevsky's enormously influential novel, *What Is To Be Done* (Chto delat', 1862) featured a heroine who liberated herself from family and bourgeois marriage and went off to medical school.

Russian populism, which surged in the 1860s and 1870s, called for benefits for the people. Populist leaders told the young gentry that their wealth and privilege came from the blood and sweat of the peasantry. Repentant noblemen were encouraged to repay their debt by performing small deeds of service on a personal basis. Many gentry women paid their debt to the peasantry as teachers or physicians. Most of the first women physicians were of this type. The popular image of the woman physician came to be one who served the poor at low salary or even without remuneration.

Nihilism was the most unusual of the incentives. The nihilists scorned the mores of the past and believed that only the study of science was worthwhile. Medicine offered a fortuitous combination of sciences and service to humanity.

In the long run the increasing need for women to support themselves was an even more powerful motivation than the popular social movements. Emancipation of the peasantry in 1861 was economically crippling for the lesser gentry, and they no longer could afford to maintain their daughters in a life of genteel ease. Dignified work for a gentry woman was very hard to find. The only two avenues that opened before the end of the nineteenth century were pedagogy and medicine, and women rushed to meet these opportunities.

Fortunately for the first Russian women physicians, the vocation of midwifery had not been preempted by men as it was in England and France. In Russia training courses for female midwives had existed since the mid-eighteenth century, but midwifery was not considered an upperclass vocation. The need for more and better trained midwives was the opening wedge for full medical education for women. Obstetrics and treatment of diseases of women and children were the first and most popular specialties for women physicians.

In most western countries the first women physicians faced great difficulties in finding an internship and establishing a practice. This was not true in Russia. Jobs were waiting for them in zemstvo service. Although the enthusiasm of many wavered in face of the appalling conditions in the countryside, they generally were wanted and gained experience which in a few years permitted them to undertake a more comfortable practice. So short was the supply of physicians in the country that many districts were staffed only by surgeons' assistants (feldshers), many of whom were women. Zemstvo boards enthusiastically supported medical education for women and helped individual students with stipends on the promise of post-graduation service. Later city dumas joined zemstvos in hiring salaried women physicians.

Not only hiring boards but also the rural population accepted women physicians. The peasants were accustomed to women caring for the ill, since that long had been the special province of peasant women.

Russian medical education in the late nineteenth century was good, comparable to that of western Europe. The delivery of health care lagged far behind, and there was a desire to catch up. The nursing profession did not develop in Russia as it did in England after the Crimean War. Whereas English and other western women were trained as nurses in roles subordinate to male physicians, Russian women were trained as physicians in roles similar to men.

Nadezhda Prokofievna Suslova was the first woman Russian physician. Her origins were humble. Her father was a freed serf who became a bailiff for the wealthy Sheremetev family. Count Sheremetev provided Nadezhda Prokofievna with education in a private boarding school, similar to those for gentry girls.

The Suslov family saw education as an avenue of social mobility, and Nadezhda Prokofievna was influenced by the new social ideas of the sixties. Medical education was not possible for women in Russia; Suslova received hers at the University of Zurich, Switzerland, where she was the first woman to enter the medical faculty. She achieved her degree in 1867. Many Russian women followed her to Zurich. Some of them were influenced by radicals in Zurich and returned to Russia with radical ideas, causing the tsar's government to prohibit further study in Switzerland. Suslova married a wealthy gentryman and spent most of her life in medical research, writing and publishing many articles on the social aspects of medicine. She also rendered free medical aid to the poor. Other women physicians who received their medical training abroad, either in Switzerland, Paris, or even the United States, served in salaried positions in rural and city hospitals, worked in the Moslem borderlands, or went into private practice.

Varvara Aleksandrovna Kashevarova-Rudneva was the first woman physician to receive her education in Russia. She was an impoverished Jewish orphan, who was motivated primarily by personal ambition. She received her education at the Russian army's Medical-Surgical Academy in St. Petersburg, the best medical school in the land, on stipend from the Orenburg military commander, who expected her to come to Orenburg on graduation to attend local Moslem women. Instead she married a Dr. M.M. Rudnev and assisted him in research and teaching. Upon his death scandal and prejudice in St. Petersburg forced her to return to her origins in Staraia Russa, where she brought honor to herself for her popular writings on hygiene and child care and her service as a country doctor. No other women were admitted to the Medical-Surgical Academy.

The need for rural doctors and the eagerness of young women to study medicine resulted in the opening of the Women's Medical Courses in St. Petersburg in 1872, under the supervision of War Minister Dmitry Alekseevich Miliutin. The courses offered a four-year program of classes taught by the faculty of the Medical-Surgical Academy, with major study in obstetrics and pediatrics. The courses were financed by the imperial government—the only higher education for women financed by the imperial government—and private endowment. Zemstvo stipends aided individual students. From 70 to 130 students were admitted yearly. Nearly all classes of society were represented, the gentry predominating. The majority entered zemstvo service upon graduation, but the need for physicians far exceeded the supply. The government grew increasingly suspicious of radical activity in the Women's Medical Courses and finally closed them, the last class graduating in 1887.

Anna Nikolaevna Shabanova graduated from the Women's Medical Courses in the first class in 1877. She served in the field of pediatrics for fifty years and published more than forty works on various aspects of medicine and pediatrics. Like many of the first women Russian physicians, she was especially interested in preventive medicine and did much research and publishing on diet and prevention of rickets. Dr. Shabanova introduced first-aid courses in the women's schools and published a textbook on first aid. She was active in the Society of Russian Doctors and participated in many national and international medical congresses. She died in 1932 at the age of eighty-four.

Aleksandra Gavrilovna Arkhangelskaia graduated from the Women's Medical Courses in 1881 and devoted her entire life to zemstvo medicine. She supervised the building of a hospital for her zemstvo board and achieved a national reputation as a surgeon. She contributed to medical knowledge in perfecting operations for the removal of gallstones and cataracts. She wrote many scientific articles and supported many causes, particularly those concerned with the delivery of good health care in zemstvo medicine.

Maria Ivanovna Pokrovskaia started out as a zemstvo doctor, but her experiences and reflections on social conditions led her to become one of the most outspoken feminists and exponents of women's rights in tsarist Russia. She conducted an extensive study of prostitution and published Woman's Messenger (Zhenskii vestnik), a feminist journal that promoted woman suffrage among other things.

After the closing of the Women's Medical Courses women again went abroad to study, but the pressure for medical education at home continued. In 1897 the Women's Medical Institute was opened in St. Petersburg. It admitted two hundred to four hundred students per year and offered a five-year course.

The curriculum included the full roster of medical courses. The government paid the major part of the operating expenses of the Women's Medical Institute. Students were prohibited from any assembly or meeting discussing political matters and were banned from any secret society and meetings prohibited by the government. In spite of the regulations, the institute was frequently the scene of protests, demonstrations, and various revolutionary activities. In 1898, after nearly forty years of argument, the government granted women doctors full equality with men in government service, and pensions. The only qualification was that women were not to have titles of noble rank, awards, decorations, and uniforms. These tokens remained the privilege of men only.

Vera Pavlovna Lebedeva, graduate of the Women's Medical Institute, was an active revolutionary and member of the Communist Party of the Soviet Union. After the October revolution of 1917 she organized the Soviet system of maternity and child care. She was the director of the Central Institute for Maternity and Child Protection from 1918 to 1931, and from 1938 to 1950 director of the Central Institute of Advanced Training for Physicians.

After the Revolution all aspects of the public health services expanded, and large numbers of staff doctors were needed. Medical schools were enlarged to train physicians to meet the need. As the Soviet Union was built workers were needed desperately in all fields of endeavor, but especially in skilled work and the professions. Young men were attracted to the building professions, especially engineering. Women flowed into the medical profession as nurses, feldshers, and physicians. Workers were encouraged to improve themselves through education. Nurses were encouraged to become feldshers, feldshers were encouraged to become physicians. A good feldsher might expect to be sponsored by co-workers to go to medical school and many did.

During the years of the New Economic Policy (NEP) in the 1920s many polyclinics could not give free medical care because of lack of funds. Physicians could choose to engage in either public or private practice. Private practice was never legally forbidden, but such a physician's taxes were heavy and the income remained, as before the Revolution, in the form of gratuities. The state supported more and more medical students and assigned them to jobs for the first three years after graduation. As for women physicians in tsarist times, the first job was most likely to be in the countryside. Disparity between country and city life continued, and most physicians did not stay in the country long. Thus positions were always available in the country to provide internships for new graduates.

The proportion of women physicians as compared to men grew rapidly. Soviet propaganda and fiction glamorized the woman doctor as having exciting adventures, flying to remote areas to bring medical relief and the benefits of socialism to the most downtrodden. Women probably entered medical school for a number of reasons: it was relatively easy to be admitted, they needed the money, they were respected, and working conditions were attractive. Undoubtedly, for many, economic motives were primary and the work was regarded as just a job. But the fact remains that multitudes of women chose medicine over other more profitable and glamorous professions open to them. By 1926, 52 percent of Soviet medical students were women, and by 1934, 71 percent. The percentage of women who were practicing physicians was somewhat lower, but reached 60 percent by 1940.

In the rearrangement of national priorities in the 1920s and 1930s the prestige of the medical profession suffered. It remained an honorable profession, whereas the aura of status rested on building for the future. Technical professions and engineering were better paid; skilled workers of all kinds received higher salaries than doctors. By the early 1930s an English doctor observed that money seemed to be spent on almost anything but doctors' salaries. A Soviet author, Georgy N. Serebrennikov, writing in 1937 on the position of women, glows with praise for women and the part they played in building the country. He comments on women engineers, inventors, skilled workers, pilots, scientific researchers, and collective farmers who, among other things, delivered litters of piglets. Women doctors, feldshers, and nurses were not mentioned in such laudatory context, although the rapid increase of numbers of women doctors from 30,000 in 1931 to 42,000 in 1935 duly was noted.

Soviet women physicians were not nearly so articulate as their grandmothers of the nineteenth century. The first women physicians wrote diaries, autobiographies, stories, books, and polemical and professional articles. Soviet women physicians were more likely to confine themselves to professional articles.

Women physicians appeared in Soviet fiction and although they were no more realistic than the novelist Chernyshevsky's character Vera Pavlovna, they presented models to emulate. Like Vera Pavlovna, the Soviet heroines are strong, positive characters.

Yury German's *Antonina* (1937) is the story of a girl orphaned in 1925 at the age of fifteen. Antonina dropped out of school and was desperately poor. Every day she went to the labor exchange, but there were no jobs, an experience known to millions of Soviet citizens during the years of the New Economic Policy. Finally she found a job working for a hairdresser, but it was despicable work, bourgeois and denigrating. Two marriages for economic purposes to men she disliked brought further indignity and physical beatings.

Antonina's destiny changed when she became acquainted with a group of communist young people involved in building a huge housing project during the first Five Year Plan. Antonina's mettle was tested by an opportunity to plan, organize, build, staff, and operate a creche and nursery for the development. She spent two days and evenings at Lebedeva's Institute of Motherhood and Childhood, learning to do this work. This was 1931 and one million women were needed in industry that year. Having the creche and nursery in operation was critical to that goal. By 1932 Antonina had decided that she must have medical training to run the creche properly, and the Medical Institute had just announced a supplementary enrollment. Antonina strained her energies to the limit to prepare for the entrance exams, but she passed and was accepted. In the real world her acceptance into medical school would have been eased by the establishment of twenty-four new medical schools from 1929 to 1935. Antonina found Latin and anatomy difficult and she was always tired. But she was no longer bored. She felt alive and happy and useful to society, inspired by the promises of socialism. She did not need men for economic support but enjoyed their respect and affection. The story ends happily in 1935 with Antonina only a few months from her thirtieth birthday and a degree as a physician.

A more romantic heroine, but one also very much in the spirit of socialist realism, is depicted by Antonina Dmitrievna Koptiaeva in a trilogy published in the 1950s. The heroine, Varvara, was born in 1917 on a reindeer hide in the taiga and was raised in a nomad hut in northeastern Siberia. Varvara was a Yakut, with shining black hair and eyes, and she too was an orphan. Her first experience with Soviet civilization came when a Russian public-health doctor in the Lena goldfields invited young Yakuts to come for feldsher training. Varvara loved the work, the Russian doctor, and her friends in the Komsomol. The Russian doctor worked hard in the difficult assignment among primitive Siberian people, but he did not consider that his lifetime work. An ideal career would be an appointment in the provinces, then an appointment in Moscow, and finally a position as a research academician.

World War II interfered with the life of Varvara and all of her friends. They set aside their careers to defend the motherland and many lost their lives. Varvara married the Russian doctor and devoted herself to medical work. After the war her husband received his appointment in Moscow, and Varvara went to medical school. By the age of forty she had become a physician and would later become an outstanding surgeon. She was also a loving and companionable wife, a cheerful and thoughtful mother who assumed all responsibility for caring for their son, a busy and efficient housewife, and a reliable friend. She never thought of herself and was only ambitious for her career when it served others. Most of all she was absolutely indefatigable.

Medicine remained a popular profession for women, as evidenced by the flow of women into medical schools. Granted, men preferred other professions and millions went off to World War II and never returned, leaving their places for women. But opportunity and desire combined to make women preeminent in Soviet medicine. Girls continued to consider medicine one of the most desirable occupations. A study published in 1970 asked 124 graduates of Leningrad secondary schools to rate 40 occupations on a scale of attractiveness. Girls indicated "physician" as their first choice. Boys rated "physician" as their tenth choice. Among other students surveyed, girls rated being a physician among their preferred ten choices, country girls considering it more desirable than did city girls.

According to 1970 Soviet census figures, 74 percent of physicians were women. This compared with 7 percent in the United States and 13 to 20 percent in major European countries. Feldshers and midwives continue in Soviet medicine, and most are women. Nursing education arrived after the Revolution; soon there were more nurses than doctors, and they were overwhelmingly women. Soviet women are unusually well represented in many fields that are considered men's fields elsewhere, such as engineering, teachers in higher education, and scientific research personnel. But it is as physicians that their place is most conspicuous.

In all the professions the female percentage declines rapidly with the higher prestige and responsibility of the job. This may be true in all countries and all times. Just as in tsarist times, positions of authority and prestige in Soviet medicine are occupied by men and not by women. Hospital directors, chief physicians, and research academicians are mostly men, and only one woman, Maria Dmitrievna Kovrigina, has been Minister of Health for the USSR (1954-1959).

A few generations of peace largely have corrected the imbalance of women in the younger population. In the 1970s official statements deplored the scarcity of men physicians, and it became easier for men to be accepted in medical school than for women. Men were accepted with lower grade averages than women, and enrollments were filled first with men students. Problems of marriage, immobility for purposes of assignment, and interruptions for family considerations, particularly in light of Soviet apprehensions about the declining Slavic birth-rate vis-a-vis Central Asian gains, were specified as making the policy necessary. In the 1980s the reforms of perestroika legalized private medical practice, increasing remuneration and making the profession more attractive. By 1984 the percentage of women physicians had declined to 69 percent, but was still high when compared to other nations of the world.

Bibliography: W. Horsley Gantt, *Russian Medicine* (New York, 1937); Yuri Pavlovich German, *Antonina*, trans. by Stephen Garry (London, 1937); Antonina Dimitrievna Koptiaeva, *Ivan Ivanovich*, (M., 1952), *Derzanie* (M., 1954), and *Druzhba* (M., 1957); Georgii N. Serebrennikov, *The Position of Women in the USSR* (Freeport, N.Y., 1937); Jeanette E. Tuve, *The First Russian Women Physicians* (Newtonville, Mass., 1984); *Narodnoe khoziaistvo SSSR, 1984 g.* (M., 1985).

Jeanette E. Tuve

WOMEN SOLDIERS IN RUSSIA AND THE SOVIET UNION. Russian culture through the ages sharply distinguished male from female roles. Even though soldiering was considered an exclusively masculine pursuit, Russian culture also knows images of strong women who take on commanding and defensive roles in critical situations. Official ideology in the Soviet period sought to break down traditional gender stereotypes; many fields previously closed to women opened for them including, in emergencies, the military. In comparison with the armed forces of such countries as the United States or Israel, the armed services have remained relatively inhospitable to women. At the same time exceptions to this rule go back to at least the eighteenth century.

Russian women's participation in the military began in 1787 when Joseph II of Austria and Catherine the Great toured the Crimea. Catherine's favorite, Prince Grigory Potemkin, organized and trained an all-female company of soldiers, whom he paraded before the monarchs. Women's military activity continued in the adventures of Nadezhda Durova, the tomboy daughter of a nobleman, who enlisted in a cavalry regiment during the Napoleonic wars, fought with great distinction, earned high decorations, and retired with the rank of captain.

During the Crimean War women saw front-line duty as medical and communications personnel. Far larger numbers of women similarly served during World War I, both in the rear and at the front. Nurses especially were exposed to all dangers of combat duty since they also served as litter bearers under enemy fire. A small number of women managed to enlist as combat soldiers, served with distinction, earned decorations, and suffered casualties. Within the Russian women's movement some leaders welcomed such participation in combat as a step in the emancipation of women, while others deplored the phenomenon of such "amazons" as unfeminine. Toward the end of the war about two thousand women volunteers served in the Women's Battalion of Death which briefly tried to defend the Winter Palace during the October revolution.

During the civil war a small but significant number of women served in the Red Army as combat soldiers or political workers, in medical and communication services, including as runners, and in partisan units behind enemy lines. By the end of the civil war about 66,000 women were in the Red Army, constituting about 2 percent of the more than three million soldiers. A few of these women served as troop commanders. The Soviet encyclopedia on the civil war lists six women who held high military rank. The most famous among them may have been Larisa Reisner, who served as commissar in the Red Fleet both on the general staff and on ships. Like the Red Army itself, most of these veterans were demobilized once the war was over, although a small number of women continued to be recruited into specialized branches. In the 1920s this participation of women in military service, however small the numbers, made the Red Army a unique institution.

During World War II women were mobilized for armed services in large number. More than 800,000 women, about 8 percent of all military personnel, served in a wide variety of functions and saw combat duty as military surgeons, nurses, and other medical personnel, as military police and truck drivers, interrogators, telephone operators, intelligence officers, and as pilots and bombardiers in the air force. There were some all-female combat formations, and women served as tank personnel, machine gunners, anti-aircraft gunners, and snipers. They were prominent also in partisan units behind German lines. They entered military service not as volunteers but in accordance with a draft.

Since the end of the World War II women continued to be recruited into military services, but voluntarily and in relatively small numbers. In thus restricting the number of women the Soviet armed services differ markedly from industry and other civilian occupations. According to legislation passed in 1967 and amended in 1973, women could enlist for terms of two to six years in various enlisted ranks and as warrant officers in all branches of the service, although not in combat units. Their recruitment corresponded to the needs of the services as determined by demographic trends. It rose in periods when draft-age men were in short supply as in the early 1960s and the 1980s, and decreased in other periods.

Female military personnel in recent decades have enjoyed the same maternity benefits as women in the civilian population. While the services used to require pregnant service women to retire into the reserves, they are now free to remain on active service, with the same prenatal care and maternity leave privileges as their civilian sisters.

Compared to the United States and some west European countries, Soviet use of women in the armed forces has been at a relatively low level, partly because the universal military service obligation imposed on men made a large pool of young men available. Despite the presence of images of strong women and historic instances of "amazonism," the military services in the USSR persisted as very much a male preserve. With the scaling down in the 1990s of what used to be the Soviet armed forces, the proportion of women serving in them can be expected to decrease even more or to disappear altogether.

Bibliography: Nadezhda Durova, *The Cavalry Maid. The Memoirs of a Woman Soldier of 1812*, trans. by John Mersereau, Jr. and David Lapeza (Ann Arbor, 1988); Nancy Loring Goldman, ed., *Female Soldiers. Combatants or Noncombatants* (Westport, 1982); Ellen Jones, *Red Army and Society. A Sociology of the Soviet Military* (Boston, 1985); Alfred G. Meyer, "The Impact of World War I on Russian Women's Lives," in Barbara Evans Clements, Barbara Alpern Engel and Christine D. Worobec, eds., *Russia's Women. Accomodation, Resistance, Transformation* (Berkeley, 1991); Vera Semenova Murmantseva, *Sovetskie zhenshchiny v velikoi otechestvennoi voine, 1941-1945* (M., 1979); Richard Stites, *The Women's Liberation Movement in Russia. Feminism, Nihilism and Bolshevism, 1860-1930* (Princeton, 1978).

Alfred G. Meyer

WOMEN'S INTERNATIONAL DEMOCRATIC FEDERATION (1945-). Communist front organization formed in 1945 in Paris.

The Women's International Democratic Federation (WIDF) was designed to support specifically the rights of women and children as well as to promote the general international front goals of "peace and disarmament," "national independence," and "democratic freedoms." Like several other Paris-based communist front organizations, it was expelled from France in 1951 for subversive activity. It then found a permanent home in East Berlin.

The organization's highest policy-making body was its Congress, which in practice has met every three to six years. The Congress elected a Council, which met yearly and was composed of at least one representative from each of its 142 affiliates located in 124 countries. The Council in turn elected a Bureau, which met when the Council was not in session and consisted of a president, vice-presidents, secretary general, and others. In theory control flowed from the Congress to the Council to the Bureau; in reality it went in exactly the opposite direction.

At the day-to-day working level WIDF was run from its headquarters in Berlin. The officers there constituted the Secretariat, which had at least ten members in 1986.

The founding president was the French communist Eugenie Cotton, who served until her death in 1967. After an interval in which there was no president, she was followed by Herta Kuusinen of Finland (1969-1975), Freda Brown of Australia (1975-1991), and Fatima Ibrahim of the Sudan (1991-).

Under President Cotton secretaries general had been first Italian (Angiotta Minella and Carmen Zanti), then Argentinean (Rosa Jasovich-Pantaleon). The

Frenchwoman Cicile Hugel served as secretary general from the time of Mme. Cotton's death at least until a new president was elected in 1969; reports conflict as to whether or not she carried on in the office until 1972. In any case, the job returned to Argentina in 1972 (Fanny Edelman) and then went to Finland in 1978 (Mirjam Vire-Tuominen). It was still considered a Finnish preserve when it was turned down by Inger Hirvela in 1989 then given to the German Bridget Triems in 1991.

Like most of the other international fronts, WIDF always has had a Soviet vice-president, who could exercise influence at the policy level, and a Soviet secretary, who was the ultimate controller of day-to-day operations at its headquarters. These Soviet citizens officially represented the Committee of Soviet Women (CSW) but ultimately were controlled by the International Department of the Communist Party of the Soviet Union. Natalia Berezhnaia had succeeded Valeriia Kalmyk as Soviet secretary by 1986 and Zoya Pukhova succeeded Valentina Nikolaieva-Tereshkova as Soviet vice-president in 1987. Mme. Pukhova also succeeded Mme. Nikolaieva-Tereshkova as chairman of the CSW.

More communist in its membership than most of the other fronts, WIDF was less affected by external events such as the onset of the Cold War and by the Soviet invasion of Hungary in 1956. There were reverberations from internal communist dissension in the 1960s, however. In 1964 the "Eurocommunist" Italian affiliate, protesting Soviet domination, reverted to associate member status and withdrew its top officers, including Secretary General Carmen Zanti. In 1966 the Chinese stopped participating in the organization. And in 1968 the powerful French affiliate protested the invasion of Czechoslovakia but was unable to influence WIDF as a whole to do likewise. It is unclear whether or not Mme. Hugel was dropped as secretary general because of this. It is clear that no Frenchwoman served in either of the two top positions after 1972.

Perhaps because of its highly communist composition, WIDF seemed to have gone downhill faster than the other fronts upon the collapse in 1989 of communism in Eastern Europe. The first hint of this occurred that year, when the organization's newly-elected secretary general, Inger Hirvela (Finland), refused to take the position, an unheard-of situation. At the end of 1990 WIDF's only major publication, the quarterly Women of the Whole World magazine, ceased publication. High quality publications heretofore had been one of WIDF's few strong points. Also in 1990 no large, broad-based women's conference was planned to coincide with WIDF's forthcoming Tenth Congress. By contrast the 1987 Moscow World Congress of Women, which immediately preceded the Ninth Congress, was the largest front meeting of the year, with over twenty-eight hundred participants. Finally, in 1991 the Tenth Congress, with a planned participation of over two hundred delegates, not only had been scaled down in size to the level of a small Council meeting, but only half of these actually showed up. Possible earlier evidence that WIDF was an unhealthy organization might have been its failure to claim the continual growth in membership characteristic of the other fronts. During the period 1955-1988 the stated membership hovered around the two hundred million mark and no subsequent claims are known to have been made.

WIDF seemed to have had some mild successes in dealing with the United Nations (UN). It was responsible for having that body designate 1975 as International Women's Year and subsequently participated in UN women's conferences in Copenhagen (1980) and Nairobi (1985). It had top consultative status (Category I) with the Economic and Social Council (ECOSOC) and a secondary one (Category B) with the United Nations Educational, Scientific, and Cultural Organization (UNESCO), and for this reason maintained permanent representatives in New York and Paris, respectively.

Close to all the other major fronts, WIDF most obviously was connected to the World Peace Council, being one of only two fronts to have held a vice-presidential slot in that organization prior to its 1990 shake-up. It is also close to the traditionally pacifist Women's International League for Peace and Freedom, a Geneva-based group that had become increasingly pro-Soviet during the 1980s under the secretary generalship of Edith Ballantyne (Canada).

Bibliography: Yearbook on International Communist Affairs, ed. by Milorad M. Drachkovich and Lewis H. Gann (1966-1967), Richard F. Staar (1970-1982, 1984-1992), and Robert H. Wesson (1983), (Stanford, 1967-1992), is a major source for all Communist front organizations. It provides yearly updates on developments in the fronts from a Western viewpoint. Clive Rose, *The Soviet Propaganda Network* (London, 1988) is a definitive study of front organization complex from the Western standpoint. Witold S. Sworasky, ed., *World Communism. A Handbook, 1918-65* (Stanford, 1973) gives pro-Western background for period indicated. US Congress, *The CIA and the Media* (Washington, 1978) describes how the US government views Soviet control of the fronts. World Congress Devoted to the International Year of Peace, Copenhagen, 15-19 October 1986, *Preliminary List of Participants* (Copenhagen, 1986) identifies many top officers of WIDF at the time. World Congress of Women, Moscow, 23-27 June 1987, *Preliminary List of Participants* (M., 1987) reveals wide scope of Congress participation. *Kansan Uutiset* (Helsinki, 20 September 1989) contains a communist newspaper account of Inger Hirvela's refusal to take up WIDF secretary generalship. *Morning Star* (London, 22 April 1991) gives a sketchy account of the Tenth WIDF Congress in Sheffield from a communist interpretation. *Women of the Whole World* (East Berlin) is the official WIDF magazine published monthly 1951-1965 and quarterly 1966-1990.

Wallace H. Spaulding

WOMEN'S MOVEMENTS IN THE USSR. In the twentieth century women's movements around the world played an active role in the improvement of women's rights and status. In the West such movements usually were linked to feminism, a social philosophy that focused on the conscious pursuit of full equality for women beyond formal, legal equality. Although improvement of women's status was on the agenda of several political movements in the prerevolutionary Russian Empire, as in the USSR and in the Commonwealth of Independent States (CIS) these rarely were linked to feminism.

In late nineteenth and early twentieth-century Russia middle and upper-class women formed a small but active feminist movement. The Russian Marxist revolutionaries, including Vladimir Ilich Lenin, did not cooperate with the feminist movement, which they labeled "bourgeois," and considered the "women's question"—their term for issues involving the status of women—as one of many problems that revolution would resolve. Some prominent women revolutionaries, including Aleksandra Mikhailovna Kollontai, Nadezhda Konstantinovna Krupskaia and Inessa Armand, actively promoted women's rights but did not identify with feminism, since feminists were considered "bourgeois" women who sought only reform within the system, not revolution. Communist women were supposed to be concerned about women's emancipation only as part of the emancipation of the working class.

The theories of Karl Marx, Friederich Engels, and Lenin formed the basis of Soviet policies on the women's question. The USSR promoted legal equality for women and inclusion of women into the work force. Although Lenin lamented the "domestic enslavement" of women, measures to reduce women's domestic burdens were only partly successful. The Soviet position on the women's question ignored Engels' argument that the traditional male-female relationship within the family was analogous to the class struggle in society. The Soviet decision around 1930 that the family was essential for social stability drew attention away from the negative characteristics which Marx and Engels attributed to the "bourgeois" family and emphasized the positive attributes of the "socialist" family.

In the early Soviet period the top leadership rejected both feminism and an independent women's movement as necessary to the solution of the women's question. In a discussion with Clara Zetkin in 1920, Lenin stated "We want no separate organizations of communist women! She who is a Communist belongs as a member to the Party, just as he who is a Communist" (Lenin, *The Emancipation of Women*, 110). Repudiation of the possibility of an independent women's movement became a basic tenet of the Communist Party of the Soviet Union (CPSU). During the 1920s measures were taken to improve the status of women under the auspices of the party through the women's section of the CPSU (Zhenotdel). Although Zhenotdel's leaders included Armand and Kollontai, whom westerners regard as feminists, within the country they were known principally as revolutionaries and party workers. Traditional attitudes toward women and women's roles were deeply ingrained into the fabric of Russian society, and Zhenotdel had difficulty implementing reforms to help women. Kollontai, the best known of the Zhenotdel leaders (1920-1922), actively promoted improved services for women and children. In 1923 Kollontai unsuccessfully recommended that the Soviet Union support feminism. Zhenotdel, which approximated a women's movement, although it was under close party supervision, was dissolved in 1930 on grounds that the women's question had been resolved successfully. This action closed a chapter of Soviet women's history.

From the 1930s to the 1980s the Soviet government passed considerable legislation on such issues as women's working conditions, maternity leave, and job security. The status of women improved, but they never achieved parity with men. Soviet women questioned traditional male-female roles far less than their western counterparts, partly because of official rhetoric that stressed the formal equality of men and women and partly because the shortage of men after World War II conditioned women to contribute more than their fair share to society.

Until the late 1980s the officially constituted Committee on Soviet Women served principally as an agent of socialization within the country and took on representative functions abroad to publicize the party's and government's position on the status of Soviet women. Women's Councils (Zhensovety), created in the 1950s and revived in the mid-1980s on the local level, engaged primarily in various service and volunteer projects involving children, women, and other groups needing assistance. In the post-Stalin era scholars wrote carefully guarded statements about "shortcomings" in the generally successful resolution of the women's question but did not directly challenge the official position itself.

The official position was confronted and cracked only under the leadership of Mikhail Sergeevich Gorbachev (1985-1991). In 1987 the Committee on Soviet Women, influenced by Gorbachev's policy of openness (glasnost), broke out of its traditional silence and criticized the implementation and enforcement of various social policies intended to benefit women. For the first time its leaders openly discussed the problems and concerns facing women. A variety of reactions emerged, including the oft-repeated, strongly expressed view that women's burden could be reduced by allowing women to return to the home as full-time homemakers and mothers.

Although official acknowledgment of women's problems came only during the Gorbachev years, quiet recognition of an unfinished women's agenda began in the 1970s. It gave rise to a minuscule underground feminist movement centered in the larger cities, principally Leningrad. It was not a renaissance of prerevolutionary Russian feminism, although contemporary Russian feminists claimed Kollontai and other feminists as their predecessors. The best known unofficial women's movement was the Almanac group whose writings were published in 1979 in samizdat, the illegal underground press. The Almanac group was influenced in part by contemporary Western feminism, although its goals and agenda were distinctly Soviet. Prominent proponents were expelled, arrested, or forced to go underground in 1980. Tatiana Arsenevna Mamonova, a leader of the Almanac group, was expelled and took up residence in the West where she wrote and lectured about Soviet women. Another group, the Mariya Club, named for the Virgin Mary, had a strongly religious, Russian Orthodox orientation. It wanted to emphasize Russian spiritual values and recapture the best of the traditional woman. Founded in the Orthodox Christian tradition, it attempted to develop a uniquely Russian feminism. Three leaders of the Mariya Club—Tatiana Mikhailovna Goricheva, Natalia Lvovna Malakhovskaia and Julia Vosnesenskaya—also were expelled in 1980.

Even in the liberal era of glasnost women's groups tended to shun the label feminism both in official and unofficial circles for fear of shattering the fragile support women had among sympathetic intellectuals and political officials. The economic crisis which struck the USSR and its successor, the Commonwealth of Independent States (CIS) in the early 1990s increased women's burdens immeasurably as affordable food became harder to find. Although consciousness of women's difficulties rose, especially among the women intelligentsia and students, they were reluctant to embrace either a women's movement or feminism as a cause at a time when the whole society faced catastrophe. This attitude resembled the views of turn-of-the-century revolutionaries who believed that all citizens of Russia faced such difficult conditions that it was inappropriate to distinguish between men and women.

The Soviet reform movements of the late 1980s did not lead to a major expansion of women's involvement in public life. A number of women academics were consultants in the reform processes initiated by Gorbachev and continued by his successor Boris Nikolaevich Yeltsin, but the role of women in the highest echelons of power continued to be modest. During the Gorbachev period there was a female deputy prime minister, and two women in succession served on the Politburo of the CPSU, primarily in the areas of economic and social services. When the Soviet Union moved toward democratization in the late 1980s the largely popularly-elected Congress of People's Deputies—and its indirectly elected powerful standing body, the Supreme Soviet—had far fewer women deputies than the former, larger, and less powerful Supreme Soviet, elected without competition.

In the latter decades of the Soviet Union Soviet women writers described women's problems in short stories and novels in keeping with the Russian tradition of raising social problems through fiction. Women writers formed a federation under the auspices of the Writers' Union to enhance attention to women's issues as well as to women writers. The poet Larisa Vasileva, a leader of the Federation, wrote numerous editorials in the Soviet central press calling attention to the role of women in society.

Various Soviet women scholars and journalists attempted to write about, and offer solutions to, the women's question. The Center for Gender Studies, established in Moscow under the auspices of the Academy of Sciences, and other research groups focused on women in society. Younger women formed informal support groups, and small feminist circles existed at the local level. Although no large-scale women's movement existed in the early 1990s, the nucleus for the establishment of future groups had been created.

During its seventy-four-year history the USSR discouraged the development of independent women's movements. Whereas various political movements arose as a result of glasnost, there was little support for a broadly based women's movement, and a fear of feminism lingered from the past.

The rise of ethnic consciousness and the assertion of the rights of national minorities overshadowed the issue of women's rights during glasnost. As of 1992 the dissolution of the Soviet Union, tensions among national minorities, the worsening economic crisis, and attempts to establish a stable base for politics in Russia and the other successor republics essentially eclipsed concern for women's rights.

Bibliography: Dorothy Atkinson, Alexander Dallin, and Gail Warshovsky Lapidus, eds., *Women in Russia* (Stanford, 1977); Lynne Attwood, *The New Soviet Man and Woman* (Bloomington, 1991); Genia Browning, *Women and*

Politics in the USSR (Sussex, 1987); Mary Buckley, *Women and Ideology in the Soviet Union* (Ann Arbor, 1989); Barbara Clements, Barbara Engle, and Christine Worobec, *Russia's Women* (Berkeley, 1991); Y.Z. Danilova, et al. eds., *Soviet Women* (M., 1975); Linda Edmondson, *Feminism in Russia. 1900-1917* (Stanford, 1984); Laurie Essig and Tatiana Mamonova "Perestroika for Women," Judith B. Seaditis and Jim Butterfield, eds., *Perestroika from Below. Social Movements in the Soviet Union* (Boulder, 1991), 97-112; Carola Hansson and Karin Liden, *Moscow Women* (New York, 1983); Barbara Holland *Soviet Sisterhood* (Bloomington, 1985); Barbara Jancar, *Women under Communism* (Baltimore, 1978); Alexandra Kollontai, *Selected Writings*, Alix Holt, ed. (New York, 1977); Gail Lapidus, *Women in Soviet Society* (Berkeley, 1978); Vladimir I. Lenin, *The Emancipation of Women* (New York, 1966); Alastair McCauley, *Women's Work and Wages in the Soviet Union* (London, 1981); Tatiana Mamonova, *Women and Russia* (Boston, 1984); Tatiana Mamonova, *Russian Women's Studies* (Oxford, 1989); Carol Nechemias, "The Prospects for a Soviet Women's Movement. Opportunities and Obstacles," Judith B. Sedaitis and Jim Butterfield, eds., *Perestroika from Below. Social Movements in the USSR* (Boulder, 1991), 73-93; Norma C. Noonan, "Marxism and Feminism in the USSR. Irreconcilable Differences?" *Women and Politics*, Vol. 8, No. 1 (1988), 31-49; Norma C. Noonan, "Women in the USSR," *Modern Encyclopedia of Russian and Soviet History* (MERSH), ed. by Joseph L. Wieczynski, (Gulf Breeze, Fla., Academic International Press, 1976-), Vol. 44, 24-31; Norma C. Noonan, "Zhenotdel," MERSH, Vol. 46, 39-43; Francine du Plessix-Gray, *Soviet Women. Walking the Tight Rope* (New York, 1989); Rochelle Ruthchild, "Sisterhood and Socialism. The Soviet Feminist Movement," *Frontiers*, Vol. 7, No. 2, 4-12; Hilda Scott, *Does Socialism Liberate Women?* (Boston, 1974); *Soviet Woman* (monthly journal) (M.); Richard Stites, *The Women's Liberation Movement in Russia* (Princeton, 1978); Philippa Strum, "Conversations with Women Policy-Makers in the USSR," *Women and Politics*, Vol. 1, No. 3 (1980), 21-33; N. Vishneva-Sarafanova, *Soviet Women. A Portrait* (M., 1981); Nataliia Zakharova, Anastasiia Posadskaia, and Nataliia Rimashevskaia, "Kak my reshaem zhenskii vopros," *Kommunist*, Vol. 4 (April, 1989).

Norma C. Noonan

WOMEN'S RIOTS. In Russian, babii bunty (pl.). Women's riots were an important and essential weapon in the arsenal of peasant protest during Soviet agrarian collectivization (1929-1933). This type of riot occurred throughout the Russian countryside in these years, but were especially prevalent in late 1929 and early 1930 when the collectivization campaign was at its height. Women's riots played a key role in forcing the state to issue a call for a temporary retreat in early March 1930 and insured that the worst abuses in matters relating to the socialization of domestic livestock, church closings, and other issues of the domestic economy would be curtailed.

The translation of the term babii bunty as "women's riots" fails to do justice to its rich cultural and political meaning. The adjective babii (pl.) is a colloquial expression for women that refers in particular to country women with country ways. The noun baba most often is perceived as ignorant, uncultured, superstitious, and given to irrational outbursts of hysteria. The modifier colors and reinforces the noun that follows. A bunt is a spontaneous and uncontrollable explosion of wrath—in this case, peasant wrath—and opposition against authority. In the mind of the official observer it is thought to be aimless, unpredictable, and extremely dangerous. A babii bunt is a women's riot characterized by female hysteria, unorganized and inarticulate protest, and violence.

Such was the understanding shared by Communist Party leaders, local activists, and other outside observers during collectivization. Women's protest rarely was evaluated in political or ideological terms. Because the baba was held to be dark and ignorant, she was neither responsible for her actions nor capable of rational protest. Her actions therefore were blamed either on the capitalist farmer (kulak) or the kulak henchman (podkulachnik) who supposedly exploited the baba for their own counterrevolutionary purposes, or on the actions of local officials, who were scapegoated for the campaign's atrocities. As a consequence women seldom were prosecuted for counterrevolutionary crimes and appear to have been dealt with far less harshly than were peasant men involved in similar protest.

The women's riots may have belied the official perception. They appear to have been a conscious stratagem employed by peasants to resist the state's policies openly while attempting to avoid the more dire consequences generally associated with more direct forms of male protest. The pattern of the riots was consistent: an altercation by women with officialdom, verbal protest ending in a shouting match, sounding of the village tocsin, and a general melee with the men standing silently in the background prepared to join in only when it became safe to enter the fray merely as defenders of their womenfolk. The action ended in a riot whereupon the officials fled the village and the collective farm dissolved. The officials generally allowed the riots to run their course, perhaps several days later reentering the village with a show of force and making several arrests. Most often the repression was minimal and the women were left unharmed.

In addition to the peasant use of such riots as stratagem it very well may have been useful for officialdom to maintain the dominant image of the riots as irrational and apolitical. Failing that the state must have had to concede the magnitude of the resistance to collectivization and the fact that it engulfed entire villages including all socio-economic categories of peasants. The official image of the women's riots may have served as a rationalization for the failure of collectivization to gain social support in the village as well as for the campaign's atrocities.

Women's riots were not confined exclusively to the collectivization era. Peasant women manipulated outside images of themselves protesting at several key junctures in modern Russian history including the 1905 and 1917 revolutions. This type of protest was not confined to Russian peasant women. Women's protest has assumed similar forms in other cultures, when open protest is not possible in the face of the state's repressive machinery.

Bibliography: Barbara Evans Clements, Barbara Alpern Engel, Christine D. Worobec, eds., *Russia's Women. Accommodation, Resistance, Transformation*

(Berkeley, 1991); Natalie Zemon Davis, "Women on Top," *Society and Culture in Early Modern France* (Stanford, 1975); Beatrice Farnsworth and Lynne Viola, eds., *Russian Peasant Women* (New York, 1992); Petro G. Grigorenko, *Memoirs*, trans. by Thomas P. Whitney (New York, 1982); Lev Kopelev, *Education of a True Believer*, trans. by Antonina W. Bouis (New York, 1980); Lynne Viola, "Bab'i Bunty and Peasant Women's Protest during Collectivization," *Russian Review*, Vol. 45, No. 1 (1986), 23-42.

Lynne Viola

WORKERS' AND PEASANTS' ALLIANCE (1921-1929). In Russian, smychka (union). This attempt to harmonize the interests between town and country and between workers and peasants was a major policy of the Russian Communist Party from 1921 to 1929. Its beginning and end marked fundamental turning points in Soviet history.

In March 1921 the Tenth Congress of the Russian Communist Party replaced the forcible requisitioning of peasants' grain with a tax in kind. This decision, which allowed the peasantry to sell its produce on the free market, signaled the end of War Communism and the introduction of the New Economic Policy (NEP). A major political goal of NEP was to forge the smychka, an alliance between workers and peasants, because the civil war years had destroyed whatever partnership had existed between these two classes.

In the early 1920s Vladimir Ilich Lenin defended NEP and need for the smychka in pragmatic terms. "Sheer necessity has driven us to this path. And this is the sole basis and substance of the New Economic Policy." "We must adapt our state economy to the economy of the middle peasant" and "take measures that will immediately increase the productive forces of peasant farming. Only in this way will it be possible to improve the condition of the workers, strengthen the alliance between the workers and peasants, and consolidate the dictatorship of the proletariat." (Lenin, *Collected Works*, Vol. 33, 158; Vol. 32, 226, 341-342).

For Lenin, the biggest obstacle to the success of NEP was the crisis of peasant farming. He warned that it would take generations to remold the small farmer, and recast his attitudes and habits. To speed that process Lenin envisioned a two-part policy. The first part aimed at adapting state economic policy to the needs of the middle peasant. This would hasten the revival of rural-urban trade, thereby raising the standard of living. The second involved the creation of patronage (shefstvo) societies through which the urban proletariat would help raise peasants' political and cultural awareness, which Lenin viewed as a precondition to strengthening the smychka and the dictatorship of the proletariat.

After Lenin's death, Nikolai Ivanovich Bukharin became the chief theoretician and interpreter of NEP and the major proponent of the smychka. Bukharin shared Lenin's beliefs that state policy must adapt itself to the economy of the middle peasant, that proletarian needs should guide the peasantry, and that the smychka served to strengthen the dictatorship of the proletariat. More than Lenin he maintained that the market offered the proletarian state the greatest opportunity to remold the peasantry and realize the smychka. So confident was

Bukharin in the market as a means of socialist transformation that in 1925 he encouraged peasants to enrich themselves. Although in 1925 the Fourteenth Communist Party Conference and Party Congress passed resolutions endorsing Bukharin's views, many in the party showed little enthusiasm for the proposals. Joseph Vissarionovich Stalin, Bukharin's political ally in 1925, quickly distanced himself from Bukharin's appeal to the peasantry.

The left opposition within the party disagreed sharply with Bukharin's enthusiasm for NEP and powers of the market. It offered a wholesale critique of NEP policies, arguing that the government endangered long-term industrial and political objectives by adjusting state economic policies to the economy of the middle peasant.

According to the opposition, NEP stimulated the economy of the middle peasants and rich peasants (kulaks) at the proletariat's expense. The working class subsidized industrial recovery through its increased productivity and inadequate living standards, while the peasantry, especially the kulaks, allegedly benefited from the resultant decrease in industrial prices. In addition NEP policies resulted in urban unemployment, slowed the improvement of working and living conditions, and actually destabilized urban-rural trade. The opposition argued that this need not be the case. Peasant demand for industrial products was relatively inelastic; by planning and carefully adjusting the prices of agricultural and industrial products, the state could widen the differential between them and generate more capital for industrial development. In this way the burden of capital accumulation would fall upon the peasantry, the largest social class and junior partner in the smychka.

The opposition did not seek to undermine or destroy the smychka. It sought to redefine its terms to serve the interests of the proletariat. But the party majority, fearful that any sharp change in policy might jeopardize economic recovery and precipitate a showdown with the peasantry, refused to support the opposition.

The heated debates over economic policy and implicitly over the nature of the smychka did not occur in an ideological vacuum but rather with the full knowledge of the costs and benefits of NEP policies and their impact upon the proletariat and peasantry.

Historically the Russian working class embodied a type of social smychka in which hereditary urban proletarians and peasant migrants to industrial sites melded into a single working class. As the pace of industrialization quickened, even more peasants swelled the ranks of the working class. Despite these bonds, during the 1920s age, gender, work experience, skill levels, work attitudes, party membership, political activism, and social origins acted as centrifugal and centripetal forces upon the working class and often generated competition and division between peasants and proletarians.

Such competition had been latent in prerevolutionary society, but two factors exacerbated this situation during NEP. The first was that the experiences of the Civil War created bitter memories for both peasants and workers. For the former the most powerful memory was the forced requisitioning of their produce by state agents and urban food teams; for the latter it was the peasantry's alleged refusal to trade their produce and the urbanites' resultant hunger and near starvation. Neither group could forget or forgive what the other had "forced" it to endure. For this reason the social foundation upon which the party hoped to build the smychka was fragile.

The second factor was that NEP's economic policies were burdensome to both workers and peasants and at times pitted the two against each other. Moreover the economic realities of village life on which the fate of the smychka and NEP depended were grim. The hardships of the civil war years had undermined the economic viability of many rural households. The amount of land under plow in 1921 was about 75 percent of that in 1913. The collapse of rural industries, artisanal activities, and wholesale and retail trade during those years further diminished rural incomes. From 1917 to 1921 few peasants could obtain the tools, equipment, and other necessities essential to maintain a rural household.

The land redistribution which occurred between 1917 and 1921 resulted in more rural households than ever before, with average landholdings somewhat larger than those in 1913. In Soviet parlance middle peasants comprised the vast majority of the rural population. The small size of the middle peasants' holdings, the scarcity of draft power, tools and equipment, and the practice of strip farming within a three-field system—all combined to ensure that most peasants engaged in subsistence farming. As a result the amount of surplus grain and other produce which peasants could sell to the urban market was limited. Policy makers hoped peasants would spend the money they received from the sale of surplus produce on industrial products and thereby stimulate industrial recovery. But throughout the 1920s the peasants complained constantly and loudly that the prices they received for their produce were too low and those for industrial commodities were too high.

To generate income and maintain their farms, many peasant households sent family members to urban centers, mines, and construction sites in search of work. Estimates of rural surplus population vary between ten and nineteen million, and untold numbers of these migrated annually to urban centers. But the urban, industrial centers to which they migrated themselves were struggling to recover from the physical and economic devastation of years of war, revolution, and collapse.

The party gave top priority to industrial recovery, for without it urban-rural trade, economic recovery, and the smychka were threatened. To hasten recovery, officials enacted a series of economic and labor policies designed to speed industrial restoration, raise industrial productivity, and hasten capital accumulation for reinvestment. Beginning in 1921 the state began to withdraw most or all direct subsidies and to force factory directors to place enterprises on a self-financing basis. To cut costs directors sought to keep labor costs as low as possible by firing personnel, forcing workers to become more productive, and when possible paying workers less. Some factories had to close. Consequently urban unemployment began to rise. In 1926 the nation's unemployment rate stood at 12 percent, and it rose steadily over the next three years. In Moscow and Leningrad the unemployment rates in 1928 exceeded 20 percent.

Massive in-migration by peasants seeking work also contributed to unemployment. Labor unions displayed little sympathy for rural migrants whom they viewed as stealing jobs from their urban, proletarian constituents. The existence of a free labor market from 1925 increased the competition between urban workers and peasants for scarce jobs and created resentment of peasants by workers. The competition between them also extended to the search for housing. The rapid repopulation of cities after the civil war quickly outstripped the supply of available housing. By 1926 Moscow had one hundred thousand homeless residents.

The economic hardships experienced by workers and peasants led each of them to believe that they bore the brunt of economic recovery and therefore slowed the realization of the smychka. Various party leaders in turn used these tensions and perceptions to strengthen their arguments for maintaining or changing NEP policies.

But there was also evidence that the smychka was being realized. From 1924 the party enacted policies to organize shefstvo societies in factories and to mobilize party activists and workers. They planned to offer villagers organizational and economic assistance and to help raise the cultural level of the peasantry by delivering books and newspapers and organizing reading rooms and libraries there. This movement hoped to strengthen the smychka. By 1927 the movement boasted one and a half million members, although for many membership seems to have been a passive affair.

In the winter of 1927-1928 the shefstvo movement experienced a crisis. Membership rolls contracted sharply, financial contributions declined, and the amount and quality of work in the villages deteriorated. The cause was the grain crisis which resulted from a conjunction of economic and pricing problems. In late 1927 peasants sold to official grain collection agencies only half as much grain as they had the year before, a shortfall which resulted in higher prices and shortages in urban markets. In response, in early 1928 the party's Politburo shifted policies and enacted the Ural-Siberian method, which by forcibly confiscating grain, undermined market equilibrium and reminded peasants of the grain requisitions of the civil war.

For many party members the destruction of the market gave no cause for lament. Bukharin and other defenders of NEP and the smychka argued that economic growth and the alliance could be achieved only by careful and patient manipulation of the market. By contrast many Bolsheviks considered those tasks far too prosaic, diverting the party from the revolutionary transformation of society and the construction of the dictatorship of the proletariat. To many Bolsheviks the problems of the market were but symptoms of a more fundamental problem: the dependence of cities, the proletariat, and industrialization on the more prosperous peasants, the kulaks.

In 1927 a political crossroads had been reached. The Fifteenth Party Congress which met that year voted to speed preparations for planned industrialization and the voluntary collectivization of agriculture and to intensify economic pressure on the kulaks. From 1928 to 1929 a new majority headed by Stalin formed within the party leadership. It repudiated NEP's compromise with capitalism, the slow pace of socialist development, and dependence upon the kulak, but did not reject the smychka, which was viewed as a canon of Leninist orthodoxy. Nonetheless Stalin's 1929 decision to collectivize agriculture forcibly marked the end of the smychka by destroying the political, economic, and social bases which were necessary to its realization.

The party leaders who supported Stalin found supporters among the urban proletariat. The deterioration of workers' living standards caused by the grain crisis and the reintroduction of rationing in 1928 and 1929 exacerbated the tensions between workers and peasants generated by the increasing competition for jobs, housing, and economic security. One indication of the widening breach during these years was the redirection and reinvigoration of the shefstvo movement, which abandoned cultural work and aimed at collectivizing agriculture and struggling against the kulaks. Another indication was the "Twenty-Five Thousander" movement, which the party organized to carry out collectivization. Between 1929 and 1930 more than seventy thousand urban workers and communists volunteered to join the Twenty-Five Thousanders.

Stalin and his political allies looked to these urban workers and worker communists for support and legitimacy in their struggle with Bukharin and the advocates of NEP. Urban workers who supported collectivization and industrialization probably did not oppose the idea of the smychka any more than many party members. They temporarily united with Stalin's supporters in the party because they perceived as unfair NEP policies which allegedly favored peasants and resulted in what Lenin termed the suffering of the proletariat. The smychka, as they saw it, was no longer—if it ever had been—determined by the interests of the proletariat. Stalin's ability to use urban workers' grievances to legitimize his policies provided him with a powerful political weapon in the struggle against Bukharin and NEP.

See Also: NEW ECONOMIC POLICY, TWENTY-FIVE THOUSANDERS

Bibliography: Sigrid Grosskopf, *L'alliance ouviere et paysanne en U.R.S.S. (1921-1928). Le probleme du blé* (Paris, 1976); William Chase, "L'Irréalisable smyčka," *Revue des Etudes Slaves*, Vol. 64 (1992), 1-22; V.P. Danilov, *Sovetskaia dokolkhoznaia derevnia*, 2 vols. (M., 1977-1979); V.I. Lenin, *Collected Works*, 45 vols. (M., 1960-1970), Vols. 32 and 33; N.I. Bukharin, *Selected Writings on the State and Transition to Socialism*, ed. and trans. by Richard B. Day (New York, 1982); Leon Trotsky, *The Challenge of the Left Opposition (1923-1925)*, Naomi Allen, ed. (New York, 1975); Leon Trotsky, *The Challenge of the Left Opposition (1925-1927)*, ed. by Naomi Allen and George Saunders (New York, 1980); R.W. Davies, *The Socialist Offensive. The Collectivization of Soviet Agriculture, 1929-1930* (Cambridge, Mass., 1980); Hiroaki Kuromiya, *Stalin's Industrial Revolution. Politics and Workers, 1928-1932* (Cambridge, 1985); Lynn Viola, *Best Sons of the Fatherland. Workers in the Vanguard of Soviet Collectivization* (New York, 1987); A.S. Sulianov, "Shefskaia pomoshch' rabochego klassa derevne v podgotovke sotsialisticheskogo preobrazovaniia sel'skogo khoziastva (1925-1929 gg.)," *Rol' rabochego klassa v sosialisticheskom preobrazovanii derevnii v SSSR* (M., 1968).

William J. Chase

WORKERS' GROUP OF THE RUSSIAN COMMUNIST PARTY (1923). Most frequently called the Workers' Group. A short-lived opposition group within the Russian Communist Party. It was formed and led by Gavriil I. Miasnikov, a working-class member of the party.

The Workers' Group grew directly out of the Workers' Opposition, a faction of the Russian Communist Party which had been condemned at the Tenth Party Congress in 1921. Like its forerunner, the Workers' Group represented a protest against the centralizing activities of the party leadership and governmental bureaucracy.

Labor unions had spread rapidly during 1917. Many workers saw them as the organizing core of the new society which the revolution of 1917 promised to create. These workers and their spokesmen, who believed the slogans of the Bolshevik party and expected to run the country after the seizure of power, formed much of the Bolshevik support in 1917. During the period of the Russian Civil War and War Communism (1918-1921) the party and bureaucracy steadily reduced the autonomy of the unions. As early as 1918 the regime began to replace workers' committees with one-man management (edinonachalie) in industry. Especially galling to the workers, these managers were often bourgeois specialists, many of whom had managed factories before the revolution. Beyond this, as the civil war continued, the party began to appoint its own men to leading positions in the labor leadership, ignoring or annulling the workers' votes. By the time of the Tenth Party Congress in 1921, the unions' role was defined as primarily educational. They were to effect propaganda, maintain discipline, and carry out the orders sent down from above.

After the condemnation of the Workers' Opposition in 1921 Miasnikov tried to organize workers in Perm, an industrial center in the Urals. In his booklet, *Vexed Questions* (Trevozhnie voprosy) he criticized the party for bureaucratism, inefficiency, and corruption. He called for complete freedom of the press for all political groups to expose these evils. Lenin wrote to Miasnikov on 5 August 1921, arguing that freedom of the press would be a powerful weapon in the hands of Bolshevism's enemies, especially the bourgeoisie. Miasnikov continued to fight against the centralizing policies of the regime and to organize workers. A commission appointed by the Central Committee of the party was sent to the Urals to investigate his activity. On its recommendation the Central Committee expelled him from the party on 20 February 1922.

Miasnikov then joined with other members of the former Workers' Opposition, including N.V. Kuznetsov and P.G. Moiseev. In February 1923 they edited *Vexed Questions*, transforming it into the *Manifesto of the Worker's Group of the Russian Communist Party*. It was published in Berlin that summer and also circulated in Moscow in typewritten and primitively reproduced copies.

This manifesto touched a number of issues, but most importantly it criticized the party leadership as a new oligarchy. Composed of intelligentsia, this new elite controlled the political power and productive wealth of the country. Although they claimed to speak in the name of the working class, the new oligarchs worked against its interests. A new bureaucracy had arisen which distrusted and alienated the workers. An example was the New Economic Policy (NEP) introduced at the Tenth Party Congress, and which appeared to the

Worker's Group a betrayal of the gains of the revolution. To them the letters NEP signified "New Exploitation of the Proletariat."

In order to cure this situation the manifesto called for full freedom of expression for the entire working class. It called for a united front of all workers' groups, including Socialist-Revolutionaries (SRs) and Mensheviks, for the reconstruction to the country. It recommended direct democracy on the factory floor. Workers must organize new elections to factory committees, displacing the party members who controlled them. They should elect their representatives to newly organized soviets. As an ultimate goal the manifesto demanded the overthrow of the current leadership of the party, the dismantling of the economic institutions of the country, and the transfer of direct control of factories to those who worked in them.

The manifesto criticized not only the party leadership, but also the Communist International (Comintern). At its Third Congress in June 1921 the Comintern held that a period of capitalist stabilization had begun. It recommended a policy of the "united front." Communist parties in the West should cooperate with other workers' parties in the struggle for shorter hours, better wages, and other economic issues. In this way they might win over the large masses of workers to communism. The manifesto, which had called for a united front of workers in Russia against the communist leadership, attacked the Comintern's version. It condemned the struggle for economic gains as a distraction from the real goal of the proletariat. It declared that the death knell of capitalism had sounded and called on the workers of the advanced capitalist countries to use all means to seize power. It foresaw a period of bloody civil war.

The Workers' Group had little to say about the peasantry except that it supported the most rapid possible mechanization of the countryside to extinguish as quickly as possible the differences between country and city.

The Workers' Group shared the hatred of the middle classes which was such a pronounced characteristic of workers during the revolution of 1917. "No arguments with the Kadet bourgeois, professors, lawyers, and doctors—here there is only one medicine: a fist in the face (mordobitie)" (Sorin, 94).

Towards the end of May 1923 Miasnikov was arrested. Despite this the leaders of the Workers' Group, roughly a dozen of them, held a conference in Moscow on 5 June and elected a Moscow Bureau. During the summer they tried to expand their group and to this end conducted talks with eminent former opposition leaders, such as Aleksandra Mikhailovna Kollontai and Aleksandr Gavrilovich Schliapnikov, but without success. The purge of some party cells in Moscow depleted their ranks, but inspired by major outbreaks of labor unrest in Moscow and Petrograd in August the leaders of the Workers' Group began to plan a general strike. Before they could accomplish anything the secret police, the GPU (Gosudarstvennoe politicheskoe uchrezhdenie), arrested their leaders and smashed their organization.

It is unclear how extensive the following of the Workers' Group was. Miasnikov and Kuznetsov themselves at one time claimed more than 5,000 followers in Moscow and the provinces. But under interrogation by the GPU they admitted to a good deal of self-delusion and said that the numbers were far more modest, limited to some 200 in Moscow. Whether this was true or whether they hoped only to avoid exposing their comrades cannot be known with certainty.

The Workers' Group was unique among the various opposition movements in that it was composed entirely of proletarians. Its lonely voice echoed the revolutionary hopes of the working masses to control society for their own benefit. Impractical in 1917, these dreams had become totally unrealistic by 1923.

See Also: WORKERS' OPPOSITION

Bibliography: The standard treatment of opposition groups within the Communist party remains Robert V. Daniels, *The Conscience of the Revolution. Communist Opposition in Soviet Russia* (Cambridge, Mass., 1965). Some brief details of Maiasnikov's life are given in Leonard Schapiro, *The Origin of the Communist Autocracy. Political Opposition in the Soviet State. First Phase, 1917-1922* (Cambridge, Mass., 1956). For Lenin's letter see Vladimir Ilich Lenin, *Collected Works* translated from the fourth Russian edition, 45 vols. (M., 1960-1970), Vol. 32, 504-509. Brief references to the Workers' Group can be found in Edward Hallett Carr, *A History of Soviet Russia*, 7 vols. (New York, 1950-1971), Vol. 4, *The Interregnum, 1923-1924*; Isaac Deutscher, *The Prophet Unarmed. Trotsky. 1921-1929* (New York, 1959); Cathy Porter, *Alexandra Kollontai* (New York, 1980). The most extensive treatment is Vladimir Gordeevich Sorin, *Rabochaia gruppa* (M. 1924), a polemic against the Workers' Group, but which quotes extensively from its manifesto.

George N. Rhyne

WORKERS' INTELLIGENTSIA (1889–1894). During the latter part of the nineteenth century Russia underwent a period of rapid industrialization. To work in the new, often technologically modern factories, tens of thousands of peasants moved to the cities, especially St. Petersburg and Moscow. Most workers maintained extensive ties with their families in the countryside, returning there for planting and harvesting each year. Nonetheless, a tiny but growing number, especially second and third generation workers, had few if any rural ties. From this growing number of full-time urban workers developed a workers' elite. They were usually young, in their early twenties on average, and were divided into two groups: craftsmen and employees of large specialized enterprises. Craftsmen included carpenters, bricklayers, printers, bookbinders, and tailors. The other segment of the workers' elite were highly skilled employees needed to operate the newly complex machinery in steel mills, railway shops and machine works.

The number of members of the workers' elite was small. Out of the total work force of 77,000 in St. Petersburg in 1890, only about 1,000 belonged to this labor aristocracy. Characteristic of the workers' elite were a high degree of literacy, a higher standard of living than other workers, highly skilled occupations, and an eagerness to learn what was happening outside of Russia.

Their higher income, often three times the average for Russian workers, allowed members of the workers' elite to spend some money on their education.

Most workers earned so little that virtually all their income went to basic necessities such as shelter, clothing, and food. Members of the workers' elite often began their education in factory, evening, and Sunday schools. After learning the basics of reading, writing, and arithmetic they attended public lectures, visited second-hand bookstores, listened to doctoral dissertation defenses, and read newspapers and the thick journals common in late tsarist Russia. Generally most of this labor aristocracy was apolitical. They sought merely cultural and economic improvement of their situation, both through formal classes and through self-education. Through education they could obtain better jobs, raise their economic standard of living, and have a richer cultural life. The furtherance of education and a hunger for the outside world was central for this workers' elite. That curiosity was the major reason many members formed circles to exchange information and news about developments in the West.

Those members of the workers' elite who decided to teach other members and who criticized and wanted to change the existing political and social order in Russia were called the workers' intelligentsia. The workers' intelligentsia was a small minority of the workers' elite. In St. Petersburg, which had the greatest number of workers' elite in Russia, perhaps no more than a few hundred out of the thousand or so of them constituted a workers' intelligentsia. Though few in number they drew the attention of both their fellow workers and educated Russians.

Contacts between the student intelligentsia and the workers dated back to the 1860s and 1870s, at the height of the Populist movement. Following the assassination of Tsar Alexander II in 1881 and the ensuing government repression, many dissident intellectuals abandoned any attempt at large-scale revolutionary acts. Instead they conducted propaganda—educating workers in the fundamentals of language, science, history, and literature. Workers needed and craved the education they received at the hands of the intelligentsia in order to improve their lives. The relationship between the working class and the intelligentsia foreshadowed a perennial dispute among Marxists. What should be the true role for the proletariat? Who should have real control over the labor movement?

During the 1880s some students formed circles, groups of six to eight people. They met several evenings a week in members' rooms to educate each other in areas not offered formally in school. These students' personal ties with workers were nonetheless minimal. Workers did not know how to find members of the student intelligentsia and vice versa, and both feared potential arrests through contacts. But some circles were successful. Among the first was the circle led by Dimitur Blagoev, a Bulgarian student, who formed a quasi-Marxist group. The goal of Blagoev's group was to educate workers who could then educate others. The group did have significant ties with the workers' intelligentsia. Within two years the police destroyed Blagoev's group.

Another foreign student, Pavel Tochissky, founded the next significant Marxist intelligentsia circle in St. Petersburg in 1885. Tochissky and his group respected the workers' right to control their own decision making and to have their own group. Tochissky's group would assist only workers, and the student intelligentsia would serve only a temporary role. Tochissky organized a library and mutual assistance fund for workers. He helped metalworkers to organize a circle loosely tied to his. Three members of the workers' intelligentsia and future leaders of the Russian labor movement became members of Tochissky's group: Egor Afanasev, Vasily Shelgunov and Nil Vasiliev. The organizational structure of both was extremely tight-knit and highly centralized. The workers' group spread to several factories in different sections of the city, where more circles formed, again mainly for self-education. Ivan Timofeev, a metalworker, assumed control of the workers' library of some several hundred volumes, quite remarkable for a worker with little formal education and a twelve-hour-day job. Neither Tochissky's group nor the workers' section ever engaged in political activities.

While the number of workers influenced by Tochissky's circle was very small, they formed the heart of St. Petersburg's workers' intelligentsia. Police arrests destroyed Tochissky's group in 1888. Because of Tochissky's concern with security, the worker's network escaped arrest and continued its operations. In 1887 another student, Mikhail Brusnev, formed a self-education circle. Under his leadership representatives of student circles from institutions of higher education from all over St. Petersburg formed a central organization called the Central Students' Circle in early 1889.

While workers lived throughout St. Petersburg, one of the major concentrations of workers was in the northern part of the city. One such densely populated, muddy, and crime-ridden area, the Nevsky Gates, played a major role in the history of Russia's labor movement. In these huge, noisy, dirty, and uncultured workers' districts many workers felt isolated and alienated. Escape depended primarily on education at factory, evening, or Sunday schools. Many members of the workers' intelligentsia learned foreign languages and even traveled to the West. To further their self-education and to find companionship many workers' intelligentsia formed circles. Workers' circles were the principal institutional expression for the emergence of the workers' intelligentsia. Each circle was quite small, usually six or eight members. Each came together spontaneously. By the late 1880s circles had spread throughout the city with an estimated membership of several hundred people. Members included joiners, blacksmiths, printers, lithographers, and iron workers. Usually a worker would lead the circle by reading a section of a book or an article and then conducting an often animated discussion. Members read Russian and non-Russian authors and often discussed historical issues such as the French Revolution of 1789. Fearing penetration by police informants, members were very selective about membership. While students led many of the discussions at the meetings, workers were careful to retain overall control and direction, and often prevented students from steering the discussions in a political direction.

All workers faced a shortage of funds and books. Most circles had a treasurer and librarian as well as a leader (starosta or rukovoditel'). Each member contributed a membership fee, often twenty-five to fifty kopecks a month. Some circles received donations from the student intelligentsia. All circles faced problems of where to meet because almost all workers lived in cramped quarters and because nosy neighbors could call the police. Most lacked good teachers, which forced them to seek potential teachers from the intelligentsia. To end their isolation some of the workers' leaders by 1888 began to consider the need to unify the disparate workers' circles throughout St. Petersburg. During the winter of 1889-1890 leaders from several workers' circles met and organized a Central Workers' Circle, consisting initially of seven workers. Each member represented the combined circles from his district (raion) in St. Petersburg or from his factory. The Central Workers' Circle coordinated the current circles and created new ones.

The members of the Central Workers' Circle were the most highly skilled, most educated, and most politicized in the Russian working class. Workers' controlled the circle and designed it to benefit the working class, and the workers' intelligentsia in particular. The Central Workers' Circle represented most of the workers' circles in St. Petersburg. All of the members of the Central Workers' Circle came from the workers' intelligentsia. The average age of members was twenty-two. They were predominantly male. Women workers tended to be less educated and less skilled; and even when highly skilled they often encountered great bias in their male counterparts. Most members were born into large peasant families in tiny villages near St. Petersburg. Their severe poverty drove them to the cities in their early teens, and most vowed never to return, even for short visits. Often members were close to their mothers, yet had unhappy relationships with their fathers, who were frequently alcoholics.

At an early age these members of the workers' intelligentsia regarded education to be the major way to escape their destitution. While having had some rudimentary schooling in the villages, most only received a genuine formal education after they arrived in the city. Virtually all spent two to three years in factory or technical schools under trying conditions after a long workday. To supplement their classes these young workers often attended libraries, public lectures, and museums. Many were metalworkers, but other skilled occupations such as printing figured into the membership. They formed an upwardly mobile group, often switching to better paid and skilled jobs. In their factories the workers' intelligentsia often stood out among their fellow workers and filled a leadership role. Their background, unhappy and confused, shaped their attitudes toward religion, drinking, their less skilled and educated co-workers, politics, and each other. Thus the workers' intelligentsia represented an aggrieved, alienated group.

The attitudes and values of members of the Central Workers' Circle are critical to understanding the group's purposes and priorities. Whereas religion was central to most workers' lives, most workers' intelligentsia rejected religion and the Russian Orthodox Church. The wealth of the Church, as well as abuses and corruption by particular priests, destroyed their faith in religion. That differing attitude about religion often caused great hostility between the workers' intelligentsia and the rest of the working class. The question of religion caused poor relations not only among workers but also between the members and their families.

Another issue that divided the workers' intelligentsia from the rest of the working class was alcohol. Almost to a man the workers' intelligentsia opposed overindulgence in drinking, one of the few pleasures available to most workers. Members tended to be very moralistic. They tended to be isolated and did not relate well to anyone except other members of the workers' intelligentsia. Frequently conflicts arose with their wives, who sought basic material needs, resented money spent on books, and feared arrest. Wives also tended to be more religious and politically conservative. Members of the workers' intelligentsia had little respect for their fellow workers and their wives, calling them "dull" and disliking their drinking and their religiosity.

Despite contacts with student teachers, the workers' intelligentsia frequently developed political views on their own. Their conception of socialism was nonideological, more an attitude of curiosity. Once they arrived at a political framework, even a hazy one, they frequently repudiated both their own past and even Russia's past. For them Russia represented arbitrariness, intolerance, and backwardness. They embraced the West. They repudiated the peasantry as backward and unorganized. The relationship between the members of the student intelligentsia and the workers' intelligentsia always remained ambivalent. They eagerly sought students as teachers and discussion leaders for their circles. Yet it seemed that many students only wanted them to become revolutionary agitators. Workers almost always said students should serve only an auxiliary role in the circles. Workers and students rarely understood each other and lived in two separate worlds. Conflicts between the two groups occurred frequently. The members of the Central Workers' Circle formed the most vocal and politicized subgroup of the workers' intelligentsia.

After those first organizational meetings the Central Workers' Circle emerged as the sole organization for most of the workers' intelligentsia. The group lasted in one form or another until 1894, when massive arrests by the police crippled the organization. The Central Workers' Circle had several purposes. First and perhaps foremost it raised money to aid its members and their families. It collected money to purchase books and journals for its library. The group also established workers' clubs and cooperatives. Furthermore the group intended to represent the interests of the workers' intelligentsia in St. Petersburg, when those workers conflicted with government authority and with factory owners or managers. The Central Workers' Circle sought to improve the political, economic, and cultural position of its members.

To further those purposes, the Central Workers' Circle had a centralized pyramidal structure. At the top was the Central Workers' Circle itself, each of whose six to eight members represented a different factory or district in St. Petersburg. The members were chosen by factory or district circles from a list sent to it. The whole network of circles never became a particularly democratic body. Directives flowed from the top down—from the Central Workers' Circle to factory or district circles, which in turn supervised local circles. Decisions were always made on a consensus basis at the Central Workers' Circle or at the district, factory, and local circles. The leader (rukovoditel') decided the activities and meeting agendas and controlled the library and treasury. The pretext for the lack of democratic procedures was the need to maintain security.

At all levels the circles were small and consisted solely of workers, except for a student teacher and advisor. Student representatives could issue recommendations only, not make policy decisions. Meetings occurred once a week in a member's room after work. Meetings were devoted to lectures and subsequent discussion based on these lectures. The lectures covered a broad gamut of subjects of interest to workers, such as Charles Darwin's theory of evolution or the works of Karl Marx. Other than books, sources for lectures and discussions were newspapers and journal articles. The Central Workers' Circle and district and factory circles decided the membership for the local circles. Thus the Central Workers' Circle maintained a centralized structure.

Two offices, the treasury and the library, were fundamental to the Central Workers' Circle. The most important was the central labor fund or the treasury. Each worker's circle had its own treasury. Most were small and raised completely through members' donations, the amount based on each person's wages. The rukovoditel' was usually placed in charge. The central labor fund not only received money through donations but from lotteries and dances as well. By 1891 the central labor fund contained 1,400 rubles. Sums from the treasury went into a strike fund to aid strikers and their families. The rest went to the purchase of books and journals and to cover daily expenses. Its assistance to striking workers allowed the reputation of the Central Workers' Circle to spread far beyond the small confines of the members' circles.

Through purchases and donations the Central Workers' Circle accumulated an extensive library. For example, Ivan Timofeev donated his huge collection of some one thousand volumes. Mikhail Brusnev, a member of the Central Students Circle, kept the illegal collection at his flat. Timofeev maintained the legal collection in his flat. That collection included histories, literary classics, books on natural and physical sciences, as well as books and pamphlets on political theory and economy. Often books from the collections were passed from worker to worker in the factories.

The Central Workers' Circle also established several consumer cooperatives to provide workers with cheap food, tobacco, tea, and coffee, circumventing the high-priced stores where workers traditionally shopped. Yet from the start the cooperatives had problems. Poor quality and selection of goods and ineffective management resulted in a failure to attract many workers. Finally the Central Workers' Circle organized workers' clubs to provide an alternative to the sordid beer bars. Few workers wanted that alternative and instead attended club social events. The various ventures launched by the Central Workers' Circle consequently met with varying degrees of success. If the Treasury and the library were very successful, the workers' cooperatives and clubs on the whole failed.

Soon after its formation the Central Workers' Circle embarked on political activity to accompany the group's social and cultural endeavors. These activities were typically intense, marked by repeated attempts, often successful, to reach out to fellow workers. In late January 1891 two spontaneous and independent strikes broke out at the port and the Thornton Textile mill in St. Petersburg. While playing no role in starting either strike, members of the Central

Workers' Circle took the opportunity to bring their nearly unknown organization greater attention. After lengthy discussion the Central Workers' Circle agreed to aid the strikers through financial donations, by writing leaflets and by providing them with leadership. Nevertheless both strikes failed. The police arrested numerous strikers and many unemployed workers were willing to fill the strikers' places. But through its actions the Central Workers' Circle built up a reservoir of good will.

In February 1891 the noted populist writer Nikolai Shelgunov was seriously ill. His works long had been popular among the workers' intelligentsia. Four leaders from the Central Workers' Circle sent a delegation to Shelgunov's house in late March to give the dying man a formal letter of condolence signed by sixty-six members of workers' circles. Through this action members from the workers' intelligentsia caught the attention of Russian society. Even the city's newspapers noted the actions. On 24 April 1891 Shelgunov died. The Central Workers' Circle quickly organized a large delegation of workers to attend his funeral and to present a large wreath. Of the one thousand people who attended his funeral three days later, about ten percent were workers, despite its being a work day. Very few women workers could attend; because their wages were much lower, they could not afford the day off. This was the first public rally in St. Petersburg by workers since the demonstration in front of Kazan Cathedral in 1876. In fact workers opened the march to the cemetery, and a worker gave a speech at the funeral. After the funeral, the large crowd dispersed peacefully. Within two weeks of the funeral several workers were arrested and exiled. Nevertheless, the power and prestige of the Central Workers' Circle grew among the workers' intelligentsia, their fellow workers, and society as a whole.

The climax of the overt activities of the Central Workers' Circle occurred in May 1891 when Russian workers, on their own initiative, participated in May Day, the new international holiday for workers. There were large-scale demonstrations the previous year in Russian Poland and Lithuania, but this was the first celebration of May Day in Russia proper. Through this action Russian workers showed they were not much behind their European counterparts in political consciousness. Discussions on organizing May Day began right after the Shelgunov demonstration. They became quite heated. Many workers at circle meetings pointed out the danger of police repression and predicted that few workers would bother to attend. The Central Workers' Circle decided nevertheless to hold May Day celebrations on the second Sunday of May, a rest day for most workers. Thus they ensured optimal attendance. Few intellectuals were invited. Workers organized the event and wrote and delivered all the speeches. After a lengthy search for an appropriate spot the representatives from the Central Workers' Circle settled on a secluded area on Krestovsky Island, sparsely populated and away from the central city. Precautions were taken to avoid police intervention.

On 17 May 1891 an estimated 60 to 200 people gathered, including several women workers. Most participants were highly skilled metalworkers. It was a holiday for the workers' intelligentsia. Only three students attended and remained in the background, dressed as workers. The whole day was spent in animated discussion by groups of workers, broken from time to time by formal speeches by predesignated workers. After each speech the crowd returned to discussion in a holiday atmosphere, eating and drinking.

The highlight of the day's activities was the major speeches written and then delivered by four of the leaders of the Central Workers' Circle: Nikolai Bogdanov, Fedor Afanasev, Viktor Proshin and Egor Afanasev. Each urged that Russian workers organize trade unions to improve their living and working conditions and to reform the autocratic tsarist system. Each stressed the need for workers to accomplish these tasks on their own without outside assistance. Soon after the speeches concluded the participants left in small groups to avoid detection by the police. Despite this precaution there were several arrests that night.

Earlier that evening sixty to seventy workers who had been unable to attend the May Day event gathered at Afanasev's apartment. There the crowd ate, drank, talked, and listened to several speeches by workers' leaders. Many women attended the gathering.

The Central Workers' Circle reaped many benefits from the May Day commemorations. After the May activities a jubilant Central Workers' Circle decided to expand activities to other cities and organize circles there. Over the next year the Central Workers' Circle appeared in Moscow, Tula, Riga, Kostroma, and Nizhni Novgorod, all of which had a much smaller and less developed labor movement. Their attempts met with resistance by other workers who regarded these Central Workers' Circle activists as "outside agitators." Yet gradually circles formed in each city and established ties with the Central Workers' Circle in St. Petersburg. The Moscow circle's network had few Muscovite workers as members. The student advisors divided into Marxist and populist factions. Despite these problems the Moscow circles established a common treasury and library. The Central Workers' Circle slowly moved toward its goal of becoming an all-Russian party of workers. Yet wide fissures between Marxists and Populists still remained. On the verge of spreading their circles to yet other cities, most of the workers' leaders were arrested in the spring and summer of 1892. By the end of 1892 most of the circles and their organization outside St. Petersburg had been broken up.

The arrests in Moscow and in other cities did not lead directly to arrests within the St. Petersburg Central Workers' Circle. Still those arrests led to weakening and greater fear in St. Petersburg. Consequently, the organization adopted much more cautious plans for May Day in 1892. The group believed it had to have a public demonstration because it had conducted few public activities over the previous year. They agreed on Sunday, 24 May, and again planned to celebrate it on Krestovsky Island. An estimated 100-200 people, including women, attended. Only 2 students attended. Once again May Day was totally a workers' event. Soon after the event began, the police arrived. The crowd quickly dispersed and no speeches were delivered. After the aborted holiday the Central Workers' Circle planned another celebration, which occurred a month later on 28 June in a woods about 5 miles from St. Petersburg. At that May Day celebration, attended by some 200 people, 8 workers delivered speeches. The police watched the gathering, and later massive arrests crippled the St. Petersburg Central Workers' Circle. Most of the leaders were jailed or deported.

Following the large-scale arrests in 1892 circle work virtually ceased for several months. Only gradually did it revive among the workers' intelligentsia. Initially the circles were tiny and isolated from each other. They had little money and feared arrest. Out of these shattered ruins of a labor movement gradually a new Central Workers' Circle reemerged to coordinate the tiny dispersed circles. The inspiration lay in the hands of a few workers who had not been arrested. During the winter of 1892-1893 Vasily Shelgunov, K.M. Norinsky, Gavril Fisher, and Ivan Keizer re-established the Central Workers' Circle. Shelgunov became the leader and made the major contribution.

Shelgunov's background was typical of other members of the workers' intelligentsia. He was born in 1867 of peasant parents in a village near Pskov. His childhood was tragic. His mother died while Shelgunov was young, and his father was an alcoholic. Shelgunov arrived first in St. Petersburg at the age of nine, but soon had to return to the countryside when he became seriously ill. At thirteen he returned to St. Petersburg and worked in a bookbindery. During his youth Shelgunov received a basic general education, and furtherance of his education became his great aspiration. Questioning the censorship of a book at his bindery, Shelgunov became interested in other forbidden books and wondered why they were banned. That small incident led Shelgunov onto the path of labor activism.

In the fall of 1885 Shelgunov became an ironworker at the new Admiralty Shipbuilding Plant. There he furthered his education through evening classes. In 1888 Shelgunov was drafted into the army, where he conducted anti-government propaganda work among the other draftees. Following the completion of his service, he returned to St. Petersburg in the fall of 1892, in the aftermath of the arrests of the workers' intelligentsia activists. He set out to reorganize the Central Workers' Circle and slowly helped revive the old organization. When it reappeared in early 1893, it had no treasury until the winter of 1893.

The new Central Workers' Circle was much smaller and poorer than its parent organization. Generational differences had appeared between the older and younger workers. The latter preferred Marxism, while the older workers preferred Populism. Ideological differences divided the group's views on tactics. The younger workers preferred to work only among the tiny workers' intelligentsia, while the older workers, who remembered the Central Workers' Circle, favored agitation among all workers.

In the meantime the Central Workers' Circle expanded into new factories to organize circles. Vera Karelina, the only female member, was the group's sole contact with women workers. Eventually twenty circles were directed by the Central Workers' Circle. The bulk of the members were metalworkers at the Putilov and Baltic factories. Educational work through lectures, readings, and discussions remained paramount.

Timidity characterized the revived Central Workers' Circle's activities. The group lacked the self-confidence of its predecessor. New ideas or tactics rarely occurred. Except in its cultural activities, successes were rare. The organization lacked the spark of its predecessor. The group became embroiled in political polemics between the Populists and Social Democrats, which included a wider issue. What would be the future of the workers' movement? And would that workers' movement allow a substantive role for the student intelligentsia who split from the younger ones? The workers' intelligentsia never recovered from that split. The May Day celebration of 1893 proved a complete failure because of poor attendance and heavy police surveillance. Arrests soon took several of the oldest and most experienced labor activists. After that the group concentrated on cultural activities, the library the center of their energies. The group had to create a new library as both sections—the legal and illegal holdings—were seized in the arrests in 1892. The new library was much smaller, and collection was dispersed to the individual circles.

Several strikes broke out in St. Petersburg from 1892 to 1894. In those strikes the Central Workers' Circle played little or no role. Through inaction the group lost a splendid opportunity to begin and develop ties with rank-and-file workers.

In St. Petersburg the principal intellectual group having ties with the workers' intelligentsia was the Populist Gruppa Narodovol'tsev (People's Will Group), founded in the summer of 1891 by Mikhail Olminskii. But its activist tactics among the rank-and-file workers drove a wedge between the two organizations. As relations worsened between Populists and Marxists in late 1893, the Central Workers' Circle was caught in the midst. The debate became bitter. Many workers disliked the acrimony and said it would harm the future of the workers' movement. To keep the workers' movement unified, in early 1894 the Central Workers' Circle invited representatives of the two ideologies to defend their views at a joint meeting.

The first of two meetings occurred in February 1894. There the Marxists declared their preference for education over agitation. A second meeting took place in early April 1894. Between fifteen and twenty workers, including several women, attended. Fearing that the agitation advocated by the populists would only mean arrest, all but two workers voted for the Social Democrats. For the first time an organized body of Russian workers definitely opted for Social Democracy. But two police informants attended the crucial second meeting, and shortly afterwards, on 21 April 1894, police raids devastated both the Central Workers' Circle and the Gruppa Narodovol'tsev. Thirty people were arrested. Of the leading figures in both groups, only Shelgunov temporarily escaped arrest. The repercussions of the arrests were several. Organized Populist activity among workers ceased. An independent Central Workers' Circle never reemerged. A new Central Workers' Circle, reformed in late 1894, was totally dependent on the intelligentsia and conducted no independent activity. A chapter in the history of the Russian labor movement had closed.

The workers' intelligentsia was a rising new force in Russia. Well read and highly skilled, they remade themselves in the image of the West, especially Germany. Some of them knew western languages, and a few even traveled to the West. Their May Day demonstrations were attempts to affirm in Russia the recent resolutions of the Second International. The workers' intelligentsia were young, usually male, often from broken homes but deeply religious backgrounds, seeking economic and cultural progress for themselves. Their numbers were tiny. Yet the people played a role far more significant than their numbers would suggest.

The Central Workers' Circle, the organization of the workers' intelligentsia, created an effective treasury and library, both of which aided workers. However, other organizations, such as workers' clubs and cooperatives, proved ineffective. The Central Workers' Circle was a labor organization with the potential to become a trade union, over a decade before trade unions were legalized in the Russian Empire.

The tragedy of the workers' intelligentsia was its inability to develop rapport with the rest of the Russian working class. They could have become the leaders of that class, had they shown greater concern for its members. But only for a period of six months, from the winter of 1891 through the summer of 1892, were there extensive contacts between the workers' intelligentsia and the working rank-and-file. This isolation gave rise to other problems and prevented the intelligentsia from assuming their proper role in the history of Russian labor. Isolation also became the major impetus for the creation of circles, as a means of seeking companionship.

Inconsistency also troubled the workers' intelligentsia. They frequently denounced students for domineering elitism, yet they showed little respect for ordinary workers, who in turn hardly were inclined to offer them assistance or look to them for leadership. The student intelligentsia was quite happy to fill that role. In Great Britain and the United States the workers' intelligentsia brought moderation to the labor movement. Lack of moderation in Russia had consequences that were fatal.

Isolation, small numbers, and opposition by the government forced the collapse of the workers' intelligentsia. After suffering arrest and banishment, few of their members returned to political work. In the aftermath of the Revolution of 1905 members of the workers' intelligentsia became active in the craft unions, such as the printers, engineers, and metalworkers. Those unions, and the workers intelligentsia among them, became casualties of the Bolshevik Revolution of 1917.

Bibliography: An excellent general survey depicting changes in late Imperial Russia is W. Bruce Lincoln, *In War's Dark Shadow. The Russians Before the Great War* (New York, 1983). A fascinating description of the ambivalent relationship between the student intelligentsia and the workers' intelligentsia is Richard Pipe's short monograph, *Social Democracy and the St. Petersburg Labor Movement, 1885-1897* (Cambridge, 1963).

Russian and Soviet authors have produced several good surveys of the labor movement, with short descriptions of the workers' intelligentsia and their activities. See N. Baturin, *Ocherki istorii sotsial-demokratii v Rossii* (M., 1906); A. El'nitskii, *Istoriia rabochego dvizheniia v Rossii*, 3rd ed. (Khar'kov, 1925); R.A. Kazakevich, *Sotsial-demokraticheskie organizatsii Peterburga kontsa 80-kh nachala 90-kh godov* (L., 1960); M.N. Liadov, *Istoriia Rossiiskoi sotsial demokraticheskoi rabochei partii, 1883-1897.* (Pb, 1906); I. Nevskii, *Ocherki po istorii Rossiiskoi Kommunisticheskoi partii* (Moscow, 1925); Yu. Z.

Polevoi, *Zarozhdenie Marksizma v Rossii 1883-1894 gg*, (M., 1959); and K.M. Takhtarev, *Ocherki Peterburskogo rabochego dvizheniia 90-kh godov* (London, 1902). An invaluable collection of memoirs is *Ot gruppy Blagoeva k "Soiuzu bor'by," 1886-1894 g*. (Rostov-na-Donu, 1921). There are also useful memoirs by K.M. Norinskii, M.S. Olminskii, V.A. Shelgunov and other workers and student leaders. See also G.M. Fisher, *V Rossii i v Anglii* (M., 1922); D. Blagoev, *Moi vospominaniia* (M.-L., 1928); S. Kanatchikov, *Iz istorii moego byt'-ia* (M.-L., 1929); V. Bartenev, "Iz vospominanii," *Minuvshie gody* (1908), No. 10, 169-197; M.I. Brusnev, "Vozniknovenie," *Proletarskaia revoliutsiia* (1923), No. 2; A.M. Buiko, "Put' rabochego," *Staryi bol'shevik* (1934), No. 6; V. Golubev, "Stranichka," *Byloe* (1906), No. 12; V. Karelina, "Na zare," *Krasnaia letopis'* (1922), No. 4; P.I. Moisenko, "Vospominaniia, 1877-1893 gg.," *Krasnaia nov'* (1924), No. 3; K. Norinskii, "Moi vospominaniia," *Staryi bol'-shevik* (1933), No. 2; and V.V. Sviatlovskii, "Na zare," *Byloe* (1922), No. 19.

Michael Share

WORKERS' MILITIA (1917). In Russian, Rabochaia Militsiia. Armed bands of volunteers formed by industrial workers during the Russian revolution of 1917.

Workers' militias came into existence during the February 1917 revolution, mostly formed by industrial workers at the factories. The first were formed on 27 February, and were one of the earliest expressions of that self-assertiveness and self-organization which became one of the primary characteristics of the revolution of 1917. After 28 February they received encouragement and some assistance from the emerging new political institutions, especially the soviets and factory committees. During the first week of the revolution hundreds of individual workers' militia detachments were formed at factories throughout Petrograd and in other cities. Militias composed primarily of students and other social groups were formed as well, but the workers' militias were the most important. Moreover, they persisted after the February revolution, unlike the student and other volunteer militias.

Several terms were used to designate these volunteer armed bands, including workers' guards, factory militia, fighting detachment (druzhina), people's militia, and Red Guard, but by far the most common during the first half of 1917 was workers' militia. City militias also formed under the supervision of municipal authorities to perform the public order and anticrime functions of the old police. The term "militia" was adopted instead of the old term "police" and survived in that usage in the Soviet Union. In Petrograd and some other large cities the workers' militias effectively patrolled the more heavily industrial districts in place of the city militia.

The purposes of the workers' militia were varied. They included protecting the factories during disturbances, policing working class districts, bringing armed force to bear in support of worker economic demands at the factory, defending and advancing working class political and other interests; and defending the revolution in general, a vague but strongly felt purpose. Originally their function was largely defensive, but as social and political tensions rose later in 1917 their role became more political and aggressive.

One of the strengths of the workers' militias as well as one of its weaknesses was its intensely local orientation. Militias were formed at the local level, usually the factory, from volunteers. The factory committees played an active role in helping form and sustain the militia, especially when the manufacturers tried to suppress them during the summer. In turn the militia supported worker interests in the factory. In some instances armed militiamen wrung concessions from management by threatening violence, and in any case they were an intimidating force. The factory committees and district (raion) soviets in Petrograd, which were created out of the February revolution as well, also helped sponsor and organize workers' militias.

The Petrograd Soviet itself had an ambivalent attitude toward them. On the one hand its leaders could not bring themselves to try to suppress genuine worker organizations. But on the other they distrusted them, fearful of where they might lead and of what kinds of "disorder" they might create. Therefore the Petrograd Soviet soon adopted a generally hostile attitude, which translated into general neglect but sometimes into efforts to restrict them. The workers' militia leaders, on the other hand, generally felt the need for broader organization and for assistance from above. Workers' militia leaders made several efforts in 1917 to create a city-wide organization, but these were unsuccessful. In organization and orientation they remained very local, linked to factory and district.

The workers' militias and Red Guards tended to attract the more aggressive and assertive workers, not surprisingly, and to stand on the more radical and impatient wing of politics. They were not associated with any one political party, and no party created or controlled them. The common reference to them as a bolshevik organization or as "Lenin's" is erroneous. They were radically inclined and therefore tended to gravitate to political and social-economic positions similar to those of the bolsheviks. Of all the major political parties, only the Bolsheviks emphatically supported the idea of such armed workers' bands, while the Mensheviks and Socialist-Revolutionaries (SRs) wavered between a neutral and an increasingly hostile stance. None of the political parties developed any clear ideas about the role such groups might play in the revolution, and even among the bolshevik higher leadership support was vague and general. The active support and direction came from lower level leaders. Therefore, it was increasingly local bolsheviks at the factory and district level who assumed leadership positions, although SRs, mensheviks, anarchists, and nonparty individuals also held such positions. By the time of the October revolution these armed worker bands, now more commonly called Red Guards, were strong supporters of "Soviet power" and hence supporters of the Bolshevik revolution in its name.

Workers' militia were found in virtually every large city of Russia. In Moscow and provincial cities they formed during the February revolution as volunteer armed bands. Their history in these cities was similar to that of Petrograd—with local variations of course—in terms of their development and functions, their factory orientation, their political attitudes and that of the parties toward them, and their difficulty in forging an effective city-wide organization and leadership.

As 1917 wore on the armed workers' bands grew more numerous, larger, better armed, and increasingly politically aggressive. Although no precise numbers are possible, a good estimate for the eve of the October revolution is about 25,000 in Petrograd and 150,000-200,000 nationwide. More important than numbers, although those were not insignificant, they were earnest advocates of "Soviet power." That is, they supported a government based on the soviets of workers, soldiers, and peasants deputies, excluding the middle classes and all nonsocialists. They were committed also to a radical social and economic transformation and an end to the war. As the gains and optimism of spring evaporated, increasingly they were willing to resort to arms to defend and advance their interests. In Petrograd, Moscow and other cities they formed by the fall a hard core of armed men committed to a new revolution. Whatever their deficiencies in training, arms, and organization, their resolve and their willingness to use armed force at a time when most potential opponents lacked both qualities allowed them to play a decisive role in the October revolution and its immediate aftermath. By that time they were more generally called "Red Guards," which term had connotations of a more radical, aggressive and political orientation than the term "workers' militia," the more common term of the spring and summer.

See Also: RED GUARD

Bibliography: The history of workers' militia and the Red Guard is Rex A. Wade, *Red Guards and Workers' Militias in the Russian Revolution* (Stanford, 1984), which has an extensive bibliography of sources and secondary literature.

Rex A. Wade

WORKERS'-PEASANTS' RED ARMY (1918-1946). Formal name of the Soviet armed forces from 1918-1946. Also known as Red Army or by its Russian acronym RKKA (Raboche-krest'ianskaia Krasnaia armiia).

On 9 November 1917 the Bolshevik party's Petrograd leadership formed a Council of People's Commissars, which included a committee on army and naval affairs and which was headed by three members of the bolshevik military organization: Mikhail Sergeevich Kedrov, Nikolai Vasilievich Krylenko, and Nikolai Ilich Podvoisky. Among its first tasks the committee oversaw the transfer of the imperial military administration to its new Soviet commissars and began to work out a plan for the demobilization of the large and disintegrating imperial army. Before long Lenin's government realized that it would need an armed force to hold back the German armies to the west and to combat the rapidly emerging domestic anti-Bolshevik forces. The provisional, improvised solution of relying on Red Guards and a few units of the old army proved inadequate to meet the mounting threats. On 15 January 1918 the Soviet government created the All-Russian Collegium for the Organization of the Workers'-Peasants' Red Army. The first units of the new Red Army began forming in the second half of January and went into immediate combat. Despite this fact the Soviet Union traditionally celebrated 23 February 1918 as the birth of the Red Army; on that day nearly sixty thousand Petrograd residents volunteered to defend their city from the German assault.

With the appointment of Leon Davidovich Trotsky as Commissar for Military and Naval Affairs on 19 March 1918, the Bolshevik regime signaled its commitment to build an effective Red Army. It thereby abandoned—at least for the duration of the crisis—a volunteer, proletarian militia based loosely on models advocated by European socialists, most prominently Jean Jaurès. Trotsky quickly introduced several controversial measures: conscription, a ban on elections of commanders, and recruitment of former tsarist officers. The latter, who ranged from General Staff officers to doctors and veterinarians, became known as military specialists. As late as 1921 after determined efforts to train Red Commanders from working-class and peasant origins, nearly 34 percent of the 217,000 command personnel remained military specialists. During the Civil War the Red Army called up nearly 50,000 former officers and 130,000 former non-commissioned officers (NCOs) of the tsarist army.

Trotsky's advocacy of widespread employment of the "military specialists" in the Red Army encountered fierce opposition, especially after several of the officers betrayed the Red cause and tried to lead their troops to the White enemies. Trotsky's critics joined forces as the Military Opposition at the Eighth Party Congress in 1919; Lenin came to Trotsky's defense and silenced most of the critics for the time being. In response to the criticisms Trotsky launched a series of crash courses to train men and women from the working class, toiling peasantry and revolutionary intelligentsia in military affairs. The graduates of these courses, together with the tens of thousands of ex-NCOs from the tsarist army who rose through the ranks during the course of the civil war fighting, became known as red commanders to distinguish them from the military specialists.

The institution of the military commissar was a further measure designed to insure the loyalty of the hybrid and often inexperienced new officer corps. The relationship between commissar and commander was fraught with tension from the beginning because the boundaries between military and political authority could never be delineated satisfactorily. The commissars came under the jurisdiction of the army's Political Administration, which acted as the representative of the Central Committee of the Communist Party in the Revolutionary Military Council of the Republic, the supreme organ of the armed forces. As a further measure to ensure firmer loyalty among the troops, the Communist Party organized mass mobilization of its members to military service. By August 1920 more than 300,000 party members were fighting in the Red Army. Among the most effective units were the special assignment detachments (chasti osobogo naznacheniia, or CHONY), which were made up entirely of party members and sympathizers. Finally the Cheka policed the lives of soldiers and officers through its special sections (osobye otdely).

In May 1918 the proletarian dictatorship retreated from its principled insistence on an urban, socialist conscript base and extended the military service obligation to peasants who did not exploit the labor of others. In accord with early Soviet legislation, only citizens of the new Soviet republic were eligible to serve in the class-based army; disfranchised persons—former policemen, clergy, landlords, among others—were banned from carrying arms and occasionally required to pay a tax or perform noncombat work in rear units. The soldiers and officers were predominantly from the Slavic peoples of the former Russian empire, largely replicating the ethnic breakdown of the imperial army. Several Turkic peoples in Central Asia were not called to service.

During the Civil War the Red Army was organized in several fronts, the most important being the Eastern, Southern, Ukrainian, Turkestan, and Western fronts. The fronts were subordinated to the Revolutionary Military Council of the Republic (RSVR), created 2 September 1918, and the All-Russian General Staff. Another office formed to coordinate the immense tasks of resource mobilization for the war effort was the Council of Workers' and Peasants' Defense (30 November 1918). By the end of the Civil War the personnel in the Red Army approached five million, although perhaps as many as one million of those listed officially as serving might have been deserters or draft dodgers.

Upon the defeat of the White armies and the major forces of foreign intervention a commission representing the Red Army and the party began to plan for demobilization and to rethink the structure of the armed forces. The improvised civil war fronts were abandoned in favor of a network of military districts that gradually embraced the entire Soviet Union. In August 1923 following the adoption of the Soviet Union's Constitution, the RVSR was renamed the Revolutionary Military Council of the USSR. Trotsky's successor as commander-in-chief, the Bolshevik Civil War hero Mikhail Vasilievich Frunze launched a number of reforms which were implemented in the mid-1920s. These resulted in a mixed system of 562,000 troops serving two-year terms of duty in the regular cadre army and a larger body of reserve formations organized as territorial militias and training citizens during summer months over the course of five years. The number of territorial units reached its peak in 1930, when 58 percent of all rifle divisions were territorial formations.

The army leadership also experimented with national formations, units composed primarily of soldiers of one non-Russian national or ethnic group. Ukrainian units never formally were called national formations, but existed as territorial militias. During the 1920s military service was extended gradually to all the peoples of the Soviet Union, albeit with the same restrictions that applied to qualification for citizenship. The practices of political control through the double agencies of Political Administration and GPU, the successor to the Cheka, were maintained. The status of the commissar was diminished upon the gradual and partial switch to "unified command," whereby commanders who were party members were held responsible for both political and military matters in their units. By the end of the 1920s the overwhelming majority of Red Army officers were party members.

Because Frunze died in 1925 his successor Kliment Efremovich Voroshilov completed the implementation of the military reforms. Under Voroshilov the Red Army grew to one million by 1934 and then expanded rapidly in the 1930s. By 1939 the Red Army's numbers were 1.943 million, and by June 1941, 5 million. During the 1930s a significant portion of the nation's industrialization effort was geared to supplying the Red Army with the modern technological weapons it would need to fight future enemies. Important changes in military doctrine required major increases in artillery, tanks, and aviation, as well as more literate and technically-skilled soldiers. Gradually the Red

Army's high command implemented measures of increasing administrative centralization. In 1934 the People's Commissariat for Military and Naval Affairs was reorganized as the People's Commissariat of Defense with a new executive organ, the Military Council. During the mid-1930s the mixed system of regular cadre forces and territorial militias was phased out, and the experiment with national formations came to an end. These changes were codified in a new law on obligatory military service, adopted 1 September 1939.

Between the Civil War and the German invasion in June 1941 the Red Army remained largely a peacetime army, but it did engage in limited combat operations. In 1929 the Red Army's Far Eastern Army, under the command of Vasily Konstantinovich Bliukher, defeated Chinese troops in a struggle over the Far Eastern Railroad. In 1936-1937 many Soviet officers were active with the Loyalist forces in the Spanish Civil War. In July 1938 Red Army units, again under the command of Bliukher, defeated Japanese forces at Lake Khassan; a year later they fought the Japanese Kwantung Army at the Battle of Khalkhin-Gol. Following the signing of the German-Soviet Non-Aggression Pact in August 1939, the Red Army entered Eastern Poland with little resistance. The conquered territories entered the Soviet Union as western Ukraine and Belorussia. Later that year Estonia, Lithuania, and Latvia accepted Soviet bases; in August 1940 these states were incorporated into the Soviet Union. During the winter of 1939-1940 the Red Army encountered stiff resistance in the Soviet war against Finland. In June 1940 the Red Army entered Romania and seized Northern Bukovina and Bessarabia. The poor performance of the Red Army in these battles immediately before the German invasion resulted in Voroshilov's dismissal as Army Commissar. His successor, Semen Konstantinovich Timoshenko, enacted a series of reforms in 1940-1941 to address some of the important shortcomings revealed in the recent fighting.

A tragic chapter in the peacetime history of the Red Army was the Great Terror of the second half of the 1930s. Beginning in 1936 high-ranking officers and commissars were arrested on charges of political unreliability. The year 1937 marked a new stage in terrorizing military men. At a military trial in June several marshals and commissars were arrested and executed as "enemies of the people," including Mikhail Nikolaevich Tukhachevsky, Iona Emmanuilovich Yakir, Yeronim Petrovich Uborevich, and Yan Borisovich Gamarnik. During 1937-1938 the repressions cut a wide swath through the high command. In his report in November 1938 to a meeting of the Defense Commissariat's Military Council, Voroshilov boasted that the Red Army had been cleansed of 40,000 men between 1937-1938 and that more than 100,000 had been transferred or promoted. The rapid and frequently murderous personnel changes had a disastrous effect on army morale and functioning.

The German invasion on 22 June 1941 resulted in large and rapid losses for the Red Army. The High Command reorganized the western military districts into a system of fronts for the duration of the fighting: Northwest, West and Southwest. On 30 June 1941 the State Defense Committee (GKO) was created, with Joseph Vissarionovich Stalin as chairman, to coordinate the war effort. The military campaigns were directed from the General Headquarters of the High Command (Stavka), headed at first by Timoshenko, but then by Stalin himself. In July 1941 Stalin also assumed the post of Commissar of Defense and Commander-in-Chief of the Armed Forces.

The Red Army's numbers grew steadily to over eleven million by May 1945. During the winter of 1941-1942 Georgi Konstantinovich Zhukov stopped the Wehrmacht at Moscow in the first defeat of the German Army since it launched the world war. Other major battles of the war included Marshal Timoshenko's attack in the Kharkov region (spring 1942), the battle of Stalingrad (1942-43), and the battle of Kursk (1943). By the end of 1944 the Red Army was chasing the German forces across Eastern Europe along three fronts—Northwestern commanded by Konstantin Konstantinovich Rokossovsky, Western under Zhukov, and Southwestern under Ivan Stepanovich Konev. The Red Army captured Berlin on 2 May 1945. Following the German surrender the Soviet government announced the first age cohorts eligible for demobilization. This chaotic process was completed by the beginning of 1948. As the Red Army made the transfer to peacetime footing a new reorganization began. In February 1946 the Commissariats of Defense and of the Navy were unified in one Commissariat of Armed Forces. Shortly thereafter the Commissariat was renamed Ministry of the Armed Forces and the Red Army renamed the Soviet Army.

Bibliography: Francesco Benvenuti, *The Bolsheviks and the Red Army. 1918-1922* (Cambridge, 1988); Herbert S. Dinerstein, *War and the Soviet Union* (London, 1959); John Erickson, *The Soviet High Command* (New York, 1962); Idem., *The Road to Stalingrad* (London, 1975); Idem., *The Road to Berlin* (Boulder, 1983); Mark von Hagen, *Soldiers in the Proletarian Dictatorship* (Ithaca, 1990); Basil H. Liddell Hart, ed., *The Soviet Army* (London, 1956); Aleksandr G. Kavtaradze, *Voennye spetsialisty na sluzhbe Respubliki Sovetov, 1917-1920 gg.* (M., 1988); Saul M. Kliatskin, *Na zashchite Okitabria. Organizatsiia reguliarnoi armii i militsionnoe stroitel'stvo v Sovetskoi Respublike, 1917-1920* (M., 1965); Dimitri Fedotoff White, *The Growth of the Red Army* (Princeton, 1944); M.V. Zakharov, ed., *50 let vooruzhennykh sil SSSR* (M., 1968).

Mark L. von Hagen

WORKING CLASS IN THE RUSSIAN REVOLUTION (1917-1921). From the February (March) 1917 revolution until the introduction of the New Economic Policy (NEP) in spring 1921, the working class in Russia experienced radical transformations in its size, composition, political power, and social role and status. During this period of profound transformation the working class was both an agent and victim of change.

On the eve of the February 1917 revolution the working class in Russia is estimated to have consisted of some 11 million workers. Only a minority of these (some 3.4 million) worked in large-scale industrial enterprises, and another 830,000 worked on the railroads. Although they comprised only a small proportion of the total population of 140 million, workers, especially industrial and railroad workers, proved to be the most powerful social agents of revolution. Their power emanated from several factors. Large-scale industry concentrated large groups of workers in relatively few enterprises. This was especially true in the metalworking industries, the workers of which played an important role in the revolution. Workers also were concentrated geographically. They comprised about one-fifth of the populations of Moscow and Petrograd, the economic and political centers of Russia. Finally the experiences of the 1905 revolution and the labor struggles of 1912-1914 provided workers with organizational experience and broadly shared political and economic demands. These factors combined in 1917 to give workers power disproportionate to their numbers.

The spontaneous general strike of Petrograd workers which was sparked by bread riots on 23 February 1917 ignited the flames of revolution throughout Russia and led to the abdication of Tsar Nicholas II. To fill the political vacuum created by the tsar's abdication, a system of dual power came into existence. The soviets represented the working class. These democratically elected, revolutionary bodies aimed at keeping a watchful eye on the Provisional Government, which represented the interests of the country's political and economic elite. They also strove to fulfill workers' revolutionary demands. Those demands included the establishment a democratic republic that would ensure democratic and civil rights and liberties, an end to the war (without annexations), the transfer of land to the peasantry, the establishment of an eight-hour workday, higher wages, and a measure of control over their working lives. In the factories workers elected factory committees to represent their interests, to keep a watchful eye on management and to give them a measure of control over factory life.

The Provisional Government resisted many of these demands and as it did workers and their demands grew increasingly radical. In July 1917 many Petrograd workers joined soldiers in demanding the overthrow of the Provisional Government and the granting of all powers to the soviets. The Provisional Government defeated this challenge. But in the aftermath of the failed coup d'etat by General Lavr Georgievich Kornilov (1870-1918) in September, workers' disgust with the temporizing policies of the Provisional Government led them to support the Bolshevik party in increasing numbers. From then until the October (November) 1917 revolution re-elections in all of the country's city soviets and many soldiers' soviets gave majorities to the most extreme parties—the Bolsheviks, Left Socialist-Revolutionaries and Anarchists. The Bolshevik party, which called for all power to the soviets, an immediate end to the war, peace without annexation, the transfer of all land to the peasantry, and the establishment of workers' control (rabochii kontrol) in industry, best expressed the frustrated workers' revolutionary agenda and won the largest number of votes in the autumn 1917 soviet elections.

On 25 October (7 November) 1917 the Second All-Russian Congress of Soviets voted overwhelmingly to create a new Soviet government, a government initially dominated by and later totally controlled by the Bolshevik party. At the time it appeared to many workers that the revolutionary agendas of the Bolshevik party and the working class were virtually identical. But during the next three and one-half years those agendas diverged widely.

Vladimir Ilich Lenin, the leader of the Bolshevik party, presented to the Congress of Soviets a series of revolutionary decrees. The decree on peace announced an immediate cease-fire and called for peace negotiations. The decree on land nationalized all land and empowered village communes to confiscate and redistribute most of it. The decree on workers' control empowered workers to participate in the management of their enterprises. But in the collapse of central governmental power and the assertion of local control that followed the October revolution, many workers moved quickly to fulfill their own revolutionary demands. As they did they came into increasing conflict with the new government.

One of the workers' primary demands was for greater control over their working lives. The decree on workers' control seemed to grant that demand. But Lenin envisioned workers' control in productivist terms; that is, the decree empowered workers not to take over their factories but rather to create committees to oversee and verify management's policies and activities. For Lenin the primary goal was to increase production. To achieve that goal workers and management were expected to cooperate. Lenin argued that granting workers the power to oversee and verify management's decisions and to share in the administration of enterprises with enterprise directors who were ultimately responsible for an enterprise would enable workers to develop the administrative skills so critical to the ultimate realization of socialism. Until late 1919 most enterprises were administered on a collegial basis (kollegialnost) by workers' representatives, trade union officials, and managerial personnel.

Many workers viewed workers' control in a more immediate and radical way. Angered by management's long-standing resistance to workers' demands for higher pay and better conditions, and suspicious of many owners' claims that they lacked the money to meet workers' demands, many factory committees interpreted the decree on workers' control as granting them the right to take over their factories. Many factory committees appealed to local soviets or newly created national offices to confiscate an enterprise and grant the factory committees full managerial powers. As more enterprises were nationalized and municipalized, greater numbers of factory committees demanded that their enterprise also be confiscated by state authorities. Once in control many workers began to enact their economic demands, especially raising their wages. In the process many factories drained their capital funds and often sold equipment, thereby endangering future production and the enterprises' viability. One observer described the process as socialism in one factory.

Workers' desire for immediate relief from their economic plight was understandable. From 1917 until 1924 spiraling inflation diminished workers' real wages. What had cost one ruble in 1913 cost 8.71 rubles by October 1917; by spring 1921 that same item cost 55,000 rubles. Workers' wages were unable to keep up with the soaring cost of living. Because food remained in short supply and the prices of basic foodstuffs rose sharply, food rationing, which had been introduced in 1916, remained in effect until late 1922.

Compounding their economic insecurity was a steep rise in unemployment in the months after the October revolution. Shortly after the Decree on Peace the Soviet government moved to end military production contracts and place the economy on a peacetime footing. The decision led to a sharp rise in unemployment among workers, especially those who worked in defense-related industries and in cities like Petrograd, the economies of which depended on military production.

When the Bolsheviks came to power Lenin had hoped to create a system of state capitalism. Socialist economic policies designed to meet the demands of working people would coexist with capitalist economic policies which were deemed essential to economic stability. But the demands of workers, the assertion of local economic interests over those of the nation, inflation, the breakdown of the nation's railroad and transport systems, the demobilization of the tsarist army, a mounting fuel shortage, food shortages, and the onset of the Civil War—all undercut that effort. Many factories, unable to meet their payroll or lacking the fuel or raw materials to maintain production, had to close. Unemployment increased, workers' anger rose, strikes occurred with increasing frequency, and workers' calls for effective policies to meet their demands grew more strident. When the government proved unable to meet their demands, workers often elected Mensheviks and Socialist-Revolutionaries to replace Bolshevik deputies in local soviets.

In June 1918 the government responded to the deepening crisis and working class discontent by breaking sharply with previous economic policies. That month the government announced a policy of requisitioning agricultural produce (a policy known as the food dictatorship) to supply the workers, cities, and the Red Army with adequate supplies. The government also ordered the nationalization of many industrial enterprises in an effort to keep them open and ordered that they direct their production toward the war effort. Thus began the policy of War Communism, which was in fact not a unified and coherent economic policy but rather a collection of increasingly severe policies designed to stem the economic collapse and supply the Red Army.

For workers the most immediate and threatening crisis was the food shortage. Since 1916 when the government introduced food rationing the size and quality of rations available to workers diminished, and prices for food in the private markets rose. After the October revolution the food crisis intensified. Although united in their anger, workers responded to the crisis in different ways. Some left the factories and returned to their villages, some devoted their workday to producing items for sale or barter in the private markets, some turned to crime and prostitution, and virtually all took time from work to search for food.

In these conditions many workers welcomed the imposition of the food dictatorship. Factories or groups of factories recruited worker volunteers to man teams which went to the villages in search of food to requisition. The requisitioned produce was sent to public dining halls where workers could receive one free meal a day or to factories where the issuance of food products increasingly replaced money wages. But requisitioning angered the peasantry, who cut back on production, thereby further undercutting rural-urban trade and reducing the supply of food available to workers. In February 1918 the average daily bread ration for a Moscow worker was 100 grams a day; in July 1919 it was a mere 80 grams. The newspaper Pravda did not exaggerate when in July 1919 it lamented that "Moscow and Petrograd are starving."

In 1917 workers also had demanded an improvement in their living conditions. Before 1917 most Russian workers lived in factory barracks or overcrowded and squalid subdivided rooms. Their living conditions stood in stark contrast to those of the Russian elite. After the October revolution many local soviets confiscated the houses and apartments of the rich and redistributed the living space to working people. Until the August 1918 decree nationalizing urban property such soviet actions had no legal basis but had considerable support among workers. The improvement in workers' lodgings proved temporary. Shortages of fuel for home heating and the breakdown of urban water and sewer systems quickly rendered many dwellings uninhabitable, thereby dashing workers' hopes for improved living conditions.

During this period the composition of the Russian working class changed profoundly. During World War I 20 percent of the nation's workers were conscripted, although in some industries the proportion was higher. The increased demand for labor resulted in a greater proportion of women, adolescents, and peasants working in factories and mines. The composition of the working class in 1917 was therefore more diverse than it had ever been. After the October revolution that class' composition underwent even more drastic changes. Upon publication of the Decree on Land many workers who were peasants by social origin returned to their villages to claim their share of the lands being redistributed. Others fled the collapsing cities and went to live with relatives in the villages. At the formation of the Red Army many workers, virtually all of them males, left the factories to take up arms against the domestic and foreign enemies of the revolution. In Moscow 70 percent of the workers between the ages of 20 and 24, 55 percent of those between the ages of 25 and 29, and 35 percent of those between the ages of 30 and 35 joined the Red Army during the Civil War. The opening of jobs in the newly forming soviet, trade union, and party bureaucracies drew thousands of other workers, most of whom were males, away from the factories. As a result women and adolescents accounted for a majority of the working class by 1920.

This exodus of workers during 1917-1921 meant that virtually every factory, mine and railroad line experienced drastic reduction in its work force. Nikolai Ivanovich Bukharin referred to this process as the "disintegration of the proletariat" and "the declassing of the proletariat." The work force of Moscow's textile and food processing industries, for example, shrank by 75 percent during the Civil War. The size of the capital's industrial work force shrank from 190,000 in 1917 to 81,000 in early 1921. In Petrograd the decline was even sharper. The loss of skilled workers grew especially acute. Factory directors and factory committees lamented the loss of skilled and experienced workers and described their work force as "yesterday's peasants." That was not entirely accurate since much of the work force consisted of women and adolescents, some of whom were family members of workers who had left the factories.

By 1921 the Russian working class was a divided class consisting of a core of experienced and skilled workers, a majority of whom were males over thirty years of age, and increasing numbers of inexperienced women, adolescents, and "yesterday's peasants." This latter group suffered from what trade union leaders called an ignorance and lack of interest in production.

Although such workers contributed to the problem, the decline in industrial productivity had several causes. Increasing shortages of fuel and raw materials resulted from the collapse of the transportation and distribution systems. Loss of territory to the White Army severely disrupted industrial production and undercut productivity. Perhaps equally important was the decline of labor discipline among workers. To procure the necessities of daily life, workers frequently took time off from work. Because epidemic diseases such as typhus and cholera swept the country, many workers were too sick or weak to work. Worker absenteeism became a common problem during the civil war years. Whereas in 1908 the average Russian worker worked the equivalent of 320 eight-hour days, in 1920 that worker reported for only 219 eight-hour days. The breakdown of workers' respect for or deference to owners, managers, technical personnel, and foremen and workers' rejection of the rules established by them further undermined labor productivity and discipline. Even when workers reported to work many devoted their time there not to producing for the enterprise, but to making products and even stealing tools to barter for food.

Soon after the October revolution trade union and government officials sought to devise means to increase productivity and improve labor discipline. As early as January 1918 many trade unions and even factory committees called for the creation of production norms and the introduction of piece-rate wages. Poor working conditions, worker resistance, and economic collapse frustrated attempts to implement these policies.

In November 1919 the Soviet state's fortunes reached their lowest ebb. The economic collapse continued unabated, starvation threatened many, and White Army victories followed in quick succession. Faced with the threat of defeat the government introduced punitive policies to combat labor indiscipline. It militarized the labor force, tied rations to productivity, and replaced collegial factory administration with one-man management.

Under the new system the powers of enterprise directors were increased dramatically and those of factory committees and trade unions were curtailed. Enterprise directors received the right to enforce labor policy as they saw fit. Worker Disciplinary Courts (also known as Comradely Courts) were organized in factories and authorized to punish violators of factory regulations and labor decrees and discipline. To instill labor discipline and thereby raise productivity, managers were allowed to withhold a portion of an absent worker's rations and to increase the rations of workers who exceeded their production norms. In June 1920 the government issued a decree authorizing the use of "natural bonuses" (that is, food, clothing, etc.) to those piece-rate workers who exceeded their production norms. Historically Russian workers had resisted the imposition of piece-rate wages. But after the introduction of that policy the number of workers receiving piece-rate wages rose sharply. For the first time in five years industrial productivity rose.

To combat the growing shortage of labor, especially of skilled labor, the government in 1919 and 1920 turned to labor conscription. Introduced on an industry-by-industry basis labor conscription was common practice by late

1919. Yet labor shortages continued. In early 1920 in an effort to draw skilled and experienced workers from the army, villages, food detachments, and bureaucratic offices, the government introduced universal compulsory labor and the militarization of labor. The latter policy subjected workers to military discipline. Stiff penalties for violators of labor discipline accompanied this policy, although the shortage of labor appears to have blunted the impact of those on most workers.

Workers responded angrily to these new policies, especially those granting sweeping powers to management. They staged strikes and protests. Given that the national trade union leadership endorsed these labor policies, workers' ability to combat these policies was limited. Stripped of their power to influence factory life and chafing under the constraints imposed by the militarization of labor, worker hostility mounted.

In late 1920 and early 1921 widespread labor unrest engulfed the country's industrial centers. Strikes occurred at 77 percent of the nation's medium and large enterprises. Approximately 90 percent of all strikes occurred in nationalized enterprises. Street demonstrations occurred in Moscow, Petrograd, and other cities. In some cases the unrest had to be quelled by troops. Improving the quantity and quality of food was the strikers' primary demand. Factory meetings and conferences passed resolutions sponsored by Mensheviks and Socialist-Revolutionaries and shouted down Bolshevik speakers.

At the February 1921 metalworkers' conference the delegates attacked Bolshevik food policy and debated production rates and the role of trade unions. Among the resolutions passed at the conference were those demanding that rations not be lowered, that the quality of food in factory and public dining halls be improved, and that issuing of the "products of production" in lieu of wages be abolished. Many delegates drew a sharp distinction between "we" and "you" when speaking of officials. As Commissar of Food Andrei Yanuarevich Vyshinsky put it: "By their words, one could sense a complete breach between the masses and the party, between the masses and the unions." (Pravda, 8 February 1921).

Given the workers' anger with the existing economic policies and their resentment of the Bolshevik party and the trade unions, as well as rebellions among the peasantry and at the Kronstadt naval base, it is hardly surprising that the Tenth Congress of the Russian Communist Party, which met in March 1921, voted to replace the requisitioning of food with a tax in kind. This vote marked the party's rejection of War Communism and heralded the introduction of the New Economic Policy.

By early 1921 the revolutionary dreams and demands of the Russian working class was unfulfilled. The alliance of workers and Bolsheviks which had brought the Soviet government to power, like the working class itself, had fallen victim to the consequences of economic collapse, war and revolution, and to government policies designed to minimize those consequences. By the end of the Civil War the working class was a profoundly different class than it had been in 1917. In 1922 there were only 4.6 million workers, less than half its size (11 million) in 1913, and fewer than half of those (2 million) labored in industry. It was a class shorn of the experienced and skilled workers of the prewar years, a class with a markedly different social composition, and a class exhausted by the privations of the previous four years.

See Also: WORKING CLASS IN SOVIET RUSSIA

Bibliography: Charles Bettleheim, *Class Struggles in the USSR. First Period. 1917-1923* (Brighton, 1977); Edward Hallett Carr, *The Bolshevik Revolution*, Vols. 1-2 (London, 1965); William Chase, *Workers, Society, and the Soviet State. Labor and Life in Moscow. 1918-1929*, Chap. 1 (Urbana, 1987); Marc Ferro, *The Russian Revolution of February 1917* (London, 1972); Marc Ferro, *October 1917* (London, 1980); Luka Stepanovich Gaponenko, *Rabochii klass Rossii v 1917 g.* (M., 1970); Aleksandr Ianovich Grunt, *Moskva-1917. revoliutsiia i kontrrevoliutsiia* (M., 1976); Diane Koenker, *Moscow Workers and the 1917 Revolution* (Princeton, 1981); Isaak Izrailevich Mints, *Istoriia velikogo otkiabria*, Vols. 1-2 (M., 1967-1968); Adolf Grigorevich Rashin, *Formirovanie rabochego klassa Rossii* (M., 1958); O.I. Shkaratan, *Problemy sotsial'noi struktury rabochego klassa SSSR* (M., 1970); Stephen Anthony Smith, *Red Petrograd. Revolution in the Factories 1917-1918* (Cambridge, 1983); Stanislav Gustavovich Strumilin, *Zarabotnaia plata i proizvoditel'nost' truda russkoi promyshlennosti, 1913-1922 gg.* (M., 1923). **William J. Chase**

WORKING CLASS IN SOVIET RUSSIA. The social group in whose name the Bolsheviks seized political power in the October revolution of 1917 and the rhetorical object of social and economic policy thereafter.

Derived from Marx and Engels' analysis of the laws of development of the capitalistic mode of production as well as the growth of industrial capitalism in tsarist Russia, the term "working class" was prominent in the vocabulary of the radical intelligentsia in the 1880s and not long thereafter among skilled industrial workers who sought enlightenment from Marxist students. Conceptually narrower than the "toiling masses" which typically included the bulk of the peasantry, the "working class" was broader in Russian Marxist discourse than the proletariat which, at least after 1917, connoted both social position and consciousness. Thus, "working class" is to be understood simultaneously as a sociological phenomenon, a cultural experience, and a discursive category.

Data on the quantitative dimensions of the working class reflect its political as well as socio-economic construction. In 1913, the last year of the tsarist regime for which more or less complete data exists, the number of workers employed in enterprises subject to the factory inspectorate stood at 2.28 million. To this figure should be added some 650,000 mine workers and 815,000 railroad workers, yielding a total of 3.7 million people. But aside from these wage earners there were approximately 4.5 million agricultural wageworkers, three million small-scale handicraft and cottage industry workers, 1.5 million construction workers and substantial numbers of domestic servants, workers in the commercial and service sectors, and office workers.

The extent to which these categories of workers can be included under the broader category of working class is highly problematic. For one thing, it is virtually impossible to determine with any accuracy the number of full time, year-round workers as opposed to those for whom wage earning was a seasonal activity supplementing income derived from the ownership, leasing, or renting of land. For another, "class" was only one of several available categories by which wage earners identified themselves or were identified by others so that even among factory workers its significance cannot be assumed. To Russian Marxists who took a keen interest in this question and fiercely debated with populists the class character of Imperial Russian society, only large-scale production created the preconditions for a collective identity and an awareness of antagonisms vis àvis officials, owners, and their "hirelings." It followed that degrees or levels of consciousness could be defined by the extent to which they corresponded to such an awareness and the (imputed) interests of that class. Much of the skirmishing between Bolsheviks and Mensheviks in the pre-revolutionary period had to do with defining those interests and competing for workers' support within the trade unions, mutual aid societies, and other precariously legal institutions permitted by the tsarist regime.

Upon coming to power in November 1917 the Bolsheviks set about making good on their claims to represent working-class interests. Aside from removing Russia from the war, the new Soviet government proclaimed workers' control in all enterprises, promulgated a relatively enlightened labor code, and organized an electoral system weighted in favor of urban residents. These and other measures comprised what Lenin and other leading Bolsheviks characterized as the dictatorship of the proletariat.

All the while the number of industrial workers, which had risen slightly in the course of the war, began to decline owing to factory shutdowns, various mobilizations in connection with the civil war and food procurement campaigns, or simply flight to the countryside whence so many workers had come. From a high of 3.4 million in 1917 the number of workers employed in "census" industry, enterprises employing more than 16 workers dropped to slightly over two million in 1918, between 1.3 and 1.5 million in 1919, and roughly 1.5 million in the latter part of 1920. Compared to 1913, losses by sector were steepest in textiles, woodworking and foodstuffs (See Table 1).

Table 1

Manual Workers in 1913 and January 1921 by Branch of Industry

Branch	Workers (thousands) 1913	1921	Percent of 1921/1913
Mining	496.8	280.8	56.5
Metalworks	601.6	473.7	78.7
Textiles	880.8	240.2	27.3
Woodworking	136.0	57.0	42.0
Chemicals	111.1	93.7	83.7
Foodstuffs	426.8	130.0	30.5
Leather goods	44.2	59.7	136.3
Clothing	47.5	65.8	140.0
Paper	56.6	26.4	46.6
Printing	61.0	51.5	86.3
Total	3,114.9	1,529.0	49.1

No less catastrophic from the point of view of Soviet authorities was the precipitous decline in the productivity of labor, variously estimated at one-third to one-half of what it had been before the war. Low productivity had many causes, not the least of which were the wear and tear of machinery and rolling stock, shortages of fuel, materials and spare parts, malnutrition among workers, and a wage/ration system based on the principle of social maintenance rather than productivity incentives. Among the "subjective factors" targeted by the regime was poor labor discipline, a term that applied to arriving at work late or leaving early, systematic absenteeism, theft, disobeying instructions, and negligence on the job.

Eventually discipline was imposed by force. In 1919 the trade unions set up comrades-disciplinary courts to punish violators of labor discipline, while peasants and other non-wageworkers who refused to do labor service had to answer to the Main Commission for the Struggle Against Labor Desertion (Glavkomtrud). On top of this, in 1920-21 as the civil war years drew to a close, entire units of the Red Army were converted to labor battalions to fell trees, clear rail lines, and load and unload freight.

Long before the end of the Civil War it was evident that a breach had opened between the Communist party and rank-and-file workers. Despite workers' participation in voluntary Communist Saturdays (subbotniki, pl.) in which Lenin placed great store, that breach continued to widen. By 1921 workers' disillusionment with the communists was registered in mass resignations from the party, strikes, and protest demonstrations. Communist disillusionment with workers was expressed in the notion of "declassing," according to which the labor force had been penetrated by "unconscious" peasants and other petty bourgeois elements who responded favorably to Menshevik and Social Revolutionary propaganda and otherwise "disorganized" workers. Resting on questionable sociological grounds, this line was contested within the party by the Workers' Opposition which viewed it as a recipe for the extension of one-man management (edinonachalie) in industry and the bureaucratization of the party itself.

Upon the introduction of the New Economic Policy (NEP) in 1921 industrial workers, the ostensible core of the working class, were subjected to a different factory regime. This regime was based on the economic principle of cost accounting (khozraschet), according to which each enterprise or group of enterprises organized as trusts must succeed without state subsidies. Along with cost accounting went the rationalization of operations, the expansion of piece work, and upward revisions of output norms. These measures, so reminiscent of contemporary advanced capitalist factory regimes, did not go uncontested by industrial workers even if they had the official sanction of the party and the trade unions.

Table 2

Unemployed Registering with Labor Exchanges, 1921-1929

Date	Total Unemployed (thousands)	Women (thousands)	Percent Women Unemployed
1 Jan 1923	641.0		
1 Jan 1924	1,240.0	530.7	42.8
1 Jul 1924	1,344.3		
1 Dec 1925	920.4	424.8	46.2
1 Oct 1926	1,070.8	519.8	48.5
1 Apr 1927	1,477.9	647.3	43.7
1 Oct 1927	1,041.2	486.9	46.7
1 Apr 1928	1,576.4	622.0	39.4
1 Oct 1928	1,364.6	642.3	47.0
1 Apr 1929	1,741.1	758.4	43.5

The overall impact of NEP on soviet workers was contradictory in the extreme. On one hand unemployment, historically the scourge of working classes, was endemic. Female workers, who comprised less than a third of the industrial work force, were particularly vulnerable when returned Red Army soldiers, male workers who had fled during the Civil War and, later, raw recruits from the countryside claimed their places. (See Table 2). On the other hand, thanks to the upsurge in consumer demand in the villages and after 1924 increased investment in capital goods industries, industrial employment rose and wage levels climbed to nearly their prewar levels. Indeed, in contrast to the 1930s, many working-class families were able to get by on the strength of the husband's wages and wives turned to domestic responsibilities.

In both economic and cultural terms the insecurities associated with NEP and peasant life insured the continuation of strong rural connections among industrial workers. In contrast to metalworkers and printers, for whom artisans' practices and the urban environment were paramount influences, textile workers, construction workers, forestry workers, peat cutters, and coal miners typically maintained strong ties with the agricultural economy through seasonal employment and/or the informal institution of the "work association" (the artel and in the cotton industry, the komplekt). These drew upon kinship and local ties to facilitate obtaining a job, finding accommodation, and learning requisite skills.

This had profound implications for the formation of the Soviet working class. Such a process did occur, but it occurred differentially. It depended not only on the occupation, degree of experience or skill, age, gender and marital status of the individual worker, but also the geographical location, scale, and strategic importance of the enterprise. Large metalworks such as Leningrad's Krasnyi Putilovets contained numerous shops, party and Komsomol (Young Communist) committees overseeing the work of shop committees and cells, a workers' club run by the enterprise's trade union committee, and a wide range of other facilities. This was less likely to have been the case in provincial factories or mines employing hundreds rather than thousands of workers and still less so in smaller workshops, cafeterias, or cooperative outlets.

The party strove to shape the formation of the working class by constructing and institutionally promoting what it referred to as "proletarian consciousness." This consisted of an aggressively collective identity, comradeship, and identification with Soviet power and the Communist party. Promoted through trade unions, Komsomol, and other "special interest" organizations, this policy secured for workers a privileged status in the hierarchy of officially sanctioned values at the same time as it obscured the subordination of workers to the dictates of cost accounting, rationalization, and productivity drives. Proletarian preference, whereby those with working-class pedigrees were granted special access to educational institutions and thence promoted into white collar positions, served a similar purpose. Finally, the recruitment of overwhelmingly male skilled workers into the party under the banner of the proletarianizing the ranks of the party succeeded in raising the proportion of party members of working-class background from 44 percent in 1922 to nearly 60 percent by 1929, even as it reinforced the Russian nationalist and anti-intellectual currents within Bolshevik political culture.

The onset of rapid industrialization and forced collectivization at the end of the 1920s shook up and radically transformed the working class as a sociological category. During the First Five Year Plan (1928-1932) some nine million peasant migrants flooded the towns, most finding jobs in the burgeoning construction and industrial sectors. Large numbers of working-class women joined the industrial work force, many for the first time, when real wages of workers plummeted in connection with the state's policy of forced savings for industrial investment. (See Table 3). The influx of peasants and women, accompanied by the promotion of some one million workers from the shop floor into technical and managerial positions, was reflected in a sharp drop in the average age and the skill levels of workers.

Crowded into barracks, dormitories, and communal apartments, working-class families had even less in the way of living space and privacy than previously. Rationing of consumer goods was reintroduced in 1928 and persisted until 1936. Unemployment effectively ceased to exist and workers took advantage of the scarcity of labor to change employment frequently, although after 1932 at the risk of losing ration cards and access to housing.

Table 3

Social Composition of Industrial Workers, 1928-1939

Year	Number of Workers (thousands)	Percent Women	Percent Youths (17-22)
1928	2,690.8	28.6	
1930	3,674.9	28.8	24.7
1932	5,152.8	32.9	38.5
1934	5,215.0	36.8	32.3
1936	6,173.0	40.1	29.3
1939	7,761.4	43.3	

Even as millions of workers passed through technical schools and other educational institutions on their way to managerial and technical positions, the dignity of labor and the production feats of manual workers were celebrated in production novels and the theater, in the press, and at party conferences. In the early 1930s the most celebrated workers were shock workers who out-performed their work mates in socialist competition. Beginning in 1935 Stakhanovites—emulators of the coal miner Stakhanov who overfulfilled his shift quota by sixteen times—replaced shock workers as the most heroic of workers. Stakhanovites eventually comprised nearly 40 percent of all production workers, although only a few achieved celebrity status and substantial material rewards.

All the while, the language of class was giving way in official discourse to that of Soviet patriotism. At the approach of war, industrial work was put on a military footing; lateness and absenteeism were subjected to criminal sanctions. Women were encouraged to enter traditionally male occupations such as machine-tools and welding, and this was even more the case during World War II. Aside from causing tremendous loss of life and hardship for survivors, the war brought about the geographical dispersal of workers. Many were evacuated to the east to work in reassembled plants beyond the Urals and in Central Asia; others were transported by the Nazi occupiers in the other direction to work as forced labor in German plants. During the first two years of the war overall industrial output fell precipitously, but through redeployment, the imposition of ruthless priorities, and improvisation, the production of aircraft and tanks rose. With a preponderance of national income devoted to "military purposes" (55 percent in 1942), the slogan "Everything for the Front" was more than a rhetorical gesture.

Although won at a heavy price, victory vindicated the centralized command system and its commanders' romance with steel. Postwar reconstruction, a massive undertaking, proceeded along the lines of prewar five-year plans. The demographic imbalance resulting from the war now placed more of the burden on women, who comprised 56 percent of all workers and employees in 1945. That percentage dropped slightly in succeeding years, but between 1960 and the early 1970s an additional 25 million women entered the work force, and by 1980 some 87 percent of working-age women in the USSR were employed or engaged in full time study.

By virtually any measure the standard of living of Soviet workers rose in these postwar decades during which millions of peasants left collective farms to receive training, or take work in the towns. At the same time, the grandiose mythology of working-class heroism in the revolution, industrialization, war, and reconstruction receded from the consciousness of a better-educated and more demanding generation of workers with nothing—not even the possibility of upward social mobility—to take its place. Occasional protest actions, but even more, high rates of absenteeism, labor turnover, alcoholism, divorce, and "hooliganism" among working-class youth belied the official image of a developed socialist society on the road to a classless communism. "They pretend to pay us, and we pretend to work" became the cynical anthem of a working class shot through with alienation.

Until 1989 Premier Mikhail S. Gorbachev's radical reforms had little impact on Soviet workers, evoking among them at most a wary curiosity. But in July of that year nearly half a million coal miners went on strike, the first such massive action since the mid-1920s. They demanded an end to demeaning shortages of consumer goods and housing, dangerous working conditions, and the complicity of the trade unions in the system of "ministerial feudalism." The failure of the Soviet government to fulfill its promises to the miners sparked a longer and more bitter strike in 1991. In the meantime other workers formed strike committees, issued lists of demands and engaged in sporadic strike action.

The collapse of the Soviet Union in 1991 and the centralized planning system associated with it since the Stalin years found workers in a precarious situation and their future as a class unknowable.

See Also: WORKING CLASS IN THE RUSSIAN REVOLUTION

Bibliography: Vladimir Anderle, *Workers in Stalin's Russia. Industrialization and Social Change in a Planned Economy* (Brighton, 1988); William Chase, *Workers, Society, and the Soviet State. Labor and Life in Moscow, 1918-1929* (Urbana, 1987); Donald Filtzer, *Soviet Workers and Stalinist Industrialization. The Formation of Modern Soviet Production Relations, 1928-1941* (New York, 1986); Sheila Fitzpatrick, *Education and Social Mobility in the Soviet Union, 1921-1934* (Cambridge, 1979); *Istoriia industrializatsii SSSR, 1926-1941 gg. Dokumenty i materialy*, 4 vols. (M., 1969-1972); Arcadius Kahan and Blair Ruble, eds., *Industrial Labor in the USSR* (New York, 1979); Diane Koenker, "Class and Class Consciousness in a Socialist Society. Workers in the Printing Trades during NEP," in Sheila Fitzpatrick, Alexander Rabinowitch and Richard Stites, eds., *Russia in the Era of NEP. Explorations in Soviet Society and Culture* (Bloomington, 1991); Hiroaki Kuromiya, *Stalin's Industrial Revolution. Politics and Workers, 1928-1932* (Cambridge, 1989); V.S. Lel'chuk, *Industrializatsiia SSSR. Istoriia, opyt, problemy* (M., 1984); A.A. Matiugin, *Rabochii klass SSSR v gody vosstanovleniia narodnogo khoziaistva, 1921-1925* (M., 1962); L.S. Rogachevskaia, *Likvidatsiia bezrabotitsy v SSSR, 1917-1930* (M., 1973); Solomon Schwarz, *Labor in the Soviet Union* (New York, 1951); V.M. Selunskaia, *Sotsial'naia struktura sovetskogo obshchestva Istoriia i sovremennost'* (M., 1987); Lewis H. Siegelbaum, *Stakhanovism and the Politics of Productivity in the USSR, 1935-1941* (Cambridge, 1989); L.I. Vas'kina, "Rabochii klass SSSR po materialam vsesoiuznoi perepisi naseleniia 1926 g.," *Istoricheskie zapiski*, Vol. 92 (1973), 7-56; A.I. Vdovin and V.Z. Drobizhev, *Rost rabochego klassa SSSR, 1917-1940 gg.* (M., 1976); Chris Ward, *Russia's Cotton Workers and the New Economic Policy* (Cambridge, 1990).

Lewis H. Siegelbaum

WORLD COMMUNIST PARTIES, CONFERENCE OF (1969). Unsuccessful attempt of the Soviet Communist party (CPSU) to bring organizational and political unity to the world communist movement. Convened in Moscow 5-17 June 1969 under Soviet auspices, it was the first global conference in almost a decade and the last such meeting of world communist parties. Far from demonstrating the unity of world communism the 1969 conference revealed unmistakably the fragmentation of the communist movement.

The year 1969 had symbolic significance as the fiftieth anniversary of the founding of the Communist International (Comintern). The 1969 conference was the climax of an intensive three-year effort by the Communist Party of the Soviet Union (CPSU) and its general secretary Leonid Ilich Brezhnev. Two major crises leading up to the conference threatened to disrupt the unity of international communism: the growing schism between the USSR and China and the Soviet invasion of Czechoslovakia in 1968. Moscow sought condemnation of China and endorsement of the so-called "Brezhnev Doctrine" which justified the invasion of Czechoslovakia. Those objectives were opposed vigorously by dissident parties which sought instead to emphasize the idea of the sovereignty of regimes, autonomy of parties, and equality of rights. Hostility to condemning China was strong in most of the Asian parties, and opposition to the Brezhnev Doctrine was led by the Romanian and Italian communist parties. So strong was the opposition to Soviet hegemony that several preconference preparatory meetings had to be convened in an attempt to iron out the differences.

A Preparatory Consultative Conference met in Budapest in February 1968. Here the Russians were forced to concede that no party would be condemned in the conference documents. Resolution of numerous differences between dissident and pro-Moscow parties was deferred to a "working group" which met in February 1969. Because of the invasion of Czechoslovakia the dissident parties, including Romanian, British, Italian, and Spanish, pushed hard for acceptance of the principle of noninterference in one another's internal affairs. Moscow found itself under unaccustomed pressure to negotiate with fellow communists. Unable to agree on the text of the main document, the parties met in Moscow for further meetings in March and May 1969. Although a majority of the sixty-six parties present in the 18-22 March session were Moscow loyalists, the dissidents fought bitterly for their position, frustrating agreement on a draft main document. A final preparatory meeting on 23-30 May failed to reconcile the polarized groups. The seventy delegations present decided to submit to the full conference a draft document along with all amendments introduced by the anti-Moscow faction. As it turned out the very holding of the conference proved to be a minor victory for the Soviet Union.

Representatives of communist and workers' parties from seventy-five countries attended the opening session. Twenty-five parties chose not to attend. Conspicuously absent were the important parties of Asia including China, North Vietnam, Japan, Burma and Indonesia. The absence of Asian representatives gave the conference a strong European orientation. Of the fourteen ruling parties, five boycotted the meeting: China, North Vietnam, North Korea, Albania, and Yugoslavia. The large number of participants could not conceal the fact that almost half of the world's party members were not represented. Press coverage was extensive. Of the 345 accredited correspondents 105 were from the Soviet Union, 90 from other socialist states, 27 from communist newspapers, and 123 from the press of noncommunist countries.

The Soviet position was presented by Brezhnev in his main speech given on 7 June. In it he called for unity in the struggle against imperialism and attacked what he called the right and left wing schisms in world communism threatening that unity. On the right he attacked the compromisers and social democrats identified with Yugoslavia. But his harshest criticism was directed against the "adventurist" and "ultrarevolutionary" policies of China and its leader Mao Zedong. Although the overwhelming majority endorsed Brezhnev's anti-Mao stance, the net impact of Moscow's assault was to harden the resistance of the minority of independent-minded parties as well as to exacerbate the Sino-Soviet dispute.

Among the ruling parties only Romania opposed the Brezhnev line. Nicolae Ceausescu rebuked Moscow for its attack on China and called upon the Soviet Union to respect the independence and national diversity of socialist states. His polycentric message was reinforced by Enrico Berlinguer who defended the autonomous path to socialism chosen by the Communist party of Italy. Ten different parties explicitly criticized the Soviet invasion of Czechoslovakia.

The main product of the conference was a declaration of some 15,000 words entitled "Tasks at the Present Stage of the Struggle Against Imperialism and United Action of the Communists and Workers' Parties and All Anti-imperialist Forces." It consisted of a collection of generalities reaffirming loyalty to Marxist-Leninist principles and acceptance of the basic formulations of Soviet foreign policy. The principal theme was a call for united action against United States imperialism, particularly in Vietnam. The dissidents succeeded in preventing any condemnation of China while Moscow avoided any censure of its invasion of Czechoslovakia. The Soviets also got endorsement of "proletarian internationalism" but the price was their acceptance of "equality, sovereignty and noninterference" in the internal affairs of other parties. But the central point which established the polycentric character of world communism was the statement that "no leading centre of the international Communist movement" existed. Further demonstrating the fissures in world communism, only sixty-one parties signed the main document without reservations. Five refused to sign altogether. For Moscow the conference was a pyrrhic victory and the last of its kind to be held.

Bibliography: Robin Edmonds, *Soviet Foreign Policy. The Brezhnev Years* (New York, 1983); A.A. Gromyko and B.N. Ponomarev, eds., *Istoriia vneshnei politiki SSSR. Vol. 2., 1945-1980* (M., 1980); Library of Congress, *World Communism, 1967-1969. Soviet Efforts to Re-Establish Control* (Washington, 1970); "Documents Adopted by International Conference of Communist and Workers Parties," *World Marxist Review. Problems of Peace and Socialism* Vol. 12, No. 7 (July, 1969).

Joseph L. Nogee

WORLD FEDERATION OF DEMOCRATIC YOUTH (1945-). One of the largest and most important Soviet-controlled communist front organizations.

Formed in Paris in 1945, the World Federation of Democratic Youth (WFDY) was expelled from the city in 1951 for subversive activities and eventually located in Budapest. At the onset of the Cold War it suffered a defection by pro-Western elements, which formed the World Assembly of Youth in 1949. Despite this loss, WFDY claimed a membership of more than 150 million in late 1975. This seems to have been its peak, even though over the next two years it claimed to have added sixty more affiliates. The major publications of WFDY were its bimonthly bulletin WFDY News and its monthly magazine, World Youth.

The highest policy making organ of WFDY was the Assembly, which generally met every four years. It was composed of representatives of all of the organization's 270-odd affiliates from 123 countries. The thirteenth Assembly met in Athens in December 1990. The Assembly traditionally elected an Executive Committee of seventy-two members (as of 1989) and was supposed to meet twice a year; in 1990 the Executive Committee was replaced by a General Council. In a departure from the usual practice in such international fronts, all the top officers—president and vice-presidents, as well as secretary general and treasurer—appear to have been full-time employees at the WFDY's headquarters.

On the other hand the normal pattern was retained in that ultimate control lay with the International Department of the Communist Party of the Soviet Union working through the Soviet affiliate. In this case the affiliate was the Committee of Youth Organizations (KMO) of the USSR. From 1979 to 1988 KMO Deputy Chairman Vsevolod G. Nakhodin served as the Soviet vice-president of the WFDY. Normally in a front organization the head of the national affiliate assumed his country's vice-presidency, but this obviously could not be the case when a full-time official was required. In another divergence from the norm, the KMO was the de facto foreign policy organ of the All-Union Lenin Young Communist League (Komsomol), which was in itself a second Soviet affiliate of the WFDY. The fact that Aleksandr Nikolaevich Shelepin served as the Soviet vice-president of WFDY before taking over the leadership of the Committee for State Security (KGB) in 1958 indicates its significance for the Communist Party of the Soviet Union.

French and Italian communists were prominent in the nominal leadership positions of WFDY not only in the early years of its existence, as in the case of the other major fronts, but much later as well. WFDY lost its Italian president and French secretary general only in 1978, when the Chilean Ernesto Ottone took over the former position and the Hungarian Miklos Barabas the latter. Enrico Berlinguer, later to become the secretary general of the Communist Party of Italy, was one of the early WFDY presidents. The presidency subsequently changed nationality twice, the Lebanese Walid Masri receiving it in 1982 and the South African Pugo Leonard Tladi taking over the post in 1991. The secretary generalship has remained in Hungarian hands; Vilmos Cserveny succeeded Barabas in 1984 and Gyorgy Szabo succeeded Cserveny in 1988.

WFDY had three subsidiary organizations: the International Committee of Children's and Adolescents' Movements, the International Bureau of Tourism and Exchanges of Youth, and the International Voluntary Service for Friendship and Solidarity of Youth. As a "nongovernmental organization" WFDY was officially recognized by several United Nations bodies: the Economic, Scientific, and Cultural Organization (UNESCO), the Economic and Social Council (ECOSOC), and the International Labor Organization (ILO).

While maintaining close relations to all the other major Soviet-controlled international fronts, WFDY's connection with the International Union of Students was most noteworthy. The two organizations co-sponsored the World Youth Festivals, the largest meetings put on by any international front. The thirteenth, held in Pyongyang in July 1989, had fifteen to twenty thousand in attendance; previous meetings claimed from seventeen to thirty-four thousand participants. WFDY appeared to have developed a close working relationship with the International Union of Socialist Youth as well.

Events surrounding the Pyongyang World Youth Festival mirrored growing Soviet tensions with other communist parties. The accommodating policies of Soviet General Secretary Mikhail Sergeevich Gorbachev toward the West contrasted sharply with the strong "anti-imperialist" stance of its North Korean hosts and its coordinator, WFDY Secretary Thierry Angles. The latter represented the Movement of Communist Youth of France and presumably its strong "class struggle" line.

Another indication of the impact of the rapidly changing conditions in the Soviet Union in the early 1990s was WFDY's decision to decentralize its activities. Paralleling similar decisions of the World Peace Council in February 1990 and the World Federation of Trade Unions the following November, at its April 1991 general council meeting WFDY gave certain of its national affiliates responsibility for their respective regions: the All-India Youth Federation for Asia and the Pacific, the Progressive Youth Organization of Lebanon for the Middle East, the Communist Youth of Columbia for Latin America and the Caribbean, and the Finnish Democratic Youth League for Europe and North America. Strangely enough it made no provision for Africa.

Bibliography: *Eleventh Assembly of the Member Organizations of the World Federation of Democratic Youth, Prague, Czechoslovakia, 3-9 June 1982* (Prague, 1982); Clive Rose, *The Soviet Propaganda Network* (London, 1988); Richard F. Staar, ed., *Yearbooks on International Communist Affairs 1981, 1986*, and *1990* (Stanford, 1981, 1986, and 1990); Witold S. Sworakowski, ed., *World Communism, a Handbook, 1918-1965* (Stanford, 1973); U.S. Congress, *The CIA and the Media* (Washington, 1978); *Guardian of Liberty*, September-October 1989 (Munich); *Rizospastis* (Athens, 12 December 1990).

Wallace H. Spaulding

WORLD FEDERATION OF TEACHERS' UNIONS (1946-). Fédération Internationale syndicale de l'enseignment or FISE. Soviet-controlled communist front organization, established in Paris in 1946.

The World Federation of Teachers' Unions was one of eleven Trade Union Internationals (TUIs) of the Soviet-dominated World Federation of Trade Unions (WFTU). It was more independent of WFTU than the others and, because of its clientele, acted more like a professional organization than a trade union. Like its WFTU "parent" it was expelled for subversive activities first from Paris (1952) and then from Vienna (1956) before settling in Prague; subsequently its headquarters were moved to East Berlin (1977) and then back to Paris (1991).

In FISE as in many other international fronts, the French played the most important titular role from its beginning. Although some organizational aspects remain obscure, Henri Wallon was apparently president from its inception until at least 1959; Paul Delanoue was apparently its secretary general and working head during this same period and its president from 1964 to 1973; Daniel Retureau was secretary general from 1973 to 1986 and was succeeded by Gerard Montant in 1987. Lesturige Ariyawansa from Sri Lanka served as president from 1977. As in the case of most of the Soviet fronts, real control of FISE at its headquarters appeared to have been exercised by its Soviet secretary, and a Soviet vice-president served to exercise the requisite influence at the policy-making level.

Like the other TUIs, FISE's policy-making structure consisted of a conference which met every two years and an Administrative Committee which held meetings between conference sessions. A small, full-time staff headed by the secretary general and three secretaries appeared to be responsible for day-to-day operations. In the late 1980s the organization claimed over 26 million members from some 150 affiliates in 79 countries. In mid-1990, like some of the other fronts—WFTU and the World Peace Council (WPC)—FISE announced its intention to decentralize its activities. It planned regional centers in Senegal, India, Chile, and Tunisia to serve respectively, (Black) Africa, Asia, Latin America, and the Arab World.

FISE had a number of institutional relationships. Its secretary general Montant was one of only two TUI officials to sit on the editorial board of WFTU's magazine, World Trade Union Movement. Beyond this FISE appeared to have links with the WPC. President Ariyawansa attended the February 1990 WPC meeting in his capacity of secretary general of the Sri Lankan affiliate of that organization. FISE had the highest consultative status (Category A) with the United Nations Educational, Scientific, and Cultural Organization (UNESCO), which also contributed to it financially. In 1985 FISE played a leading role in the formation of the more broadly based Teachers for Peace organization, just as three years earlier FISE's "parent" WFTU had played a leading role in setting up the similarly broader based International Trade Union Committee for Peace and Disarmament or "Dublin Committee."

FISE published the quarterly Teachers of the World in four languages.

Bibliography: Clive Rose, The Soviet Propaganda Network (London, 1988); Session of the World Peace Council, Athens, Greece, 6-11 February 1990, *Documents* (Helsinki, 1990); Richard F. Staar ed., *Yearbook on International Communist Affairs 1991* (Stanford, 1991); U.S. Congress, *The CIA and the Media* (Washington, 1978); *Flashes from the Trade Unions* (Prague), 27 November 1987. *Teachers of the World* (East Berlin), September 1989 (special edition) and July-September 1990.

Wallace H. Spaulding

WORLD FEDERATION OF TRADE UNIONS (1945-). A major communist front organization, established in 1945.

The World Federation of Trade Unions (WFTU) was second in size only to the World Peace Council (WPC) among the post-World War II international communist front organizations. Claiming 60 million members at its 1945 inception, it rose to approximately 214 million during 1987 to 1989, before the defection of East European unions. In the opinion of both pro-and anti-Soviet writers, among such "nongovernmental organizations" only the "peace movement" exceeded trade union activity in importance.

WFTU was the first of a series of three important international fronts founded in late 1945 with headquarters in Paris. The other two organizations were the Women's International Democratic Federation (WIDF) and the World Federation of Democratic Youth (WFDY). All three had for the most part nominal French or Franco-Italian leadership, as France and Italy, with their strong communist parties, were the two areas in Western Europe most prone to Soviet influence.

WFTU was unique among communist front organizations in the degree to which pro-Western elements participated in its early years. Most notably the Britishers Sir Walter Citrine and Arthur Deakin, whose socialist Trades Union Congress took the initiative in setting up WFTU, were its successive presidents from 1945 to 1949. At Soviet insistence Louis Saillant of France, also a socialist but a Soviet-oriented one, became WFTU's first general secretary. As the full-time working head, he packed the organization's headquarters with like-minded persons and turned it into a sounding board for Soviet foreign policy objectives. This almost totally eliminated the early British and other pro-Western influences in WFTU.

The changed character of WFTU, coinciding with the onset of the Cold War, subjected it to a series of external pressures by pro-Western forces. In 1949 its British, Dutch, and American affiliates withdrew and formed the rival International Confederation of Free Trade Unions. In 1951 the French government, suspecting them of subversive activities, forced all the Paris-based front organizations to remove their headquarters. WFTU moved to the Soviet sector of Vienna. After regaining its sovereignty in 1956 the Austrian government expelled WFTU for the same reasons as the French. WFTU then found a more permanent home in Prague.

The most important bodies in the central structure of WFTU were the World Trade Union Congress, the General Council, the Bureau, and the Secretariat. The Congress, which generally met every four years, drafted and adopted the major programs and policies of the organization and ratified the selections made by constituent organizations for membership on the General Council. Each member union selected the number of Congress delegates allocated to it according to size and pursuant to a WFTU constitutional formula. From 1953 on General Council invited an increasing number of observers from non-communist unions to the Congress. These took part in the deliberations but could not vote in internal WFTU organizational matters. On this basis, the Twelfth (1990) World Trade Union Congress could claim to have represented 405 million trade unionists, although WFTU itself never claimed more than 214 million.

The General Council, which generally met once a year, was composed of one full and one alternate member from each of WFTU's national affiliates (ninety-three claimed in early 1990) and eleven Trade Union Internationals (TUIs). It worked out the plan for implementing the Congress decisions, elected the top WFTU officers and other members of its Bureau and Secretariat, took action on matters submitted to it by the Bureau, and approved the organization's budget.

As of 1988 the Bureau consisted of WFTU's president, its thirteen vice-presidents, its general secretary, and one full and one alternate member from each of thirty-seven national affiliates and three TUIs. It directed the Secretariat in carrying out the decisions of the Congress and Council, took urgently needed actions submitting them to the Council for ratification, and monitored WFTU finances. The Bureau generally met twice a year.

The Secretariat was WFTU's permanent executive body. Its tasks included implementing the decisions of the Congress, Council, and Bureau; directing the headquarters apparatus of at least nine departments and five commissions (1990); gathering all relevant material and presenting urgent questions arising therefrom to the Bureau, after having taken immediate action when necessary; maintaining contact with national affiliates and TUIs; and supervising WFTU publications. Two features regarding this latter activity are of special interest. From 1978 to 1990 at least, the head of the Press and Propaganda Department apparently always was Russian. And at the beginning of 1991 it was announced that the organization's World Trade Union Movement magazine henceforth would come out quarterly rather than monthly and its Flashes from the Trade Unions news sheet would be reduced from a weekly to a bi-weekly.

WFTU had close ties to international organizations devoted to specific occupations called Trade Union Internationals. There were eleven of these, representing workers in agriculture, building and wood trades, chemical and oil industries, offices and commerce, energy, food and hotel industries, metallurgy and engineering, government, textile and clothing, transport, and education. Their representatives held seats on the General Council. Apparently looser connections were maintained with the International Trade Union Committee for Peace and Disarmament ("Dublin Committee"), which was linked to WPC, and with the International Center for Trade Union Rights, which similarly was linked to the International Association of Democratic Lawyers, a relatively minor Soviet-line front.

In line with WFTU's desire to expand its influence beyond its own member unions, it invited nonmembers to attend its congresses from 1953 onward and established close relations with four regional trade union organizations containing a mix of WFTU and non-WFTU affiliates. Two of these, the Organization of African Trade Union Unity (OATUU) and the International Confederation of Arab Trade Unions (ICATU), were semi-governmental in nature in that they were organs of the Organization of African Unity and Arab League, respectively. The other two, the AsianPacific Trade Union Coordination Committee (APTUCC) and especially the Permanent Congress for the Trade Union Unity of Latin American Workers (CPUSTAL), more closely resembled traditional communist fronts.

Although WFTU's post-1949 leadership accepted the expulsion of the Yugoslav affiliate in 1950 and the cutting of ties with the Chinese and Albanian ones by 1967, it balked at the Soviet invasion of Czechoslovakia the following year. As a result of WFTU criticism of this action, the Italian president of WFTU, Renato Bissoti, who followed his countryman Giuseppi di Vittorio in the job, and the French general secretary Louis Saillant, lost their respective positions in 1969. They were replaced by the Uruguayan communist Enrique

Pastorino as president and a more pliant French communist, Pierre Gensous, as general secretary. The ouster of Bitossi paralleled the growth of a more independent "Eurocommunism" within the Italian Communist party. The latter's General Confederation of Italian Labor reverted to "associate membership" within WFTU in 1973 and withdrew altogether in 1978.

The above implied the ultimate control of WFTU by the Soviets without their occupying either of the leading positions—president or general secretary—in the organization, confirming its nature as a front. During the bulk of the period from 1950 to 1988 the Soviet All-Union Central Council of Trade Unions (AUCCTU) provided over half the membership of WFTU, and the unions of the Soviet-dominated East European nations constituted much of the other half. Because delegates to WFTU's "highest" body, the Congress, were apportioned according to the size of each affiliate, the Soviets could have run the organization on the basis of a straight majority rule if they had so wished. Instead they appeared to have run it as they did the other fronts, using the Soviet secretary at the organization's headquarters to give day-to-day guidance and the Soviet vice-president to insure conformity in the periodic meetings of the Bureau, Council, and Congress. Both represented the AUCCTU officially, but it was likely that they answered directly to the International Department of the Communist Party of the Soviet Union. In 1989 prior to the rapid political deterioration in the USSR these two were, respectively, Vsevolod Mozhaiev and AUCCTU chairman, Stepan Shalayev. In early 1990 Aleksandr Zharikov, chief of the AUCCTU International Department, noted: "A lot of people consider WFTU as an organization representing only the interests of the world communist movement and the socialist system...and to a certain extent this was true" (Flashes from the Trade Unions [Prague], 27 April 1990). This appeared to be yet one more example of Soviet openness, so prevalent during the period.

In November 1990 WFTU's Twelfth Congress, or more specifically, the General Council approved by it, made significant organizational changes, including changes in the Soviet methods of operation. The meeting, held in Moscow, elected for the first time a Soviet citizen as general secretary, Aleksandr Zharikov. This was consistent with the practice followed in the new types of fronts that appeared in the 1980s where Soviets took leading positions in an apparent attempt to prove to Western audiences that their government was treating the organization seriously enough to make it worth dealing with. Consistent with the old system, the Soviets retained a vice-presidency, this time in the person of Vladimir Shcherbakov. He was chairman of the new General Confederation of Soviet Trade Unions, which succeeded AUCCTU.

There was little of note in the election to the presidency of the Sudanese Ibrahim Zakariya, who served as general secretary from 1980 to 1990. He replaced the Hungarian Sandor Gaspar when the latter resigned prematurely in early 1989, in line with the growing independent and democratic tendencies in his home country. But, curiously, the Council appointed to the reinstated office of deputy general secretary the Frenchman Alain Stern, representative of the General Confederation of Labor, whose line of aggressive class struggle then was opposed by the Soviet government.

Having a Soviet and a Frenchman in the two top WFTU headquarters jobs seemed logical considering the mid-1990 allegation that the Soviets, the

French, and a "handful of Arab unions" constituted the sole WFTU paying membership. It also gave a definite European flavor to the headquarters, especially since the Pole Jan Nemoudry appeared to be the only other chief officer left there after the establishment of WFTU regional centers in 1991. At its Twelfth Congress WFTU established these centers in Havana, New Delhi, Brazzaville, and Damascus, the first three manned by secretaries Jose Ortiz (Chile), Debkumar Ganguli (India), and Messeambia Koulimaya (Congo), respectively. As in the case of a similar dispersal of WPC assets a year earlier, all this appeared to reflect the Soviets' desire to use the organization to facilitate ties with the industrialized nations while divesting themselves of third world financial responsibilities and anti-imperialist rhetoric.

How the new WFTU regional centers related to the regional trade union organizations was not known by early 1992, but it was noteworthy that ICATU and APTUCC have headquarters in the same cities as their WFTU counterparts, Damascus, and New Delhi respectively. And it must be remembered that WFTU may have achieved its greatest success in forging "unity of action" with noncommunist trade unions in the regional associations—both through cooperation agreements with the latter's top leaderships and the interaction of WFTU and non-WFTU affiliated members in each of these area organizations (specifically OATUU, ICATU, CPUSTAL, and APTUCC). There have been few similar gains by pro-Western or neutralist worldwide trade union federations here.

While WFTU was close to all other major international communist fronts, cooperation was most obvious in the case of WPC. In the latter's pre-February 1990 structure WFTU was one of only two international fronts to have had a WPC vice-presidency allocated to it in its own name, the other being WIDF. And WFTU was able to lend its considerable and largely complementary resources to such WPC-led campaigns as the Stockholm Peace Appeal against atomic weapons in 1950, the anti-neutron-bomb campaign in 1977, and the movement to keep Pershing II and cruise missiles out of Western Europe in 1983.

With respect to the United Nations, WFTU is the only one of the international fronts to have achieved the highest, most-consulted, status with the two specialized agencies dealing most extensively with "nongovernmental organizations;" it has Category I status with the Economic and Social Council (ECOSOC) and Category A status with the United Nations Educational, Scientific and Cultural Organization (UNESCO). WFTU also has conducted joint seminars in trade union education with the UN's International Labor Organization. This evidence of acceptance by the UN would appear to have enhanced WFTU's credibility most effectively in the third world, the very place where it has been most successful in cooperation with nonaffiliates through the regional mechanism.

Bibliography: Yearbook on International Communist Affairs, ed. by Milorad M. Drachkovich and Lewis H. Gann (1966-1967), Richard F. Staar (1970-1982, 1984-1992), and Robert H. Wesson (1983), (Stanford, 1967-1992), is a major source for all communist front organizations. It provides yearly updates on developments in the fronts from a Western viewpoint. Clive Rose, *The Soviet Propaganda Network* (London, 1988), is a definitive study of organization of communist fronts from a Western standpoint. Witold S. Sworakowski, *World Communism. A Handbook, 1918-65* (Stanford, 1973) gives background for the period indicated. W.J. Vogt, *The International Front Organizations of Communism* (Johannesburg, 1960), is another pro-Western view stressing Soviet control of the fronts. US Congress, *The CIA and the Media* (Washington, 1978), provides an official US government view of the fronts. *World Federation of Trade Unions, 1945-1985* (Prague, 1985) is the official WFTU history of itself over the first forty years of its existence. René Milon, "Le XII Congress de la FSM, répit dans l'effondrement du communisme ou noveau depart?" *Est et Oust* (Paris, January 1991), 23-26, describes the Soviet and French communist disagreements within the trade union movement. G. Shakhnazarov, "On the Problems of Correlation of Forces in the World," *Kommunist*, No. 3 (February, 1984), sets the trade union movement in context from the Soviet standpoint. Eleventh World Trade Union Congress, *List of Participants* (East Berlin, 1986) and Twelfth World Trade Union Congress, *List of Participants* (M., 1990), show the breadth of participation and give information on headquarters organizational structure. *Flashes from the Trade Unions* (Prague, 1973-1991) is the official WFTU news sheet. *World Trade Union Movement* (Prague, 1959-1991) is the official WFTU magazine. As of early 1992 it was published quarterly.

Wallace H. Spaulding

WORLD MARXIST REVIEW (September 1958-May 1990). Journal with editorial offices in Prague but published in a number of locations. Some editions were entitled Problems of Peace and Socialism. During its lifetime it was the only permanent institutional symbol of unity for the world's pro-Moscow and independent communist parties.

The World Marxist Review (WMR) was the lineal descendant of the journals Communist International, published 1919-1943 by the Communist International (Comintern, 1919-1943) and For a Lasting Peace, For a People's Democracy, published 1947-1956 by the Communist Information Agency (Cominform). Like its predecessors it was designed to coordinate the activities of the world communist movement. This was especially the case after 1969 when, because of the opposition from Eurocommunists and pro-Chinese parties, the periodic conferences of the world communist parties ceased to be held. In these circumstances WMR's staff and conferences on the work of the journal served as substitutes.

At its inception its Editorial Council consisted of representatives of 20 communist parties; by its demise the number had risen to 69. In the beginning it published in 19 languages and was distributed in 80 countries; by its thirtieth anniversary the respective figures were 40 and 145. National editions rose from 22 in 1958 to 75 in 1983.

Control of WMR rested ultimately with the International Department of the Communist Party of the Soviet Union. Until 1990 the chief editors were high-ranking members of that party: Central Committee member Aleksei M. Rumiantsev (1958-1964); alternate Central Committee members Georgy P. Frantsev (1964-1968), Konstantin I. Zarodov (1968-1982), and Yury A. Skliarov (1982-1986); and Central Auditing Commissioner Aleksandr Subbotin (1986-1990).

In 1990 a relative unknown, Lubomir Molnar, presumably a Czech, held the post. During much of the magazine's life one of the editor's two deputies called "executive secretaries" or "managing editors" also had been Soviet citizens.

At the next level down, the Editorial Board, consisting of these three plus the representatives of some thirteen or so other parties, appeared always to have a strongly pro-Soviet majority. In April 1982 the official newspaper of the Japanese Communist party (Akahata) stated that the top three editors formed the "core of the Editorial Office" and that the Editorial Board was "instrumental" in maintaining Soviet control.

The third level, the Editorial Council, on which all participating communist parties were represented, was organized in such a way as to make Soviet supervision easy. Each council member sat on one or more of ten regional or problem-oriented commissions which monitored articles for publication and planned conferences in their respective fields. These commissions had the following responsibilities: problems of socialist construction (communist countries); the class struggle in capitalist countries (developed capitalist countries); the national liberation struggle in Asian and African countries; the national liberation struggle in Latin America and the Caribbean; general problems of theory; exchanges of experience of party work; problems of peace and democratic movements (international front organizations); problems of science and culture; communist press criticism and bibliography; scientific information and documents. Each of these commissions appeared to have a Soviet secretary who doubled as chief of a counterpart and predominately Soviet department of the magazine, which in turn exercised the requisite supervision.

Although all this guaranteed a generally Soviet slant to the journal's articles, opposition was notable and to some degree tolerated. Individual national editions were allowed to delete articles from the Prague master copy or insert articles of local interest. But they were not supposed to make any changes in the originally approved articles, a principle that appeared to have been violated most notably by the Rumanians in 1964 in their support of the Chinese, who with the Albanians had withdrawn from the journal two years earlier. The September 1968 issue leaned toward the reformist Czechoslovak communists with respect to the Soviet invasion to oust them the previous month. This resulted in an issue being skipped—the next one was labeled October-November—and the appointment of a new, presumably more orthodox, Soviet chief editor. The Spanish Eurocommunists since at least 1969 and the Japanese independent communists since at least 1971 had criticized the journal's one-sided, pro-Soviet stand, the latter especially in reference to the Sino-Soviet dispute. From 1981 on the Japanese Communist party called for the demise of WMR but continued to have a representative on the journal's Editorial Council until the very end. By contrast the Eurocommunist Italian Communist party withdrew its representative altogether in 1988. Ironically, by the latter year WMR had begun to open up, carrying articles of various shades of opinion, even anti-Soviet. This was consistent with the concurrent growth of democracy and pluralism in the USSR. It is also ironic that just as the journal was becoming interesting its circulation allegedly dropped to zero after having peaked at 500,000. WMR ceased publication altogether in May 1990.

Bibliography: *Yearbook on International Communist Affairs* eds. Milorad M. Drachkovich and Lewis H. Gann (1966-1967), Richard F. Staar (1970-1982, 1984-1992), and Robert H. Wesson (1983) (Stanford, 1967-1992). See especially the entries by Wallace H. Spaulding, "World Marxist Review," in volumes for 1983-1991. Other sources are *Akahata* (Tokyo), 27-28 November 1981, 11 December 1981, and 30 April 1982. Trans. in *Information Bulletin for Abroad* (Tokyo), No. 475, December 1981 and No. 485, May 1982; Kevin Devlin, "Carrillo's Independent Stand at Prague Conference," *Radio Free Europe Research* (Munich, 13 March 1974); "International Communist Journal Closing Down," Radio Free Europe/Radio Liberty, *Report on Eastern Europe*, 8 June 1990; Christian Duevel, "Yuriy Frantsev Replaced by Konstantin Zarodov as Chief Editor of 'Problems of Peace and Socialism,'" *Radio Liberty Research* (Munich), CRD 433/68, 29 November 1968; "'Problems of Peace and Socialism' Romanian Style," *Radio Free Europe Research* (Munich, 23 September 1964); Wallace H. Spaulding, "New Head, Old 'Problems of Peace and Socialism,'" *Problems of Communism*, Vol. 31 (November-December 1982), 57-62; "To the Reader," *World Marxist Review* (Toronto, September 1988), 5-7; "How Our Journal Functions," *World Marxist Review* (London, August 1981), 128, and "How Our Journal Functions," *op. cit.*, (September 1981), 8.

Wallace H. Spaulding

WORLD PEACE COUNCIL (1948-). The largest and most important of the Soviet-line international communist front organizations, formed in Paris at a series of conferences between August 1948 and November 1950.

In view of the strength of the Communist Party of France in the immediate post-World War II period, the Soviet Union concentrated much of its propaganda efforts here. For this reason the World Peace Council (WPC), like several of the most important front organizations, was based first in Paris, and Frenchmen took leading roles in it until the growth of "Eurocommunism" made this inconvenient. Its headquarters was expelled from Paris in 1951 and then from Vienna in 1957 for subversive activities. It eventually settled in Helsinki in 1968.

Although WPC appeared never to have publicized its total strength, a Soviet estimate in the mid-1970s put the membership of its national affiliates at about 400 million. If this was anywhere near correct, it would have made WPC by far the largest of the international fronts. WPC's own figures indicated that it began with national affiliates in 70 countries in 1949, rising to 145 in 1988 before the East European defections of 1989 and 1990. This is a record for such organizations. As for the number of persons involved in its activities, a peak apparently was reached between 1975 and 1978, when WPC claimed that "over 700 million persons signed or endorsed" its New Stockholm Appeal for ending the arms race, another record.

Until 1990 WPC was the only such organization to have representatives from the other major international communist fronts on its major policy organs, thus serving a de facto coordination function. It is little wonder that Soviet writers in the past have declared "the peace movement" as the most important area for the activity of "nongovernmental organizations." Since the late 1980s WPC appeared to have lost ground to the traditionally more even-handed and truly neutralist peace movement called European Nuclear Disarmament (END), which several national WPC affiliates joined with or without disaffiliating with their old parent body.

The largest meetings sponsored by WPC were the fourteen congresses it held between April 1949 and October 1986. These were not official WPC meetings as such but were meant to gather as wide a spectrum of persons as possible to support Soviet foreign policy objectives. They were characterized by the approval by acclamation of predigested resolutions. Apparently the October 1986 congress held in Copenhagen was the last. Aside from the expense involved in bringing some 250 delegates together the 1986 congress was subjected to disruptions on the floor by anticommunist activists and hostile commentary by much of the local press.

Until a series of wide-ranging changes in 1990 the highest and largest official organ of WPC was the Council. It was composed of representatives chosen by WPC-affiliated organizations and generally met every three years. Its membership hovered around five hundred for years. The Council started to grow in the 1970s and by 1983, the last year the WPC list was published, it had nearly sixteen hundred. The function of this body was to make the organization's major policy decisions and to determine both its own structure and that of any subsidiary bodies that might be set up. It appeared that the Soviets and other financial benefactors tired of paying to bring all the Council members together. The last two Council meetings, in Sofia in April 1986 and in Athens in February 1990, had only about five hundred delegates each. It seems fairly certain that the Assembly, set up by the Council at its last meeting to replace itself, will be a smaller body.

From 1959 to 1990 a Presidential Committee, elected by the Council, served to carry out the decisions of the latter and otherwise take care of the organization's business between Council sessions. It also appointed the Secretariat. As the Presidential Committee grew over its lifetime, from 24 to over 280 members, it reduced its normal meeting frequency from twice to once a year and elected another body that could meet more frequently. This body was the Bureau, set up in 1974 with twenty-five members but growing to fifty-two by 1983 and to a still larger number by the time of its 1990 demise; that is, its June 1989 meeting had ninety-seven participants. The Bureau met between two and four times a year to take care of WPC business between sessions of the Presidential Committee. The February 1990 replacement of the Presidential Committee with a forty-three-member Executive Committee and the Bureau with a standing committee of nine regular and two ex-officio members to serve under the president illustrated the downsizing necessitated by the organizations' reduced financial circumstances.

The foregoing organizational structure applied solely to the periodically-meeting policy-making side of WPC. The permanent, full-time organization at WPC's headquarters consisted of an executive body called the Secretariat, an Information Center in charge of publications activities, and attendant clerical personnel. Just prior to the reorganization of February 1990 the officers of these two bodies, which together constituted the editorial board of New Perspectives magazine, totaled twenty-one. As a result of the 1990 reorganization, an executive secretary and six other former Secretariat officers (secretaries) reconstituted themselves as a Liaison Office, which in turn incorporated the old Information Center as one of its departments.

The top position in WPC served to unify the policy-making and executive organs. At least the Indian communist Romesh Chandra seems to have done this from the time of his 1966 appointment as secretary general, a post which made him technically full-time director of headquarters staff, rather than from that of his election as president when that office was reinstated in 1977. The post of president had been abolished after the death of WPC's first president, the French communist Frederic Juliot-Curie, in 1958. The top spot was then taken over first by J.D. Bernal (UK) as chairman of the Presidential Committee from 1959 to 1965 and then by Isabelle Blume (Belgium) as coordinating chairman of the presidential Committee from 1966 to 1967. Neither appeared to have had the authority wielded by Juliot-Curie. The position of chief Soviet agent may have continued for a time in French hands in the person of Fernand Henri Vigne, who though giving up the WPC secretary generalship when that position was abolished in May 1959, continued on as managing secretary of the International Institute for Peace (IIP).

The office of secretary general, vacant since 1977, was reinstated in 1986 with the Finnish communist Johannes Pakaslahti in the post but coexisting with the presidency, still held by Chandra. The two appeared to have become respective focal points of "hard line"/Third World vs. "soft line"/industrialized nation conflict within the organization over whether anti-imperialism or disarmament—the two major thrusts of propaganda activities—should be paramount. The February 1990 Council meeting replaced Chandra with the Greek Evangelos Maheras, a noncommunist, as president and again abolished the post of secretary general. The less-exalted post of executive secretary, held by Frank Swift (UK) during 1983-1985 without causing any known major organizational tension, was re-established with Ray Stewart (New Zealand) in the job.

The foregoing discussion illustrates the point that, befitting the nature of a front organization, the Soviet Committee for the Defense of Peace (SDCP) which actually controlled WPC, furnished none of its top leaders. At the policy level, this control appears to have been exercised through the Soviet vice-president and at the day-to-day operating level by a Soviet member of the Secretariat (after 1990, Liaison Office). In 1990 these individuals were, respectively, SCDP Chairman Genrikh Borovik and former SCDP First Vice-Chairman Vladimir Orel. A major means of Soviet control was through finances, as the USSR and its East European allies provided the bulk of the organization's funding, a point openly acknowledged from at least 1989 onward. This admission, as well as open self-criticism within WPC for having been too pro-Soviet in the past, coincided with the growth of democratic tendencies within the USSR and were not necessarily indicative of any lessening of Soviet control. All this helped to explain both a drastic reduction of Soviet financial support to WPC and a growing reliance on END for peace activities, even by the more "hard line" among the Soviet elements.

Aside from the reduction in size of WPC's central institutions, another notable result of its February 1990 Council meeting was the purported dispersal of the bulk of its activities to the regional level. Since the regional structures, which are supposed to mirror those at the center but on a more modest scale, are to be self-financed, this allows the Soviets to concentrate their funding on Europe, the region in which they were placed organizationally and in which they appear now to be primarily interested. Most certainly this gets the new financially strapped and anti-imperialist-oriented regional organizations for Africa (Dakar), the Arab World (Cairo), Asia (New Delhi), and Latin America (presumably Havana) out of the way. The European Regional Center (presumably Paris) was to handle North America, while that of Asia did the same for the South Pacific.

The regional structure of WPC was tied into the central one at the top. In 1990 four regional coordinators sat on the WPC Standing Committee: Vital Balla (Congo) for Africa, Khalid Muhyi-al-Din (Egypt) for the Arab World, Chandradjit Yadev (India) for Asia, and Jacques Denis (France) for Europe. All but one of the Standing Committee members were on the forty-three-member WPC Executive Committee, just as the bulk of the latter are on their own respective Regional Executive Committees.

Of the numerous organizations related to WPC, including virtually all the other major fronts and many of their regional offshoots, the closest appear to be IIP and the International Liaison Forum of Peace Forces (ILFPF). IIP was set up in Vienna in 1957 to provide cover for the continued operation of WPC headquarters after that body was expelled from the city. Since the establishment in 1968 of WPC headquarters in Helsinki, IIP has continued in Vienna as a research organization for the parent body.

Even though WPC was successful in uniting communists with others, mainly left socialists in Western Europe and Latin America and semi-Marxist "revolutionary democrats" in Africa and Asia, it aimed to incorporate more elements toward the political center. For this reason ILFPF was set up in 1973. It was somewhat successful in so widening the constituency served by WPC, most notably at four broadly based "Vienna Dialogue" conferences between 1982 and 1987, which treated Soviet foreign policy objectives in a less directly confrontational manner than would have been normal for WPC itself. This success was especially notable since the ILFPF president has been the former WPC secretary general/president Romesh Chandra, its secretary general the former Soviet WPC secretary Oleg Kharkhardin, and its headquarters in Moscow.

WPC, as a "nongovernmental organization," has the highest, most-consulted (Category A) status with the United Nations Educational, Scientific, and Cultural Organization (UNESCO) and consultative status with its Economic and Social Council (ECOSOC), United Nations Conference on Traded Development (UNCTAD), and United Nations Industrial Development Organization (UNIDO). In 1981 it withdrew its bid for the highest (Category I) status with ECOSOC after failing to accede to demands for a full disclosure of its finances. After having been made honorary president of WPC in February 1990, Romesh Chandra's main job was to represent WPC to the UN complex. WPC had permanent representation to the UN offices in New York and Geneva as well as to the UNESCO office in Paris.

As of early 1992 WPC continues to publish the quarterly International Mobilization magazine in cooperation with the UN Center Against Apartheid. On its own WPC published the monthly newspaper Peace Courier and the twice-monthly Peace News Bulletin. Until early 1990 it had also published New Perspectives magazine every two months.

Bibliography: Yearbook on International *Communist Affairs*, ed. by Milorad M. Drachkovich and Lewis H. Gann (1966-1967), Richard F. Staar (1970-1982, 1984-1992), and Robert H. Wesson (1983), (Stanford, 1967-1992), is a major source for all communist front organizations. It provides yearly updates on developments in the fronts from a Western viewpoint. See also Clive Rose, *The Soviet Propaganda Network* (London, 1988); US Congress, *The CIA and the Media* (Washington, 1978); World Peace Council, *List of Members, 1983-1986* (Helsinki, undated); *The World Peace Council. What It Is and What It Does* (Helsinki, 1978). *ECOSOC Report* (New York, 16 March 1981); Ye. Kuskov, "The Most Active and Influential Force," *Kommunist*, No. 17 (Moscow, November 1972); Réné Milon, "Le XII Congrès de la FSM, répit dans l'effondremont du communisme ou nouveau départ?," *Est et Ouest* (Paris, January 1991), 23-26; G. Shakhnazarov, "On the Problem of Correlation of Forces in the World," *Kommunist*, No. 3 (Moscow, February 1974). Publications of WPC are *Perspectives* (Helsinki, 1966-1971) and its successor *New Perspectives* (Helsinki, 1971-1991); *Information Bulletin* (Helsinki, 1966-1971) and its successor *Peace Courier* (1971-1991); and *Peace News Bulletin* (Helsinki, 1988-1991).

Wallace H. Spaulding

WORLD REVOLUTIONARY PROCESS. A concept used by Soviet ideologists to predict, describe, and justify the "historically necessary victory" of communism over capitalism.

In 1983 Vadim Valentinovich Zagladin, deputy chief of the International Department of the Communist Party of the Soviet Union (CPSU), defined the world revolutionary process (WRP) as "...a complex conglomerate of antagonistic classes, social movements, trends and organizations, the sum total of revolutions, uprisings, strikes, the most diverse class, national liberation and other social battles. In other words, it is the active, creative aspect of history, its most forceful constructive force and at the same time its product at each given stage" (New Times [Moscow], No. 18, 1983). It was this "product at each given stage" that was most often described by Soviet writers. In this more narrow and static sense, WRP appeared to be simply the collectivity of "progressive" and "inevitably triumphant" forces pitted against those of "world capitalism" in the "basic transformation of our times." These forces appeared to peak in the 1970s and then began to disintegrate in the period 1988-1991.

Soviet writers identified three major WRP components. The first and the most important was the world communist movement, which was composed of the total membership of the Communist parties recognized by the Communist Party of the Soviet Union (CPSU). G. Shakhnazarov, writing in the ideological journal Communist (Kommunist) in February 1974 described it as "the most influential political force of our time," exercising "the leading, vanguard role."

An official directory of world Communist parties published in 1988 (*First Hand Information*) claimed 85 million communists in almost one hundred countries. The Hoover Institution's *Yearbook on International Communist Affairs, 1991* estimated only slightly more than seventy-one million in those Communist parties recognized by the Soviets, the losses of over fifteen million registered in Europe and North Korea not being offset by smaller gains in most of the rest of the world.

The second major component of WRP was the national liberation movement in the former colonies and semicolonies. Although linked with the world communist movement in the common struggle against "imperialism," the national liberation movement was clearly considered subordinate. The chief contradiction of the contemporary era remained the struggle between capitalism and communism.

Within the national liberation movement "revolutionary democratic parties" were held to be the distinctive progressive element and the "countries of socialist orientation" that they ruled were said to perform a "vanguard" function. These parties allegedly differed from communist ones; they reflected multiclass interests and lacked a uniformly cohesive doctrine and discipline. The "countries of socialist orientation" were said to remain in the world capitalist system although in most of them the state sector dominated the economy.

Some revolutionary democratic parties were held to be closer to communism than others. This elite group consisted of "vanguard parties" which had stricter class and ideological standards for membership and had opted openly for "scientific socialism," the Soviet brand of communism. *First Hand Information* listed the following as vanguard parties in power as of 1988: People's Democratic Party of Afghanistan, MPLA-Workers' Party (Angola), Party of the People's Revolution of Benin, Congolese Party of Labor, Workers' Party of Ethiopia, Frente de Libertacao do Mozambique (FRELIMO), Sandinist National Liberation Front (Nicaragua), and Yemen Socialist Party. The Madagascar Independence Congress Party was listed as a vanguard junior partner in its country's government. The following were identified as illegal opposition groups: National Liberation Front of Bahrain, National Democratic Union (Chad), National Democratic Front of South Korea, and People's Front for the Liberation of Oman. By the end of 1991 the African parties appeared to be moving away from Marxism one way or another, the Sandinistas had reverted to a legal opposition party, and the Yemeni socialists saw their country absorbed by their larger, more conservative northern neighbor.

As for the other non-elite and non-vanguard revolutionary democratic parties, the African Party for the Independence of Guinea and Cape Verde (Guinea-Bissau) and the Zimbabwe African National Union-Patriotic Front certainly stood at the head of the list, for they attended the 1988 meeting on the work of the journal World Marxist Review along with seventy-nine pro-Soviet and neutralist Communist parties and eleven of the thirteen vanguard parties. Other parties recognized as revolutionary democratic in the early 1980s included the Algerian National Liberation Front, the Burmese Socialist Program Party (inoperative as of 1991), the Democratic Party of Guinea, the Movement for the Liberation of Sao Tome and Principe, the Seychelles Peoples Progressive Front, the Arab Socialist Renewal (Ba'ath) Party of Syria, and the Revolutionary Party of Tanzania. It is noteworthy that persons associated with the Guinean, Syrian, and Tanzanian parties in 1990 were elected vice-presidents of the most important communist front organization, the World Peace Council (WPC). So too were persons apparently associated with other "revolutionary democratic" possibilities, the ruling groups in Burkina Faso, Ghana, Mali, and Zambia.

Coupled with the revolutionary democratic parties in the national liberation movement were the national liberation movements proper, illegal opposition groups generally involved in armed struggle against their respective governments but without the elite status of vanguards. In this category in the early 1980s were the Southwest Africa People's Organization, which in 1991 became the ruling party of Namibia; the African National Congress (ANC), which by 1991 was negotiating for participation in the South African government; the Polisario of Western Sahara; and three coalitions: the Farabundo Marti National Liberation Front (FMNLF) in El Salvador, the Palestine Liberation Organization (PLO), and the Association of Revolutionary Organizations of Guatemala. The ANC, PLO, and presumably the FMNLF received vice-presidential seats in the 1990 reorganization of the World Peace Council. In addition the Salvadorean and Palestinian Communist parties participated as such in the FMNLF and PLO respectively, and all members of the South African communist party were also members of the ANC.

Instead of distinguishing between the world communist movement and national liberation movement in the WRP, some Soviet authors conceived of a three-fold division: the "world socialist system," composed of communist-ruled countries; the "revolutionary movement of the working class in capitalist countries", composed of the Communist parties of the "Free World"; and the national liberation movement as described above. This breakdown had the advantage of including the institutions in communist-ruled countries in addition to the ruling parties themselves. In any case, here again the first element was superior to the second. As M. Mitin stated in Izvestiia (20 April 1974), the world socialist system is "the main bulwark" of WRP whereas the revolutionary movement of the working class in capitalist countries is merely "another chief force" therein.

Shakhnazarov, who ranked the world communist movement and the national liberation movement as the two most important elements of WRP, ranked "the social democratic movement, especially its left wing," an entity third in importance as "one of the influential political currents of our time," but did not specifically identify it with WRP. In practice two groups of left socialists were important here, members of left wing socialist parties per se and those on the left wings of the more moderate socialist parties. These constituted one major faction within the international communist front organizations, the other being composed of communists, revolutionary democrats, and members of national liberation movements.

The international fronts appeared to be the institutional embodiment of WRP or, more accurately, its non-Chinese, non-Albanian, and non-Yugoslav majority component. For example the largest and most representative of the fronts, the World Peace Council, had twenty communists, twelve revolutionary democrats, three left socialists, and two liberation movement leaders among its politically identifiable vice-presidents just prior to its reorganization in February 1990. Just after the reorganization the respective figures were fourteen, thirteen, four, and three. The other major international fronts, in approximate order of importance were The World Federation of Trade Unions, the World Federation of Democratic Youth, the Afro-Asian Peoples' Solidarity Organization, the Women's International Democratic Federation, the International Union of Students, the International Organization of Journalists, and the International Association of Democratic Lawyers.

The monthly World Marxist Review, with sixty-eight pro-Soviet and neutralist Communist parties represented on its staff at the time of its dissolution in 1990, served as a forum in which revolutionary democrats, liberation movement spokesmen, left wing socialists, and international front leaders belonging to various of these groups could publicize their officially approved statements. In this way it served as a WRP mouthpiece as well.

By early 1992 of the countries involved in the world socialist system just three years earlier, five—China, Cuba, Laos, Vietnam, and North Korea—were run by communists in the old way. Four—Bulgaria, Czechoslovakia, Hungary, and Poland—ceased to be ruled by communists altogether. Albania, Mongolia, and Rumania were ruled by communists but within a new, pluralistic framework, whereas the USSR and Yugoslavia were disintegrating into their constituent republics, some ruled by communists, some not. Cambodia was evolving into a pluralistic nation where the communist position was still unclear and East Germany had been absorbed by its non-communist rival. Logically then, the world socialist system as of early 1992 consisted of the eight countries and the Soviet and Yugoslav republics ruled by Communist parties. The concept of WRP had become irrelevant in its homeland, and the cause it was to promote had become increasingly tenuous.

Bibliography: Ralph M. Goldman, ed., *Transnational Parties. Organizing the World's Precincts* (Lanham, Md., 1983); *Session of the World Peace Council, Athens, 6-11 February 1990. Documents* (Helsinki, 1990); V.G. Solodovnikov, A.B. Letnev, and P.I. Manchkha, *Political Parties of Africa* (M., 1970); Richard F. Staar, ed., *Yearbook on International Communist Affairs, 1991* (Stanford, 1991); Alexander Subbotin, ed., *First Hand Information. Communists and Revolutionary Democrats of the World Presenting Their Parties* (Prague, 1988); Vadim Zagladin, ed., *The International Communist Movement. Sketch of Strategy and Tactics* (M., 1972); Pavel Auersperg, "International Meeting of the Forces of World Progress," *Tribuna*, No. 48 (Prague, 26 November 1980); A. Kiva, "Countries of Socialist Orientation. Some Aspects of Their Political Development," *International Affairs* (October, 1973), 30-37. "Sotsialisticheskaia orientatsiia. Nekotorye problemy teorii i praktiki," *Mirovaia ekonomika i mezhdunarodnye otnosheniia*, No. 10 (October, 1976), 19-32; Nikolai Dmitrievich Kosukhin, "Development Trends of the Countries of a Socialist Orientation," *Rabochii klass i sovremennyi mir*, No. 4 (July-August, 1981); Ye. Kuskov, "The Most Active and Influential Force,"

Kommunist, No. 17 (November, 1972); Vl. Li, "Social Revolution in Afro-Asian Countries and Scientific Socialism," *Aziia i Afrika Segodnia*, No. 3 (March, 1981); M. Mitin, "A Doctrine Which Is Transforming the World," *Izvestiia* (20 April 1974); *New Perspectives*, No. 1/90 (Helsinki), 2; Boris Ponomarev, "V.I. Lenin and the International Communist Movement," *Kommunist*, No. 2 (January, 1974); G. Shakhnazarov, "On the Problem of Correlation of Forces in the World," *Kommunist*, No. 3 (February, 1974); Vadim Zagladin, "A Few Problems in the Communist Movement and the Policy of the CPSU," *Neues Deutschland* (East Berlin, 4 May 1972); Idem., "Immortal Teaching," *New Times*, No. 18 (Moscow, 1983), 9-11; Idem., "A New Historical Stage," *Voprosy istorii*, No. 6 (June, 1974); R.A. Ulianovskii, "Great October and Revolutionary Process in Asian and African Countries," *Problems of the Far East*, No. 2 (1977).

Wallace H. Spaulding

WORLD VIEW OF THE SOVIET UNION (1917-1991). The Soviet view of the world and of the Soviet Union's place in it.

The Soviet world view underwent considerable metamorphosis during the seventy-four-year history of the USSR. Rooted in Karl Marx's dialectical interpretation of the history of class struggle and Vladimir Ilich Lenin's theory of imperialism, until the mid-1980s the world view of the USSR was characterized by a fundamental belief in a worldwide class struggle between the forces of capitalism and socialism. An important component of the Soviet world view was the theory of peaceful coexistence, first pronounced by Lenin and reinterpreted by each of his successors to fit changing times and perspectives. The Soviet world view evolved as the Soviet Union developed from a fledgling state struggling to survive in the early 1920s to a military superpower in the 1970s and 1980s. In the mid-1980s the Soviet Union gradually modified its traditional world view when it adopted "new thinking," the hallmark of Soviet foreign policy under the leadership of Mikhail Sergeevich Gorbachev. Eventually this new thinking resulted in the abandonment of traditional tenets of Soviet foreign policy which had evolved over seventy years.

The Marxist-Leninist Foundations. The origins of the Soviet world view can be found in the theories of Karl Marx. Marx's writings concentrated primarily on capitalism and its anticipated demise. He discussed post-capitalist society only briefly in a few essays. He believed that, once proletarian revolution began in advanced capitalist societies such as Germany or England, it would spread from country to country. Revolution would come to less developed countries such as Russia only if sparked by revolution in more advanced capitalist countries. Marx foresaw the end of nationalism and the nation-state and therefore ignored the need for traditional diplomacy in the postcapitalist world. The major ideological principle he bequeathed to Lenin and indirectly to the Soviet state was the belief that class struggle was the moving force of historical development.

In *Imperialism, The Highest State of Capitalism* (1916) Lenin used Marx's perception of the world, along with that of several European economists, to develop his own world view and to explain why Marx's anticipated world revolution had not yet occurred. The theories found in *Imperialism* provided the genesis for the Soviet world view. Lenin argued that mature capitalism generated market conditions which led to monopolies, close ties between finance and industry, and excess capital. To relieve social pressures in society, capitalists sought investments abroad, especially in colonies, where labor was cheap and natural resources plentiful. Workers in the mother countries began to earn higher wages, and the development of proletarian class consciousness was delayed. As more and more capitalist countries attempted to acquire colonies competition became intense, ultimately leading to the outbreak of World War I in 1914. Lenin's analysis resulted in a world view that provided the nucleus of the five basic principles that later guided the Soviet state. First, capitalism had matured to a final stage, namely imperialism, from which it would succumb to socialist revolution. Second, the Soviet state was a model and leader of world transformation, so that its survival was a paramount concern. Third, socialism as embodied in the USSR represented the mortal enemy of capitalism, which would try to destroy it, leading to Lenin's basic question: "Kto kogo?" (Who will defeat whom?). Fourth, competition among capitalist and imperialist states would prevent them from uniting to destroy socialism; the Soviet state could take advantage of this competition and rivalry to gain a "breathing space" for survival. Fifth, to defeat imperialism, the colonies had to be wrested from the imperialist states so that social pressures in the latter would explode. These five concepts, in varying combinations, influenced Soviet foreign policy for most of the history of the Soviet Union.

The Early Soviet Period (1917-1924). When Lenin came to power in 1917 he believed that World War I provided the seeds for international revolution leading to the demise of capitalism and that further revolutions were imminent in Europe, especially after Germany's anticipated defeat. The Decree on Peace (26 October/8 November 1917) and the early negotiations with Germany at Brest-Litovsk sought to provoke revolution rather than promote negotiations. Although reality dawned during the negotiations with Germany, hope remained that revolution would follow after the war. Faced with a civil war (1918-1920), Soviet Russia could not concentrate on foreign policy until its own survival was assured. Foreign intervention on behalf of the White forces in the Civil War served to reinforce the belief that the outside world was fundamentally hostile to the Soviet Republic.

When Lenin turned his attention more fully to foreign policy in 1920, his policies reflected a world view that retained a distinctly revolutionary tone. The survival of the Soviet state was the primary concern, but hope lingered that revolution could spread to other countries. Lenin's world view in 1920 described a world divided into two hostile forces, the capitalist and the socialist camps. The economic crisis facing the Soviet republic tempered his revolutionary views. Rising discontent led Lenin to seek cooperation with the West. The introduction of the New Economic Policy (NEP) in 1921 permitted economic cooperation with the capitalist world and the granting of concessions to western firms to invest in the Soviet republic. In the short run, they could cooperate under peaceful coexistence, described as a "breathing space" to enable the new state to regain the strength depleted by World War I and civil war.

During the early 1920s the Soviet Union aspired to normalize relations with the capitalist states and at the same time to sow discord and encourage revolution both in the capitalist world and in the "East," Lenin's term for the colonial and semicolonial states. The Soviet government focused its attention principally on state-to-state relations, while the Communist International (Comintern), the international communist organization formed by Lenin, sought to foment revolution. By the time Lenin died hope of revolution in Europe had dimmed, but communists were still assisting national liberation movements, especially in Asia.

The Early Stalin Period, 1924-1934. Socialism in One Country. By the mid-1920s hope in world revolution gave way to the belief that the survival and well-being of the Soviet Union were the primary concerns of Soviet policy-makers, although the Comintern still promoted revolution when circumstances seemed encouraging. Joseph Vissarionovich Stalin, who played the single most important role in determining Soviet policy in the late 1920s and 1930s, interpreted peaceful coexistence and the theory of two camps more narrowly than Lenin. He warned his countrymen of the dangers of capitalist encirclement, often expressing fear that war could be unleashed at any time. Setbacks in Soviet foreign policy toward Germany, England, and China, in the aftermath of Comintern activity in those countries, reinforced belief in the accuracy of Stalin's perception. By 1928 the Comintern, after several defeats, retreated from cooperation with noncommunists in national or popular front movements, and the Comintern was transformed into an organization whose primary purpose was support for the USSR.

Stalin's approach to the world can be summed up in the idea of "Socialism in One Country," which became the slogan of his early rule. In contradiction to the traditional views based in Marx's writings, this concept asserted that the USSR could build socialism independently, without waiting for world revolution. "Socialism in One Country" had several practical advantages since it appealed to Russian nationalists for whom Marxist internationalism held little attraction. It also justified the sacrifices made in support of the Russian revolution and provided a rationale for distancing Russia from active involvement in promoting revolution. It also served as an effective ideological counterweight to Trotsky's concept of "permanent revolution" in Stalin-Trotsky struggle for power.

After the USSR adopted a Five Year Plan for rapid economic development in 1928, foreign policy assumed secondary importance in favor of a policy of economic self-sufficiency and guarded isolation. The Five Year Plan assumed a stable world in which the USSR could develop without fear of imminent invasion. In a well-known speech given in 1931 Stalin nonetheless argued for the urgency of transforming the USSR into a great power; he maintained that in the past Russia had been attacked because it was weak. Russia had to make up decades of development in one decade in order to survive possible attack by its enemies.

Stalin and International Affairs (1934-1941). By the mid-1930s external events contrived to end the USSR's decade of relative isolation. The dangers of Japanese militarism and its conquest of Manchuria on Russia's eastern border and the rise of Hitler in Germany and his expansionist agenda in Eastern Europe caused Stalin and the USSR to seek greater cooperation with the outside world. In 1934 the USSR joined the League of Nations and became an advocate of collective security against aggression. In 1935 the USSR signed mutual defense treaties with France and Czechoslovakia. The Comintern in 1935 modified its stance on cooperation with noncommunists; the "Popular Front" strategy became the hallmark of Comintern and Soviet policy in Europe and Asia in the late 1930s. The Soviet Union even sent "volunteers" to Spain to fight in the "Popular Front" against General Francisco Franco.

Concerned by the lack of concerted western response to German, Italian, and Japanese aggression during the 1930s, the USSR eventually sought to avoid war by making agreements with all sides. In 1939 the Molotov-Ribbentrop Pact gave Hitler the license to start an early war against Poland, at the same time that it gave Stalin the hope that the USSR could avoid involvement in the impending war. The secret protocol that recognized Russian influence in the Baltic States, eastern Poland, Finland, and Bessarabia, however, entangled the USSR in the European conflict even before Germany invaded the Soviet Union in June 1941. The USSR also made peace with Japan, recognizing the puppet state of Manchukuo (Manchuria) and selling to Japan the decrepit Chinese Eastern Railway. A pact of neutrality with Japan in 1941 was designed to keep the USSR out of the Sino-Japanese conflict.

In the years immediately preceding World War II Soviet foreign policy, although expressed in Stalinist rhetoric rooted in Marxism-Leninism, was pragmatic. It reflected more the traditional instincts of Russia as a great power than those of a communist revolutionary state. Once war began there were revolutionary overtones in the actions initiated by the USSR to take over the Baltic states and Finland and impose communist regimes there.

World War II And The Early Cold War (1941-1953). After Germany attacked the USSR on 22 June 1941 the USSR entered an alliance with England and the United States. During World War II (for Russia, the Great Patriotic War) the Soviet Union shifted its strategy, subduing communist revolutionary zeal in favor of defense of the fatherland against the German invaders. This was an intensely nationalist approach to the war, acceptable both to the Soviet peoples and to the Western allies. Although Stalin de-emphasized his confrontational world view during the war, his new pragmatism did not outlast the war. As Soviet troops liberated the country from the Germans and led the offensive into Eastern Europe, the Soviet Union simultaneously absorbed the Baltic states, Bessarabia, and eastern Poland. Soviet troops ensured that governments friendly to the USSR came to power in the liberated nations of Eastern and East Central Europe. The Cold War, although induced by multiple causes, was influenced strongly by Stalin's view that the defeat of Hitler's Germany had not eliminated all dangers to the USSR. Anxious to avoid a recurrence of an invasion from the West, Stalin insisted that the Soviet Union play a major role in postwar Eastern Europe. Over the next few years the USSR created a bloc of Soviet client states in Eastern Europe. Prior to Stalin's death the Soviet world view and the resultant closely entwined foreign policy emphasized the newly formed socialist bloc, but was hostile or indifferent to most other developments around the world. The governments of Eastern Europe were united with the Soviet Union in ideology and policy. The process of intermingling the economies of the Communist-party states began during the Stalin years, but required several decades to implement. Western antagonism toward the USSR after World War II played a role in accelerating the Soviet hold over Eastern Europe although, given Stalin's attitude toward monolithic agreement within and among Communist parties, it could be argued that an East European bloc would have developed even without the solidifying influence of Western opposition. The victory of Mao Zedong and the Communist party in China reinforced and advanced the notion of a large communist bloc in the world.

The Cold War intensified during the Berlin Crisis (1949) and the Korean War (1950-1953). The formation of NATO in 1949, a response to the Soviet bloc in Eastern Europe, contributed to worldwide perception of a bipolar world in which the Soviet bloc often was called the "East" and the NATO allies the "West." The "East-West" conflict, fueled by Soviet-American rivalry, dominated international relations for several decades.

Khrushchev And Competitive Peaceful Coexistence (1953-1964). In the early post-Stalin years the pressures of the Cold War eased as the Soviet Union took a good look at the changing world. Although still interpreting the world through a Marxist-Leninist screen, the new leaders of the 1950s recognized the possibilities inherent in developing relations with new states in Asia and Africa, according to the "Five Principles of Peaceful Coexistence," first adopted in Sino-Indian relations in 1954. Soviet leader Nikita Sergeevich Khrushchev and his colleagues reopened a dialogue with the West on the basis of a revised concept of peaceful coexistence, which included both cordial relations and competition between the two social and economic systems. The changing nature of warfare in the nuclear age led the Soviet Union under Khrushchev to abandon Lenin's idea of a final military showdown. Instead Khrushchev projected the possibility of socialism's economic victory over capitalism in peaceful competition. His ideas were incorporated into Soviet ideology at the landmark Twentieth Party Congress in 1956, the Party Congress which launched de-Stalinization. Although the western states did not accept Khrushchev's definition of competitive coexistence, de facto competition in which the stakes were the Third World and other noncommitted states, characterized East-West relations. The post-Stalin leadership resolved a number of lingering problems. It contributed to ending the Korean War (1953), it helped negotiate the Geneva Protocols on Indochina (1954) and with the United States, Great Britain, and France it signed a peace treaty with Austria (1955). Other problems like Berlin continued to haunt East-West relations during the entire Khrushchev period.

Khrushchev's world view encompassed a vision of a future under communism. His internal goals centered on building the material bases for communism by 1980, a goal which required greater emphasis on consumer goods and services in an economy in which the military-industrial complex continued to determine the basic pattern of economic development. The Soviet standard of living gradually rose in the 1950s and 1960s, giving rise to hope among the people that a brighter future awaited them.

Khrushchev's world view recognized that the socialist bloc countries of Eastern Europe and Asia could not follow the Soviet example in every particular. He was inclined to allow greater freedom to these states under the precept "many roads to socialism," which the 1956 Party Congress also adopted. This doctrine was tested almost immediately by events in Hungary and to a lesser degree by Poland and China. The result was the Hungarian Revolution of 1956 and the resulting Soviet invasion. In Poland differences were resolved without intervention. Differences multiplied between China and the USSR, leading to a full-fledged ideological war between the two socialist giants by the early 1960s. Nonetheless the concept of "many roads to socialism" remained. It was tested over the years through trial and error in Eastern Europe by various leaders, anxious to establish their own pattern of development within the general parameters of acceptable socialist behavior.

The Brezhnev Era, 1964-1982. The Soviet world view during the Brezhnev era retained the major features of Khrushchev's world view, although there were some differences. Leonid Ilich Brezhnev and Aleksei Nikolaevich Kosygin dropped the competitive component from peaceful coexistence in the 1960s, recognizing that the USSR was unlikely to surpass the United States or any other major western power by 1980. At the same time they presided over the maturation of the USSR as a military superpower, a status guaranteeing the Soviet Union respect in international relations. During the Brezhnev Era the term "detente" was used to describe the new forms of cooperation in East-West relations which developed in the late 1960s and the 1970s. As a concept detente was more acceptable to the western powers than the ideologically laden peaceful coexistence. Nonetheless the Soviet leadership did not abandon the ideological goals embodied in the traditional world view. In the 1960s considerable effort was expended on attempting to reunify the fragmented socialist camp. China, Albania, Romania, and Yugoslavia, for differing reasons, resisted Soviet efforts. After the invasion of Czechoslovakia in 1968, unification of the socialist camp became even harder than before.

An important component of the Soviet world view during this period was the Brezhnev Doctrine, a policy put forward after the Czech invasion in 1968. The Brezhnev Doctrine stated that socialist states had a responsibility to intervene in any socialist state where socialism was endangered. The 1968 reforms initiated under Alexander Dubcek (1921-1992) were considered evidence that socialism was in jeopardy in Czechoslovakia. The Brezhnev Doctrine originated in the communist belief that socialism was a higher stage of historical development than capitalism and was buttressed by the Soviet belief that Eastern Europe was its sphere of influence.

The Brezhnev period also was characterized by Soviet interest in revolutions in the Third World. Through aid and the use of military proxies the USSR became involved in several civil wars and revolutionary movements, most notably in Angola and Afghanistan.

Although the USSR's status as a superpower was assured in the late Brezhnev era, the intense arms race with the United States took its toll on the Soviet economy. Up to 75 percent of the Soviet economy is believed to have been dedicated to the military effort, creating a dichotomous economy: a military superpower and a third-world consumer economy. The Brezhnev administration was myopic about the long-term effect of its policies, arguing that the world "correlation of forces" favored the Soviet Union and socialism. The Soviet world view under Brezhnev focused only on Soviet gains, not on the price paid to gain global military power.

In the brief interregnum between the death of Brezhnev (1982) and the ascendancy of Gorbachev as general secretary of the Soviet Communist party (1985), the Soviet Union operated under the existing world view, a world view soon to be challenged by openness (glasnost).

Gorbachev And New Thinking (1985-1991). Despite changes in emphasis and focus, the essentials of the Soviet world view remained relatively unchanged until the mid-1980s when Gorbachev came to power. With his advisers he significantly modified the Soviet world view through a process known as "new thinking" (novoe myshlenie).

New thinking among the Soviet leadership, in its most general application, gave rise to restructuring (perestroika), openness, democratization (demokratizatsia), and new thinking in foreign policy. The term "new thinking" itself was used to describe changes in the Soviet world view and foreign policy, whereas perestroika applied to domestic policy changes. In Gorbachev's words, "The fundamental principle of the new political outlook is very simple: Nuclear war cannot be a means of achieving political, economic, ideological or any other goals" (Gorbachev, 140). In the West the term new thinking did not receive the attention accorded to perestroika and glasnost, even though new thinking was one of the most successful accomplishments of the Gorbachev era.

Initially the concept of new thinking did not mean abandonment of the traditional, Soviet Marxist-Leninist world view and its derivative ideological precepts. In its earliest manifestations new thinking allowed Soviet policy makers to look at the world from a decreasingly dogmatic, yet Marxist-Leninist perspective. Intended to open a discourse about the direction of Soviet foreign policy, it also had significant military and economic implications. The new approach was multidimensional in orientation and practice, opening the door to a more flexible, less ideological diplomacy conducted in a spirit of open and frank exchange. As a consequence of glasnost and new thinking, the Soviet Union opened its doors to the outside world, especially to the West. Cooperation and contacts between the Soviet Union and the West, once confined primarily to official exchanges, soon encompassed joint ventures, extensive cooperative cultural and scientific contacts, and citizen diplomacy. New thinking also encouraged foreign investment, reminiscent of the 1920s NEP period, to stimulate the sagging Soviet economy and acquire new technology.

New thinking gradually transformed the Soviet world view, propelling its understanding of global reality beyond peaceful coexistence or detente. The peaceful coexistence of the 1950s sought cooperation and competition between systems, while maintaining ideological distance. Detente, a bridge between peaceful coexistence and new thinking, expanded options for cooperation without denying basic ideological distinctions between socialism and capitalism. Under new thinking, ideological differences were downplayed in recognition of the need to avoid global nuclear holocaust. New thinking sought to put aside both the Marxist-Leninist view of class struggle and the world's reliance on military solutions advocated by theorists like the Prussian general Carl von Clausewitz (1780-1831). Gorbachev stated, "Security is indivisible. It is either equal security for all or none at all" (Gorbachev, 142). This was a significant departure from Lenin's "Kto kogo?".

Security concerns and the Soviet military budget were central to new thinking, which proceeded from the assumption that military sufficiency, not supremacy, should determine policy. The United States and the USSR had engaged in an arms race for many years, especially in the neo-Cold War era of the early 1980s. Both states had exceeded military sufficiency and had paid a high national price for their armaments. The USSR had invested in the military sector at a greater sacrifice to the consumer economy and agriculture, resulting in the economic crisis in the early 1990s.

Until the abortive coup of August 1991 the Soviet world view was determined, at least theoretically, by Marxism-Leninism. After the coup the situation abruptly changed as Russian President Boris Nikolaevich Yeltsin outlawed Communist party activities, and the Soviet leaders distanced themselves from the party's traditional perspectives. The demise of the old USSR and the birth of the new Commonwealth of Independent States (CIS), established by eleven of the former fifteen Soviet republics in December 1991, can be regarded as a logical extension and culmination of the new thinking which took root in the USSR in the late 1980s.

Postscript. Post-Soviet Russia and the CIS, 1992—. Of the fifteen component republics of the USSR three Baltic states—Latvia, Estonia and Lithuania—and Georgia decided not to join the CIS and chose to develop their own independent foreign policies. The largest, most powerful of the new republics is Russia, the successor state to the USSR in the United Nations' Security Council and in international negotiations. The remaining ten republics, in which former communist officials often play a leading role, abandoned the traditional Soviet world view and appeared anxious to establish new, friendly relationships with the outside world on a bilateral and multilateral basis without an ideological context. Nonetheless, new thinking did not totally revolutionize society. The bureaucracy and the old Communist party elite continued to be important voices in many republics of the former USSR. The world view of the CIS and its eleven independent republics was not fully defined in mid-1992 as Russia and the other CIS republics struggled to implement economic reforms to relieve severe shortages of food and consumer goods. Apart from affirmations of intent to establish friendly relations with the outside world, there was no one unifying world view among the CIS states.

Bibliography: Mikhail S. Gorbachev, *Perestroika. Thinking for Our Country and the World* (New York, 1987); George F. Kennan, *Russia and the West under Lenin and Stalin* (New York, 1961); Robert J. Kingston, *Perestroika Papers. An Exercise in Supplemental Diplomacy* (Dubuque, 1988); Vendulka Kubalkova and Albert Cruikshank, *Marxism and International Relations* (New York, 1989); Margot Light, *The Soviet Theory of International Relations* (New York, 1988); Richard Lowenthal, *World Communism. Disintegration of a*

Secular Faith (New York, 1966); R. Judson Mitchell, *Ideology of a Superpower. Contemporary Soviet Doctrine on International Relations* (Stanford, 1982); *New Political Thinking. Soviet Journalists Discuss Mikhail Gorbachev's Address at the United Nations* (M., 1989); Alvin Z. Rubinstein, *The Foreign Policy of the Soviet Union*, 3rd ed. (Boston, 1988); Gordon B. Smith, *Soviet Politics. Continuity and Contradiction* (New York, 1988); Peter Zwick, *Soviet Foreign Relations. Process and Policy* (Englewood Cliffs, 1990). J.L. Black, ed., *USSR Documents Annual*, 1987- (Gulf Breeze, Fla., Academic International Press, 1988—); Rex A. Wade, *Documents of Soviet History*, Vol. 1 ff. (Gulf Breeze, Fla., Academic International Press, 1991—).

Norma C. Noonan

WYNNE, GREVILLE MAYNARD (1919-1990). British businessman and spy. Served as liaison between British intelligence (MI5) and Colonel Oleg Vladimirovich Penkovsky, the most highly placed Soviet informer during the period of the Cold War.

Greville Wynne was born in 1919 in Shropshire, England. Two years later he moved with his family to Ystrad Mynach in South Wales, where his father took a job as foreman in a firm which serviced mining equipment. As a child he suffered from dyslexia, which made school difficult for him but forced him to develop his memory. When he left school at age fourteen he had compiled a mediocre record but had developed a fascination with electricity. After working for an electrical firm for a year and a half and taking a night course in electricity, Wynne moved to Nottingham, where on a government scholarship he served as an apprentice with the Ericcson Telephone Company and studied electrical engineering at University College in Nottingham.

In 1938 Wynne enrolled in the Officer Training Corps (OTC) program at Nottingham University. In November of that year at the Ericcson plant, which had taken on some military contracts, he accidentally discovered a German agent sending messages on a secret radio. His reporting of the incident to his OTC colonel and his ability to keep his silence played an important role in his future. In January 1939 he was put through a testing program by the British internal security agency, MI5, and he came under its control when he was called to the service in the summer of 1939. He spent World War II working for MI5 observing and reporting on potential security risks.

Following the war, Wynne established himself as a successful businessman selling electrical and industrial machinery. In 1955 his wartime superior, now working for MI6, the British intelligence agency responsible for espionage, contacted him and suggested selling machinery in Eastern Europe. Following this suggestion proved to be lucrative and also provided Wynne with a cover useful to MI5.

Early in 1958 MI6 asked Wynne to help them evacuate from Odessa one of their chief agents, Sergei Kuznov, a major in Soviet military intelligence, (GRU, Glavnoe razvedyvatelnoe upravlenie). The first part of Wynne's job was to carry a block of gold concealed in a cigarette pack to Kuznov, to pay for his transportation on a Western freighter. The second part was to create a diversion of the port guards by falling from the deck of a Black Sea cruise ship, the Uzbekistan, on which he had booked passage for this purpose, onto the dock below. The first part went according to plan, but unexpectedly Kuznov gave Wynne an envelope of documents for transmission to London. Afraid that they would be found, Wynne concealed them in an air vent on the cruise ship. He successfully created the diversion that allowed Kuznov to board the freighter, but in the process of falling from the Uzbekistan he broke his leg. He was taken to hospital and shortly thereafter airlifted to England. In August 1959 he contrived to meet the Uzbekistan during its stop in Varna, Bulgaria, and retrieve Kuznov's documents which had remained hidden there for over a year.

In November 1960 MI6 again contacted Wynne, asking him to establish relations with the State Committee for the Coordination of Scientific Research Work (gosudarstvenny komitet po koordinatsii nauchno-issledovatel'skikh rabot, or GKKNIR). GKKNIR's stated function was to develop a coordinated policy for science and technology, but it also served as a cover for Soviet agents seeking Western technology. GKKNIR met with Wynne on 1 December and approved his plan to bring a delegation of industrialists to Moscow. At the same time he was introduced to Penkovsky, one of GKKNIR's members. Only on his debriefing in London did MI6 tell Wynne of Penkovsky's postition in the GRU and its suspicion that he was a likely turncoat. Wynne was told to establish closer relations with the Colonel. He managed to Penkovsky's friendship and confidence on his second trip to Moscow in April 1961. At this time Penkovsky revealed his intention to supply the British with highly sensitive information. As earnest of his convictions and value he gave Wynne an envelope of documents for transmission.

Wynne's business interests and Penkovsky's position on the GKKNIR gave them a number of occasions to meet. Penkovsky made two trips to England and one to France in 1961 as a member of trade delegations. Between commercial meetings and Penkovsky's debriefings by MI6, Wynne accompanied Penkovsky in London and Paris and joined him on an overnight trip to Washington to meet President John Fitzgerald Kennedy. In the same year Wynne travelled twice to Moscow, carrying in film and a radio set for receiving coded messages, and carrying out exposed film of secret documents. The information provided by Penkovsky was enormously important. He unmasked some 300 East Bloc intelligence agents and provided vital details of Soviet weapons production. Not least it provided details on the development, placement, and reliability of Russia's intercontinental ballistic missiles. This information enabled President Kennedy to face down Soviet leader Nikita Sergeevich Khrushchev in the Cuban missile crisis.

By early 1962 Penkovsky had come under suspicion, and MI6 decided to bring him West. Wynne was to organize a caravan of trailers to serve as a travelling exposition of British industrial products in Eastern Europe. One of the trailers was equipped with a secret compartment in which Penkovsky was to be carried from Bucharest or Budapest, depending on which of these cities he was able to reach. Before this plan reached fruition, Penkovsky was arrested in Moscow on 22 October. In the meantime Wynne, unaware of this event, waited for Penkovsky in Budapest. He was arrested there on 2 November.

Wynne was taken to Moscow the following day and imprisoned in the infamous Liubianka prison. Here he was subjected to cold, hunger, and frequent and intensive questioning in preparation for the public trial at which he and Penkovsky were to be condemned as spies. Penkovsky's apartment had been raided, and incriminating evidence, including films of top secret documents, was found. For this reason the trial, which took place from 7 to 11 May 1963, was not a dispassionate examination of the evidence or an attempt to ascertain guilt. It was instead a show trial designed to demonstrate to hardliners in the regime that Khrushchev's policies of peaceful coexistence had not weakened the vigilance of his regime against the West and its machinations. Both Penkovsky and Wynne stuck to the story that Wynne, a naive businessman, had been unknowingly transferring documents to the British. Penkovsky was sentenced to death and Wynne to three years in prison to be followed by five years at hard labor.

After his trial Wynne spent eleven months in prison in Vladimir. Here again he was subjected to frequent questioning and severe conditions in the continuing effort to make him confess to espionage. On 22 April 1964 he was exchanged in Berlin for the Soviet spy Konon Trofimovich Molody, better known as Gordon Lonsdale.

Upon his release Wynne returned to his business ventures, which prospered. He wrote two memoirs of his espionage activity, as noted below. He died in London of throat cancer on 27 February 1990.

See Also: PEN'KOVSKII, OLEG VLADIMIROVICH

Bibliography: Basic sources are Wynne's memoirs, *Contact on Gorky Street*, published in England as *Man from Moscow*, (New York, 1968) and *the Man from Odessa* (Bath, England, 1983). A number of notes and documents by Penkovsky, including the reasons for his betraying his country are collected in Frank Gibney, ed., *The Penkovsky Papers* (New York, 1965). Wynne and Penkovsky are mentioned in a number of books dealing with espionage activities. Some older ones such as Boris Levytsky, *The Uses of Terror. The Soviet Secret Police, 1917-1970* (New York, 1965) and Richard Deacon, *A History of the Russian Secret Service* (New York, 1972) discount the value of Penkovsky's information. Ernest Volkman, *Warriors of the Night. Spies, Soldiers, and American Intelligence* (New York, 1985) accentuates the reluctance of the Central Intelligence Agency to give Penkovsky's information the credence it deserved. The latest work on this subject is Jerrold L. Schecter and Peter S. Deriabin, *The Spy Who Saved the World* (New York, 1992). Despite its sensationalist title, it is a serious work, based on a wealth of recently declassified governmental documents.

George N. Rhyne

X

XINJIANG PROVINCE, CHINA, RELATIONS WITH RUSSIA AND THE SO-VIET UNION. Xinjiang's (Sinkiang) importance in Russo-Chinese relations has been mainly political, involving the indigenous Turki population of Islamic faith akin to that on the Russian side of the border. This has prompted Russian intervention in anti-Chinese uprisings during the tsarist and Soviet eras, both in support of and subversive of Chinese authority. Local trade has been of secondary importance.

The Russian and Chinese empires first came into contact along the Central Asian frontier in the latter half of the nineteenth century. In 1864 St. Petersburg and Peking agreed on the border separating Kazakh, Kirgyz, Uygur, and other peoples. Common imperial interests prompted Russia to side with China in the following period after a local adventurer, Yakub Beg, led a successful uprising and expelled Chinese rule for thirteen years. Russian troops entered the Ili River Valley that crossed the border and remained in occupation despite the promise to leave once order had been restored. An initial agreement granting St. Petersburg nearly 30 percent of the Ili Valley was repudiated in Peking. An 1881 treaty returned most of the land in question but China agreed to pay a sizeable indemnity for losses suffered by Russian merchants and residents in Xinjiang during the uprising.

Further tsarist pressure in the Altai region adjoining Russia and Mongolia territory became an issue between the two capitals on the eve of World War I. Tsarist interest stemmed in part from competition with Britain in the "Great Race" for spheres of influence in Central and South Asia. The collapse of the Qing Empire in 1911 raised the prospect of Xinjiang's being informally divided between London and St. Petersburg. World War I diverted both imperial powers and Xinjiang remained nominally Chinese, albeit in effect subject to local authority.

Revolution in Russia in 1917 and Outer Mongolia temporarily involved Xinjiang, as fleeing "Whites" sought refuge from the "Reds." But the Chinese governor, Yang Tseng-hsin, disarmed and interned these troops and then negotiated with Moscow to win amnesty for those returning peacefully. In 1924 the establishment of diplomatic relations between the Soviet Union and China expanded the Russian consulates in Xinjiang from two to five. Completion of the Turksib Railway in 1930 facilitated trade. In 1931 eight Soviet trade agencies were established, customs duties on Soviet goods were reduced, and new telegraph and radio communications crossed the border.

Politics returned in 1931 when local rebellions again threatened the Xinjiang government, this time led mainly by powerful Chinese Moslem forces. In 1933 the newly installed warlord governor, Sheng Shih-t'sai, won Soviet support, including aircraft as well as small arms and ammunition, advisers, and money. Sheng professed belief in Marxism-Leninism and sought admission into the Chinese Communist Party but was persuaded by Stalin to enroll secretly in the Soviet party. Thus from 1934 to 1941 Xinjiang became a virtual satellite of Moscow, complete with Soviet secret police, military units, mining concessions, and financial backing.

In return Sheng carried out merciless purges of alleged "Trotskyite, Japanese, and imperialist spies," while pursuing Stalin's nationality policy, thereby raising the political status if not the actual power of the non-Chinese peoples. This provided Moscow with a buffer against feared Japanese expansionism from Manchuria across Inner Mongolia to Central Asia. It also provided a secret pipeline to the Chinese Communist Party which in 1935, after its "Long March," had set up its base in North China. The Nazi invasion of 1941 prompted Stalin to abandon Sheng who quickly repudiated his satellite status and supported Chiang Kai-shek. All Soviet forces withdrew from Xinjiang together with the geological survey and mining personnel.

Yet the approaching end of World War II permitted Stalin to resume intervention in Xinjiang by assisting a major anti-Chinese revolt in 1944. Reinforced by ethnically kindred troops from across the Soviet border, Uygur and Kazakh rebels established the "East Turkistan Republic" and quickly won control over much of the western region. The rebellion soon threatened the capital, Urumqi, where the Soviet consul facilitated negotiations that ceded virtual autonomy to the dissident area but left the rest under Chinese rule.

In 1949 Chinese Communist forces entered Xinjiang, forcing Stalin to pull back once more. The rebel regime accepted Beijing's renewed control. Most of its leadership reportedly died in an airplane crash en route to the Chinese capital. Only after determining the loyalty of all local forces did Beijing proclaim the Xinjiang Autonomous Uygur Region in 1955. Joint Sino-Soviet stock companies in oil, minerals, and various industrial enterprises prompted a dramatic rise in output between 1952 and 1957.

Chinese suspicion of Soviet intentions returned in 1961-1962 when Moscow's consulates suddenly granted visas to those non-Chinese residents seeking refuge from the economic ravages of China's disastrous economic reform, the Great Leap Forward. With upwards of 60,000 Uygurs, Kazakhs, and others taking this route, Beijing closed the Soviet consulates, sealed off the border, and accused Moscow of seeking to separate Xinjiang from China. Tension rose further in 1969 following incidents between opposite military forces prompted by Beijing's claims of disputed areas. Only in the 1980s as detente developed between the two capitals did tension disappear and trade begin to resume its traditional role.

Soviet leader Mikhail Sergeevich Gorbachev's policy of openness (glasnost) released demands for greater autonomy among the non-Russian nationalities in the Soviet Union. The spillover effects of this in Xinjiang worried Beijing, despite the fact that forced in-migration by millions of Chinese between 1958 and 1980 decreased the non-Chinese population to a minority. Establishment of an Institute for Uygur Studies in Alma-Ata, USSR, in 1987 evoked a Chinese protest of "interference in internal affairs." Soviet Uygurs, some 200,000 of whom live in Kazakhstan, were permitted to visit relatives in Xinjiang for up to three months, but no newspapers or periodicals could cross the border and tourism remained closely controlled.

The promulgation of fully independent republics in Central Asia added new concern in Beijing. Prior to the massacre of political protestors in Beijing on 4

June 1989 Uygur demonstrations had protested the use of Xinjiang for nuclear weapons testing and alleged discriminatory treatment in literature. In 1990-1991 Chinese officials repeatedly toured the region warning against "splittism" and calling for "stability" and "vigilance" by military and civilian groups. In March 1990 Beijing reported a small "armed counterrevolutionary rebellion" in a southern Xinjiang city. In 1991 official accounts told of larger riots and demonstrations near the Soviet border. Neither situation approached the crises of 1944 and 1962, but dissolution of Moscow's control and the rise of such independent Central Asian states as Uzbekisan, Turkmenistan, and Karakhstan apparently encouraged local dissidence.

Xinjiang's natural trading relationship is across the Russian and Soviet border through passes and valleys rather than with central China, from which it is separated by extensive desert and mountains. In the past cotton from the southern area and livestock from the northern portion comprised the main exports. This trade increased dramatically in the 1980s as a result of Deng Xiaoping's "open door" economic reforms and promised further expansion after completion of the railroad linking Xinjiang and the Kazakh Republic. Livestock, meat, corn, sugar, and oil to Kazakhstan raised border trade in 1991 to four times the total in 1987-1990. In 1990-1991 the respective leaders of the Kazakh Republic and Xinjiang exchanged visits and concluded agreements on economic and cultural exchange. Thus decentralization in China and dissolution of the Soviet Union combined to transform the century-old Russo-Chinese relationship into a quasi-Central Asian one, with unforeseeable implications for the future.

Bibliography: Andres D.W. Forbes, *Warlords and Muslims In Chinese Central Asia. A Political History of Republican Sinkiang, 1911-1949* (Cambridge, 1986); Owen Lattimore, *Pivot of Asia* (Boston, 1950); Donald H. McMillen, *Chinese Communist Power and Policy in Xinjiang, 1949-1977* (Boulder, 1979); Allen S. Whiting and Sheng Shih-t'sai, *Sinkiang. Pawn or Pivot?* (East Lansing, 1958).

Allen S. Whiting

Y

YABLOCHKOV, PAVEL NIKOLAEVICH (1847-1894). Russian scientist and inventor. Specialized in the theory and application of electric light. Inventor of the "Yablochkov candle." Ardent promoter of practical uses of electricity in Russia and abroad.

Yablochkov was born in Zhadkova, Saratov province, on 14 (26) September 1847 to a family of impoverished landowners. He attended Saratov gymnasium from 1859 to 1862 but left before graduating in order to prepare for admission into the prestigious Nicholas Engineering School in St. Petersburg. His studies there deepened his interest in a new technology, electricity. Upon graduation from this institution in 1866 he entered the military, where he served in an engineering battalion in Kiev. While in service he attended the Technical Galvanic Institute, the only educational institution in Russia at the time that gave instruction in the theory of electricity.

Only on completion of his military service in 1872 did he have the time to devote himself to scientific work. He took a job with the Moscow-Kursk railway in one of the few positions that dealt with the practical uses of electricity, the telegraph service. In Moscow he met others who shared his fascination with the new science. He helped organize a scientific exposition in Moscow in 1872 and then participated in the creation of the Moscow Polytechnical Museum. At the end of 1874 he opened a laboratory with his friend N.G. Glukhov.

The following year while conducting an experiment in electrolysis, Yablochkov accidentally discovered how to apply practically the principles of arc lighting. Soon after in October 1875, convinced that Russia's technical level was too low to support electric lighting on a large scale, he moved to Paris. There he met French Academician Louis François-Clément Breguet (1808-1883), who employed him in his laboratory. Within a few months he received a patent for an electromagnet, and on 23 March 1876 he patented his most famous invention, the "Yablochkov candle."

This apparatus consisted of two parallel, vertical rods of carbon (coal or coke) connected to an electrical circuit. An electrical charge applied to one rod continued to its tip and then jumped the gap to the other rod, thus completing the circuit. When the rods were held at the correct distance from each other, the result was a brilliant light, which continued until the carbon was gradually consumed. This much had been known before Yablochkov's work. The problem was that the rods needed continual adjustment so that the gap remained constant. Yablochkov's contribution consisted in separating the rods with an insulating medium (gypsum or kaolin), which was consumed as fast as the carbon, thus averting the need for regulation.

While perfecting the "candle" he pioneered the practical use of alternating current and made significant discoveries in induction coils, transformers, and condensers. The candle in its perfected form was exhibited at the Paris exposition of 1878, where it was a major attraction. His process soon was applied commercially in France, Great Britain, the United States, and elsewhere for the illumination of streets and public places, such as stores, theaters, and train stations.

In 1879 Yablochkov returned to Russia to promote the spread of electrical lighting there. He devoted special efforts to pushing the construction of central electric generating plants. His efforts led to the creation of an electrotechnical section of the Russian Technical Society, the holding of an exhibition of electrical technology in St. Petersburg in 1880, and the founding of the journal Electricity (Electrichestvo). He helped prepare the Russian exhibits at the international exhibition of electrical technology in Paris in 1881, and while there he participated in the First International Electricians' Congress.

In 1879 Yablochkov established his own lighting firm and an electromechanical factory in St. Petersburg. During the 1880s he invented lighting systems for naval vessels and secured patents on several devices related to alternating current, induction, and other electromechanical properties. He spent much time and effort in developing batteries of various sorts.

Despite his scientific genius Yablochkov was an unsuccessful businessman. He never received much income from his inventions or enterprises. The development of a practical incandescent bulb by the American inventor Thomas Alva Edison in 1881 made the Yablochkov candle obsolete. In 1889 he fell ill and could work only sporadically. In 1893 he returned to Saratov, where he died in poverty on 31 March 1894.

Yablochkov and his achievements are largely forgotten outside his homeland. In 1947 a Yablochkov Prize, to be awarded every three years for exceptional achievement in electrical engineering, was instituted in the Soviet Union.

Bibliography: There is little in English on Yablochkov, other than descriptions of his "candle" in such older books as T.C. Mendenhall, *A Century of Electricity* (New York, 1887) and Benjamin Park, *The Age of Electricity. From Amber-Soul to Telephone* (New York, 1886). A brief entry on Yablochkov is in the English edition of *The Great Soviet Encyclopedia*, ed. by A.M. Prokhorov, 32 vols. (New York, 1973-1983), 30, 406. A brief, informative article on Yablochkov is L.D. Bel'kind, "Pavel Nikolaevich Iablochkov," in I.V. Kuznetsov, ed., *Liudi Russkoi nauki. Ocherki vydaiushchikhsia deiateliakh estestvoznaniia i tekhniki* (M., 1965), 355-363. Other works include K.D. Perskii, "Zhizn i trudy P.N. Iablochkova" in *Trudy Pervogo Vserossiiskogo elektrotekhnicheskogo s"ezda 1899-1900 gg.* (SPb., 1901); B.G. Kuznetsov, *Istoriia energeticheski tekhniki* (M.-L., 1937); N.A. Kaptsov, *Pavel Nikolaevich Iablochkov. K 50-letiiu so dnia smerti* (M.-L., 1944); L.D. Bel'kind, *P.N. Iablochkov* (M.-L., 1944); O.N. Florinskaia, *Pavel Nikolaevich Iablochkov (bibliograficheskii ukazatel')* (M.-L., 1949); L.D. Bel'kind, *Pavel Nikolaevich Iablochkov. Zhizn i trudy* (M., 1950); "Ocherki o zhizn i trudakh Iablochkova," in *Pavel Nikolaevich Iablochkov. Trudy, dokumenty, materialy* (M., 1954); M.A. Shatelen, *Russkie elektrotekhniki XIX v.* (M., 1955); L.D. Bel'kind, "Konfederatov I.Ia. i Shneiberg I.A.", *Istoriia tekhniki* (M., 1956); N.A. Kaptsov, *Pavel Nikolaevich Iablochkov, ego zhizn' i deiatel'nost'* (M., 1957); L.D. Bel'kind, *Pavel Nikolaevich Iablochkov* (M., 1962).

George N. Rhyne

YAK AIRCRAFT (1937-). A wide variety of aircraft produced by the Aleksandr Yakovlev design bureau, including combat aircraft, passenger planes, trainers, sport planes, and helicopters.

During his career, Aleksandr Sergeevich Yakovlev (1906-1989) supervised the design and development of seventy-five types of aircraft, almost 70,000 of which have been produced. His first aircraft bore the designation AIR, the initials of Aleksei Ivanovich Rykov, Vladimir Ilich Lenin's successor as chairman of the Council of People's Commissars. After Rykov fell from grace in 1937 during Soviet leader Joseph Vissarionovich Stalin's bloody purges, Yakovlev designated his planes YAK.

As war clouds gathered over Europe the USSR took close interest in the aviation advances in other countries, especially in Germany and Great Britain. Stalin took particular interest in a new fighter that the Yakovlev design bureau was working on in 1939. The fighter, designated YAK-1, was unveiled on 1 January 1940. Constructed mostly of wood and fabric on a steel-tube frame, it was armed with a 20mm cannon and two rapid-firing 7.62mm machine guns.

Its Klimov 1,050 horsepower VK105P engines attained a top speed of 363 miles (585 km) per hour. In the rush to produce the plane a number of short-comings were overlooked: its modest power/weight ratio, unreliability of gears and flaps, and severe engine vibration, to name a few. Nevertheless, in May and June of 1940 the YAK and two aircraft from other design bureaus, the MIG and LAGG, were chosen for mass production.

The Soviet aircraft industry was almost devastated by the German surprise attack on 22 June 1941. As German armies swept deep into the USSR the Soviet government decided to evacuate critical industries to the east, out of reach of German armies and bombers. Yakovlev's enterprise moved to western Siberia, a process requiring several months of precious time and resulting in sharp drops in aircraft production. Nonetheless, by mid-1942 the reconstruction of evacuated aircraft plants was virtually complete, and the output of planes and engines was 30 percent higher than on the eve of the war. The total 1942 production figure for the YAK-7 fighter was 2,431, as compared with 166 in 1941.

Yakovlev's YAK-1, -3, -7, and -9 were the principal fighters used during World War II, comprising two-thirds of the Soviet air force's 36,000 planes. The YAK-3, possibly the most agile monoplane of World War II, excelled in close combat at low and medium altitudes. Its qualities included ease and precision of control, excellent rate of roll, turning circle, and maneuver in the vertical plane. It had a maximum speed of 410 miles (660 km) per hour and a range of 441 miles (710 km). Once cleared for production, it was built with remarkable speed: 21 in July 1944, over 100 in August of the same year, and by May 1945 4,848 had been produced. During the war Yakovlev continually made improvements and modifications to his fighter aircraft. For example, by decreasing the weight of the YAK-3 he added significantly to the plane's maneuverability and speed, and in 1944 his YAK-3 achieved a speed of 463 miles (745 km) per hour, the highest ever for a Soviet piston aircraft.

When the war ended the USSR urgently set about studying captured and interned aircraft of friend and foe. As the only major power which had not produced a jet fighter by the end of World War II, a high-priority examination of German jet aircraft began. Over Yakovlev's objections, the Soviet leadership made the decision to put into production a copy of the German ME-262 jet plane and its Junkers Jumo-004 engine. Yakovlev believed that copying the Messerschmitts would absorb all attention and resources, to the serious detriment of work on a domestically-designed jet. Artem Ivanovich Mikoyan was working on his MIG-9 twin-jet fighter, while Yakovlev was constructing a single-jet fighter which began development tests in October 1945. The result of Yakovlev's work was the YAK-15. Capable of speeds to 435 miles (700 km) per hour, it flew for the first time in April 1946. On the same day the test pilot for Mikoyan and Mikhail Iosifovich Gurevich took up the first MIG-9 from the same airfield. Stalin reacted by ordering the production of both planes. Both the YAK-15 and MIG-9 used German engines, while British jet engines were installed in the MIG-15, LA-15, and YAK-23. In 1952 Yakovlev designed his first all-weather interceptor, the YAK-25, and it took its place in PVO Strany

(Air Defense of the Country). Several years later, in 1958, the first Soviet supersonic two-seat tactical bomber, the YAK-28, made its appearance. The modified YAK-28P was designed for the interceptor role.

Yakovlev turned to the development of vertical-takeoff-and-landing (VTOL) aircraft, producing the first such Soviet aircraft in 1967. In 1976 Yakovlev's VTOL plane, the YAK-36, began to appear on the new aircraft carriers Kiev and Minsk. Like the British Hawker Harrier, the YAK-36 used vectored thrust. The YAK-36, according to *Jane's All the World's Aircraft*, was capable of speeds up to 870 miles (1,400 km) per hour, could operate up to 7.5 miles (12 km) kilometers in altitude, and had a mission radius of about 149 miles (240 km).

Other models produced by Yakovlev's design bureau included the YAK-14 troop carrying glider; the YAK-100 helicopter, completed in 1950 but not mass produced since the Soviets had adopted the MI-1; the versatile YAK-24 helicopter, the first Soviet helicopter in which the rotors were placed in tandem, and which was capable of accommodating forty persons or four tons of freight; the YAK-11, YAK-18, and YAK-18T trainers; the multi-purpose YAK-12; and the sport planes, YAK-18P, YAK-18PM, and YAK-50, which set world and European records. Forty-five world records were made in airplanes built by Yakovlev. His passenger planes were the YAK-40 and YAK-42. The YAK-40, designed for relatively short-range flights, from 373 to 932 miles (600 to 1,500 km), had a cruising speed of 342-373 miles (550-600 km) per hour. It appeared in 1966. Aeroflot, the Soviet airline, adopted the YAK-42 which carried 120 passengers at a speed of 506 miles (820 km) per hour, for 1,150 miles (1,850 km).

See Also: YAKOVLEV, ALEKSANDR SERGEEVICH

Bibliography: Alexander Yakovlev, *The Aim of a Lifetime. The Story of Alexander Yakovlev, Designer of the YAK Fighter Plane* (M., 1972) and *Fifty Years of Soviet Aircraft Construction* (Jerusalem, 1970); "Iakovlev, Aleksandr Sergeevich," *Sovietskaia voennaia entsiklopediia*, Vol. 8 (M., 1980), 657; A.N. Ponomarev, *Sovietskie aviatsionnye konstruktory* (M., 1980), especially 138-148; Robin Higham and Jacob W. Kipp, eds., *Soviet Aviation and Air Power. A Historical View* (London, 1977). Another highly useful source is Bill Gunston, *Aircraft of the Soviet Union. An Encyclopedia of Soviet Aircraft Since 1917* (London, 1983), especially 355-404. Some of Gunston's figures are from *Jane's All the World's Aircraft* (London, annual).

Otto Preston Chaney

YAKIR, PETR IONOVICH (1923-1982). Prominent human rights activist. Helped to establish dissident movement in Moscow in the late 1960s. Publicly recanted his participation at a notorious trial in August 1973.

Yakir was born in 1923 in Kiev. His father Iona Emmanuilovich Yakir was commander of the Kiev Military District and a member of the Central Committee of the Communist party. He was arrested and executed in the spring of 1937 during a major purge of the Red Army officer corps.

Petr Yakir and his mother were exiled to Astrakhan. For the next seventeen years Yakir experienced the full range of Stalin's labor camp system, spending time in a series of prisons and camps. He frequently attempted to escape and once even eluded his pursuers for almost a month before he was captured. As a punishment for his defiant behavior Yakir was placed in solitary confinement. He later described his years of imprisonment in a vivid memoir *A Childhood in Prison* (Detstvo v tiurme), which reached the West in 1972.

After Stalin's death Yakir was released from the camps and allowed to study and live in Moscow. He became a historian and often lectured about the Stalin period to students and workers. In 1961 he even met Soviet leader Nikita Sergeevich Khrushchev who mentioned him and his father's case during an important denunciation of Stalin at the Twenty-second Party Congress later that same year.

Following Khrushchev's removal from power in October 1964 and the case of the two writers Andrei Platonovich Sinyavsky and Yuli Markovich Daniel, who were convicted of "anti-Soviet agitation and propaganda" in February 1966, intellectuals began to emerge who were willing to challenge the Kremlin's abuses of human rights. Petr Yakir was among them.

His first widely publicized appeal took place in 1968. Joined by his friends Ilya Yankelevich Gabai and Yuli Mikhailevich Kim, Yakir warned against the rebirth of Stalinism in a letter to Soviet cultural and scientific figures. "During recent years ominous symptoms of the restoration of Stalinism have appeared in our public life," they declared. "The most striking of them is the repetition of the most terrible deeds of that time—the organizing of cruel trials of persons who dared to uphold their dignity and to defend their inner freedom, who made so bold as to think and to protest.... The naive hopes for a complete purification of our public life with which the resolutions of the Twentieth and Twenty-second Party Congresses [in 1956 and 1961] inspired us, have not materialized. Slowly but surely the process of restoring Stalinism goes on. And here chief reliance is being placed upon our social inertia, our short memory and our bitter experience and acceptance of the absence of freedom." (Reddaway, 241-244).

Yakir was for a time a central figure among the dissidents. He met often with foreign journalists in order to share information about the regime's abuses. People came to him day and night, eager to pass along information and obtain copies of his uncensored, self-published (samizdat) protests and appeals.

Yakir was particularly active in collecting information for A Chronicle of Current Events, which began publication in 1968 and lasted until 1982. It was the principal, uncensored journal of the human rights movement. He worked with the Chronicle's editors from its inception in 1968. In May 1969 he helped to establish the Initiative Group to Defend Human Rights, the first human rights association formed in Moscow. Its initial appeals to the United Nations focussed on the persecution of Ukrainian activists, nationalists in the Baltic republics, Crimean Tatars, Jewish activists, and believers who were trying to defend freedom of religious expression.

Despite his popularity Yakir's behavior grew increasingly erratic. He talked too much on the telephone about sensitive matters and often pressured uninvolved people to sign intemperate petitions that easily could lead to trouble with the authorities. Yakir was a heavy drinker and he greatly feared violent reprisals against himself and his family. Several active dissidents even came to mistrust him and avoided sharing information with him.

Their caution proved to be justified. Yakir was arrested on 21 June 1972 at the height of a major attempt by the regime to disrupt political samizdat and specifically to destroy A Chronicle of Current Events. Isolated and threatened with execution as traitors, both Yakir and his co-defendant Victor Aleksandrovich Krasin broke down and gave evidence against their dissident colleagues. In subsequent months the regime interrogated over two hundred people. Yakir and Krasin tragically contributed to this official campaign of repression.

At their trial in August 1973 they admitted to "anti-Soviet activity" and repented their "crimes." A week later they appeared at a news conference with foreign journalists and repeated the claim that information in the Chronicle was "libelous." The dissident movement, under tremendous pressure, had to back down; the Chronicle suspended publication for two years.

Yakir and Krasin were sentenced originally to three years of labor camp and three years of internal exile, Yakir to Riazan and Krasin to Kalinin. An appeals court annulled the labor camp term and initially let stand the years in exile. But this portion of their term was set aside as well and Yakir soon returned to Moscow from Riazan.

Yakir never recovered from the humiliation of his trial. His old friends shunned him and he died, a lonely and tragic figure, in November 1982.

See Also: YAKIR, IONA EMMANUILOVICH.

Bibliography: Ludmilla Alexeyeva, *Soviet Dissent* (Middletown, Conn., 1987); Peter Reddaway, ed., *The Trial of the Four*, trans. by Janis Sopiets (New York, 1972); Joshua Rubenstein, *Soviet Dissidents. Their Struggle for Human Rights* (Boston, 1985); Petr Yakir, *A Childhood in Prison* (New York, 1973).

Joshua Rubenstein

YAKOVLEV, ALEKSANDR SERGEEVICH (1906-1989). Eminent Soviet aircraft designer, Academician of the Academy of Sciences of the USSR, Colonel General of Engineers (1946), twice Hero of Socialist Labor (1940, 1957), member of the Communist Party of the Soviet Union since 1938.

Yakovlev was born on 19 March (1 April) 1906 in Moscow, the son of a fairly prosperous family. His father was in charge of the shipping department of the Nobel Petroleum Company. Completing secondary school at the age of seventeen, he decided to become an aircraft designer. His first job was as an ordinary worker in the carpentry shop of the Aeronautical Academy. He then became a mechanic's helper in the academy's flight training unit before becoming an engine mechanic.

As a young man Yakovlev became a pioneer in aircraft modeling, gliding, and aviation sports. In 1924 he built the AVF-10 glider which took part in the second All-Union glider competition. He entered the N.E. Zhukovsky Air Force Engineering School in 1927 and while there continued to work on aircraft design. In 1927 he built a light two-seated sport biplane, the AIR-1, powered by a Cirrus engine. The acronym AIR, which stood for Aleksei Ivanovich Rykov, Vladimir Ilich Lenin's successor as chairman of the Council of People's Commissars, lasted until Rykov's denunciation in 1937 during the great purges; then Yakovlev changed his aircraft designation to YAK, for Yakovlev. His test pilot, Julian Piontkovsky—whose close association with Yakovlev ended suddenly on 27 April 1940 when the pilot was killed in an experimental YAK-1—successfully flew the AIR-1 from Moscow to Sevastopol and back. Yakovlev's future was assured. As a student in the Zhukovsky School, Yakovlev developed the AIR-2, -3, -4, and -5.

After graduation in 1931 he went to the Menzhinsky works as an engineer, where he worked with the well-known aircraft designers Dmitry Pavlovich Grigorovich and Nikolai Nikolaevich Polikarpov. In 1932 he became engineering supervisor for light aircraft and in 1935, chief designer. In these years he turned out the AIR-5 "Flying Ford," a monoplane with a five-seat automobile-type cabin, powered by a 220 horsepower Wright engine of American make; the AIR-6, a modified AIR-5 seating three and using a domestically manufactured engine; and the exceptionally maneuverable AIR-7 monoplane, capable of speeds up to 199 miles (320 km) per hour. During a test flight the AIR-7 lost an aileron and crashed without injuring Piontkovsky and a passenger. Nevertheless a commission appointed to investigate the accident recommended that Yakovlev be barred from aircraft construction. His plant's party organization and the Party Central Committee interceded on his behalf, and he was permitted to continue his design work, but at another plant. At this time his team consisted of five or six designers and fifteen to twenty workers housed in a bed factory. Other planes built in this make-shift plant included the AIR-9 and AIR-10, prototypes of the UT-2 trainer.

In July 1935 Yakovlev entered several of his aircraft in a demonstration at the Tushino airfield attended by party and government leaders, including Joseph Vissarionovich Stalin and defense commissar Kliment Efremovich Voroshilov. Stalin took a personal interest in Yakovlev's UT-2 trainer because of its speed (124 miles (200 km) per hour) and more modern monoplane design. It was selected for initial pilot training in the air force. Eventually 7,150 UT-2s were produced by several Soviet factories. Also in 1935 Yakovlev's team built the AIR-14, later redesignated the UT-1, designed as a sport and training plane. In 1939 Yakovlev designed a tactical short-range bomber, the BB (capable of speeds up to 352 miles (567 km) per hour), which was far more advanced than other aircraft of the same type, and entered mass production. In April 1939 he was summoned to the Kremlin, where Stalin awarded him the Order of Lenin.

Stalin took a close, personal interest in a new fighter which Yakovlev's team was designing and pressured him to complete the project by December 1939. Stalin wrote a personal note to the well-known engine designer, Vladimir Yakovlevich Klimov, urging him to expedite delivery of his M-105 engines to Yakovlev's bureau. Stalin also discussed with Yakovlev how the British were arming their Spitfires, and the Germans their Messerschmitt-109s. High priority was attached to arming the new fighter with a cannon as well as machine guns. The fighter, designated the YAK-1, was rolled out on 1 January 1940. Constructed mostly of wood and fabric on a steel-tube frame, it was armed with a 20mm cannon and two rapid-firing 7.62mm machine guns. Its Klimov 1,050 horsepower VK105P engine attained a top speed of 362 miles (585 km) per hour. In the rush to get the YAK-1 into production, certain shortcomings were overlooked: its modest power/weight ratio, unreliability of gears and flaps, and severe engine vibrations, to name a few. Nevertheless in May and June 1940 the YAK and two aircraft from other design bureaus, the MIG and LAGG, were selected for mass production.

On 9 January 1940 Yakovlev again was summoned by Stalin who informed him that he had relieved Mikhail Moiseevich Kaganovich as People's Commissar of the Aircraft Industry and had appointed Aleksei Ivanovich Shakhurin in his place. Stalin also told him that, in addition to running his design bureau, Yakovlev would serve as deputy people's commissar in charge of scientific research and experimental aircraft construction, a post he occupied until 1946.

Just before the outbreak of war in Europe in 1939 the USSR and Germany ratified the Molotov-Ribbentrop Non-Aggression Pact. During the period of cooperation between these two countries Yakovlev formed part of a delegation of Soviet aviation specialists who visited Germany to study its aircraft industry and to select planes which the USSR would be interested in buying. Hitler broke the pact by suddenly attacking the Soviet Union on 22 June 1941. By noon the Germans had destroyed 1,200 Soviet planes, giving them total air superiority over the battlefield. Yakovlev and other aircraft builders were confronted with the Herculean task of resupplying the air force with new planes of all types. Complicating their work was the governmental decision of 5 July 1941 to stop production and evacuate much of the factories' equipment to western Siberia, out of the reach of the Germans. The design bureau and the factory constructing the YAK fighters were moved in September 1941 to a new plant beyond the Urals. In October 1941 the State Defense Committee ordered Yakovlev to take over an engineering plant in Siberia and organize the production of fighter aircraft. During October, November, and December 1941 the output of planes and engines fell drastically, as plants relocated and organized new assembly lines. By mid-1942 the reconstruction of evacuated aircraft plants was virtually complete, and output 30 percent higher than on the eve of the war in June 1941. The total 1942 production figure for the YAK-7 fighter was 2,431, as compared with 166 in 1941.

Yakovlev's YAK-1, -3, -7, and -9 were the principal Soviet fighters used during World War II, comprising two-thirds of the Soviet air force's 36,000 planes. By mid-1943 the Soviet air force was twice the size of the German, and total output in 1943 was 37 percent greater than in 1942. During the war Yakovlev continually made improvements and modifications to his fighter aircraft; for example, by decreasing the weight of the YAK-3 he added significantly to the plane's maneuverability and speed, and in 1944 his YAK-3 achieved a speed of 463 miles (745 km) per hour, the highest ever for a Soviet piston aircraft.

After the war Yakovlev turned to the development of jet aircraft. In May 1947 his YAK-15 passed official government tests. It was the first Soviet jet aircraft to do so and was the first jet fighter adopted by the air force. In 1952 he developed the first Soviet all-weather interceptor, the YAK-25. Several years later, in 1958, the YAK-28, the first Soviet supersonic tactical bomber, made its appearance. He turned to the development of vertical-takeoff-and-landing (VTOL) aircraft, producing the first such Soviet aircraft in 1967. Other models produced by his bureau included the YAK-14 troop-carrying glider; the YAK-24 helicopter, accommodating forty persons or four tons of freight; the YAK-11, YAK-18, and YAK-18T trainers; the multi-purpose YAK-12; and the sport planes, YAK-18P, YAK-18PM, and the YAK-50, in which world and European records were set. Airplanes built by Yakovlev set forty-five world records. His passenger planes were the YAK-40 and YAK-42. Altogether he supervised the design and development of seventy-five types of aircraft, of which almost 70,000 were produced.

Yakovlev was a deputy to the second through the ninth convocations of the Supreme Soviet of the USSR. He was awarded the Lenin Prize in 1972 and the State Prize of the USSR in 1941, 1942, 1943, 1946, 1947, 1948, and 1977. He was presented with eight Orders of Lenin, the Order of the October Revolution, Orders of Suvorov First and Second Class, the Order of the Patriotic War First Class, the French Legion of Honor (Grand Cross), and the Grand Gold Medal of the Federation Aeronautique Internationale.

Yakovlev authored several books. His highly-readable *Aim of a Lifetime* has been translated into several languages, including English.

Yakovlev died in Moscow on 22 August 1989. His son, Sergei Aleksandrovich, carried on his work.

See Also: YAK AIRCRAFT.

Bibliography: An invaluable source is Bill Gunston, *Aircraft of the Soviet Union. The Encyclopedia of Soviet Aircraft Since 1917* (London, 1983), especially 355-404. Robin Higham and Jacob W. Kipp, eds., *Soviet Aviation and Air Power. A Historical View* (London, 1977); A.N. Ponomarev, *Sovetskie aviatsionnye konstruktory* (M., 1990), especially 138-148; *Istoriia Velikoi Otechestvennoi Voiny Sovetskogo Soyuza, 1941-1945*, 6 vols. (M., 1960-1965); *50 let vooruzhennykh sil SSSR* (M., 1968); Alexander Yakovlev, *The Aim of a Lifetime. The Story of Alexander Yakovlev, Designer of the YAK Fighter Plane* (M., 1972); and *Fifty Years of Soviet Aircraft Construction* (Jerusalem, 1970); "Aviatsiia" *Bolshaia Sovetskaia entsiklopediia*, 2nd ed., Vol. 1 (M., 1949) and 3rd ed., Vol. 1 (M., 1970); "Iakovlev, Aleksandr Sergeevich, *Sovetskaia voennaia entsiklopediia* Vol. 8, (M., 1980), 657.

Otto Preston Chaney

YAKUNCHIKOVA, MARIA VASILIEVNA (1870-1902). One of the first women in Russia to work professionally in the world of art.

Yakunchikova belonged to the symbolist generation of artists at the turn of the century. Like them she was interested in the spiritual nature of art and in its ability to express delicate and ineffable emotions through color and form. She created a distinctive version of Russian symbolism, combining West European trends with national folk-art. The originality and lyricism of the art of country people influenced her work, and she actively participated in the revival and preservation of folk arts and crafts.

Born in Wiesbaden on 19 January 1870, Maria Yakunchikova grew up in Moscow amidst the artistic intelligentsia. Her family, which was closely related to the distinguished Tretiakov and Mamontov families, belonged to a cultured Russian mercantile circle which patronized artists and collected art. Yakunchikova displayed an artistic flair by the age of twelve. Beginning in 1883 she studied art at home, and in 1885 she enrolled as an external student at the Moscow School of Painting, Sculpture, and Architecture. Between 1887 and 1889 Yakunchikova met the artists Konstantin Alekseevich Korovin, Mikhail Vasilievich Nesterov, Valentin Aleksandrovich Serov, and Isaak Ilich Levitan at the popular Thursday painting evenings at the home of the artist Vasily Dmitrievich Polenov. She found Levitan especially congenial. The feeling of doom and poetic sadness and the sense of the transience of life in Yakunchikova's landscapes owe much to Levitan's influence. Her view of life was always joyless but distinctive and very personal. Her painting The Flame (1897) may be seen as a symbol of her own life—a flickering candle, vivid but short-lived.

The tuberculosis which she contracted early forced Yakunchikova to make frequent trips abroad. For the most part she returned to Russia only in the summer. Her first trip to Europe was to Austria and Italy in 1888, and in March 1899 she traveled to France and Germany. Her letters home are full of wonder, and her work revealed a delicate appreciation of the places she visited. Although in Paris she became a student at the Académie Julian and worked in the studios of the academic painters Bougereau and Fleury, the sinuous lines, symbolic swans, and the decorative but mysterious atmosphere of her works reflect her profound ties to modernism.

Yakunchikova's paintings embodied both the poetic sadness of the Russian symbolist Viktor Elpidiforovich Borisov-Musatov and the expressionism of the Norwegian Edvard Munch. She vehemently opposed the excesses of the French symbolist group the Rose + Cross (La Rose + Croix) and the works of Odilon Redon for their heightened interest in scenes of blood and depravity. She was captivated by the melancholic visions of Eugene Carrier, but her own art was based more on reality than on imagination. Her paintings are simple but full of passion and emotions. The empty avenues and parks draw the spectator into the depths of their shadowed paths to the steps of neglected churches and deserted pavilions and mansions.

Yakunchikova was equally versatile and innovative in graphic and book illustrations, and in applied and decorative art. In the early 1890s she started to work in graphics, especially in colored etching, a technique long neglected in Russia. Many of these works such as Death and Flowers, Fear, The Unattainable, and Irretrievable made mostly between 1893 and 1895, are permeated with presentiments of death. Yakunchikova's combination of clear-cut contours and diverse spots of flat color introduced rhythms suggesting music, which the symbolists, who considered it the absolute art, especially valued. These rhythms, combined with Yakunchikova's profound spirituality, appealed to the symbolist Blue Rose (Golubaia roza) group, led by Pavel Varfolomeevich Kuznetsov.

Yakunchikova's colored engravings were received warmly both in Russia and abroad and were prized by artists of the World of Art (Mir iskusstva) group. Yakunchikova received commissions to create covers for The World of Art magazine in 1899. Her image of a swan on a lake in delicate blue and yellow with the title in ancient orthography was one of the most evocative and elegant covers ever designed for this magazine. Her graphic art was exhibited at the Salon Champs de Mars in Paris. In 1895 the English magazine The Studio published an article on Yakunchikova and in 1897 featured her ex-libris bookplates.

Although Yakunchikova spent many years abroad, her art remained essentially Russian in spirit. With her friend Elena Dmitrievna Polenova she took part in the development of the neo-national movement and enthusiastically supported the concept of the relationship between fine and decorative arts. In 1894 in Paris she helped organize an exhibition of applied art by Russian women artists. Her own interests in applied art were virtually limitless, including embroidery, textile, furniture designs, toys, and ceramics.

In the mid-1890s she began to work in an original style of pokerwork, which was derived from folk art. In this technique line drawings are burned on wood with metal implements. Yakunchikova then covered the remaining flat surfaces with oil colors. A series of these panels was shown in the 1896 Paris Exhibition of the Experiments of Artistic Creation organized by Ilia Efimovich Repin.

After the death of Elena Polenova in 1898 Yakunchikova, who collaborated with her in many projects, took charge of the Abramtsevo embroidery workshop. Following Polenova's plan, she organized an exhibition of Russian handicrafts at the Exposition Universelle in Paris in 1900. Yakunchikova's own embroidered panel, Little Girl and Wood Spirit, executed for this exhibition, won a silver medal.

Yakunchikova spent her last years at Chène Bougerie, Switzerland, with her husband Lev Nikolaevich Weber, whom she married in 1896, and her children. She died there at the age of thirty-two. The World of Art group dedicated a special issue of their magazine to her. A posthumous exhibition of her work, supported by artists of many different fields, took place in Moscow in 1905. Although she died young, Yakunchikova played a significant role in the development of twentieth-century art.

Bibliography: N. Barok (N.V. Polenova), "M.V. Iakunchikova," *Mir iskusstva*, No. 3 (1904); S.D. Diaghilev, "M.V. Iakunchikova," *Mir iskusstva*, No. 12 (1902); Oktav Uzanne, "Modern Colour Engraving with Notes on Some Work by Marie Yakounchikoff," *The Studio*, 6, No. 6 (1895); E. Sakharova, Vasily D. Polenov, Elena Dmitrievna Polenova, *Khronika sem'i khudozhnikov* (M., 1964); M. Kiselev, *Maria Vasilievna Iakunchikova* (M., 1979); M.N. Yablonskaia, *Women Artists of Russia's New Age. 1900-1935* (New York, 1990).

Musya M. Glants

YAKUT AUTONOMOUS SOVIET SOCIALIST REPUBLIC (1922-1990). Autonomous republic within the Russian Federation.

The Yakut ASSR covers approximately 1.198 million square miles (3.103 million square km) in eastern Siberia. It is almost six times as large as France. The Arctic Sea forms the northern border of the Yakut ASSR. It extends from Krasnoiarsk territory (krai) in the west to the Khabarovsk territory and Magadan region (oblast) in the east. In the south it borders on the Irkutsk, Chita, and Amur regions. Its major rivers are the Kolyma, the Indigirka, the Olenek, the Vitim, and the Lena with its tributaries, the Aldan, Olekma, and Viliuy.

Archeological evidence locates human settlement in the Yakut region from the upper paleolithic era 20,000-10,000 B.C. These people dwelt along the major river systems, as did the successive neolithic, bronze, and iron age cultures. The earliest people seem to have been hunters who followed herds of reindeer and elk and who fished in the rivers. At the turn of the modern era the Tungus people began to enter the area. From the tenth through the sixteenth centuries cattle-herding Turkish peoples, ancestors of the Yakuts, came into the region from the south.

By the seventeenth century the Yakut people settled in the area between the Lena and the Amga rivers and around the headwaters of the Yana and the lower reaches of the Viliuy rivers and constituted the most numerous of the indigenous peoples there. These seminomads raised cattle and horses. Fishing, hunting, and gathering were important sources of sustenance too. Politically they were divided into a number of warring tribes. The religion of the Yakuts was shamanistic.

In 1630 with the arrival of the Russians the region became a part of the Russian state and the people subject to the yasak tribute. This was a tax imposed by the Russian authorities on the indigenous population of Siberia. Originally it was paid in furs, but later it could be commuted into a money payment.

In 1632 a detachment of Yenisei Cossacks under the leadership of Petr Beketov constructed on the Lena River a fort which was to become the city of Yakutsk, the major military and administrative center of the region. It also served as the base for much of the Russian expansion of eastern Siberia, including the expedition of Vitus Bering. Originally Russians—cossacks, merchants, artisans, and exiles—constituted the major part of the population of the city. Later Yakuts began to settle there, forming over one third of the population by the beginning of the nineteenth century.

During the eighteenth century Russian settlement of this vast and inhospitable land was sparse and had only marginal impact on the culture of the native inhabitants. Gold was discovered to the southwest of Yakutsk in the 1840s, and in the next decades lead and other mineral deposits began to be worked. These new sources of wealth attracted new settlers and stimulated the economy of the region. To support the increased population a number of small-scale manufacturing establishments sprang up, and agricultural activities increased. These developments affected not only the Russian population but the natives as well. The latter increasingly were drawn into urban occupations and agriculture. In addition to these economic forces, accelerating conversion to Christianity, the development of an alphabet for the Yakut language, and schools for the natives began to erode native culture during the latter half of the nineteenth century.

The Yakut region long served as a place of punishment and internal exile. Disobedient serfs and religious dissenters were sent there as were participants in subversive activities. Decembrists (Aleksandr Aleksandrovich Bestuzhev-Marlinsky and Matvei Ivanovich Muraviev-Apostol), Polish rebels, populists (Nikolai Gavrilovich Chernyshevsky, Vladimir Galaktionovich Korolenko, and Mark Andreevich Natanson), and a number of Marxists and Bolsheviks (Yury Mikhailovich Steklov, Viktor Pavlovich Nogin, Grigory Konstantinovich

Ordzhonikidze, Nikolai Alekseevich Skrypnik, and Emelian Mikhailovich Yaroslavsky). By 1910 more than three thousand exiles resided in the area. Over the years many of these contributed to raising the economic and cultural level of the area. During the regime of Joseph Vissarionovich Stalin and particularly during the 1930s some of the worst of the political prison camps came to be located in Yakut ASSR.

The Yakut area, despite its distance from European Russia, reverberated from the political developments there. Disturbances took place in a number of towns during the revolution of 1905-1906. The massacre of over two hundred striking workers in the Lena goldfields in April 1912 signaled a rise in labor unrest in the empire. In May 1917 a soviet of workers' and soldiers' deputies arose in Yakutsk. Most of the Bolshevik exiles left for European Russia during 1917. Not until 1 June 1918 did the Bolsheviks establish their control over Yakutsk. This victory was short-lived, as the White forces of Admiral Aleksandr Vasilievich Kolchak took over two months later. Bolshevik control was reestablished on a permanent basis only in January 1919, but sporadic opposition from sizable anti-Bolshevik forces continued as late as the summer of 1923.

During the 1930s the Yakut ASSR was subjected to collectivization. At the same time, the Five Year Plans expanded the area's industry as well as the forest, fishing, construction, and particularly the extractive industries, where coal and gold were the most important products.

In the post-WWII years vast new resources were discovered, and many were developed. The republic possessed significant deposits of brown coal at Sangarskoe and Kangalasskoe. There are several deposits of bituminous coals in the South Yakut basin, an area stretching about 466 miles (750 km) east to west. Geological reserves are estimated at 40 billion tons. These include the Neryungri, Chulmanskoe, and Denisovskoe deposits. There are also iron deposits in the South Yakut basin. In 1984 the government verified reserves at the Taezhnoe deposit of over 1.2 billion tons.

Gold continued to be a major product. As of the early 1990s mines operated in the Aldan district, in the Dzhugdzhur district, and in the Kular Range.

The republic produced about 80 percent of the Soviet Union's diamond supply. The Mirny deposit was discovered in 1954-1955 and the concentrator opened in 1957. Production began at Aikhal in 1964 and at Udachny on the Daldyn River in 1968.

There are also significant deposits of other minerals, including tin, phosphate, apatite, phlogopite, lead, zinc, antimony, and copper. Some of these, such as the copper deposits, had not been exploited by the early 1990's because of the difficult climatic and geographical conditions and the expense involved in their development.

As of 1 January 1991 explored or proven reserves of crude oil and gas condensate were estimated at 142 million metric tons and natural gas at 894 billion cubic meters. Oil and gas have been found in four of the republic's nine tectonic regions. Fifteen of twenty-three fields discovered to date are along the Nepa Botuoba anticline.

Rivers account for about 80 percent of the freight delivered. The Lena River (2,750 mi.; 4,400 km) is navigable for about 150 days a year in its middle reaches and about 120 days in the lower reaches. Both the Viliuy (1,656 mi.; 2,650 km) and the Aldan (1,421 mi.; 2,273 km) also average about 150 days navigation a year. The northern rivers are useful a much shorter time: Yana 113-127 days, Indigirka (1,079 mi.; 1,726 km) 117-135 days, the Kolyma (1,330 mi.; 2,129 km) 120-130 days in the middle reaches and 100-115 in the lower.

The Yakut ASSR has a sharply continental climate. It gets about 50 percent of its precipitation between June and August. Winters are very cold and dry.

The longest frost-free periods (about 100 days) are in the valleys of the Lena, Aldan, Amga, and lower reaches of the Vitim rivers. There the last frost is usually at the end of May and the first frost is at the beginning of September. In valleys higher than 2,000-2,500 feet (650-750 m) there are no frost-free days. For these reasons, agriculture is marginal. Despite substantial expenditures, the republic cannot feed itself. In 1991 the central government shipped in about 95 percent of its food.

The 1989 census recorded 1,094,065 inhabitants, of whom 731,963 (67 percent) were urban and 362,102 (33 percent) rural. Yakuts made up 33.4 percent of the population and Russians 50.3 percent. Women outnumbered men. For every 1,000 women there are only 987 men. Yakutsk, the principle city of the republic, reported a population of 187,000; Neryungri had about 68,000 (1987).

In 1990 about 544,000 people worked in the Yakut economy. That is about half of the total population. The average monthly wage in 1990 was 489 rubles, but workers in the arts, culture, public health, and education received only 293 to 320 rubles a month. Housing always has been in short supply and waits of years are common. This is partly because construction costs generally run three to four times that of the central provinces in European Russia. The difficulty of living in the North may be seen in the migration patterns. In 1989 28,868 Russians arrived and 28,126 left, for a net gain of only 742.

The Yakut department of the All-Union Scientific Research Institute of the Hunting Industry opened in 1946, followed by the Tuberculosis Institute of the Academy of Medical Sciences in 1949. The Yakut Scientific Center, part of the Academy of Sciences, was formed in June 1947, although it did not become an actual branch until 1949. In 1956 Yakutsk State University was inaugurated.

Administratively, the area of the Yakut ASSR was included in Siberia province (guberniia) when it was formed in 1708 and was annexed to Irkutsk province 1764. In 1805 Yakut region (oblast') was created within Irkutsk province, and Yakut province came into existence in its own right in 1851. When it became the Yakut ASSR in 27 April 1922, Nizhne-Tungussky district was left with Siberia province. Today that area is part of Irkutsk province. In 1990 the republic had thirty-three districts.

In September 1990 the Yakut ASSR Supreme Soviet proclaimed the republic's sovereignty within the RSFSR. In keeping with the desires of the Yakuts, who call themselves "Sakha," it renamed the republic the Yakut-Sakha Republic. In December 1991 the republic elected a president and changed its name again to the Republic of Sakha.

See Also: YAKUTS, YAKUTSK, YAKUTSK PLACE OF BANISHMENT, "YAKUTSK PROTEST OF 1904," "YAKUTSK TRAGEDY OF 1889," and YASAK and their bibliographies.

Bibliography: Basic sources are Innokenti Petrovich Gerasimov, *Iakutiia* (M., 1965), Aleksei Pavlovich Okladnikov, ed., *Istoriia Iakutskoi SSSR*, 3 vols. (M., 1955-1963), and Gurii Vasilievich Naumov, *Zapadnaia Iakutiia. Ekonomiko-geograficheskaia kharikteristika* (M., 1962). Several articles in *Sovietskaia istoricheskaia entsiklopediia*, Vol. 16, (M., 1976) are good sources for matters touched on here: I.G. Spiridonov, "Iakutsk," 868-869; F.G. Safronov, "Iakutskaia Avtonomnaia Sovetskaia Sotsialisticheskaia Respublika," 869-875; I.S. Gurvich,"Iakuty," 878; I.F. Gindin, "Iasak," 992; and Sh. F. Mukhamediarov, "Iasachnie liudi," 992.

Robert B. Valliant

YAKUTSK (1632-). A city of about 170,000 population located on the Lena River in northeastern Siberia. It is the capital of the former Yakut Autonomous Soviet Socialist Republic, and since December 1991 of the Republic of Sakha.

Yakutsk was founded in 1632 by Yenisei Cossacks commanded by one Petr Beketov. At first it was only a log fort (ostrog) on the east bank of the Lena, but it became a town in 1680 after being moved about 1642 to the west bank. Yakutsk was intended to serve as a base for further explorations and conquests in eastern Siberia and served this purpose well, explorers moving outward from Yakutsk east to the Sea of Okhotsk and northeastward to the Bering Strait and Kamchatka.

Perhaps the most notable explorations were to the south. Grain could not be raised so far north, so in 1643, after hearing of a grain-producing region called Daurien to the south, the Yakutsk governor (voevoda), Petr Golovin, sent an expedition of more than 130 men in that direction under Vasily Poiarkov to find it. Poiarkov reached the Amur Valley but aroused the hostility of the native peoples there and returned to Yakutsk via the Sea of Okhotsk, after losing two-thirds of his men. In 1648 Yakutsk Cossacks established an ostrog at the mouth of the Okhota River, which became Okhotsk, and in 1649 the famous explorer Khabarov also set out from Yakutsk and reached the Amur. On his return in 1650 he proposed conquering the Amur Valley with 6,000 men.

That same year he went back to the Amur with a far smaller force of about 140 men and set up a fortified base. This led to an armed clash with China in which the Russians prevailed. Russians rushed into the Amur area in a movement that brought strong Chinese reaction, Russian defeat, and the Treaty of Nerchinsk in 1689. This treaty made the Amur Valley Chinese for nearly 200 years.

Yakutsk, although located amid Siberian tribes, was itself always predominantly Russian, its population consisting mostly of cossacks, traders, and huntsmen. Within ten years of its founding it became the military and administrative center of a wide area in northeast Siberia. In 1708 it was made a part of the Province of Siberia, and in the late eighteenth century it became part of Irkutsk Province.

In the nineteenth century political exiles were sent to Yakutsk, including some Decembrists and the revolutionary writer Nikolai Gavrilovich Chernyshevsky. By the end of the century about three thousand exiles were living there. In 1889 these political exiles staged a demonstration to protest bad conditions. Six were killed and seven others wounded, after which a military tribunal ordered three more exiles hanged. Others were sentenced to hard labor, some for life.

Another disturbance occurred in 1904 after Irkutsk Governor General Kutaisov ordered a more strict regime for the exiles. On 18 February of that year about fifty-six exiles gathered under arms at the house of one Yakut Romanov to protest the order and to compose an open letter to Kutaisov. Two soldiers and one exile were killed in the shootout that followed. On 7 March the surviving "Romanovtsy," as they became known, surrendered and were sentenced to twelve years at hard labor each. As a result of the October Manifesto of 1905 all were freed.

In July 1918 Bolshevik rule was established at Yakutsk, but White forces ejected them and took over the city the next month. After the misrule of Admiral Aleksandr Vasilevich Kolchak, the Communists retook Yakutsk in December 1919. On 27 April 1922 it became the capital of the Yakut ASSR, the largest political unit in the Soviet Union except for the giant RSFSR, of which it is a part.

In the later twentieth century Yakutsk is well known for its arctic agriculture. This agriculture is concerned mainly with beef and dairy products, but specialists there also have developed strains of small grains which ripen within a remarkable sixty days from planting. The yield from this strain is small. But in the Siberian northeast the growing season is extremely short, and such a fast-ripening strain is necessary. Potatoes and some other foods are raised, but much food must be imported in the best of times.

Light industry has developed rapidly at Yakutsk since World War II. In 1980 the industrial output was forty times that of 1940. Extractive industries account for most of this, with the products being gold, diamonds, natural gas, tin, mica, and coal. Lumber and forest products are also important.

Yakutsk is to be linked by rail to the new Baikal-Amur Mainline (BAM) to the south. For the construction workers of this "YAM" (Yakutsk-Amur Mainline) food must be brought in from places with a more temperate climate.

In 1956 Yakutsk State University was founded. In 1976 it had a library with more than 400,000 volumes, departments of mathematics, physics, biology and geography, agriculture, medicine, foreign languages, history and philology, and engineering. There is also a graduate school. In 1981 there were about 6,500 students and a faculty of 462.

Yakutsk has schools for the technical training of river workers, specialists in electrical communications, non-professional medical personnel, musicians, teachers, and artists. The Yakutsk branch of the Siberian Division of the Soviet Academy of Sciences is located there, as is the Siberian Division's Institute for Permafrost Studies. There are several theaters and museums.

See Also: YAKUT AUTONOMOUS SOVIET SOCIALIST REPUBLIC, YAKUTSK PLACE OF BANISHMENT, "YAKUTSK PROTEST OF 1904," "YAKUTSK TRAGEDY OF 1889," and YASAK.

Bibliography: *Istoriia Yakutskoi ASSR* 3 vols. (M.-L., 1955-1963); Z.V. Gogolev, *Sotsial' no-ekonomicheskoe razvitie Yakutii* (Novosibirsk, 1972); F.G. Safronov, *Russkie krest' iane v Yakutii* (Yakutsk, 1961); *Materialy po istorii Yakutii XVII v.* (M., 1970); S.A. Tokarev, *Ocherki istorii yakutskogo naroda* (M., 1940).

Patrick R. Taylor

YALTA. Renowned recreational and health resort near the southern tip of the Crimean Peninsula on the Black Sea. Yalta lies in a broad plain between the Vodopadnaia and Bystraia rivers. These descend the southern slopes of the Iaila Range of the Crimean Mountains, which protect Yalta from colder weather to the north. Nearly isolated, Yalta is forty-nine miles (79 km) from the Simferopol railroad terminal and is connected by road and trolleybus. Ships connect the city with Odessa, Rostov-on-Don, and Batumi. Administratively, Yalta belongs to the Crimean province of the Republic of Ukraine. Its population in 1980 was 83,000.

The exact date of the founding of Yalta is obscure. By the seventh century B.C. Greeks had established trade relations with the Cimmerians, who inhabited the Crimean Peninsula, at a site known as Chersonesus Taurica. During the next century Greek settlers established a number of colonies on the peninsula. They built the coastal towns of Chersonesus (Kherson) and Theodosia (Feodosia) near the primitive settlement of Yalta. It is probable that a substantial town existed on the site of Yalta during the Roman Empire. Yalta first was mentioned in historical writing at the beginning of the twelfth century by the Arab geographer, Ibn-Endrizi. He referred to the town as Dzhalyta (Galyta) and described it as a Byzantine port and fishing village inhabited by the Cumani, called Polovtsy (pl., Polovetsians) by the early Russian chroniclers. Various medieval Italian cartographers called the town Etalte, Callyta, and Yalyta on their maps.

In the fourteenth century Yalta was a Genoese colony known as Etalita. At that time the town had a consul and apparently was prosperous. In 1475 the Turks occupied the northern Black Sea coast and Yalta fell under their control. Near the end of the century a tremendous earthquake completely destroyed the town. The inhabitants sought refuge in neighboring towns, and for nearly a century it remained deserted. Greeks and Armenians eventually rebuilt the town and gave it the present name Ialta or Yalta. It remained under Turkish rule until 1783 when under Catherine the Great the Russian Empire annexed the Crimean Peninsula.

Yalta grew in size and prosperity after 1783. In 1837 Tsar Nicholas I, impressed by its many villas and coastal beauty, proclaimed it a town. A year later Yalta was chosen as the administrative center of a district in Tavrida Province. In 1854 during the Crimean War French Admiral Changarnier landed his forces at Yalta, and his crews robbed the towns' inhabitants. By the end of the nineteenth century Yalta had become a favorite resort of the Russian people. In 1910-1911 the Livadia Palace was erected in early Renaissance style about 1.9 miles (3 km) from Yalta as the summer residence of Tsar Nicholas II.

During the Bolshevik revolution Yalta was spared from political turmoil. But in January 1918 an armed uprising by Red Guard workers and sailors in Sevastapol led to the establishment of Soviet power in Yalta. Soviet control in the Crimean region was completed by November 1920, and in the process Yalta became a part of the Crimean Autonomous Socialist Soviet Republic. During World War II the German army captured Yalta on 8 November 1941. The city suffered under the German occupation but regained its role as a tourist center after its liberation by the Red Army on 6 April 1944. It became part of the Crimean province in the Russian Soviet Federated Socialist Republic in 1945. The Crimean province was transferred to Ukraine in 1954.

Yalta was the location of the last great WWII conference between the allied leaders in February 1945. President Franklin D. Roosevelt, Prime Minister Winston S. Churchill and Premier Joseph V. Stalin planned the final defeat and subsequent occupation of Germany at this meeting. Stalin achieved considerable gains for the Soviet Union in exchange for his promise to enter the war against Japan.

Yalta has grown dramatically as a resort and recreational city since 1945. The city's estimated population in 1897 was 13,269. Since then the number of tourists and patients in Yalta has made it difficult to assess the permanent population. The more recent official figures are 1956, 34,000; 1971, 60,000; and 1980, 83,000. The population is ethnically mixed but the majority is Russian. Yalta's climate is Mediterranean. It has the mildest winters of all the resorts of the former Russian Empire and Soviet Union. Frost is rare and any snow that may fall at Yalta quickly melts. The summer heat is not uncomfortable because of its sea breezes. The average January temperature is 39°F (3.9°C) and the average July temperature is 75°F (23.8°C).

Yalta is called the "Pearl of the Crimea." The pleasant climate attracts over one million people a year to the beaches and recreational facilities. Hotels line the Lenin Embankment, and ornamental gardens and parks are scattered throughout the city. The city is also a popular health spa. When Soviet authority was established in 1920 the private hotels, guest houses, and palaces belonging to the Russian nobility were converted into public facilities and medical centers. The greater Yalta area has nearly 135 institutions and vacation homes that can accommodate nearly 40,000 visitors at a time. There are nearly seventy sanatoriums and twenty rest homes. The most famous center is the I.M. Sechenov Research Institute, which was founded in 1914. Other renowned institutions include the Chernomorsky Sanatorium, the Ai-Danil' Sanatorium, and the Polyclinic.

Yalta is divided into three distinct districts. The busy thoroughfare called Roosevelt Avenue dominates the "Old City"; the "New City" is the residential, tourist, and hotel center; and the area beyond the river, called Zarechye, is the hospital and sanatoria district. Prominent names and residents associated with Yalta include the authors Leo Nikolaevich Tolstoy, Maxim Gorky, and Anton Pavlovich Chekhov and poets Vladimir Vladimirovich Mayakovsky and Nikolai Alekseevich Nekrasov.

The city has four major museums—The Museum of Regional Studies, the History and Archaeology Museum, the Literary Museum, the Alupka Palace Museum, and the Chekhov Museum. It also boasts a Philharmonic Concert Hall, the Chekhov Theater, the Yalta Film Studio, and the Nikitsky Botanical Gardens. The city has several libraries. Among the educational institutions in Yalta are a medical college, a nursing school, an agricultural college, a pharmaceutical college, a pedagogical school, and a trade technicum. Other scientific institutions are the Magarach Central Research Institute of Viticulture and Viniculture and the Vinicultural Combine of Massandra which experiment with over eight hundred varieties of grapes.

In addition to the horticultural schools studying the grape industry Yalta has the Massandra Industrial-Agricultural Association which represents the winemaking industry. The city also has a tobacco curing plant, a milk plant, a brewery, a fish processing firm, and an asphalt-cement plant. Smaller factories produce regional souvenirs, headgear, and nonalcoholic beverages. The Massandra combine employs many people in five bottling plants.

Yalta, sometimes called the capital of the Crimean Coast, is the center of a network of resort villages that include Foross, Gaspra, Alupka, Gurzuf, Koreiz, Livadia, Simeiz, Miskhor, Castropol, Massandra, Krasnokamenka, and Botanicheskoe. The Yalta city soviet has jurisdiction over these resort suburbs and small villages.

See Also: YALTA CONFERENCE.

Bibliography: There are entries on Yalta in the major Soviet reference works, including the English translation of the third edition of the *Great Soviet Encyclopedia*. A useful general reference work is Victor Louis and Jennifer Louis, *The Complete Guide to the Soviet Union* (London, 1976). Other works containing information on Yalta include O. Sobolev, *Ialta. Kratkii putevoditel'* (Simfiropol', 1974) and E.A. Vorontsov, *Bol'shaia Ialta. Kraevedcheskii ocherk* (Simferopol, 1968). Some information about the city is found in M.P. Chekhova, *The Chekhov Museum in Yalta* (M., 1958).

Phillip E. Koerper

YARILO. A mythological personage whose celebration fell into the general complex of spring and early summer celebrations of the Russian folk.

Most commentators believe that Yarilo was a pre-Christian god of fertility, although a few consider this hypothesis unfounded in view of the absence of his name in ancient texts (Propp). The root "iar-" suggests associations with "spring," "sexual prowess," and "fury" (as in contemporary Russian "iarovoi" [spring], "iaryi" [ardent], and "iarostnyi" [furious]), and rituals connected with this figure suggest that peasants regarded him as a bringer of vegetational fertility and sexual exuberance.

Celebrations in honor of Yarilo, while varying somewhat in date and content from region to region, were known in many provinces of European Russia and in Belorussia in the first half of the nineteenth century. By the end of the century his cult had diminished significantly in these regions, although a few ethnographic reports were recorded. By the late twentieth century the figure of Yarilo had all but faded from peasant consciousness except for occasional mentions of the name in association with general merriments occurring after planting and in place names.

In eighteenth-century Voronezh an elaborate Yarilo celebration occurred for several days in mid-June in conjunction with a fair held just outside the city's Moscow Gates. A man playing the part of Yarilo was rouged and decorated with flowers, streamers, bells, and a pointed cap. Crowds of men and women accompanied him in his carousing and dancing. The celebration included dancing, singing, eating sweets, drinking, boxing in which people were occasionally maimed or killed, and a good deal of sexual license. All this ceased soon after Tikhon Zadonsky, then bishop of the city, condemned the "idol-worshiping, devilish, and unlawful" nature of the holiday in 1763. Like the Voronezh celebration, most Great Russian celebrations of the nineteenth century occurred in mid-June, during the period preceding the fast for Saints Peter and Paul; a few occurred at Trinity and a few just after Peter and Paul Day (29 June). Almost all reports mentioned debauchery and eroticism as typical for this celebration, and a few specified that peasants associated Yarilo with sexual love.

In some places peasants conducted a ritual funeral for Yarilo. Its general outlines resembled those practiced in commemoration of other mythological personages (Kostroma, the rusalka, Kostrubon'ko) and which some commentators, such as Propp, interpret as an embryonic rite of a dying/rising divinity of vegetational fertility. In Kostroma Province an old man dressed in rags and accompanied by drunken, wailing women carried a coffin containing a doll of Yarilo bearing an erect phallus. In one village of Yaroslavl Province a man-sized clay effigy with exaggerated genitals represented Yarilo. It was positioned opposite a female counterpart called Yarilikha. At the end of the merriment peasants broke these statues and threw them into the river. Sometimes an old man played the part of Yarilo; the peasants made him drunk, amused themselves with him, and then the village girls bowed to him before joining in the khorovod, a dance in which the participants form a circle. In Poshekhonsk District of Yaroslavl Province peasants divided the celebration into that of Young Yarilo and Old Yarilo; the former occurred a week before the day of Ivan Kupalo (24 June) and the latter one day before Kupalo. In some areas the holiday consisted of a general merrymaking without specific rituals devoted to the figure of Yarilo; his name might be lost or retained only in the name of the celebration (Yarilki) or the place of the merrymaking (Yarilina dolina, Yarilina roshcha). In Belorussia the feast of Yarilo was celebrated 27 April. Here a barefoot young man wearing a white garb and a garland of fresh flowers represented the figure. He rode about on a white horse with stalks of rye in his left hand and a representation of a human head in his right. He was accompanied by a young girl on a white horse tethered to a pole around which the other girls, wearing garlands of fresh flowers, danced the khorovod.

Controversy exists concerning the saint-replacement of Yarilo. Some emphasize that the cult of Yarilo merged primarily with that of St. George (Georgy, Yury), who in the peasant imagination was a patron of livestock and a bringer of vegetational fertility and whose spring feast occurred 23 April (Efimenko, Ivanov, and Toporov). Others note that the choice of St. George is based too exclusively on limited Belorussian materials and ignores the more extensive reports from Great Russia, which indicate that Yarilo celebrations tended to fall close to the summer solstice. They contend that Yarilo is largely interchangeable with Kupalo, the more usual midsummer's figure (Sokolova).

Bibliography: A.N. Afanas'ev, *Poeticheskie vozzreniia slavian na prirodu*, Vol. 1 (M., 1865), 432-468; P.S. Efimenko, "O Iarile, iazycheskom bozhestve russkikh slavian," *Zapiski Imperatorskogo russkogo geograficheskogo obshchestva po otdeleniiu etnografii*, Vol. 2 (M., 1869), 77-112; Felix Haase, *Volksglaube und Brauchtum der Ostslaven*, (Breslau, 1939), 88-111; V.V. Ivanov and V.N. Toporov, "Iarilo i ego sootvetstvie u slavian," in *Issledovaniia v oblasti slavianskikh drevnostei. Leksicheskie i frazeologicheskie voprosy rekonstruktsii tekstov* (M., 1974), 180-216; Roman Jacobson, "Slavic Mythology," *Funk and Wagnall's Standard Dictionary of Folklore, Mythology, and Legend* (New York, 1949-1950), 1026-1027; E.V. Pomerantseva, "Iarilki," *Sovetskaia etnografiia*, No. 3 (1975), 127-130; V. Ia. Propp, *Russkie agrarnye prazdniki* (L., 1963), 87-104; I.M. Snegirev, "Iarilo," *Russkie prostonarodnye prazdniki i suevernye obriady*, Vol. 4 (M., 1837), 51-61; V.K. Sokolova, *Vesenne-letnie kalendarnye obriady russkikh, ukraintsev i belorussov* (M., 1979), 180-181, 250-255; S.A. Tokarev, ed., "Iarila," *Mify narodov mira*, 2 vols., Vol. 2 (M., 1982), 686-687.

Linda J. Ivanits

YAROPOLK II VLADIMIROVICH (1082-1139). Prince of Periaslavl-Yuzhny; Grand Prince of Kiev.

From the point of view of any political theory, the method of rule conceived by Yaroslav the Wise for the first Russian principality, the Kievan state, must be considered idealistic. He devised a rota system, under which members of the senior branch of the ruling house were supposed to move up from a lesser town in the realm to a greater one, following each other in a fixed sequence until the most senior among them would in time become grand prince of Kiev. But by the twelfth century regional towns were growing stronger, while Kiev was becoming weaker. A host of sovereign independent duchies, or appanages, appeared. Thus the rota system began to break down almost as soon as it started.

The system lasted longer than it otherwise might have because Vladimir Monomakh and Mstislav, the eldest of Monomakh's eight sons, strove to abide by its conditions. They were committed to the principle of seniority. They believed that junior princes had an obligation to join forces against a common foe at the bidding of the senior prince in Kiev on pain of losing their patrimonies. Ironically the career of Yaropolk, Monomakh's third son, was one of the initial examples of the breakdown of the rota system.

The Kievan state long had suffered severely from the attacks and raids carried out by marauding groups of Turko-Tataric steppe nomads. In the twelfth century the Polovtsy (Polovetsians) constituted the major threat. As prince of Pereiaslavl-Yuzhny and as grand prince of Kiev, Monomakh conducted four major campaigns against the Polovtsy: in 1103, 1107, 1111 and 1113, mainly in the Don River region. Leaving for Kiev in 1113, Monomakh installed his son Yaropolk as ruler of Pereiaslavl-Yuzhny, which he was destined to rule for nineteen years. Yaropolk conscientiously sought to carry out his father's behests during Monomakh's lifetime, accompanying him on these successful campaigns; he captured Polovtsy towns and took a bride from among the north Caucasus people he found inhabiting one of them.

Yaropolk also joined Monomakh in a contest with their irreconcilable enemy, Prince Gleb of Minsk. During the course of the campaign of 1116 against him, Yaropolk captured the town of Drutsk and settled many of its inhabitants in a new town he founded, Zhelni. He also subdued a number of towns along the river Seim and established his own officials in them. In 1119 Vladimir and

Yaropolk again assailed Minsk and captured Prince Gleb, who died in captivity in Kiev the following year.

In 1125 Monomakh, who had fought the Polovtsy so long and stubbornly, died. The steppe nomads believed they had received a splendid opportunity to attack Russia, especially the Pereiaslavl region, but Yaropolk anticipated their move. With no more than a single band of soldiers from Pereiaslavl and no support from other princes, he fell upon the Polovtsy and inflicted a series of such sharp defeats upon them that they did not invade Russia again for nearly a decade.

Mstislav, Monomakh's eldest son, succeeded his father as grand prince of Kiev. When he died in 1132 the influential popular assembly (veche, sing.) in Kiev invited Yaropolk to become grand prince. He accepted and took up his duties there, but his temperament provoked disturbances in the city which weakened his power base in the struggles with the outside foes he soon faced. Furthermore in making dispositions for Pereiaslavl he created another problem that illustrates some of the difficulties that the rivalries and jealousies among the princes could cause for Russia.

On departing for Kiev Yaropolk had assigned Perialsavl-Yuzhny to Vsevolod Mstislavich, his oldest nephew. His action made the younger members of the Monomakh family, Yury of Rostov and Andrei of Volynia, suspicious that Yaropolk intended eventually to install Vsevolod as grand prince in Kiev, which they considered a violation of their rights. This aroused his uncle Yury to expel Vsevolod from Pereiaslavl on the day he arrived there. Yaropolk then had to persuade Yury to leave Pereiaslavl. In vain hopes of restoring amity among the brothers, he assigned the region to another nephew, Iziaslav Mstislavich.

This only made the situation worse, especially when Yaropolk shortly afterwards made Iziaslav surrender Pereiaslavl to another uncle, Viacheslav, compensating his nephew with the towns of Turov and Pinsk. Viacheslav thereupon proceeded to Turov, expelled Iziaslav, and took up residence in the town himself. It now was Yury Vladimirovich's turn once again to seize Pereiaslavl, compensating Yaropolk with a portion of his holdings in the Rostov area.

This series of confusing maneuvers attracted the attention of Vsevolod Olgovich, prince of Chernigov. The members of his family, descended from Grand Prince Sviatoslav Yaroslavich, were strong champions of the new concept of regional autonomy. Vsevolod did not shrink from summoning the Polovtsy to assist him in an effort to recover territories he previously had lost. He was joined by Iziaslav Mstislavich and his brother Sviatopolk, and was opposed by Yaropolk and his brothers Yury and Andrei. At first the fortunes of war fluctuated, but at last with the help of the Polovtsy, who laid waste the west bank of the Dnieper River, Vsevolod got the upper hand.

Next Yaropolk and Vsevolod agreed to a truce, among the terms of which Periaslavl went to Andrei Vladimirovich while the Vladimir-Volynia appanage went Iziaslav Mstislavich. The truce did not last long. In 1135 Vsevolod advanced on Periaslavl; Yaropolk rushed to relieve it, but sustained a defeat. He hastened to raise a fresh army beyond the Dnieper. Vsevolod was reluctant to follow up his initial success and withdrew to his home base of Chernigov to make further tentative overtures to Yaropolk about renewing the truce.

Then abruptly changing his plans, early in winter Vsevolod called upon the Polovtsy once more and brought them across the Dnieper to ravage the environs of Kiev. Although Yaropolk had succeeded in assembling a large army he seemed unwilling to resume fighting the Olgovichi family. Perhaps in a last despairing effort to heed Monomakh's adjuration to "love thy brethren," he concluded another peace with them and assigned towns he controlled along the Seim River to members of the Olgovich family.

Even so conditions did not improve. Sviatoslav, Vesevolod Olgovich's brother, was expelled from Novgorod in 1138; this served as a pretext for renewing hostilities. The Olgovichi (pl.), aided by the Polovtsy, this time attacked the part of the Pereiaslavl-Yuzhny district that lay along the Sula River. Yaropolk collected a large force and headed for Chernigov. Alarmed, Vsevolod tried to take refuge with the Polovtsy, but the people of Chernigov compelled him to seek a further accommodation with Yaropolk. Another uneasy truce ensued until Yaropolk died in 1139. Vsevolod then ascended the throne of Kiev.

By attempting to advance the interests of certain members of his family at the expense of others, Yaropolk violated and undermined the concept of the rota system to which his father and older brother had been strongly committed. He brought down the wrath of the Olgovichi upon the House of Monomakh and transformed an intraprincely struggle into an interprincely contest. His action helped to usher in the gloomy appanage period of Russian history, which did much to paralyze the country during the times of national crisis soon to descend upon it.

Bibliography: Polnoe sobranie russkikh letopisei, especially Vols. 1-3; A.E. Presniakov, "Kniazhnoe pravo v drevnei Rusi," *Zapiski istoriko-filologicheskago fakul' teta Imperatorskago s-peterburgskago universiteta*, Vol. 90 (1909), 72-79. *Russkii biograficheskii slovar* (1913), 161-162. *Ocherki istorii SSSR, period feodalizma, IX-XV vv.*, Vol. 1 (M., 1953), M.P. Kuchera, "Pereiaslavskoe kniazhestvo," in *Drevnerusskie kniazhestva X-XIII vv.* (M., 1975), 118-143. Vladimir Andreevich Kuchkin, *Formirovanie gosudarstvennoi territorii severo-vostochnoi Rusi v X-XIV vv.* (M., 1984).

Hugh F. Graham

YAROSHENKO, NIKOLAI ALEKSANDROVICH (1846-1898). Artist. Socially committed genre painter who became the "conscience" and head of the association of Russian realist artists known as the Wanderers (Peredvizhniki) after the death of Ivan Nikolaevich Kramskoy in 1887.

On 1 December 1846 in Poltava, Ukraine, Nikolai Aleksandrovich Yaroshenko was born into the family of A. M. Yaroshenko, a retired artillery officer and member of the Chernigov nobility. He completed training at the Mikhailovsky Artillery Academy in St. Petersburg in 1870 and remained in the service over twenty years with responsibility for the army's St. Petersburg cartridge factory, retiring in 1893 with the rank of major general.

Drawn to art from his youth, Yaroshenko began attending evening art classes at the drawing school of the St. Petersburg Society for the Encouragement of the Arts in the mid-1860s, where he attracted the attention of his teacher and mentor Ivan Kramskoy. Yaroshenko's sociopolitical commitment to the cause of populism dates from the 1860s. It can be attributed to the influence both of Kramskoy and of the writers Mikhail Evgrafovich Saltykov-Shchedrin, Aleksei Nikolaevich Pleshcheev, Gleb Ivanovich Uspensky, and Vsevolod Mikhailovich Garshin who had formed a circle connected with their journal Notes of the Fatherland (Otechestvennye zapiski). All of them became friends of Yaroshenko and sat for portraits.

Nevsky Prospect at Night (Nevsky prospekt nochiu), the artist's first major genre painting, which depicted people forced by circumstances to spend a cold, rainy night on the street, won the artist admission to the Wanderers in 1876 but unfortunately was destroyed during World War II. Two years later Yaroshenko created a stir at the Sixth Wanderers' Exhibition with two bitter indictments of late imperial social conditions. Stoker (Kochegar) featured a powerful laborer with a body bent from ceaseless, repetitious toil. Imprisoned (Zakliuchennyi) was a dramatically light study of a bearded revolutionary gazing upward and outward through the small grated window of his prison cell. The famed Moscow merchant patron Pavel Mikhailovich Tretiakov bought both of these works and hung them in his gallery.

On 1 March 1881, the day revolutionaries of the People's Will (Narodnaia volia) assassinated Tsar Alexander II, the Ninth Wanderer's Exhibit opened in St. Petersburg. It included two works in which Yaroshenko addressed the profound generational and political conflict of that era. In the first, The Old and the Young (Staroe i molodoe), a heated argument between father and son was dramatized. The second, By Litovsky Fortress (U litovskogo zamka), presented a young woman dressed entirely in black hurrying past the heavily guarded fortress and trying furtively to make contact with one of the inmates via a small prison window. According to V.V. Sekliutsky, the police removed By Litovsky Fortress from the Wanderers' exhibit, and Yaroshenko was summoned to make an explanation to Minister of the Interior Mikhail Tarieovich Loris-Melikov. The artist's military and artistic careers nonetheless flourished thereafter.

An 1883 work, Female Student (Kursistka), Yaroshenko's next major canvas, received a rapturous response from liberal critics such as Gleb Uspensky and presented the definitive type of the activist woman. The political resonance of this canvas was particularly great because the simply dressed young woman with cropped hair tucked under a man's cap and a substantial tome under her arm called to mind Vera Ivanovna Zasulich, who had tried to assassinate the St. Petersburg chief of police in 1878, and other female student revolutionaries, such as the regicide Sofia L'vovna Perovskaia, who recently had stood trial. The artist's actual model was Anna Chertkova, the wife of Tolstoy's disciple, publisher Vladimir Grigorievich Chertkov. Continuing his depiction of strong, politically and socially committed Russian women, Yaroshenko offered a striking portrait of Aleksandrinsky Theater actress Pelageia Strepetova (1850-1903) at the 1884 Wanderers' exhibit. The actress was famous for her depiction of suffering, wronged women in plays by Aleksander Nikolaevich Ostrovsky and Aleksei Feofilaktovich Pisemsky. Yaroshenko was a gifted portraitist. He completed nearly one hundred portraits. Some of the best date from the 1890s when he had ceased to produce significant genre works. An example is his splendid 1890 portrait of the artist Nikolai Nikolaevich Ge, now in the Russian Museum, St. Petersburg.

Life is Everywhere (Vsiudu zhizn, 1888) was Yaroshenko's last important genre painting. With its depiction of various types—including a somewhat incongruous madonna-like female in a blue veil—all neatly framed in the window of a prison railway car as they feed pigeons through its bars, it seems contrived. The painting provides a classic example of the sentimental, poster-like quality so disliked by the young artists and critics who fostered the Silver Age of Russian culture in the last decade of the nineteenth century. Inspired by Tolstoy's polemics, the painting became the most popular and frequently reproduced of Yaroshenko's works, winning praise from Vladimir Ilich Lenin in later years.

Yaroshenko suffered from tuberculosis of the throat, evidently as a result of his work in the St. Petersburg cartridge factory. In 1892 he moved to the healthier mountain climate of Kislovodsk, where he built a villa, entertained, and continued to paint. He found himself at odds with fellow Wanderers such as Ilia Efimovich Repin when they joined the staff of the reformed Academy of Arts in the mid-1890s and was critical of all those who strayed from the stylistic and conceptual norms of the first generation of the Peredvizhniki. Among younger artists his influence can be seen in the work of Nikolai Alekseevich Kasatkin which depicts laborers in difficult working conditions. Yaroshenko died of a heart attack on 25 June 1898 while at work on a canvas. His close friend, genre and religious painter Mikhail Vasilievich Nesterov, delivered the graveside eulogy. In 1962 the painter's Kislovodsk estate became the Museum of N.A. Yaroshenko.

Bibliography: V.V. Sekliutskii, *Nikolai Aleksandrovich Iaroshenko* (Stavropol, 1963), is the best general biography. V.A. Prytkov, *Nikolai Aleksandrovich Iaroshenko* (M., 1960), is the most substantive discussion of his work, richly illustrated with a catalog raisonée. I.V. Polenova, *Iaroshenko v Peterburge* (L., 1983), provides a less politicized reading of his most important works and detail on his activities in Petersburg. See also "Iaroshenko," *Entsiklopedicheskii slovar'*, Vol. 65, 784, and *Bolshaia sovetskaia entsiklopediia*, 3rd ed., Vol. 30, 559-60.

                                                                    John O. Norman

YAROSLAVL (1010?-). City of 619,000 (1983) and the economic and administrative center of Yaroslavl district in the Russian republic. Yaroslavl is situated on both banks of the Volga River at the confluence with the smaller Kotorosl River. It is 156 miles (260 km) northwest of Moscow. Yaroslavl, an important engineering, chemical and industrial city, is a major river port and a junction for railroad and highway lines to Moscow, Kirov, Vologda, Kostroma, and Rybinsk.

Archaeological records indicate a sparse habitation at Yaroslavl long before the village of Medvezhi Ugol was settled in the ninth and tenth centuries. In 1010 Prince Yaroslav the Wise (1019-1054) conquered the villagers of Medvezhi Ugol and established a fortress which was named after him. Yaroslavl grew rapidly because of its advantageous location along the Volga River trade routes. A city named Yaroslavl first was mentioned in Russian chronicles in the year 1071. The town crest is a bear rampant with a halberd on his shoulder. The traditional legend told that the local inhabitants released a bear from a cage to chase Yaroslav away but that he slew the bear with his halberd. In 1218 the city became the capital of the independent feudal principality of Yaroslavl. Early in the thirteenth century the first school in northern Russia was established in Yaroslavl. The city was sacked and partially burnt by the Tatars in 1238.

In 1463 the Yaroslavl principality was united with Moscow when Prince Alexander Brukhatyi exchanged his ancestral holdings with Tsar Ivan III the Great (1462-1505) for a feudal estate near Moscow. Tsar Ivan IV, the Terrible (1533-1584), established trade relations in 1555 with England through the White Sea port of Archangel. Consequently, the English established a trade center at Yaroslavl to exploit commerce along the Volga and on into the Near East. In the seventeenth century commerce expanded so rapidly that by mid-century Yaroslavl was surpassed in foreign trade only by Moscow and Kazan.

During the Time of Troubles (1605-1613) the capital of Russia was moved temporarily to Yaroslavl following the Polish invasion of Moscow. Kuzma Minin and Prince Pozharsky formed the Peoples' Home Guard in Yaroslavl during the summer of 1612. The city was damaged severely by both the Poles and the cossacks but was rebuilt and maintained its commercial importance.

In the eighteenth century Yaroslavl's industrial development began with a ukase (decree) in 1722 by Peter I the Great (1685-1725) which created the Yaroslavl Textile Works. Industrialization continued throughout the century. In 1710 Yaroslavl was incorporated into St. Petersburg Province and became a subprovincial center in 1719. The city was merged into Moscow Province in 1727. In 1777 it became the capital of Yaroslavl Vice-Regency (Namestnichestvo) and capital of Yaroslavl Province in 1796.

Upon establishment of St. Petersburg as a commercial port during the eighteenth century Yaroslavl's commercial role decreased in importance. The city remained as Moscow's Volga port until the Moscow-Volga Canal was inaugurated in 1937. During the nineteenth century Yaroslavl remained a medium-sized city but it became a more diversified center. The Demidov Juridicial Lyceum was established in the city in 1803. Its growing textile, tobacco, chemical, and flour-milling industries employed the eighth largest labor force in Russia by 1900. During the last quarter of the century railroad lines were constructed connecting Yaroslavl with Moscow, Kostroma, Vologda and St. Petersburg. A railroad bridge was built across the Volga River in 1913. The economic development of Yaroslavl accelerated rapidly after the revolution in 1917.

Aleksandr Mitrofanovich Stopani organized the first Marxist circle in Yaroslavl in 1895. In 1901 the city became the center of the Northern Workers' Union, later reorganized and renamed the Northern Committee of the Russian Social Democratic Labor Party (RSDLP). When the revolution of 1905-1907 broke out Yakov Mikhailovich Sverdlov, Viacheslav Rudelofovich Menzhinsky and Nikolai Ilich Podvoisky led the workers of Yaroslavl in demonstrations and strikes. During the Bolshevik revolution Soviet authority was established by a revolutionary committee in the city on 27 October 1917. When the White Guards, under the leadership of Boris Savinkov, staged an anti-Bolshevik revolt in July 1918, they were subdued by the local Red Army Regiment and Workers Detachments. The Revolutionary Military Committee headed by Yan Davylovich Lentsman coordinated the suppression of the rebellion. Many city buildings and hundreds of residents perished during the armed clashes that drove out the White Guards.

During the early years of the Soviet Union Yaroslavl continued to develop as an industrial center. In addition to its food-processing, chemical, and textile industries, it became a center for the production of machinery, petroleum refinement, light industry, and energy. The chemical industry is led by the Lakokraska Association and by other plants producing tires, rubber, asbestos products, synthetic rubber, paint, and lacquer. The Novoiaroslavsky Refinery receives its crude oil from the pipeline from the east. The machinery industry produces automobiles, diesel engines for heavy vehicles, fuel equipment, refrigeration units, electric machinery, and polymer machines. The large Krasnyi Maiak Plant produces electric oscillators. The Perekop Yaroslavl Industrial Fabrics Combine is one of the oldest factories in Yaroslavl. The city also manufactures wood products, building materials, food products and consumer goods. Yaroslavl has district power and heat plants in its energy production systems.

The city of Yaroslavl covers an area of approximately 105 square miles (170 sq. km). The city's estimated population in 1897 was 72,000; 1917, 125,000; 1937, 309,000; 1959, 407,000 and 1978, 592,000. The population is predominately Russian. The January average temperature is 13°F (-10°C) and the average July temperature is 64°F (18°C).

Yaroslavl has not declined culturally because of industrial development. The city has several educational institutions including the University of Yaroslavl and a branch of the Moscow Agricultural Academy. Other schools specialize in medical, pedagogical, polytechnical, engineering, economics, and finances. There are twelve specialized secondary educational institutions related to the various industries in the city.

The city has several museums of local history, the Yaroslavl Art Museum, Museum of Natural History and a museum outside the city honoring Nikolai Alekseyevich Nekrasov, the famous poet. There are two renowned theaters, the Yaroslavl Puppet Theater and the F.G. Volkov Theater, established in 1750 and the first public theater founded in Russia. There are also a circus, a planetarium, and a philharmonic concert hall with a thousand-seat capacity. The Spaso-Preobrazhensky Monastery contains several examples of the Yaroslavl school of architecture and art which flourished from the thirteenth through seventeenth centuries. Other examples of Russian art and murals dating from the seventeenth century can be found in the Nikola Nadein Church, the Church of Elijah the Prophet, the Church of St. John Chrysostom, the Church of Nikola Mokryi, the Church of St. John the Precursor, and several other churches. Near these churches are the remnants of the ancient earthen ramparts and brick towers that once enclosed the Old City. Because it was not damaged during World War II, Yaroslavl is the best city for visiting old Russian churches and the ancient mansion houses in the center of the mostly unspoiled Old City.

See Also: YAROSLAVL THEATER and YAROSLAVL, UPRISING OF, 1918.

Bibliography: There are entries on Yaroslavl in the major Soviet encyclopedias, including the English translation of the third edition of the *Great Soviet Encyclopedia*. Books and monographs include: F.I. Kozlov, *Iaroslavl'. Putevoditel'* (Yaroslavl, 1974); E.V. Arapov, *Iaroslavl'. Putevoditel'* (M., 1976); K.D. Golovshchikov, *Istoriia goroda Iaroslavlia* (Yaroslavl, 1899); and E.D. Dobrovol'skaia and B.V. Gnedovskii, *Iaroslavl', Tutaev* (M., 1971). References on the Yaroslavl revolt of 1918 are D.L. Golinkov, *Krushenie antisovetskogo podpol'ia v SSSR (1917-1925)* (M., 1975); *Boris Savinkov pered Voennoi kollegiei Verkhovnogo Suda SSSR* (M., 1924); and *Shestnadtsat' dnei. Materialy po istorii Iaroslavskogo belogvardeiskogo miatezha (6-21 iiulia 1918g)* (Yaroslavl, 1924). A useful general reference work is Victor Louis and Jennifer Louis, *The Complete Guide to the Soviet Union* (London, 1976).

Phillip E. Koerper

YAROSLAVL THEATER (1750-). The first professional theater in Russia, founded in 1750 by Fedor Grigorievich Volkov (1729-1763), in the city of Yaroslavl, northwest of Moscow.

Before the founding of the Yaroslavl theater troupe Russian dramatic productions took place largely under the auspices of the imperial court. Influenced by French and German dramas and Italian commedia dell'arte, they were staffed by European personnel. Audiences consisted of members of the court, nobles, and foreigners. This western dominance of Russian theater has its origins in the Imperial Theater established in Moscow by Tsar Alexis (1645-1676), who imported German actors and plays for his enterprise. Peter the Great (1682-1725) continued the westernization of Russian theater in 1702 by subsidizing a theater which employed wandering troupes of folk performers devoted to propaganda. This venture was ultimately unsuccessful. It was only during the reign of Peter's daughter Elizabeth (1741-1762) that a truly Russian theater began to flourish.

In 1750 Elizabeth authorized theater performances in private homes. This led to the growth of many provincial theaters, such as that founded in the home of the merchant Grigory Serov in January 1750. The most successful of these was Volkov's troupe in Yaroslavl which, according to modern scholarship, marked the emergence of Russian professional theater.

Fedor Volkov, the stepson of a merchant, eventually rejected the merchant's life because of his avid interest in theater. In fact his passion for theater developed while he was in Moscow training for a commercial career. At this time the court was in Moscow (1742-1749) and Volkov had the opportunity to attend amateur performances, productions of German troupes, stagings of Italian opera, and French plays. As a result his exposure to theatrical art was broader than that of his contemporaries in Yaroslavl. Upon his return to his hometown, he established a theater troupe. His brothers, Grigory and Gavrilo, and various members of the Yaroslavl population, including seminary students, participated. Among the original members were several actors who were later to become important figures of Russian theater, including the tragic classical actor

Ivan Afanasievich Dmitrevsky and Aleksei Popov. The performances of the fledgling troupe were so popular that Yaroslavl residents financed the building of a thousand-seat theater there in 1751.

Word of the troupe's successful efforts, exceptional talent, and professionalism reached Elizabeth in St. Petersburg. She summoned Volkov and his actors to the capital by official order issued 3 January 1752. They arrived a month later and by all accounts the court treated them with respect and provisioned them well. On 6 February 1752 on the stage of the German Theater the troupe presented a performance of Khorev, the tragedy by Alexandr Petrovich Sumarokov (1718-1777). Thus began Volkov's association with Sumarokov, the founder of Russian classical drama. In March of the same year they performed for the court Dmitry Rostovsky's comic morality play The Repentance of a Sinner with Volkov in the main role, as well as a repeat performance of Khorev.

Elizabeth, greatly impressed by these performances, decided to provide a better education for the troupe's more talented members. In February 1754 she enrolled them in the Infantry Corps of Nobles (Shliaketnyi korpus), a military school for the sons of the nobility. Here they studied not only traditional courses in literature, science, and languages, but also special courses in declamation and stage technique. Volkov himself was noted for meticulous study and detailed research, which in turn accounted for his intelligent guidance of all of the troupe's productions. The Yaroslavl actors gained experience performing in school dramas staged by the students.

By 1756 Volkov and the members of the Yaroslavl theater troupe with Sumarokov as director became the first permanent professional theater open to the general public. It is for this reason that Volkov is considered both the father and the first actor of the Russian theater. His contemporaries, including the poet Gavriil Romanovich Derzhavin (1743-1816), the playwright Denis Ivanovich Fonvizin (1745-1792), and the publisher and critic Nikolai Ivanovich Novikov (1744-1818), acknowledged his superior knowledge of theatrical arts. As an actor, Volkov won acclaim for his passionate style and declamatory skill.

In 1911 the theater was officially named for its founder. Henceforth it was called the F.G. Volkov Yaroslavl Drama Theater. In 1966 it became an academic theater, but lost its leading role in Russian theatrical culture.

Bibliography: P.A. Markov et al., eds., *Teatral'naia entsiklopediia,* 5 vols., Vols. 4-5 (M., 1963); Konstantin Evgrafov, *Fedor Volkov* (M., 1989); *Istoriia russkogo dramaticheskogo teatra,* 7 vols., Vol. 1 (M., 1977); B.V. Varneke, *History of the Russian Theatre* (New York, 1951).

Therese M. Malhame

YASA. Legal code of the Mongols.

The Yasa (yassa, jasa, jasay, jasaq, jasak, yasaq, tura) of Chingiz Khan (1162-1227) (Genghiz Khan, Jenghiz Khan, Cinggis Qan, Temüjin) was a compilation of Mongol law allegedly promulgated by him in 1206 upon his election as great khan. It was supplemented in 1210 and 1218 at the assemblies of Mongol notables called kuriltays. Completed or formally promulgated about

1228-1229, it became the basis of Mongol law. Whether it existed in any form during the life of Chingiz as well as whether it was a codification of Mongol common law or imperial law as formulated by Chingiz Khan have been matters of contention.

No written text of the Yasa exists and it is known only through retellings by thirteenth-century Arabic, Armenian, and Persian authors. These and other authors through the fifteenth century mentioned the work or claimed to have seen it. Some alleged that it was kept in the treasury of the Chingizids or that there was a copy in the library of al-madrasa al-Mustansirigya in Baghdad. The extant fragments of the Yasa, none of which date from Chingiz Khan's lifetime, are in the Mongol language in Uighur script.

What has come down to us makes it appear that the alleged initial 1206 version concentrated on sanctions for serious crimes. The later alleged redactions compiled while Chingiz Khan was campaigning in Central Asia and China changed and broadened the work.

Chingiz was extraordinarily arrogant about his legal norms and forbade from them. Doubtless this was because he, who was totally illiterate, considered the Yasa to be of divine, heavenly (the "Blue Sky") origin, much like Moses' Ten Commandments or the Tablets that commenced the Roman Law tradition. If Chingiz had little or nothing to do with the Yasa then it is fair to suspect that divine trappings were attributed to its norms by legislators who wanted to maximize the legitimacy of their enterprise. His successors considered—or advocated—that Chingiz was the Son of Heaven and the Yasa divinely inspired. Alleged deviations from the Yasa were among the most damning accusations Chingis's rival heirs could make against one another. The Yasa was believed by the Mongols and Turks to have semi-magical power.

The late historian George Vernadsky attempted a hypothetical reconstruction of the Yasa and surmised that it consisted of the following sections: general precepts, international law, government, army and administration, criminal law, civil law, and commercial law. His organization will be followed for heuristic purposes in this presentation. There is no doubt, it must be stressed, that these norms existed in the mid-thirteenth century. The issue is whether they originated with Chingiz and whether they were an organized, coherent code of law.

The general precepts were a few rules for everyone such as love one another, do not commit adultery, do not steal, some hospitality rules, and the notion that all nations and religions were to be tolerated equally—some would say treated equally as slaves.

In the international sphere, the Yasa did not recognize an order of sovereign states. Instead it proclaimed that everyone who refused to acknowledge the supremacy of the Mongol khan was a rebel and could anticipate dire sanctions.

The statutes on the government dealt with the titles of the khan and his family members and the maintenance of the ruling household. This section also may have prescribed norms for the governance of the Mongol nation and the operation of the kuriltays which elected new rulers. Another section dealt with hunting as an aspect of military training. An army statute prescribed a near universal conscription of all males over the age of twenty; possessors of mental magic—priests, scholars, and physicians—were exempted. This statute also stipulated the death penalty for deserters and those who recruited them and provided for the army's decimal organization. This organization had the utility of breaking down the tribal structure and putting all manpower at the disposal of the khan. Women were required to do the work of men while the latter were on campaign. The requirement that nearly all serve gave the Mongols a tremendous advantage over their often numerically superior adversaries. These laws also dealt with postal relay stations and various taxes.

The criminal law was among the most severe known to mankind. Nomads have little use for jails, fines were an insufficient deterrent, and so death was prescribed for many infractions. Considered as crimes were offenses against customs, morals and religion, against the ruler and the state, and against individuals. Jailing, banishment (which probably was considered equivalent to capital punishment), corporal punishment, and fines (often nine-fold restitution) were subsidiary sanctions. A baneful collective responsibility held family members criminally responsible on certain occasions for a culprit's behavior. Homicide and horse theft were punishable by fine. In many societies fines which could not be paid were converted into slavery, but the Mongols replaced them with the death penalty. Vernadsky surmised that the criminal law in the Yasa must have been more severe than the traditional Mongol law. The severity of Mongol law greatly distressed adherents of Islam.

The civil law section was minuscule. One statute provided that the property of a person who died without heirs was to pass not to the ruler but to the person who looked after him when he was dying. This was a rational provision from the perspective of the economics of law.

A provision on commercial law provided the death penalty for a third bankruptcy. It is assumed that, given the importance of commerce in the Mongol realm, there must have been additional laws in the Yasa on commerce, but none of them seem to have survived. In general the Yasa concerned itself with nomadic warriors and ignored the spheres of artisans and farmers.

According to one account the Mongols of the Golden Horde, which was adjacent to Rus', did not observe the Yasa as strictly as did the Mongols of the Chagataid Khanate and the Mongols in China.

As the Mongols converted to Islam from the later thirteenth century on, the issue arose as to what should be done when the Yasa conflicted with Islamic law. In general the Yasa prevailed for a while in the procedural sphere, but Islamic law (the ordinances of the Shari'a) pushed it aside in the criminal sphere. Some specialists speculate that the Yasa was maintained by Chingisids who wanted to retard the spread of Islam and the influence of the mullas. In any case, Babur (Babar), founder of the Mogul dynasty in India, abolished the Yasa in the first quarter of the sixteenth century because it had outlived its purpose.

The Yasa was used in other societies conquered by the Mongols. Chaghatai (Chingis's second son, d. 1242), the ruler of Central Asia, was the guardian and preserver of the Yasa and zealously instituted it in his Iranian and Turkic lands. The Yasa was referred to in China as a source of law until the end of the thirteenth century, some authorities say precisely the code of ca. 1280. Tax exemptions granted the Russian church by the Mongols in the fourteenth century referred to the Yasa.

Bibliography: David Ayalon, "The Great Yasa of Chingiz Khan. A Reexamination." *Studia Islamica*, 33 (1971), 97-140; 34 (1971), 151-180; 36 (1972), 113-158; 38 (1973), 107-156; John Andrew Boyle, ed., *The History of the World Conqueror by 'Ala-ad-Din 'Ata-Malik Juvaini. Translated from the Text of Mirza Muhammad Qazvini*, 2 vols. (Manchester, 1958); Paul Heng-chao Ch'en, *Chinese Legal Tradition under the Mongols. The Code of 1291 as Reconstructed* (Princeton, 1979); S.D. Dylykov, *Ikh Tsaaz ("Velikoe ulozhenie")*. *Pamiatnik mongol'skogo feodal'nogo prava XVII v. Oiratskii tekst* (M., 1981); Mansura Haider, "The Mongol Traditions and Their Survival in Central Asia (XIV-XV Centuries)," *Central Asiatic Journal*, 28 (1984), 57-79; Klaus Lech, *Das Mongolische Westreich, Al-'Umari's Darstellung der mongolischen Reiche in seinem Werk Masalik al-absar fi mamalik al-amsar* (The last named item constitutes the entirety of *Asiatische Forschungen* [Wiesbaden 22 (1968)] and often is cited as such); David O. Morgan. "The 'Great Yasa of Chingiz Khan' and Mongol Law in the Ilkhanate," *Bulletin of the School of Oriental and African Studies*, 49 (1986), 163-176; A.N. Nasonov, *Mongoly i Rus'. Istoriia tatarskoi politiki na Rusi* (M.-L., 1940); P. Popov, "Iasa Chingis-khana. Ulozhenie Mongol'skoi dinastii Iuan'-chao-dian'-chzhan," *Zapiski Vostochnogo otdeleniia imp. Russkogo arkheologicheskogo obshchestva*, 17 (1907), 150-163; Valentin A. Riasanovskii, *Fundamental Principles of Mongol Law* (Bloomington, 1965 [reprint of the 1937 Tientsin edition]); Idem, *K voprosu o vliianii mongol'skoi kul'tury i mongol'skogo prava na russkuiu kul'turu i pravo* (Harbin, 1931); Idem, *Mongol'skoe pravo (preimushchestvenno obychnoe)* (Harbin, 1931); George Vernadsky, "Juwaini's Version of Chingis Khan's Yasa," *Annales de l'Institut Kondakov (Seminarium Kondakovianum)*, 11 (1939), 33-45; Idem, *The Mongols and Russia* (New Haven, 1953), 99-110; Idem, "The Scope and Contents of Chingis Khan's Jasa," *Harvard Journal of Asiatic Studies*, 3 (1938), 337-360.

Richard Hellie

YAZYKOV, NIKOLAI MIKHAILOVICH (1803-1846). A Romantic poet of the Pushkin pleiade.

Yazykov was born on 4 March 1803 to a wealthy ancient landowning family of Simbirsk Province. At age eleven he entered the School of Mining Engineering in St. Petersburg. After six years of uninspired study he decided that poetry was his true calling. His poems began appearing in journals in 1819.

In 1822 he enrolled as a philosophy student at the University of Dorpat (now Tartu, Estonia), which retained relative autonomy although at that time it was under the aegis of the Russian Imperial government. This was possible because of its historical association with the European university tradition. The seven years that Yazykov spent there were the best and most productive of his poetic life. He defined himself as a poet of joy and intoxication. His verse of the period is distinguished by an effervescent spirit, created by a driving rhythm and an unconventional intermingling of the fluent style cultivated by the followers of Karamzin with elements of the heavy rhetorical style of the day. This combination gave Yazykov's verses a fresh and original ring, earning him acclaim among the literary elite. He became personally acquainted with a number of leading poets, including Pushkin who saw in Yazykov exceptional poetic promise.

In the cycle "Songs" (1823) Yazykov created the lyric persona of a freedom-loving, libertine, and politically defiant student-poet. He deftly grafted such standard motifs of Anacreontic poetry as wine, love, and song to the "student song" genre, mixing wine, love, friendship, and rebellion in his verse. The credo of his merry-making student fraternity was expressed in the lines "Freedom, songs and wine/These are our Holy Trinity." Verses from "Songs" and other Yazykov poems of 1823-1826, which circulated in handwritten copies, show that although his personal convictions were vague he sympathized with the dissident political movement that ultimately led to the Decembrist uprising in 1825. In poems written in the aftermath of the failed uprising he lamented the execution of its leaders and continued his rhetorical struggle against the tyranny of autocracy. He also began to express the nationalistic sentiments that later made him a zealous ally of the Slavophiles.

In 1829 Yazykov left the university without taking his graduation exams. He went to Moscow where he made a number of friends in the Slavophile circle. He became especially close with the Kireevsky brothers and took active part in Petr Vasilievich Kireevsky's project of gathering Russian folk songs for what became the still famous collection known under P.V. Kireevskys name. After two years of perfunctory government service he retired, in 1833, to his Simbirsk estate. In that same year his first collection of poems was published. The book received mixed critical reviews which Yazykov blamed in part on heavy editing by the censor. Some reviewers, among them Ksenofont Alekseevich Polevoy, criticized Yazykov's exuberant style for its lack of serious thought and genuine feeling. Words of praise and encouragement came chiefly from his friends, notably from Ivan Vasilievich Kireevsky, who in his review extolled Yazykov's poetry for its "vastness of soul and life."

The next five years Yazykov spent at his estate, often bedridden, suffering from tabes dorsalis, a syphilis involving the spinal cord. He spent 1838 to 1843 abroad, seeking a cure at European spas. There he developed a close relationship with Nikolai Vasilievich Gogol who, assuming the role of a spiritual mentor, urged Yazykov to write poetry with a socially edifying message.

In his works written in 1833-1843 Yazykov attempted to revive the effervescent ambiance of his student songs and also tried his hand at long verse narratives, but his forced labors produced little of merit. His tone grew didactic, and the theme of freedom gave way to declarations of xenophobic patriotism. In Earthquake (1844), one of the more effective of his later poems, he proclaimed the role of poet as prophet, the agent of salvation through faith.

At the end of 1844 Yazykov wrote several polemical epistles addressed to his ideological opponents. The poems To the Aliens (K nenashim) and To Chaadaev contained a vicious and tasteless attack on Alexander Ivanovich Herzen, Timofei Nikolaevich Granovsky, and Petr Yakovlevich Chaadaev, accusing them of betraying Holy Russia. In another poem, addressed to the Slavophile Konstantin Sergeevich Aksakov, Yazykov called for a decisive break with Russia's detractors. These poems were destined to serve as a catalyst for the final split between the Slavophiles and the Westernizers.

In the last three years of Yazykov's life two more editions of his work were published under the titles *Fifty-Six Poems of N. Yazykov* (1844) and *New Poems* (1845). They were received with harsh criticism. The leading critic of the day, Vissarion Belinsky, characterized Yazykov as the poet who survived his talent, and this severe sentence was upheld by posterity. Yazykov died on 26 December 1846.

Bibliography: N.M. Iazykov, *Polnoe sobranie stikhotvorenii*, M.K. Azadovskii, ed. (M.-L., 1934) and *Sochineniia* (L., 1982); *Stikhotvoreniia i poemy*, 3rd ed. (L., 1988); *Pis'ma N.M. Iazykova k rodnym za derptskii period ego zhizni* (1822-1829); *Iazykovskii arkhiv*, Vol. 1. (SPb., 1913); *Pis'ma P.V. Kireevskogo k N.M. Iazykovu* (M.-L., 1935); I.M. Semenko, *Poety pushkinskoi pory* (Moscow, 1970).

Irina Gutkin

YČAS, MARTYNAS (1885-1941). Deputy to Fourth Russian State Duma, Constitutional Democrat, Lithuanian finance minister, and nationalist leader.

Yčas (pronounced Ichas) was born on 13 November 1885 in Simpliskiai, Lithuania, then part of the Russian Empire. His father, also named Martynas, emigrated to the United States after having trouble with the Russian authorities for his role in smuggling Lithuanian books into the Russian Empire. With the help of his older brother Jonas, an educator who was working in Siberia, Martynas graduated from the legal faculty of Tomsk University in 1911. He then returned to Lithuania to practice law.

Yčas's political career began in 1912 when Lithuanian candidates formed a bloc with Jewish voters in the election campaign to the Fourth Russian State Duma. He was elected deputy from the Kaunas region. In St. Petersburg he joined Pavel Nikolaevich Miliukov's Constitutional Democratic (Kadet) bloc in the Duma, and became active in Lithuanian affairs. In 1913 together with Jonas Basanavicius, the "patriarch of the Lithuanian National Renaissance," Yčas visited Lithuanian colonies in the United States to raise funds for a Lithuanian National House in Vilnius.

Yčas used his position in St. Petersburg to lobby for the Lithuanian cause, but without great success. He found that in the Russian capital the "national question" involved only the Jews and the Poles. Lithuanian deputies in the Duma remained aloof from the nationalities' bloc for fear of being dominated by the Poles. After the outbreak of war in August 1914 Yčas read to Russian Prime Minister Ivan Logginovich Goremykin a formal declaration calling for the unification of "Lithuania Major" (Lithuanian territory in the Russian Empire) and "Lithuania Minor" (Lithuanian territory in the German Empire). The Russian responded curtly, "Such nonsense! What are you really asking for?"

In the Duma's session of 8 August 1914, which approved Russian war credits, Yčas hailed the Russian "crusade" and called for "smashing the German forces" and reuniting Lithuanians "under a single Russian banner." During the war the Russian Union of Zemstvos designated him as its agent for Lithuania and Belorussia, and in 1917 he became vice-chairman of the "Tatiana Committee" for relief of refugees in the empire. An estimated one third of Lithuanian adults became refugees as a result of the war, and in 1915 Yčas established two high schools (gimnaziums) in Voronezh, one for boys and one for girls.

The German occupation of Kaunas and Vilnius in 1915 divided Lithuanian political leaders into three camps. Yčas led the Lithuanians still in the Russian Empire, Antanas Smetona emerged as the leader of Lithuanians under the German occupation, and Juozas Gabrys in Switzerland claimed to lead the Lithuanians in the West.

In the spring of 1916 as part of a Russian parliamentary delegation organized by Miliukov, the leader of the Constitutional Democratic Party, Yčas toured Scandinavia and Eastern Europe. Miliukov complained that Yčas and the two Poles in the delegation spent most of their time with compatriots and that the nationalities' question seemed to dominate the delegation's discussions. Yčas introduced Miliukov to Lithuanian émigré leaders. Together the two met personalities ranging from the anarchist Petr Alekseevich Kropotkin to Pope Benedict XV and the writer Sir Arthur Conan Doyle.

At the same time Yčas conducted his Lithuanian business. In October 1915 he had met Gabrys and a German agent, the Estonian Alexander Kesküla, in Stockholm. In Switzerland in 1916 he opposed actively Gabrys' anti-Russian propaganda efforts and the planned formation, under concealed German sponsorship, of a League of Alien peoples of Russia. After the parliamentary mission concluded its work Yčas visited Lithuanian colonies in the United States, and in the fall of 1916 he again met German agents in Stockholm to discuss Lithuanian affairs.

The collapse of the tsarist regime in February-March 1917 opened the way for the Constitutional Democrats to form a provisional government. Yčas, still loyal to the cause of liberalizing Russia, took the post of deputy minister of education. But as Lithuanian leaders began to formulate thoughts of independence Yčas abandoned his activities in Russian affairs and became more active on behalf of the Lithuanian cause. In October 1917 he chaired a Lithuanian meeting in Stockholm that recognized the Lithuanian Council (Taryba), formed in Vilnius under the German occupation, as the supreme organization for the establishment of a Lithuanian state.

By the time of the Bolshevik revolution he was back in Petrograd where the new Russian rulers imprisoned him briefly. After moving to Voronezh he again experienced imprisonment; in the spring of 1918 he made his way to Lithuania where the Lithuanian Taryba, now renaming itself the Lithuanian State Council, coopted him as a member.

Once back in Lithuania Yčas joined the ranks of the conservative Progress (Pažanga) group, which eventually became the Nationalist (Tautininkai) Union. In the summer of 1918 he supported the move to preempt pressures from Berlin by electing Wilhelm of Urach as King Mindaugas II of Lithuania. In September he participated in the Third Lithuanian Conference in Lausanne, at which he apparently backed Smetona in the belief that the Germans would win the war. He became minister of finance in Lithuania's first government in the fall of 1918, and the next year he joined Lithuania's delegation at the Paris Peace Conference as a financial specialist.

Between the wars Yčas remained out of the public eye, although as director of the Commercial and Industrial Bank he was often considered one of Lithuania's kingmakers. In 1921 he participated in the commission setting

Lithuania's border with Latvia, and in 1922 he played an important role in establishing Lithuania's independent currency, the litas. An evangelical, he was active in his church organization, and behind the scenes he worked for rapprochement with Poland.

When Soviet forces occupied Lithuania in 1940 Yčas fled to Germany and then made his way to Portugal. In Lisbon he participated in Antanas Smetona's abortive talks with the Poles, and in January 1941, together with Smetona, he sailed for Brazil. He died there shortly thereafter on 5 April 1941.

Bibliography: Martynas Yčas, *Atsiminimai nepriklausomybés keliais*, 3 vols. (Kaunas, 1935-1936); Pavel Miliukov, *Natsionalnyi vopros* (n.p., 1925); "Martynas Yčas," *Lietuviu Encyklopedija*, 36 vols. (Boston, 1957-1969); "Dnevnik P.N. Miliukova," *Krasnyi arkhiv*, Vols. 54-55 (1932), 3-48; "Russkaia parlamentskaia delegatsiia za granitsei v 1916 g.," *Krasnyi arkiv*, Vol. 58 (1933), 3-23; Alfred Erich Senn, *The Emergence of Modern Lithuania* (New York, 1959); A.E. Senn, *Jonas Basanavičius. Patriarch of the Lithuanian National Renaissance* (Newtonville, Mass., 1980); A.E. Senn, *The Russian Revolution in Switzerland, 1914-1917* (Madison, 1917); A. E. Senn, "Smetona ir lenkai 1941 metais," *Akiračiai*, Vol. 3 (1990), 13.

Alfred E. Senn

YEMEN, SOVIET RELATIONS WITH (1928-1991). Throughout much of the Cold War the Soviet Union supported an anti-Western, revolutionary foreign policy orientation in North and South Yemen. Moscow apparently hoped that revolution would spread from the Yemens to Saudi Arabia and the other monarchies of the Arabian Peninsula. While the Soviet Union did achieve a substantial degree of influence in both Yemens, attempts to spread revolution to other parts of the peninsula failed. By the end of the Cold War Moscow essentially had abandoned its position in the Yemens.

Located at the southwestern corner of the Arabian Peninsula, Yemen had been divided into two spheres of influence during the nineteenth century by the Ottoman and British Empires. North Yemen became independent in 1918 after the collapse of the Ottoman Empire at the end of World War I.

In 1928 the USSR established diplomatic relations with the absolute monarch (imam) of North Yemen with whom Moscow shared a common anti-British foreign policy. In 1928 the USSR and Yemen also signed a ten-year treaty of friendship. Although the treaty was renewed for another ten years in 1938, the entire Soviet diplomatic mission to Yemen was recalled that year. Relations were not restored until 1955, when a five-year treaty of friendship was signed. In 1956 the USSR and North Yemen reached a trade agreement, and the USSR began supplying weapons to the Imam's government.

Despite its good relations with the royalist regime, Moscow immediately recognized the new republican government which came to power as a result of a coup d'etat on 26 September 1962. The coup had been organized with the support of Egypt (then the United Arab Republic), which under Nasser was Moscow's primary ally in the Arab world. Over the next five years the Soviet Union provided substantial military assistance to Egypt's military effort to defend the new Yemen Arab Republic (YAR) in a civil war against Saudi-backed royalist opposition forces.

Although the USSR and YAR signed a treaty of friendship in 1964 Moscow sought to avoid offending Egypt by competing with it for influence in North Yemen. YAR sought a direct arms supply from Moscow, but the Soviets complied with Egypt's demands that Moscow route military assistance to YAR through Cairo.

In the aftermath of Egypt's defeat by Israel in the June 1967 Middle East War, Nasser no longer was willing to continue the long counter-insurgency effort in North Yemen. He agreed to withdraw his troops from North Yemen in return for a cessation of Saudi support to the royalists. After Egyptian forces departed royalist forces surrounded the capital, Sanaa, and laid siege to it in December 1967. As a result of direct Soviet military assistance, including Soviet pilots flying combat missions for YAR, the siege was broken in February 1968.

Despite this direct Soviet involvement in the affairs of the North, Soviet-North Yemeni relations cooled in 1968. This occurred partly because the republican government became more conservative and improved its relations with Saudi Arabia, which helped the republicans end the civil war in 1970. It also occurred because Moscow turned its attention to the new radical regime that had emerged in South Yemen.

Local opposition to British rule in South Yemen began in the 1950s and developed into an armed insurgency by 1963. There were two primary opposition groups: a Nasserist one supported by Egyptian forces in North Yemen and a Marxist one. Until British forces withdrew from South Yemen in November 1967, Moscow did not aid the Marxist group but favored the Nasserist one which its Egyptian allies backed. Upon withdrawal of Egyptian forces from North Yemen the Nasserist group in the South lost its main source of military support. The British also focused their counter-insurgency efforts on the Nasserist group. As a result, it was the Marxist group that came to power on 30 November 1967 after the British withdrew.

The new regime in the South supported a Marxist insurgency in Oman, its neighbor to the east, and had poor relations with Saudi Arabia and North Yemen. Saudi Arabia and YAR supported the opponents of South Yemen, which became known as the People's Democratic Republic of Yemen (PDRY) and vice versa. The two Yemens fought brief border wars with each other in 1972 and 1979.

South Yemeni support for revolution against its neighbors earned it the enmity of those neighbors and of the West. South Yemen turned increasingly to the Soviet Union for support which gave it military and economic assistance. The South Yemeni regime also moved closer to the USSR as a result of coups in 1969 and 1978, the latter involving considerable violence.

After the 1978 coup, the pro-Chinese wing of the ruling party was eliminated. A staunchly pro-Soviet leader, 'Abd alFattah Isma'il, gained full power. He in particular promoted revolution in neighboring states, even though the insurgency against Oman collapsed in 1975 and Saudi Arabia never experienced one. Under Isma'il's leadership, the PDRY signed a treaty of friendship and cooperation with Moscow in 1979. Moscow also acquired access to naval and air facilities in South Yemen.

While the Soviets progressively gained influence in the South during the 1970s, their relations with the North deteriorated. During the border war between the Yemens in the spring of 1979 North Yemen requested military assistance from the United States. US President Jimmy Carter announced that Washington would ship almost $500 million worth of weapons to the North.

Since Saudi Arabia agreed to buy these weapons on YAR's behalf, the US did not give them directly to North Yemen. Instead, Washington shipped them to Saudi Arabia, which undertook to send them on to YAR. Once a cease-fire to the North-South border war was arranged in mid-March 1979 after about three weeks of fighting, Saudi Arabia stopped sending the American arms to North Yemen. While fearful of Marxist South Yemen, the Saudis also were concerned about how a heavily-armed North Yemen would behave toward the kingdom.

While the border war had ended, North Yemen faced a new security threat in the form of a South Yemeni-sponsored insurgency against the YAR government. The North appealed to the Saudis to resume the arms shipments and to the United States to send American weapons directly to YAR, but to no avail. In a stunning diplomatic reversal, North Yemen asked for and received large-scale military assistance from the Soviet Union later in 1979. It was primarily with Soviet weapons that North Yemen was able to defeat the South Yemeni-backed Marxist opposition by mid-1982. In 1984 the USSR and YAR signed a twenty-year treaty of friendship and cooperation to replace the treaty they had signed in 1964.

Moscow's decision to support the non-Marxist North Yemeni government's counter-insurgency effort against Marxist rebels appears to have resulted from a general Soviet assessment at the end of the 1970s that Marxist revolution was unlikely to spread beyond South Yemen to the other countries of the Arabian Peninsula. Moscow at this time launched a diplomatic campaign to improve relations with Saudi Arabia and the other conservative monarchies of the region. This effort was hindered by South Yemeni leader Isma'il's support for opposition forces in North Yemen and continuing call for revolution in Oman—even though the insurgency there had been defeated in 1975.

On 21 April 1980 the hard-line Isma'il was ousted by a more moderate Marxist, 'Ali Nasir Muhammad. Moscow immediately welcomed the new leader, whose conciliatory foreign policy toward the neighboring states was more in line with Soviet diplomacy.

The leadership of the PDRY's ruling Yemeni Socialist Party (YSP) remained divided between hard-line and moderate factions. The hard-line faction became worried that 'Ali Nasir's policy of allowing increasing numbers of Western oil and other enterprises to operate in South Yemen would result in weakening socialism there. In early 1985 the Soviets allowed the former hard-line leader Isma'il, who had gone to Moscow after his ouster in 1980, to return to South Yemen.

Moscow's motive for doing this remains unclear. Perhaps the Soviet leadership thought that it could manipulate the rivalry between the two leaders in order to ensure South Yemeni compliance with Soviet policy preferences. But if this was Moscow's reasoning, it turned out to be incorrect.

On 13 January 1986 a fierce civil war erupted between the Isma'il and the 'Ali Nasir factions of the ruling party. In approximately two weeks Isma'il and most of his senior allies were killed, 'Ali Nasir and his allies were defeated and fled to North Yemen, approximately 10,000 South Yemenis (of whom 4,000 were members of the YSP) died, and the South Yemeni capital, Aden, suffered extensive damage. The war ended relatively quickly mainly because, after some initial hesitation, Soviet armed forces present in the PDRY provided assistance to the forces opposing 'Ali Nasir and because Moscow warned all other countries not to interfere in the conflict.

The new hard-line regime that came to power in Aden continued to pursue a moderate policy toward the neighboring states of the Arabian Peninsula—a policy which Moscow wanted it to pursue. This new regime, however, soon became factionalized. Paralysis in decision-making, slow recovery from the 1986 civil war, and declining Soviet assistance all served to make the regime increasingly unpopular.

Apparently as a result of Moscow's acquiescence in the down-fall of communism in Eastern Europe during the autumn of 1989, the South Yemeni leadership concluded that the USSR would not act to save its regime. On 22 May 1990 the North and South merged into a united Republic of Yemen. The leadership of the more populous North became the dominant force in the new government; the non-Marxist president of the North became president of united Yemen.

Moscow made no effort to halt the merger. By the end of 1991 Moscow retained only marginal influence and interest in Yemen.

Bibliography: John Baldry, "Soviet Relations with Saudi Arabia and the Yemen, 1917-1938," *Middle Eastern Studies*, Vol. 20 (January 1984), 53-80. Norman Cigar, "Soviet-South Yemeni Relations. The Gorbachev Years," *Journal of South Asian and Middle Eastern Studies*, Vol. 12 (Summer 1989), 3-38. Fred Halliday, *Revolution and Foreign Policy* (Cambridge, 1990). Mark N. Katz, *Russia and Arabia* (Baltimore, 1986). Stephen Page, *The USSR and Arabia* (London, 1971).

Mark N. Katz

YIDDISH LANGUAGE IN RUSSIA AND THE SOVIET UNION. The major language of Ashkenazic Jewry, including of most Jews in Russia and the Soviet Union. Ashkenaz is the name used in medieval Jewish texts for the Jewish cultural area associated with Germanic territory. During subsequent Jewish history the term Ashkenazim refers to the descendants of these settlements.

The beginnings of Yiddish, like the genesis of Ashkenaz, are usually traced back to the ninth century when Jews from old French and old Italian cultural areas settled in the region of the Rhine and Moselle rivers. Although the first identified written Yiddish text dates from 1272, socio-historical information suggests earlier origins. Despite devastations caused by the Crusades, plagues, and local expulsions, the German Jewish settlements expanded to include not only a variety of locations in southern German lands but also Prague in western Slavic territory. By the thirteenth century, mainly in response to the invitation of Polish nobility, Yiddish-speaking Jews from West and Central Europe settled in Poland, Lithuania, and western Ukraine. By the beginning of the eighteenth century this movement shifted the center of Ashkenaz to Eastern Europe. Russia acquired most of these territories after the partitions of Poland (1772-1795) and the Napoleonic wars, putting under tsarist rule the largest Jewish community in the world at that time.

Scholars and speakers alike characterize Yiddish as a fusion language, made up of components derived from the stock languages and cultures: Germanic, Hebrew and Aramaic, Romance, and Slavic. Like all languages and cultures, Yiddish is an integrated, interlocking whole; consequently, it is not always simple to ascribe language elements to the different components. In particular the role of the Slavic languages in the evolution of Yiddish has provoked scholarly controversy. The neighboring Slavic languages and cultures having the greatest influence on the development of Yiddish were Polish, Ukrainian, and Belorussian. These were the languages spoken in the Pale of Settlement, coinciding with the borders of the old Polish kingdom, the area to which Jewish residence was restricted in the Russian Empire. Within the Jewish community the Yiddish language maintained a functionally separate (diglossic) relationship with Hebrew, which generally was reserved for religious and communal functions. As the language of everyday discourse and folklife and folklore, Yiddish was subjected to denigration and scorn, both from within and without the Jewish community. Nevertheless in the 1897 census 97 percent of Russian Jewry declared Yiddish as their mother tongue.

During the nineteenth century modern societal functions for Yiddish developed in Congress Poland and other parts of the Russian Empire despite restrictions imposed by the regime on publishing, theatrical performance, and education in the language. In the nineteenth century the literary language that evolved was no longer archaic and Germanized but reflected the spoken language more closely, especially including the Slavic component of Yiddish of Eastern Europe. A full range of modern belles-lettres emerged, aided by a weekly newspaper, The Voice of the Messenger (Kol mevaser), started in Odessa in 1862 by Aleksandr Tsederboym. Yehoshua-Mordkhe Lifshits published a Russian-Yiddish dictionary in 1869 and a Yiddish-Russian dictionary in 1876. By the beginning of the twentieth century the functions of Yiddish included popular theater, revolutionary propaganda, and secular education. Although the first Yiddish dailies appeared in the United States at the end of the nineteenth century, it was not until 1903 that The Friend (Der fraynd) was launched in St. Petersburg. Yet despite governmental restrictions much of modern, secular Jewish culture based on Yiddish and Hebrew took form within the Russian Empire.

During the years following the Russian revolution Yiddish-language institutions—schools, newspapers, courts, soviets, and workers' cooperatives—flowered in the regions with sizable Ashkenazic Jewish populations. These included Ukraine, Belorussia, and to a lesser extent the Russian republic. In the 1930s Yiddish institutions also were formed in Birobidzhan, the Jewish autonomous region in the Soviet Far East.

For many of these purposes new terminologies were created. In Yiddish as in other non-Russian languages of the Soviet Union government-sponsored language planning took place. This was a collaborative effort involving writers, journalists, teachers, lawyers, judges, engineers, and Communist party leaders as well as linguists. Stylistic recommendations were based on diverse sources: innovations of Yiddish belles-lettres of the previous century, the Jewish workers' movement of tsarist Russia, and postrevolutionary developments in the Russian language. The hegemony of the Yiddish language within the Jewish community was strikingly new for Jewish culture, since synagogues and religious schools were closed and secular Hebrew literature and theater were suspended. Although competition from Hebrew culture was eliminated, the influence of the dominant high status language, Russian, grew. The leaders of the Communist party's Jewish sections, which existed from 1918 to 1930, best illustrated the ambivalence toward Yiddish. Although active in building the new Yiddish institutions, they often spoke Russian at home, sent their children to Russian schools, and privately encouraged linguistic assimilation.

During the 1920s and 1930s issues relating to standards for Yiddish as a language of culture were discussed in the press and at language conferences. A multiplicity of standards was adopted at different times for various purposes, ranging from the living language of the uneducated folk, to a Russified Yiddish, to the sophisticated style of certain authors. This variation and vacillation reflected adjustment to specific societal needs, adherence to short-lived political pressures, and avoidance of strict loyalty to a position which party officials might vilify.

Most Yiddish language planners and cultural leaders were independent, nonparty members. The outstanding linguistic researchers and planners included Nokhm Shtif, the expert stylist and literary historian, who led the Philological Section of the Institute for Jewish Proletarian Culture at the Ukrainian Academy of Sciences in Kiev from 1926 until his death in 1933; his successor, Elye Spivak, pedagogue, morphologist, and authority on the lexicon and specialized terminologies; Mordkhe Veynger, dialectologist, who headed the corresponding institute in Minsk, Belorussia, from 1925 until his death in 1929; and Ayzik Zaretski, dean of Yiddish grammarians, whose *Practical Grammar* (Praktishe gramatik, 1926) remained a model into the 1990s.

Orthographic reform, because of its visual, symbolic power, became the most debated issue regarding Yiddish language in the Soviet Union. After the revolution, the spelling of the Hebrew component of Yiddish was naturalized. An approximation of phonemic spelling replaced the traditional practice in which, like the Hebrew model, vowels were missing. In addition, in the late 1920s spelling was simplified by eliminating special consonants used only at the end of words. This coincided with the pressure for Soviet cultural workers to distance themselves from their compatriots in the West. In the 1930s Yiddish cultural leaders in the Soviet Union used the term Soviet Yiddish, but from an historical perspective change within the living language was quite conservative and the language and culture shared most elements with Yiddish across the globe. Effects of the planner's tendencies on the language included greater receptivity to the influence of modern German than was the case in the West and to the prevalent syntactic influence of contemporary Russian that resulted in the use of multiple clauses and positioning the adjectival determinant after the adjective. But more radical reforms such as purging all Hebrew elements from Yiddish, suggested briefly by planners around 1930, were never accepted.

Yiddish flourished in the USSR as a language of literature, the arts, and education between the world wars largely because of governmental support, which did not exist in other parts of the world. Several Yiddish cultural and political leaders and authors were arrested, charged as enemies of the state, and executed during the late 1930s. Yiddish linguists did not share the fate of their co-territorial contemporaries, who were persecuted for their work on the Belorussian and Ukrainian languages in the early 1930s. Although Yiddish language institutions were dismantled during the late 1930s, the government did not halt all public cultural activity until the late 1940s. The massive arrest of writers and cultural leaders was followed by the secret trial and execution of twenty-four of the best known personalities, including the linguist Spivak, on 12 August 1952 in Moscow's Lubianka prison.

Starting in the late 1950s, the government permitted Yiddish song concerts and book publishing, and since 1961 literary activity centered around the new journal Soviet Homeland (Sovetish heymland). The newspaper Birobidzhan Star (Birobidzhaner shtern) continued to publish, but with little original material of Jewish cultural interest. This stood in stark contrast with the myriad Yiddish publications and cultural events of the earlier period. In 1979 Yiddish classes began in Birobidzhan, home to a small Jewish population, and a Yiddish primer was published there in 1982. Monthly Yiddish lessons in Russian were introduced in 1969 in Sovetish heymland, and a Russian-Yiddish dictionary, in preparation for forty years, was published in 1984. A group of young writers, some of whom attended advanced courses in Yiddish literature, clustered around Sovetish heymland in the 1980s. The Jewish nationalistic movement that arose in the late 1960s sparked an interest in Hebrew and in Israel, but not Yiddish. Nevertheless, starting with political liberalization in 1989, Yiddish cultural clubs appeared in many parts of the Soviet Union. A Yiddish day school was founded in Riga, Latvia. Limited Yiddish instruction developed within the Soviet Union, and Jewish institutions abroad provided teachers and seminars.

Census data registers a dramatic decrease in the use of Yiddish by Soviet Jews, as the following figures, adjusted for border changes, show. The percentage of those declaring Yiddish their mother tongue declined from 73 in 1926, to 41 in 1939 and 18 in 1959. Uncorrected figures for later years, 18 percent in 1970 and 14 percent in 1979, tell the same story.

Although census data on language are difficult to interpret and often represent attitudes and solidarity rather than language use, the dramatic decrease is evident, especially when contrasted with the situation in the Russian Empire (97 percent in 1897). Studies on immigrants to the West in the 1970s and 1980s showed that maintenance of Yiddish was greater in cities in Ukraine and in the territories acquired during World War II, such as Latvia, Lithuania, and Moldavia than in Moscow and Leningrad. Yiddish in the Soviet Union, which had exhibited outstanding cultural achievements in belles-lettres and theater, was maintained by Ashkenazic Jews in only a limited fashion as a language of the home and the family.

See Also: YIDDISH LITERATURE

Bibliography: Solomon A. Birnbaum, "Soviet Yiddish," *Soviet Jewish Affairs*, 9 (1979), 29-41; David E. Fishman, "The Politics of Yiddish in Tsarist Russia," *From Ancient Israel to Modern Judaism. Essays in Honor of Marvin Fox*, ed. by Jacob Neusner, Ernest S. Frerichs, and Nahum M. Sarna, 4 vols. (Atlanta, 1989), 155-171; Rakhmiel Peltz, "The Dehebraization Controversy in Soviet Yiddish Language Planning. Standard or Symbol?" *Readings in the Sociology of Jewish Languages*, ed. by Joshua A. Fishman (Leiden, 1985), 125-150; Rakhmiel Peltz and Mark Kiel, "Di Yiddish-Imperye. The Dashed Hopes for a Yiddish Cultural Empire in the Soviet Union," *Sociolinguistic Perspectives on Soviet National Languages. Their Past, Present and Future*, ed. by Isabelle T. Kreindler (Amsterdam, 1985), 277-309; Mordkhe Shekhter, "Dos loshn fun *Sovetish heymland*," *Yidishe shprakh* 29 (1969), 10-42; 30 (1971), 32-65.

Rakhmiel Peltz

YIDDISH LITERATURE. Literature of East European Jewry. With the Yiddish language, Yiddish literature provided a cultural identity for Jews of Eastern Europe generally and of Russian and Russian-dominated Poland in particular. In more recent times Jewish emigration has spread its influence beyond its original base to America and to Israel.

Although old Yiddish literature developed first in Germany and northern Italy in the Middle Ages and the Renaissance, modern Yiddish literature is the creation of eastern European Jewry. By the end of the eighteenth century eastern European Jewry began to dominate Yiddish cultural productivity, spurred on by the European Enlightenment. In the nineteenth century the Jewish Enlightenment movement, the Haskalah, disseminated Western ideals in Yiddish texts while satirizing religious obscurantism, particularly the Khasidim, a mass popular movement of the mid-eighteenth century which started in Podolia, with possible links to the eighteenth-century schismatics in Russian Orthodoxy. Modern Yiddish literature only emerged as a self-conscious, aesthetic, and social force in the late nineteenth century. Whereas the classical era spanned the years 1860 to 1914, the period from 1918 to 1940, although influenced by ideological and political factors, revealed the full sophistication and modernist tendencies of the literature. The catastrophe of European Jewry in World War II, the suppression of Yiddish culture in the USSR during the latter years of the Stalinist era by 1948, and the continuous acculturation of Jews in the Americas and Israel (into Hebrew) limited further creativity in Yiddish literature.

Old Yiddish Literature. The recovery of Old Yiddish literature is the accomplishment of the eastern European Jewish pioneering scholars of the 1920s Max Weinreich (1894-1969), Max Erik (1898-1937), Meyer Viner (1893-1941), and Israel Tsinberg (1873-1939), whose articles, histories, and critical editions revealed a literary inheritance reaching back to the medieval period. The earliest examples are epic fragments and biblical poems found in a 1382 codex. Two major sources were German popular literature and Hebraic religious material, the *Pentateuch*, *Talmud*, and *Midrashim*. The poetry adopted German stanzaic structures and meters and often knightly romance matter devoid of all

Christological allusions, such as Elia Levita's (1469-1549) legendary *The Bovo Book* (Bovo Bukh, printed 1541) and *Paris and Vienna* (Paris un Viene, 1594). Biblical epics like Moshe Esrim Vearba's *The Samuel Book* (Shmuel Bukh, 1548) and *The Book of Angels* (Melokhim-Bukh, 1543) also flourished. Certain ethical tracts and homelitic texts often were reprinted: the anonymous *Book of Tales* (Mayse-Bukh, 1602); the *Brantshpigl* (1602) by Moshe ben Hanoch Altshul; the ever popular *Tsena Urena* (1616) by Jacob ben Isaac Ashkenazi (1550-1625), the woman's handbook (free translations and homilies on the Hebrew bible) into the twentieth century; and Tkines (16th century), devotional prayers for women, ascribed to the legendary Sarah bas Tuvim. Glückl of Hameln (1646-1724) chronicled in her unique *Memoirs* (Zikhroynes, 1913) the life of a Jewish wife and business woman.

The origins of Yiddish theater emerged in the seventeenth and eighteenth centuries with the Purim play (Purimshpil), Jewish "mummer" plays performed by Yeshiva students and later folk actors. They were witty dramatizations of the biblical Esther story with topical allusions.

A large hagiographic literature developed about the Khassidic rabbis such as *In Praise of the Baal Shem Tor* (Shivhei ha Besht, 1815). The Rabbi Nakhman of Bratslav (1772-1810) composed the mystic *Tales* (Sippure Masiot, 1815), fusing folk narrative and Khasidic lore which influenced modern Yiddish short story writing.

At first the Jewish adherents of the Haskalah in Eastern Europe Mendel Lefin (1749-1826) and Joseph Perl (1773-1839) wrote Yiddish texts to satirize the Khassidic community and open traditional Jewry to Western forms and liberal values.

Haskalah literature served as a conduit by adapting Western forms into Yiddish. Isaac Meyer Dik (1814-1893) built a vast audience for his moral tales as did Israel Aksenfeld and Abraham Baer Gottlober. A contemporary, Shloyme Ettinger, wrote the first Yiddish comedy, Serkele, in the 1830s and Abraham Goldfaden (1840-1908), the father of Yiddish theater, debuted in it (1862).

Goldfaden established the modern Yiddish theater in Jassy, Romania in 1876. By fusing text, spectacle, and music into "operettas" and by building a repertoire around Jewish folk types and heroes of Jewish history and Bible, he not only entertained but also stirred Jewish national patriotism and reinforced Jewish moral values while pursuing Haskalic ideals of modernizing East European Jewry. Many of his works continue to be adapted and performed and his songs have entered Jewish folklore. He moved to New York City (1887) and helped develop Yiddish theatre there after all performances in Yiddish were banned by the tsarist regime. This ban was lifted in 1908.

Modern Yiddish Literature. In the classical period (1862-1917) almost all Yiddish writings first appeared in journals. The first journal was Voice of the Messenger (Kol Mevasar, 1862-1872) which helped standardize modern literary Yiddish and introduced new writers. Mendele Mokher Sforim (Sholem Abramovitch, 1836-1917), traditionally dubbed "the grandfather" of modern Yiddish literature, first appeared in its pages with The Mannikin (Dos Kleyne Mentshele, 1863), a satire on corruption in communal leadership. Mendele's verve, wicked portraiture, and accurate depiction of the socio-psychological reality, crafted in a unique style, served as a model of Yiddish prose. Other successful loosely constructed novels, *The Mare* (Di Klyatshe, 1873) and *Fishke the Lame* (Fishke der Krume, 1868-1888), depicted the downtrodden condition of Eastern European Jewry and its inability to reform itself when faced with internal and external pressures. The picaresque novel, *Travels of Benjamin the Third* (Benyomin Hashlishi, 1878), contrasts ironically Jewish utopic dreams with the hostile reality of tsarist Russia. His autobiographic narrative *Reb Khoyim's Son Shloyme* (Shloyme Reb Khayims) distilled the life of many Jewish youths in the Jewish settlements (shtetl). Mendele established the shtetl and its depiction as the focus of classical Yiddish literary concerns. Yitskhok Yoel Linetsky's *The Polish Lad* (Dos Polishe Yingl, 1867) continued the satire of religious obscurantism, but Mendele's other contemporaries, Yakob Dinezon, Shomer (Nakhum Shaykevitsh) and Mordkhe Spekter preferred highly sentimental fiction.

Sholem Aleichem (Sholem Rabinovitsh, 1859-1916) is considered the most original and most cherished Yiddish author. His massive array of Jewish characters in various genres captured Jewish shtetl life in all its daily complexity. He developed a tragicomic humor which fused the Gogolian grotesque with Chekhovian empathy. His narrating persona engages the reader with the intimacy, warmth, and familiarity which marks the Sholem Aleichem style. Both Marxist and Western critics praise his formidable narrative skills, acute social analyses, and witty characterizations. *Menakhem Mendl* (1892-1913), an epistolary novel, describes the comic trials of a would-be capitalist writing to an uncomprehending traditional wife. This work serves as a subtext to Ilf and Petrov's *The Twelve Chairs*. *Tevye the Dairyman* (Tevye der Milkhiger, 1894-1916) illuminates a man and his shtetl world buffeted by modernity through comic and despairing monologues. This, Sholem Aleichem's most beloved prose, reached a world audience as the musical *Fiddler on the Roof* (1964). *Motl Peyse, the Cantor's Son* depicts a child immigrant's wry passage from the shtetl to America. Many stories revolve around Kasrilevke, the quintessential shtetl Aleichem created, using his preferred genre, the monologue. His last unfinished work, *From the Fair* (Furem Yarid), provides an inventive autobiography for the pen name, Sholem Aleichem. The author's death in New York brought out two hundred thousand mourners.

Yitskhok Leybush Peretz (1852-1915), the third classic author debuted with *Monish* (1888), a satiric poem which furthered lyric growth in Yiddish. His home in Warsaw became a mecca for young writers. As the most intellectual, experimental, and theoretical among the classic writers, Peretz sought to create a modern Yiddish culture fusing contemporary European forms with Judaic ethics by reworking Jewish folk matter, which he found in scorned Khasidic hagiography. This resulted in his best short story collections, *Hasidic* (Khasidish, 1908) and *Folktales* (Folkstimlikhe Geshikhtn, 1909). His verse dramas, At Night on the Old Market Square (Bay Nakht Oyfn Altn Mark) and The Golden Chain (Di Goldenekeyt), sought to rekindle Jewish spirituality and communal vitality. The Peretz circle included Abraham Reyzin (1880-1953), the short story writer in the Chekhovian tradition; Sholem Asch (1880-1957), who became internationally known for his conventional Christological novels but who treated first the grimy shtetl life in *The Shtetl* (Dos Shtetl, 1904), *Motke the Thief* (Motke Ganev, 1917), and later New York immigrant life in *Uncle Moses* (1918); and I.M. Vaysenberg whose *The Shtetl* (Dos Shtetl, 1906) responded to Sholem Asch's treatment. Lesser figures included David Pinski, later a dramatist in America, Mordecai Spektor, Hersh David Nomberg (1876-1927), and Yone Rosenfeld.

Yiddish poetry began with wedding bards and folk poets like Mark Varshavsky (1848-1907) and Mordecai Gebirtig (1877-1942), whose songs still are sung. Shimon Samuel Frug's (1860-1916) verse marks the transition into conscious artistry.

The Sweatshop Poets of New York City, all immigrants from Eastern Europe, David Edelshtat, Yosef Bovshover, Morris Vinchevsky and especially Morris Rosenfeld (1862-1923) made the Yiddish lyric a vehicle for the social and personal aspirations of the immigrant workers by voicing the Jews' communal suffering, exploitation, and hopeful future. Then followed poets stressing more individual experience: Abraham Liessin, editor of the major literary journal The Future (Tsukunft), Yehoash (Solomon Bloomgarden, 1872-1927) who introduced contemporary themes and forms from world literature and completed a modern Yiddish Bible translation, and Yosef Rolnik (1879-1955) who introduced old country nostalgia into his verse.

The literary movement The Young (Di Yunge, 1907-1926) in New York City established the Yiddish impressionist lyric as a personal esthetic object, stressing form and effect with an appreciation of musicality and understatement. The novelist David Ignatov was the nominal leader. Their main journal, Writings (Shriftn, 1912-1926), published their leading poets: Ruvin Iceland (1884-1955), a miniaturist, Zishe Landau (1889-1937), and the humorist Moyshe Nadir. Mani Leyb (1884-1953), the outstanding Di Yunge poet, fused form, musicality, and mood into intense sonnets. I.I. Shvarts composed an epic, *Kentucky* (1925), about a Jewish immigrant peddler. The most original of Di Yunge was Moyshe Leyb Halpern (1886-1932) whose self-deprecating, savagely ironic, strident verse is built on chains of personal and metaphoric associations revealing his loneliness, anguish, and cries for social justice. The best Di Yunge novelist was Yosef Opotoshu who wrote *In Polish Woods* (In Poylishe Velde, 1921), but Lamid Shapiro's prose style competed with him in his short stories about pogroms. Isaac Raboy's *The Jewish Cowboy* (Der Yidisher Koboy, 1942) captured the immigrant experience in a lyric mode.

Before World War I, on New York's Second Avenue, Yiddish theatre flourished free of censorship and awash with eager immigrants from Russia, as well as Poland and Romania. The dramatist Yankev Gordon (1853-1909) wrote Mirele Efros or God Man and the Devil (Got, Mensh un Tayvil), and plays by Sholem Asch, Leon Kobrin, David Pinski, and Perets Hirshbeyn were produced, as were the verse dramas of H. Leyvik (1888-1962) such as The Golem (Der Golem, 1921).

New writings from Kiev (1908-1914) brought a fresh subtlety of style in prose, refined psychological depiction and original structural strategies and solutions. David Bergelson (1884-1952), the finest stylist in Yiddish, wrote impressionistic stories of shtetl decay in silvergrey tints. His masterpiece, After All Is Said and Done (Nokh Alemen, 1913), portrays an emancipated heroine, a Jewish Anna Karenina, trapped between shtetl ennui and vapid urban modernity. *Yosef Shur* (1918), a novella, analyzed the ironic distance sharply separating secular city Jewry from their traditional country cousins. A quality of Oblomovshchina—a lethargy exemplified by Ivan Aleksandrovich Goncharov's famous character Oblomov—glazed all of Bergelson's pre-Soviet writing. Der Nister (Pinkhas Kaganovitch, 1884-1950) constructed symbolic short stories collected in *Thought* (Gedakht, 1922) and *From My Possessions* (Fun Mayne Giter, 1929), inspired by the mystical tales of Nakhman of Bratslav. Der Nister's spiraling syntax, Aesopian language and stylistic elaborations grip the reader as much as the unique imaginative realms he spins.

By World War I Yiddish literature was firmly established, and at an international conference on language, held in 1908 at Czernowitz, Austria, the participants declared Yiddish and Hebrew the national languages of the Jews.

Soviet Yiddish Literature. The Russian revolution unleashed Yiddish creativity in every genre. Bergelson and Der Nister drew new talent to their journal, Our Own (Eygns, 1918, 1920), in Kiev. Three major poets debuted: David Hofshtetyn (1889-1952), Leyb Kvitko (1890-1952), and Perets Markish (1895-1952). Their poetry expressed the joy of freedom and discovery; they stressed nature, the body, release from the past, and utopic aspirations. In 1919 theoretical debates on the function of literature pitted Bergelson, defending the autonomy of art against Moshe Litvakov (1875-1937), the Bolshevik critic, who demanded that art serve the revolution. By December 1920 the Kiev-grupe, a loose association of secular writers of socialist tendencies devoted to the use of Yiddish as the language of modern Jewry, stripped of its cultural autonomy by the local Bolsheviks, left Kiev.

In the Soviet period Moscow, Kiev, and Minsk became the chief centers of Yiddish literary production. In Moscow a group of "fellow travelers" formed about the journal Stream (Shtrom, 1922-1924) which possessed an international modernist outlook. Influenced by Russian post-Symbolism and futurism, the founders included the critic Yeheskel Dobrushin (1883-1952), the prose writer Shmuel Godiner (1883-1942), and the poets Aron Kushnirov (1890-1949) and David Hofshteyn (1889-1952). They drew together the main Soviet Yiddish poets Shmuel Rosin (1890-1941), Ezra Fininberg (1889-1946), and Shmuel Halkin (1897-1960); the party poet, Itsik Fefer (1900-1952); and the Minsk poets Selik Akselrod (1904-1941) and Izi Kharik (1898-1937). Their verse treated the Civil War pogroms, nostalgia for the old shtetl, urbanism and optimistic faith in the future. Litvakov, named head of the Moscow Yiddish daily Truth (Emes), attacked the journal's orientation and brought about its demise. The Minsk critics Ber Orshansky, Yashe Bronshteyn and Khatzkl Duniets were even more fanatical communists who established the rules for the new Yiddish proletarian literature. Their dangerous vituperations against nonconforming Soviet Yiddish poets are still hair-raising rhetorical performances.

Soviet Yiddish prose passed quickly from impressionism to socialist realism and affected the works of Shmuel Persov (1890-1952) and Itsik Kipnis (1896-1974). The thirties brought strict conformity: "Soviet in content, Yiddish in form." Even Bergelson in *On the Banks of the Dniepr* (Baym Dniepr, 1932, 1939) and Der Nister in *The Family Mashber* (Di Mishpokhe Mashber, 1939, 1948) squirmed cleverly but ultimately conformed. A unique prose masterpiece, *Zelmenyaner* (Part I, 1931; Part II, 1935), by the poet Moshe Kulbak (1896-1940), portrayed in heartfelt humor a provincial Jewish family clumsily adapting to Soviet realities. The 1937 great purge swallowed Kulbak, the Minsk writers and critics, Litvakov, and others. All Jewish national allusions dissolved in the literature, replaced by praise of the Communist party and of Stalin.

Soviet Yiddish theater, founded as a studio by Aleksander Granovsky in Petrograd (1918), became in Moscow (1919) the Yiddish Chamber Theater (Goset). Reworking plays of Goldfaden, Sholem Aleichem, Perets and Asch, with décors by M. Chagall, N. Altman, R. Falk, Aleksandr Grigorievich Tyshler (1893-) and Israel Rabinovitch (1894-1964), and music by A. Krein, L. Pulver and M. Milner, and joining unique ensemble acting with two master actors, Salomen Mikhoels and Benjamin Zuskin, Goset displayed Soviet Yiddish culture at its best. Many poets wrote popular plays: L. Resnik, P. Markish, M. Kulbak, and Shmuel Halkin. The Kiev Yiddish theater, under Efrayim Loyter, followed Goset, but the Minsk Yiddish theater stressed leftist revolutionary plays. A Yiddish state theater studio also thrived in Birobidzhan. Ten Yiddish theaters were functioning throughout the Soviet Union in 1939, and seven in 1946. In 1948 the murder of Mikhoels by agents of the secret police initiated the closing of all Yiddish cultural institutions. Most Yiddish writers were arrested and later shot on 12 August 1952 in Lubianka Prison.

In 1961 the Soviet government permitted one journal to appear, Soviet Homeland (Sovetish Heymland), of which Aron Vergelis (1918-) was editor-in-chief. It serialized Natan Zabare's novel set in medieval Provence, *The Revolving Wheel* (Galgal Hakhozeyr, 1972-77), and Eli Shekhtman's *Evening* (Erev, 1962), later completed in Israel. Between 1970 and 1992 only five to eight Yiddish books were published annually and one daily newspaper, Birobidzhan Star (Birobidzhaner Shtern), was printed. In 1992 Sovetish Heymland changed its name to On the Jewish Street (Oyf der yidisher gas), a journal devoted to tying Russian Jews with world Jewry.

Poland and Eastern Europe. The poet, playwright and journalist Moshe Broderzon (1890-1956) with his Yung-Yidish group (1919) in Lodz brought modernism in poetry, art, and theater to Polish Jewry. He organized Khad Gadya, the first Yiddish marionette theater and the little art theaters, Ararat and Shor ha-Bor. By 1922 full blown expressionism appeared in The Street Gang (Di Khalyastre), the journal (1922-1924) and avant garde group so dubbed by Hillel Tseytlin (1872-1943), the leading traditionalist critic of the daily Moment. The stinging hyperbolic verse of P. Markish in *The Mound* (Di Kupe, 1921), the apocalyptic vision of Uri Tsvi Grinberg (1896-1981) in *Mefisto* (1921) and in his own journal, Albatros (1922-1923), and the neo-primitivism of Melekh Ravitsh in *Naked Poems* (Nakete Lider, 1921) electrified the new generation. The major themes were the agony of war, pogroms, the dismal present, and the bleak future. Other participants were the poet Israel Shtern and the realist novelists Oyzer Varshavsky (*The Smugglers* [Di Shmuglers, 1920]) and Israel Joshua Singer (1893-1944) (*The Brothers Ashkenazi* [Di Brider Ashkenazi, 1935]) and Alter Katsisne.

By the late 1920s modernism was waning. The besieged Jewish worker became a central theme in the works of S. Horonchik and Israel Rabon (1900-1941) (*The Street* [Di Gas, 1928]). Yosef Perle (1898-1943) captured the Polish-Jewish condition of the interwar years in *Normative Jews* (Yidn fun a gants yor, 1935). The prose master and Nobel Prize winner (1978), Isaac Bashevis Singer (1904-1991), debuted with his most distinguished novel, *Satan in Goray* (Satn in Goray, 1935), a forerunner of magic realism. He published in Globus, a journal where the poets Yehiel Lerer (1910-1943) and Aaron Tseytlin, the editor, appeared with their mystical verse. A cubist-modernist poetess, Dvoreh Fogel (1902-1942), linked the expressionist movement The Gang (Khalyastre) to the modernist-surrealist Young Vilna (Yung-Vilne, 1934-1936), the last literary movement in Poland. The most talented of these young poets were the surrealist Abraham Sutzkever (1910-), Leyzer Volf (1910-1943), Hirsh Glik (1922-1944), and Khayim Grade (1910-1982), who chronicled this lost Vilna world in *The Abandoned Woman* (The Agunah, 1961).

Yiddish literary production continued in the ghettoes of World War II. Fragments of poems by Miriam Ulinover (1890-1944) remain and Yitskhok Katsenelson's (1866-1944) The Song of the Murdered Jewish People (Dos Lid Funem Oygehargetn Yidishn Folk, 1944) survived complete. Yehiel Yeshayah Trunk (1887-1961) escaped to complete his prose epic, *Poland* (Poyln, 1944-1953). Many autobiographical texts and memoirs of the Holocaust serve as both tragic witnesses and as potent examples of Yiddish belles-lettres.

Yiddish theater flourished in interwar Poland. The Vilna Troupe in Warsaw presented The Dybbuk (Der Dibuk) by S.A. Ansky (Solomon Rappoport, 1863-1920) in 1920, two years before the Hebrew version directed by Vakhtangov and performed in Moscow's Habima theater. By the 1930s over twenty Yiddish companies were active. After the Holocaust the Jewish State Theater (1950-) was founded. Yidbukh (1947-1968) publishing house attempted to revive Yiddish letters but closed after a wave of antisemitic manifestations in 1968.

Romania provided two of the major Yiddish Poets: Eliezar Shteynbarg (1890-1934) with his pessimistic but witty *Fables* (Mesholem, 1932), and Itsik Manger (1901-1969) whose ballads, *The Ballads of Itsik* (Medresh Itsik, 1935-1936), retell biblical stories set in 1900 Carpathian-Jewish folk surroundings. Between the wars Romania was a minor Yiddish cultural center with one town, Lipkan, producing the fabulist Shteynbarg, the dramatist Yacob Shternberg, the novelist Moyshe Altman (1890-), and the poet Eliezar Grinberg. Five Yiddish theaters existed before World War II and one Jewish State Theater in Bucharest during the Communist era.

The United States (1918-1992). Arriving from Siberian exile, H. Leyvik (1888-1962) entered New York Yiddish culture with intense verse (1918) tying personal suffering with Jewish messianism. He encouraged the Introspectivists (In

Zikh) and the journal of the same name (1919-1940). They created a modernist Yiddish American movement fusing imagism, futurism, and expressionism. In free verse or fixed forms, these poets rejected mimesis and sought to reflect the outside world filtered through the authentic Self, using modernist techniques of simultaneity, fragmented imagery, associative thinking, and varied rhythms. Two major poets, A. Leyeles (Aron Glants, 1889-1966), a master of fixed forms and the chief theoretician, together with Yankev Glatshteyn (1896-1971), the quintessential modernist, wrote their manifesto (1920), joined by Nochum Boruch Minkoff (1893-1958) who later produced valuable scholarship on Yiddish poetry. Of the nearly one hundred poets and writers in the movement, Anna Margolin (Rosa Lebensbaum, 1887-1952), and the fiery eroticist, Celia Dropkin (1888-1956), were the outstanding poets of the feminist perspective.

In the 1930s a late Yunge, Abo Shtoltsenberg, and true modernists, Judd Teller (1912-) and Shloyme Shvarts, with Berish Vaynshteyn, a proletarian expressionist, entered Yiddish poetry. The Holocaust and the aftermath turned Yiddish poetry back from the personal to the collective: to remember and to lament. Kadia Molodovsky (1894-1975) captured her grief in prickly verse. Glatshteyn became a national poet. Women poets came to the fore after World War II: Rokhl Korn (1898-), Reyzl Zhikhlinski, and Malke-Heyfets-Tussman (1896-).

The Jewish Art Theater (1918-1950) created by the actor Maurice Shvarts set high theatrical standards and exposed New York City to the modern classics of Eastern Europe. The workers' theater group (Arbeiter Teater Farband, ARTEF, 1923-1940), which complemented the proletarian writers' movement (Proletpen), staged true left-wing social protest productions fusing revolutionary Marxist ideology and Jewish folk traditions with innovating ensemble work, drawing much critical acclaim. These two theaters exposed America to theatrical traditions of the Moscow Art Theater and Soviet agitational and propaganda (agitprop) techniques. Yiddish theater began to wane by World War II due to the Americanization of its audience. Yet art theater productions were still staged by the Folksbine Theater in Manhattan (1915-).

Yiddish literary criticism began with Baal Makhshoves (Isidore Eliashev 1873-1924), Abraham Coralnik (1883-1937) and S. Gorelik. The Russian tradition of civic criticism, which stretched from Vissarion Grigorievich Belinsky in the 1840s to Russia's Silver Age at the turn of the century, affected all Yiddish critics. Their critical essays fused literary appreciation with philosophy, cultural politics, ideology, and sentiment. Widely read, these essayists were concerned with both improving Yiddish esthetic expression and the Jewish condition-in-the-world. Shmuel Niger (1883-1955) exercised the greatest influence on the writers and the general public as the arbiter of taste. A literary critical impressionist, Niger expected art to serve the collective cultural resurgence and opposed the modernists with their personal agendas. Nakhman Mayzel (1887-1966) represented the Yiddish Marxist tradition. He played a major role in helping the Kiev Eygns-grupe and the Kultur-Liga in Warsaw before becoming the editor of the New York leftist journal Yiddish Culture (Yidishe Kultur). Borukh Rivkin (1883-1945), basically an anarchist original, wrote a seminal work *Basic Tendencies of Yiddish Literature in America* (Grunt-tendentsn fun der yidisher literatur in Amerike, 1948). Shlomo Bikl (1896-1969) continued the Niger tradition but emphasized the "Romanian" contribution. Abraham Baer Tabachnik (1902-) provided a last insider's appreciation of his contemporaries. YIVO (Yidishe Visnshaftlikhe Institut), the Jewish Scientific Institute for Social Research founded in Vilna in 1925 and transferred in 1939 to New York City, serves as the archival center today for all critical and scholarly research on Yiddish literature and culture. The passage of the last and oldest newspaper, The Forward (Forverts), from a daily to a bilingual weekly in 1983 symbolizes the fading of Yiddish literature.

Israel. A few pioneers in the 1930s who came from Eastern Europe to rebuild Israel preferred to use Yiddish: Yosef Papernikov, Arye Shamri, and Rikudah Potash. In 1949 Abraham Sutskever, the last surviving major Yiddish poet, created The Golden Chain (Goldenekeyt), the last major Yiddish literary journal worldwide.

The postwar period also brought new poets Moshe Yungman (1922-) and Yankev Fridman. Later the Soviet immigration of the 1970s brought the poets Rokhl Boymvol (1913-), Shloyme Roytman, Meir Kharats, and others. The 1990s immigration has brought a few more poet/survivors. One publishing house still remains, the I.L. Perets Farlag in Tel Aviv.

See Also: YIDDISH LANGUAGE, ZIONISM

Bibliography: In Yiddish: *Leksikon fun der nayer yidisher literatur*, 8 vols. (Biographical Dictionary), 1956-1981; Y. Lubomirski, *Melukhisher Yidisher Teater in Ukrayne* (Kharkov, 1933); Z. Zilbertsvayg, *Leksikon fun yidishn teater*, 5 vols. (Warsaw-Mexico City, 1934-1957); Elias Shulman, *Soviet-Yidish literatur* (New York, 1971); Khone Shmeruk, *Prokim fun der yidisher literatur geshikhte* (Tel Aviv, 1988).

In French: Béatrice Picon-Vallin, *Le Théâtre juif soviétique pendant les années vingt* (Lausanne, 1973); Régine Robin, *L'Amour du Yiddish* (Paris, 1984).

In Russian: *Evreiskaia Entsiklopediia*, 16 vols. (Pg., 1915); A. Sneer, "Evreiskii teatr," *Istoriia Sovetskogo dramaticheskogo teatra*, Vol. 3, (M., 1967), 557-567; L. Tamasin, "Evreiskii teatr," *Istoriia Sovetskogo dramaticheskogo teatra*, Vol. 2, (1966), 430-443.

In German: Claudio Magris, "Randbemerkungen zum heutigen Sinn der jiddischen Literatur," *Neohelicon Acta, Comparationis Litterarum Universarum 1979-1980*, Vol. 7, No. 2, 203-211.

In English: *The Field of Yiddish*, Vols. 1-5 (New York, 1954-); F. Burko, "The Soviet Yiddish Theater in the Twenties" (Ph.D. diss., Southern Illinois University, 1978); Benjamin Harshav, *The Meaning of Yiddish* (Berkeley, 1990), is to be used with caution; Kathryn Hellerstein, "A Question of Tradition. Women Poets in Yiddish," *Handbook of American-Jewish Literature*, ed. by Lewis Fried (Westport, Conn., 1988); Kathryn Hellerstein, "Poetry, Yiddish in America," *Jewish-American History and Culture. An Encyclopedia*, ed. by J. Fishel, S. Pinsker (New York, 1992); Benjamin Hrushovski, "On Free Rhythms in Modern Yiddish Poetry," *The Field of Yiddish*, ed. by Uriel Weinreich (New York, 1954); David Lifson, *The Yiddish Theater in America* (New York,

1965); Sol Liptzin, *A History of Yiddish Theater* (Middle Village, N.Y., 1972); Charles Madison, *Yiddish Literature. Its Scope and Major Writers* (New York, 1968); Nahama Sendrow, *Vagabond Stars. A World History of Yiddish Theater* (New York, 1986); Ruth Wisse, *A Little Love in Big Manhattan* (Cambridge, Mass., 1988); Ruth Wisse, *I.L. Peretz and the Making of Modern Jewish Culture* (Seattle, 1991).

Scholarly Journals of Yiddish Literature: In English: *Yiddish*, and *Prooftexts*; in French, *Pardes*.

Seth L. Wolitz

YOM KIPPUR WAR, SOVIET ROLE IN (1973). Also known as the Arab-Israeli War and the October War. Third war between Israel and its Arab neighbors, the Yom Kippur War of 6-24 October 1973 was one in a series of the "proxy" conflicts in the Cold War in which the United States supported one side and the Soviet Union the other.

Students of Soviet foreign policy actively debated Moscow's role in the Yom Kippur war. Those who saw the Soviet role as being a defensive one point to Moscow's warning the United States prior to the war, Soviet efforts to secure a cease-fire at the beginning of the war, its cooperation with the US to bring about a cease-fire at the end of the war, and the noninvolvement of Soviet troops in the conflict. On the other hand those who see an offensive role point to Moscow's violation of the Basic Principles of Mutual Relations agreement reached with the US in 1972, its failure to push strongly for a cease-fire at the start of the war, its urging of other Arab states to join Egypt and Syria in the war against Israel, its strong support of the Arab oil embargo against the United States, and its threat to intervene in the latter stage of the war.

At the high point of their detente in June 1972 the United States and the Soviet Union signed an agreement titled the Basic Principles of Mutual Relations. Under the agreement the two countries promised to warn each other in case of a threat to the peace, to avoid exacerbating international conflicts, and not to take unilateral advantage of each other. Moscow violated all three of these agreements during the Yom Kippur war.

The Soviet Union had resumed supplying arms to Egypt in early 1973 after the expulsion of the Soviet military from their Egyptian bases in July 1972. The Soviets clearly knew that Egypt and Syria were about to attack Israel, but never formally warned the United States and thus violated the Basic Principles agreement. Several days before the war dependents of Soviet advisors were sent back to the USSR from Egypt. While some interpret this withdrawal as a tacit signal from Moscow to the US that war was imminent, alternative explanations for this action such as a renewed cooling of Soviet-Egyptian relations make the theory of a serious Soviet signal a doubtful one.

Once the war broke out the US called for a cease-fire. Moscow, perhaps fearing a rapid defeat of its Arab clients or acting on a prearranged agreement with Syria, initially concurred but quickly stopped calling for a cease-fire when Egyptian President Anwar Sadat rejected it.

Three days into the war, after the Arab states made impressive military gains both on the Golan Heights (Syria) and in the Sinai (Egypt), the Soviet

Union, in response to Algeria's request for Soviet military aid for the Arab states, urged other Arab states to join Syria and Egypt in the war against Israel. To many observers this appeared to be an effort to exacerbate an already dangerous situation. Those who evaluate Soviet behavior as defensive note that its action was a ploy to avoid direct Soviet intervention. Whatever its motivation, the end result was a Soviet call to widen the war. These were not the actions of a defensively inclined state seeking to contain and limit a conflict; rather they constituted another violation of the Basic Principles agreement.

A further exacerbation of the war came with the Soviet decision to resupply Egypt and Syria with armaments, an action that led the United States to begin a massive effort to resupply Israel. On the diplomatic front the USSR now opposed any cease-fire unless it meant a withdrawal of Israeli forces to the borders Israel held before the June 1967 war. Meanwhile the tide of battle had turned, and by 16 October the Israelis not only had crossed the old cease-fire lines with Syria and moved toward Damascus but also had crossed the Suez Canal and begun to develop a salient that would soon threaten Cairo. On that same day Soviet Premier Aleksei Kosygin, perhaps recognizing the developing crisis in the Egyptian military position, flew to Cairo for three days of talks with Sadat, who continued to deprecate the Israeli canal crossing. Although the Arab military position was now in jeopardy, the Soviet leaders could take comfort from continued "anti-imperialist Arab solidarity." This was demonstrated by an Arab oil embargo against the United States because of its support of Israel. Participating in the embargo were Saudi Arabia, once the closest ally of the United States in the Arab world, Kuwait, and a number of other Arab countries. Radio Moscow cheered the oil embargo. The Soviet Union, in clear contravention of the Basic Principles agreement, sought to gain unilateral advantage from the weakening of the United States and the divisions in the North Atlantic Treaty Organization (NATO) alliance which the oil embargo caused.

The use of the oil weapon could not stop the rapid deterioration in the position of the Egyptian army. This development resulted in US Secretary of State Henry A. Kissinger's trip to the Soviet Union on 20 October at the Soviet leaders' "urgent request." The result of Kissinger's visit was a "cease-fire in place" agreement, a major retreat from the USSR's previous position calling for a return to the 1967 boundaries as a price for the cease-fire. The US-Soviet cease-fire agreement, which the United Nations Security Council approved in the early hours of the morning on 23 October, did not end the hostilities. Both sides, despite their agreement to the cease-fire, continued fighting, and by 24 October Sadat was forced to appeal to both the United States and the Soviet Union to send troops to police the cease-fire.

Egypt was about to suffer a major defeat, which would have meant a major defeat for Soviet prestige as well, for the USSR openly had backed the Arabs. The Soviet leaders apparently decided to pressure Israel and the United States by alerting Soviet airborne troops. At the same time Soviet leader Leonid Ilich Brezhnev sent a stiff note to US President Richard M. Nixon that reportedly stated "I say it straight that if the United States does not find it possible to act together with us in this matter, we should be faced with the necessity urgently to consider the question of taking appropriate steps unilaterally" (Kissinger,

503). While the Soviet leader may have been bluffing, Nixon apparently decided not to take any chances and called a nuclear alert. It now appeared not only that detente had died but that the two superpowers were on the verge of a nuclear confrontation. Brezhnev quickly backed away from his implied threat to intervene unilaterally. The United States, equally unwilling to see the conflict develop further, brought pressure on Israel to stop the Israeli army before it destroyed the surrounded Egyptian Third Army and marched to Cairo. The superpowers then agreed to bring the issue back to the United Nations, and a UN emergency force was established to police the cease-fire.

On balance, despite the risks that Moscow ran on behalf of the Arabs during the war, with the concomitant damage to Soviet-American detente because of its clear violations of the Basic Principles agreement, Soviet gains from the war were ephemeral. The "anti-imperialist" Arab unity engendered by the war collapsed at its end, the oil embargo was lifted several months later and, most damaging of all to Soviet interests, the war provided an opportunity for the skilled diplomacy of Kissinger. Kissinger succeeded in building an American-Egyptian alignment while maintaining US ties to Israel, thus eliminating Soviet political influence in Egypt. He also set the ground work through the Sinai I and Sinai II agreements for the Egyptian-Israeli peace treaty of 1979, thus relegating Moscow to the sidelines of Middle East politics. The USSR had not recovered from this position when it collapsed in December 1991.

Bibliography: For differing views of Soviet behavior during the Yom Kippur war, see Robert O. Freedman, *Soviet Policy Toward the Middle East Since 1970*, 3rd ed. (New York, 1982); Galia Golan, *Yom Kippur and After. The Soviet Union and the Middle East Crisis* (New York, 1977); Alvin Rubinstein, *Red Star on the Nile. The Soviet-Egyptian Influence Relationship Since the June War* (Princeton, 1977); and William Quandt, *Soviet Policy in the October 1973 War* (Santa Monica, Cal., 1976).

Robert O. Freedman

YOUNG BUKHARANS (1910?-1923). A secret society founded around 1910 in Bukhara in the Russian Central Asian province of Turkistan (later divided into Turkmenistan and Uzbekistan) by young intellectuals, minor government officials, small merchants, and students. Influenced by the liberal revolution in Persia in 1906 and the Young Turk revolution in Turkey in 1908, the Young Bukharans eventually allied with the Bolsheviks and succeeded in overthrowing Emir Alim Khan. Their program centered on three goals: educational reform, government reform, and the struggle against religious conservatism and reaction.

The Young Bukharan origins lay in the "new method" (jadid) reform movement which was composed of a number of liberal intellectuals seeking educational reform. Inspired by the 1905 Russian revolution and new ideas among Tatars, many Bukharan reformers attempted to start newspapers and open schools for the emirate's subjects. By 1908 the majority of these endeavors had closed, failed, or moved underground. In 1909 under Russian· pressure Emir Abd al-Ahad (1885-1910) authorized the opening of a new method school. The conservative clergy reacted against what they perceived to be a challenge to

Koranic law (shariat) and launched a verbal attack against the school. The emir ordered the school closed in October of the same year.

In 1910 the new emir, Alim Khan (1910-1920), provided the reformers with encouragement shortly after he ascended the throne. Bowing to the pressures of the reformers, to a clash between Sunnis and Shia Muslims in January of that year, and the tsarist government's threats of annexation, he presented a liberal "manifesto." It had four points designed to eliminate serious abuses in Bukhara's political arena: it forbade gifts to government officials and other dignitaries, it prohibited lesser officials from imposing taxes, it forbade Islamic judges (gazis) from fixing the price of legal deeds at will, and it promised to increase salaries to state officials. But the conservative clergy influenced the population to reject the reformers and their goals. Gifts poured in to government officials, and they showered the emir with like affection. The emir, finding it difficult to comply with his own manifesto, rescinded it.

Shortly thereafter a secret association was founded to combat the continued repression of reform. The Union of Bukhara the Noble (Shirkat-i Bukhara-yi Sharif) had the goal of procuring books for future reformed schools. Another group, Society for the Education of Youth (Jamiyat-i Tarbiyat-i Atfal), merged with Sharif, drawing together many of Bukhara's reform leaders, such as Abdul Rauf Fitrat, Usman Khodzhaev, Abd al-Vahid Burkhanov, Ahmad Makhdum, the wealthy Mirza Muhitdin Mansurov, and Fayzallah Khodzhaev. Many supporters of the reformers were drawn from Bukhara's Jewish community and minority Shia population. Both groups were seeking to end the historic discrimination which had been directed against them.

Fitrat was the ideological leader of the Young Bukharans and his thoughts and actions dominated the movement after 1913. He had the opportunity to further his education in Constantinople and was inspired by the Young Turks. In 1909 he published his first newspaper, A Talk (Munzizira), in Persian. It became the manifesto for the Bukhariote Jadids.

From its inception until the start of the First World War the society remained a clandestine organization reluctantly tolerated by the government. It was organized under strict rules and had a complicated initiation which subjected every candidate to a rigorous background investigation. After its successful completion the candidate was given the chance to express his views before the assembly; the opposition of a single member disqualified the applicant for membership.

In the years between 1910 and 1913 the Jadids operated with little pressure from Bukharan officials or verbal attacks from the emirate's clergy. Numerous reformed schools opened throughout Bukhara, usually in the home of the sponsor. Both Shia and Sunnis opened schools. Often the teaching was in Persian, although one school, started by Mulla Vafa, placed significant emphasis on the Russian language. Enrollment varied and it is uncertain how many children received an education in these schools.

The Jadid press also operated with some degree of freedom. In the four years before the First World War several publications opened. The most influential newspapers were Bukhara-yi Sharif and Turan. Most of the newspapers were financially unsuccessful and usually survived only due to the generous support of wealthy individuals.

In January 1913 the emir's government cracked down on the reformers. Schools and newspapers were banned and no immediate successors were produced. Most Young Bukharans fled to Tashkent, Samarkand or Russian New Bukhara, a Russian settlement bordering Bukhara. At the outbreak of World War I the majority of them were still in exile throughout Turkestan and they had little hope of successfully implementing their ideas. But they continued their secret agitation as best they could.

During the years of exile the movement divided along two lines. The moderate wing advocated limited reforms based on civic freedoms, elimination of fanatical religious leaders, strict control of taxation, and educational reform. The left wing sought radical economic reforms and, in addition to educational reform, demanded that the emir's powers be reduced greatly. It was this latter group that actively used the name "Young Bukharans" and organized themselves into a party. Their central committee included Burkhanov as president, Fitrat as secretary, and U. Khodzhaev as treasurer.

It was not until the February revolution that the Young Bukharans were able to emerge from their illegal status and actively seek reform. The new party turned towards the Provisional Government for support, but none was to be found. Few in Petrograd understood the nature of Bukhara's society and system of government. The Russian government's representative in Bukhara, A. Miller, agreed to intercede with the emir on behalf of the Young Bukharans. A modest manifesto was produced by Miller and signed by the emir in April 1917. The conservative clergy exploded in anger at what they believed to be an infringement upon their traditional role. They had not been consulted, the population did not have the chance to read the manifesto and, worse still, it had been drafted by a Russian infidel. The Young Bukharans attempted to organize a popular demonstration in favor of the reforms. On 8 April 1917 members of the party, at the head of about a thousand marchers, demonstrated in the capital, gathering sympathizers along the way and reaching a total of almost five thousand people. The clergy also mustered their supporters, about eight thousand people, who confronted the Young Bukharans. To avoid bloodshed, Burkhanov ordered the reformers to disperse; many were arrested and several fled the city under Russian protection.

During this tense period it became apparent to Miller that the cause of reform in Bukhara was hindered by Petrograd's indifference and the comparative weakness of the Young Bukharans against the strong hold of the clergy over the emir and the population. For their part the Young Bukharans realized the Provisional Government's impotence and most remained in New Bukhara under Soviet protection after the October revolution.

In December 1917 F. Khodzhaev went to Tashkent to meet with Fedor Ivanovich Kolesov (1891-1940), president of the Turkestan Council of People's Commissars (Sovnarkom), to obtain Soviet support for an uprising. Initially, Kolesov refused, but in early March 1918 he agreed to the Young Bukharan plans. Kolesov assembled almost 700 men and marched on Bukhara with about 200 armed Young Bukharan supporters. They presented the emir with an ultimatum. After a brief skirmish the emir agreed to the terms. Kolesov sent a small delegation to meet with the emir's representatives. But it was a trap and several people were killed, including three members of Kolesov's delegation. The emir had time to assemble his forces and attacked. He was better armed than either Kolesov or the Young Bukharans believed and the small Soviet contingent was forced to flee. The emir demanded the surrender of all members of the Young Bukharan leadership, but Kolesov refused. Once again the Young Bukharans were forced into exile and had proven their weakness to their only allies. For the next two years party members, about 150 people, remained politically inactive.

In the fall of 1919 the Young Bukharan revolutionary program, which had been written two years earlier by Fitrat, was published. In outlining the group's specific goals for government and society it recognized the need to redistribute Bukhara's land to the population and to increase and regulate Bukhara's water supply. In addition the program called for the creation of a "special body" to administer the lands held by the clergy. Profits from the use of this land were to be used to repair schools and mosques. New secular schools, orphanages, hospices for the poor, and refectories would be built with the funds. The Young Bukharans also envisioned maintaining an army of twelve thousand men. They wanted to create ministries of finance, interior, foreign affairs, justice, police, agriculture, war, transport and mines, clerical lands, and public education. The minister of foreign affairs would act as president of the council of ministers. The program also called for a free press. It included few socialist slogans. Instead, expounding pan-Islamic ideas, it sounded more nationalist than communist.

In March 1919 the Soviet journal Life of the Nationalities (Zhizn nationalnostei) published an appeal of the Moscow "Socialist Committee of Young Bukharans" encouraging the Bukharan people to liberate themselves. One month later several Young Bukharans decided to break away and formed the Bukharan Communist Party (BCP). There was little difference in membership or goals between the two parties. Burkhanov and Sadriddin Aini, both former Young Bukharans, held positions of authority in the BCP. Fitrat and F. Khodzhaev made every effort to convince Moscow that the Young Bukharan party was better prepared to arouse support for revolution among Bukhara's masses.

On 2 July 1919 a major riot consumed the city of Bukhara. Over sixty of the participants were executed. The Young Bukharans and the BCP were encouraged by the apparent growing popular discontent. They believed it would neutralize the support the emir and the clergy had known in the past. Moscow was convinced that any revolution in Bukhara must have the appearance of a nationalist rebellion and worked diligently to bring about a reconciliation between the two groups. In the summer of 1920 both parties agreed to cooperate for the sake of reform and revolution.

In August 1920 the Young Bukharans, supported by the Red Army, started the much anticipated siege of Bukhara. The emir fled the city and on 2 September a new government, headed by F. Khodzhaev, was formed. Nine days later the Young Bukharans, fulfilling a promise in return for Soviet armed support, merged with the BCP and assumed the name and organization of the communist party. On 6 October the Bukharan People's Soviet Republic was established with F. Khodzhaev as premier and Fitrat as minister of public education.

Despite the merger, tensions between BCP and the government dominated by the Young Bukharans continued. The BCP wanted to proceed with the transformation of Bukhara into a socialist society, whereas Fitrat and others wanted to continue with their program. The issue was complicated further by the Basmachi revolt (1918-1926), a popular uprising against Soviet rule which eventually spread throughout Turkestan. Several former Young Bukharans actively participated in this movement.

Russian protection alone allowed those who governed in Bukhara to remain in power. The Young Bukharan program was never implemented because of an indifferent and uneducated population and continued resistance by members of BCP. Only F. Khodzhaev sincerely accepted Marxism. In December 1921 Moscow, increasingly frustrated by the Basmachis and the pace of change in Bukhara, ordered an investigation as to how Bukhara's government could be transformed into a worker's state. Moscow decided to remove most Young Bukharans from power. By 1923 Stalin reported that the purge of noncommunists in Bukhara was almost completed. Many Young Bukharans, such as Fitrat, were arrested and deported to Russia. Only F. Khodzhaev remained in power. Most died in Stalin's purges of the 1930s. The Young Bukharan party effectively was removed from power at the advent of Soviet policy in Bukhara.

The Young Bukharans were a small, generally well-educated group of idealists who attained political power only through Bolshevik support. Their reformist goals usually alienated Bukhara's traditional leadership, particularly the clergy. They often overestimated their support among Bukhara's people, which discredited them in the eyes of their Soviet allies. Once in power their program was pushed aside in favor of a socialist one.

Bibliography: Hélène Carrere d'Encausse, *Islam and the Russian Empire. Reform and Revolution in Central Asia* (Berkeley, 1988); Seymour Becker, *Russia's Protectorates in Central Asia. Bukhara and Khiva, 1865-1924* (Cambridge, 1968); Alexander Garland Park, *Bolshevism in Turkestan, 1917-1927* (New York, 1957); Serge A. Zenkovsky, *Pan-Turkism and Islam in Russia* (Cambridge, 1960); B.Kh. Ergashev, "K voprosu o mladobukhartsakh," *Istoriia SSSR*, No. 4 (1990), 58-70; F. Khodzhaev, "O mlado-bukhartsakh," *Istorik-Marksist* Vol. 1, part 1 (1926), 123-141; "Proekt reformy v Bukhare komiteta Mlado-Bukhartsev," in *Programmny dokumenty musul'manskikh politicheskikh partii 1917-1920 gg.* Society for Central Asian Studies, Reprint Series No. 2 (Oxford, 1985).

Steven O. Sabol

YOUNG COMMUNIST LEAGUE. See KOMSOMOL

YOUNG KHIVANS (1905-1920). A small group of Uzbek Muslim reformers centered on the ancient city of Khiva, located in Central Asia east of the Caspian Sea and south of Lake Aral. First manifestation of Uzbek national feeling in the Russian Empire.

Like the Young Bukharans, their counterparts further to the east in Bukhara, the Young Khivans formed shortly after the 1905 Russian revolution. Unlike the Young Bukharans, they had no structured program of reform and their leadership was composed of ineffective men of little note. Principally, the movement included young intellectuals and small merchants. It played little role in Khivan affairs before 1917 and its efforts at reform appeared to be sporadic and weak.

After the February 1917 revolution the movement, which at that time had fewer then fifty members, allied with the newly formed soviet in Khiva's military garrison. Together they pressed Khan Isfendiyar, who ruled from 1910 to 1918, for reforms. On 5 April 1917 he produced a manifesto that included Young Khivan demands. It promised civil liberties, a constitutional government with a parliament (majlis) and council of ministers, new schools, and strict fiscal accounting. The first majlis, composed of thirty members, met three days later. Seventeen Young Khivans had seats, which gave them a clear majority.

The new government was unable to deal with the enmity between Khiva's rival Uzbek and Turkmen populations. Consequently it was ineffective. Turkmen leaders were angered by the new government's apparent lack of concern for taxes and water issues and their lack of representation in the majlis. Turkmen raids against Uzbek settlements continued to enrage the Young Khivans. Seven Turkmen leaders eventually were added to the majlis, but this failed to appease them. Muhammad Karim Baba Ahun, a Young Khivan leader and speaker of the majlis, turned to the Russian Provisional Government for military assistance against the raids. Petrograd was reluctant to become involved and provided no support.

In June 1917 conservative factions in Khiva, taking advantage of Baba Ahun's absence, persuaded Isfendiyar to oust the Young Khivans from power. Most of the party leaders either were arrested, went into hiding, or fled to Tashkent. Ultimately the party was outlawed.

In late July 1917 Petrograd reached an agreement with the khanate to supervise Isfendiyar's government and implement reforms. The Young Khivans were excluded from power. Following the October revolution Turkmen clan leader Junaid-Khan established his own government and created a virtual dictatorship, with Isfendiyar as the nominal head. In late November the khan ordered the Young Khivans who had been arrested the previous June to be tried. The Russian garrison commander in Khiva, Colonel I.M. Zaitsev, intervened in time to prevent their executions. However, in January 1918 Zaitsev withdrew his forces from Khiva. The imprisoned Young Khivans, whose lives had been spared, were shot in May 1918.

One month later in Tashkent the remaining members formed a Young Khivan revolutionary committee-in-exile. Chairman of the party was Palvanniyaz Yusupov. Branches were set up in Petro-Aleksandrovsk and in Chardjui. Because there was no other organized revolutionary group for the Bolsheviks to back, support was given to the Young Khivans. The soviets attempted to get the party to adopt a more revolutionary program, but had little success. The Young Khivans had no formal plan and their hopes of reform encompassed little more than the creation of a constitutional monarchy.

The party spent the next year waiting for Soviet interest and strength to grow in the region. In October 1919 a Turkestan Commission was formed under the All-Russian Central Executive Committee and the Council of People's Commissars of the Russian Soviet Federated Socialist Republic (RSFSR). Its task was to exercise Soviet authority in Turkestan at a time when the region was isolated from Soviet Russia. In November 1919 Bolshevik and Young Khivan sources reported that Khiva's citizens, both Uzbek and Turkmen, had rebelled against Junaid and were requesting Soviet aid. The Turkestan Commission decided to act and, if indeed it was a genuine popular revolt, to attack. In December a campaign was started with the intention of defeating Junaid and initiating Khiva's revolution. The Red Army troops were assisted by a small Young Khivan detachment that was formed in Petro-Aleksandrovsk.

On 25 December 1919 Soviet forces occupied Novyi Urgench. The Young Khivans were very distrustful of Soviet intentions and had refused to take any action until Khiva was attacked. Most feared the Soviets would abandon them, leaving them exposed and vulnerable before Junaid was defeated. In late January 1920 Khiva fell and Junaid fled into the Kara Kum Desert. Isfendiyar's brother, Khan Abd Allah, who ruled for only two years from 1918 to 1920, abdicated in favor of a revolutionary committee headed by Dzhumaniyaz Sultanmuradov, chairman of the Petro-Aleksandrovsk Young Khivan Committee.

The replacement of the khan was not one of the Young Khivans' original goals, but they had little true authority and it was the Bolsheviks operating through the Turkestan Commission who decided to remove the khan. The Soviets continued to pressure the new government to adopt a socialist program. On 8 February 1920 a small wing of the Young Khivan party requested Moscow's assistance to establish a worker's government. On 1 April 1920 a delegation, sent by the Turkestan Commission, arrived in Khiva from Tashkent. It was led by G.I. Broido and included several Tashkent Young Khivans who had not participated in the assault. Three days later the Young Khivans announced their dissolution, while simultaneously joining the Russian Communist party.

A new political body was created to rule Khiva: a seven-member Council of People's Ministers (Nazirs). It was headed by Yusupov, chairman of the Tashkent Young Khivan Committee, with posts filled by Turkmen clan leaders and former Young Khivans. None of the Young Khivans who joined the Communist party before Khiva fell was included.

In late April 1920, at the first All-Kurultai of People's Representatives, the khanate was renamed the Khorezm People's Soviet Republic, utilizing Khiva's ancient name. A fifteen-member council was created also. Yusupov retained his post and former Young Khivans occupied ten of the fifteen ministerial positions. In addition, the Khorezm Communist party (KhCP) was created formally. A member of the Bukharan Communist party was elected chairman of the central committee and Sultanmuradov was made deputy chairman. The new KhCP membership swelled. By September over 1,000 people had joined, although most Young Khivans were communists in name only. This fact frustrated the Turkestan Commission and Moscow. Another aspect of Khiva's political atmosphere that angered Moscow was the continued tension and distrust that permeated relations between Uzbeks and Turkmen.

In August 1920 after many Bukharan communists departed Khiva to participate in the overthrow of the emir of Bukhara, Sultanmuradov and others assumed control of the KhCP. The murder of Turkmen leader Gochmamed-khan and dozens of his men prompted Moscow to purge the Young Khivans from power. Their representative in Khiva, M.V. Safonov, proceeded to organize rival party cells in Khiva's embryonic army, which undermined Young Khivan support. Safonov also courted the Turkmen population. By December 1920 Safonov orchestrated a new election of the KhCP's central committee, ousting the Young Khivans from the party.

On 10 March 1921 a mass demonstration was held in Khiva protesting against the government. Most Young Khivan leaders including Yusupov and Sultanmuradov resigned their positions and fled the republic. Many joined Junaid's forces, whose ranks swelled, in the Kara Kum Desert. In June Communist party membership was reduced by 97 percent to only sixty people, effectively eliminating all Young Khivans from participation in the new government. Most fought on with Junaid or other insurgent groups, but Soviet control over Khiva was complete.

The Young Khivan movement, which never attained any influence among Khiva's divided population, continually was plagued by its reliance on Russian or Soviet support. In return for that support the movement's leaders often compromised their reform plans. Attempts to implement the reforms constantly failed. Resistance from Turkmen leaders, the Provisional Government, and finally the Bolsheviks prevented them from participating actively in Khiva's government.

Bibliography: Seymour Becker, *Russia's Protectorates in Central Asia, 1865-1924* (Cambridge, 1968); Alexander Garland Park, *Bolshevism in Turkestan, 1917-1927* (New York, 1957); Ann Sheehy, "The End of the Khanate of Khiva," *Central Asian Review*, 15 (1967), 5-20; Ann Sheehy, "The Khorezm Communist Party, 1920-1924," *Central Asian Review*, 16 (1968), 308-321; D.B. Yaroshevski, "The Central Government and Peripheral Opposition in Khiva, 1910-24," *The USSR and the Muslim World. Issues in Domestic and Foreign Policy*, ed. by Yaacov Roi (London, 1984), 16-39.

Steven O. Sabol

YOUNG TATARS (1905?-1910). An informal body of Crimean Tatar intellectuals and activists, mostly young teachers and students, who emerged as a political and nationalist force in the years around 1905.

More a movement than a party, the Young Tatars developed little organization of their own, preferring to ally themselves individually with certain of the major Russian political parties, especially the Socialist-Revolutionaries (SRs) and Mensheviks. The epithet "Young Tatar" was not a self-designation but was coined by Russian authorities and was not always used with precision. The movement flourished between 1905 and 1909.

Although some Crimean Tatar youths actively participated with SRs or Social Democrats in underground revolutionary activities as early as 1903, they apparently began to form parallel and independent collectives only in 1905. These tended to mimic the slogans and ideological positions of the Russian socialists, emphasizing the overthrow of the tsarist regime, establishment of some kind of democratic order and, as with the SRs, resolution of agrarian problems, which happened to be particularly acute among Crimean Tatars. Beyond these issues the Young Tatars continued the interests of an earlier generation of reformers by displaying concern for the overall "enlightenment" of Tatar society. This took several forms. It involved support for the so-called "new method" schools advocated by the elder figure Ismail Bey Gasprinsky, with their "modern" pedagogy, flexible, broad, and practical curriculum, as well as for females. The "enlightenment" goals further called for development of teacher-training facilities and production of a national (Tatar) cadre of professional teachers; encouragement of advanced education for Tatar youth in both Russian and foreign institutions of higher learning; and a commitment to learning the Russian language.

If the Young Tatars failed to create a centralized party organization or to articulate a comprehensive political program, they did manage to establish a network of cells across Crimea in both urban and rural areas. Some of the most important circles could be found in the towns of Bakhchisarai, Akmescit, Gözleve, Kefe, Yalta, and Karasubazar, the latter recognized as the most significant. Each of these in turn served as regional headquarters for cells that reached into the Tatar villages, where activists carried on agitation in favor of educational, economic, and social reform, collected money to support their activities, organized mutual-assistance efforts, and read to the villagers from the Tatar press, especially from the long-established Tercüman (The Interpreter) and after May 1906 from their own Vatan Hadimi (Servant of the Fatherland). The Young Tatars, particularly in Karasubazar, worked to achieve greater ethnic participation in municipal administration, whereby Tatars could gain both a greater voice and experience in public affairs. One result was the election of Abdürreşid Mehdi first to the Karasubazar city duma, then as deputy mayor, and finally in 1907 as mayor. He later served in the second State Duma as well.

In addition to Abdürreşid Mehdi some of the most prominent Young Tatars included Cafer Odamon, Celâl Meinov, Hasan Sabri Ayvazov, Süleyman Idrisov, and Ali Bodaninsky, young men from varied social backgrounds, but all well educated and substantially integrated into Russian society. Devoid of any strong sentiment of Russophobia, the Young Tatars wedded their cause and the fate of their particular ethnic group to the emergence of a progressive, democratic Russia. This explains, for example, their commitment to such institutions as the zemstvos, which they hoped, through public pressure, to turn more fully to the needs of the Tatars.

Unquestionably the most important legacy of the Young Tatar movement was its role in generating a political and national consciousness among the Crimean Tatars. Even though they frequently expressed opinions and positions that reflected loyalties transcending those focused on their native population— to the larger Turkic and even larger Islamic communities—they systematically emphasized local issues and problems and spoke directly to the Crimean Tatars as a nation with a defined territory. More than anything or anyone else, they helped define the identity of the Crimean Tatars, using literature from poetry, drama, the short story, and novel, as well as satire, and historical writing to enlighten and influence a growing readership.

By 1910 the movement waned owing in part to its still tenuous links to a mass base, and more importantly to a reassertion of tsarist pressure that proved especially effective in its strikes against the major activities and forums of the Young Tatars: the modern schools, the press, and publishing generally. Some Tatars reverted to the less politically oriented approach of Ismail Bey Gasprinsky, while others bided their time either in Crimea or abroad, especially in Turkey and Egypt, until circumstances for political action were once again propitious. In the evolving experience of the Crimean Tatars since the mid-nineteenth century, the Young Tatar movement represented a brief but important transitory phase between those community spokesmen who pursued cultural and revivalist measures and those who later struggled for national self-determination.

Bibliography: The only meaningful source in English is a detailed, although unpublished, doctoral dissertation by Sirri Hakan Kirimli, "National Movements and National Identity among the Crimean Tatars (1905-1916)," University of Wisconsin, 1990. Numerous articles by participants, contemporaries, and later Tatar analysts have appeared over the past eighty years in languages ranging from Tatar to Turkish and Russian. All have been incorporated in the Kirimli study.

Edward J. Lazzerini

YOUTH IN THE USSR (1919-). The 1919 party program of the Russian Communist Party (Bolshevik) announced that one of the goals of the new leaders of Soviet Russia was "the creation of a generation capable of establishing communism." Addressing the Twentieth Congress of the All-Union Young Communist League (Komsomol) in 1987 the leader of the Communist party, Mikhail Sergeevich Gorbachev, said, "Young people are the creative force of revolutionary renewal." In both 1919 and 1987, as well as at many points in between, the leadership of the Soviet Union expressed optimistic revolutionary hopes and expectations for the youth of that country.

All of the speeches and ideas about young people over the entire period of Soviet history had two aspects in common. They were made by older leaders to or on behalf of the younger citizens of the USSR, and they stressed not what young people needed or wanted during their minority, but instead emphasized the historic roles they would play once they reached adulthood. These two features typified the passive position young people occupied in the USSR from 1917 onward. Despite their many appeals to youth to act, the authorities insisted on defining their directions, concerns, and programs. As the break-up of the USSR continued into 1992 there were no signs that this long-established pattern had changed.

Who were the youth and who should oversee their growth and development were complex questions that received various answers during the approximately seventy years of Soviet history.

Legal, Educational, and Political Definitions of Youth. Many societies define the term "youth" by determining the age of criminal responsibility, the age at which courts cease to view a person in legal difficulties as a juvenile and treat him as an adult. During the Soviet period this age ranged from as low as twelve years during the mid-1930s to as high as eighteen. The Soviet definitions of the age of legal responsibility changed not because of new concepts about the transition from juvenile to adult offender, but because of the varying political needs of the time. The age of criminal responsibility was lower during times of crisis and rebuilding, such as during the 1930s, the years of World War II, and the immediate postwar reconstruction period. It was higher in more settled times such as the 1970s under the leadership of Leonid Ilich Brezhnev.

From the 1960s onward the age of legal majority, the age at which an individual becomes an adult in legal and civic terms, was set at eighteen. The age of criminal responsibility was sixteen officially, but in practice a person aged seventeen to eighteen still could be regarded as a juvenile offender. A survey of felonies in the Baltic republics during the 1980s revealed that individuals eighteen years old and younger had committed 50 percent of them; the authors of the study concluded that these areas faced significant amounts of juvenile crime. A factor that further complicated the legal definition of "youth" in the USSR was the raising of the legal drinking age to twenty-one in 1985 as part of Gorbachev's antialcoholism campaign. Soviet history thus reveals no standard legal definition of "youth."

Another traditional criterion for defining "youth" is the age at which an individual may cease schooling and acquire full-time employment and possible economic independence. This too has varied over the years of Soviet history from twelve in the 1920s to sixteen to eighteen in the early 1990s, depending on the type and level of education. Like the changing definitions of the age of criminal responsibility, the various ages at which one could leave school were determined more by the availability of education in a particular region than by any fixed notion of when a child became an adult in terms of educational preparation. As the numbers of schools and teachers spread across the country from the beginning of the Soviet regime in 1917 to its collapse in 1991, the numbers of young people receiving education increased, as did the age at which they could drop out legally. By 1950 in the USSR the average sixteen-year old had received 5 years of education at a time when the Union-wide goal was for every young person to receive 8 years of primary and secondary education. By 1960 the average sixteen-year-old had received 5.9 years of education; by 1970, 7.3 years. In the 1970s the state's new educational goal became 10 years of primary and secondary education with graduation at age seventeen, and the statistics began to reflect even higher levels of educational attainment for sixteen-year olds, the average being 9.1 years of education reported in the 1989 census.

Literacy rates for the entire Soviet Union dramatically increased as the regime invested in the education of young people. Among the population aged 9 to 49 years literacy was 44 percent in 1920, 87.4 percent in 1939, and 99.7 percent in 1970. The formation and establishment of a coeducational, universal, and compulsory educational system stood as one of the Soviet success stories. This achievement derived more from the use of education to modernize society than from any concept that young people form a specific social group with special needs and concerns.

Establishing the ages of membership in the Communist youth organizations reflected yet another way of defining youth. The youngest children, aged seven to nine years, joined the Young Octobrists. This children's organization was founded during 1923 and 1924 to start the political preparation of children that some adult Communist Party members considered lacking in the schools. In the post-World War II period nearly 100 percent of children this age became Octobrists. Older children, aged ten to fourteen or fifteen, joined the Young Pioneers, an organization which was started in 1922. At its founding the upper age limits for participation were left imprecise so that adolescents in the final years of schooling or in the first years of employment could remain active in this organization. The founders hoped that these children would stay in school but recognized during the early years of Soviet history that many could not do so. Since 1945 the Pioneer organization also enjoyed membership of nearly 100 percent of the youngsters in that age category. In the post-1945 period the Pioneer movement was active primarily through the schools. This mirrored the increasing numbers of young people who could continue their education well into their teens, when they became eligible for membership in the next organization, the Komsomol.

The Komsomol, founded in 1918, recruited much wider age cohorts than the other two. An individual could join the Komsomol at the age of fourteen. During the history of this organization the age at which one ceased belonging to the Komsomol ranged from twenty-three to twenty-eight. This broad age distribution originally was developed to reach and motivate politically youths who already worked in the economy as well as those who still pursued an education. This reflected awareness of the various educational or vocational options available to people in their teens and early twenties, an awareness that continued through 1990. Therefore, unlike the Octobrist and Pioneer experiences, active Komsomol cells existed in many actual workplaces and not just primarily in educational establishments. During the years of membership in the Komsomol an individual could petition to join the Communist party, so some eighteen-year olds were full-fledged members of the party while others the same age remained in the Komsomol.

One result of this built-in overlapping age structure was that no clear lines correlated age with the level of political participation in party-sponsored groups. One scholar concluded from the 1949 party rosters that eleven to fourteen million young people aged fourteen to twenty-five were members of either the Pioneers, the Komsomol, or the Communist party itself. Again, these variations derived not from a consistent or even consistently developing sense of the nature and needs of young people but from changing external circumstances such as the availability of education and employment.

State Institutions and Youth. A major issue that received much attention during the Soviet period, particularly during the first decades after 1917, was the question of which social and governmental institutions should bear the primary responsibility for devising programs for young people. As in other societies, in the USSR jurisdiction over youth eventually was placed in a variety of institutions instead of in just one organization such as a ministry of youth. Additionally there were many questions about what roles young people should play in a socialist society. These questions were answered by the historical experience of the USSR, and not by any major ideological formulation.

Some members of the new Bolshevik government considered the formation of a central organization dedicated to issues and concerns relating to minors in Soviet society in the years immediately following 1917. The proponents of a unitary institution charged with overseeing the health, education, upbringing, and rights of children and adolescents acted in response to the mistakes they believed the imperial government had made. The new youth advocates such as Zlata Iovanovna Lilina (Zinovieva) argued that it was senseless to have, for example, experts in children's physical health located in one agency, lawyers specializing in juvenile delinquency in another, and educational experts in yet a third. Following the models of the Women's Section (Zhenotdel) and the Jewish Section (Evsektsiia) within the Communist party, these people proposed that the new state establish some kind of children's and adolescents' section. The state never did this, but this argument served as a background factor in the creation of the party's organizations for youth, since the Communist party was an all-Union body while commissariats dealing with social issues operated at the republic level only.

During the 1920s many institutions claimed jurisdiction over the younger members of Soviet society. In the Russian Soviet Federated Socialist Republic (RSFSR), for example, the People's Commissariat of Enlightenment argued that all issues relating to children, adolescents, and even people in their early twenties should fall under its purview. This organization saw itself as the logical meeting place for a variety of experts on education, childhood development, the rehabilitation of homeless and abandoned children, and so on. The People's Commissariat of Health believed that anything relating to the health and physical well-being of minors rightfully concerned that body. The Commissariat of National Minorities within the RSFSR stressed that it should supervise all non-Russian minors, although it promised to consult with other relevant agencies. Other claimants to the right to determine the nature of childhood and youth in the RSFSR included the Komsomol and its special children's organizations: the Children's Commission, established in 1921 to resolve specifically the problem of children's homelessness as well as the legal status of children in general; the Commissariat of Social Welfare, which was interested in addressing issues relating to the family upbringing of young people; the People's Commissariat of Justice, which in 1918 abolished adoption and foster care before determining socialist replacements for those necessary functions; the Commissariat of Labor, which saw inspection of the working conditions of children as a logical component of its duties; and the Women's Section of the Communist party, which concerned itself both with children in their connection to the lives of adult women and with female adolescents who could be liberated from traditional, gender-based restraints.

In order to resolve these conflicting claims over children, the central authorities from both the party and the RSFSR government had to determine which agency held which responsibility. For example in 1919 the Council of People's Commissars in the RSFSR decided that the People's Commissariat of Enlightenment would be responsible for the social upbringing and general education of children, while the Commissariat of Health took charge of children's mental and corporal health. A series of decisions such as this meant that issues relating to children and adolescents would fall under the divided supervision of a variety of governmental agencies, a condition which persisted throughout the Soviet experience. All of the previously named organizations and other new ones since the 1920s continued to share, frequently uneasily, the responsibility for minors.

The duties and responsibilities of these and other child-related institutions were defined so fully that every minute of a youngster's day fell under some organization's jurisdiction. This phenomenon led one western specialist to refer to the continued and continual bureaucratization of childhood and adolescence in the USSR.

The other major issue regarding young people that generated debate in the 1920s concerned the specific goals and roles for children and adolescents in the new Soviet society. Two broad views emerged during the first decade following 1917. The first held that childhood and adolescence were stages of human life where the skills, habits, and knowledge that would create a healthy and harmonious individual were acquired. The adherents of this idea were concentrated primarily in the RSFSR's Commissariat of Enlightenment under the administration of Anatoly Vasilevich Lunacharsky. They argued that Soviet upbringing should liberate children and adolescents from all the constraints and repressions of the past. They therefore focused on questions about the socialization of children and young people; that is, how to give children a sense of self-identity while still preparing them to interact positively in society as a whole. It was this group that pondered the issues relating to the creation of "the new Soviet Man."

The other view tended to dominate in Ukraine's Commissariat of Enlightenment, especially during the tenure of Grigory Fedorovich Grinko, from 1920 to 1926. The members of this group argued that the primary aim of child rearing and education was to prepare young people to meet the future manpower needs of the economy. They saw that the preparation of "a generation capable of establishing communism" meant the development of workers able to assist in modernizing the economy. They therefore tended to stress the mastery of basic skills rather than the formation of the well-rounded individual.

This particular dilemma was resolved during the period of the first Five Year Plan, 1928-1932. During those years questions of economic modernization outweighed issues of personal development, and in 1931 the central authorities determined that the foremost task of education and upbringing was mastery of basic skills. This led to major emphasis on the teaching of mathematics and the natural sciences. Within a little more than twenty years this policy helped to produce Sputnik, the first artificial satellite, and to inspire western educators to re-examine their systems. Ironically, the decision to adopt a modernizing rather than a socializing approach did not completely eliminate the other point of view. Soviet education in the 1930s and 1940s also experienced development of children's literature and other forms of popular entertainment specifically devoted to young people. This demonstrated a continuation, however small, of the socializers' concept of childhood and adolescence as formative phases with their own special needs and requirements. Two later leaders, Nikita Sergeevich Khrushchev and Gorbachev, tinkered with the notion of shifting the focus of education more toward individual development than toward the needs of the economy, but ongoing fiscal and industrial crises led both of them soon to revert to what became the traditional Soviet focus in educational matters.

Despite extensive changes in Soviet society since 1917 and despite occasional attempts at reform, the general outlines of the policies and institutions relating to Soviet youth formed by the early 1930s continued with little revision to the early 1990s.

Youth in Periods of Soviet History. During the first decade after 1917 many of the general outlines of the Soviet system were established. Many utopian ideas arose during these years, such as the guarantee of free meals for schoolchildren at a time when the new authorities had minimal control over or even access to the food distribution system. Resolving issues like these took some time because of the poverty and size of the country the Bolsheviks had inherited. Two examples should suffice to illustrate the confusion and problems relating to policies for young people in the 1920s. Throughout that decade the officially atheist state permitted the continued operation of religious schools in the Muslim parts of the former Russian empire. Because the new authorities believed that any education was better than no education at all, young Muslim boys received an education not much different from that of their fathers and grandfathers. Girls traditionally were excluded. The new authorities were not able to challenge these older educational patterns until the late 1920s when the political and economic situation had stabilized enough to create coeducational and secular schools in those areas. Then there was the poverty and social breakdown of the country following the years of wars, revolutions, famines, and epidemics. In 1921 more than nine million homeless and abandoned children lived in the former Russian empire. These unfortunates represented a multifaceted challenge as the new state attempted, with minimal success, to marshal the resources necessary to rescue and rehabilitate them. During the 1920s the government made promises about a better life for children and young people, but it rarely realized them.

The 1930s—or more precisely the period from 1928, the initial year of the First Five Year plan, to the outbreak of World War II in 1941—introduced both stabilization and new opportunities for young people. The educational and social experimentation characteristic of the 1920s ended; young people experienced again the traditional nexus of school, home life, and extracurricular activities. At the same time educational opportunities and the chances for upward mobility significantly increased as the industrialization drives necessitated acquisition of technical skills and virtually guaranteed employment. A protective social welfare network, guaranteeing the physical and emotional well-being of children and adolescents as envisaged in the 1920s, began to emerge, although slowly and sporadically. Daily life still could be tumultuous as the collectivization of agriculture helped to produce a new generation of homeless children and as the state greatly increased its expectations of productivity from all of its citizens.

The years of World War II halted most of the child and youth-related programs that started in the 1930s. Educational opportunities declined severely; schools and institutions of higher education either remained in areas occupied by the Nazi forces or suffered depopulation by the recruitment of male teachers and students into the military effort. The Communist youth movement attempted to organize young people on the home front to support the struggle through collection of crucial materials and organization of civil defense. The state made a concerted effort to evacuate children and young people from occupied or threatened areas and managed to move great numbers into safe areas in Central Asia, particularly to Tashkent. The war produced many orphans. Records from 1946 indicate that over 393,000 orphans were in children's homes in the RSFSR alone. One legal revision resulting from the war years was the reinstatement of adoption and foster care since there were too many orphans and too few state institutions to care for them.

The immediate postwar years led to several changes affecting young people in particular. New waves of homeless teenagers appeared when adolescents fled war-shattered areas and attempted to survive on their own in major cities. Many government officials perceived them to be delinquents since they did not participate in the war-recovery effort and, for the first time in Soviet history, large numbers of minors wound up in prison or work camps. As late as 1957 the Soviet government was issuing orders on how to combat the problem of unsupervised teens.

This crisis lessened during the Khrushchev and Brezhnev years. Postwar reconstruction was completed by 1955, when Khrushchev emerged as the Soviet leader, and he was able to institute some changes that had a positive impact on young people in general. These continued under his successor. The major developments were the expansion of the educational opportunities already discussed and fuller implementation of the long-dreamed-of social welfare network. The state finally could afford significant sums for child-care allowances; one-third of the neediest children in the USSR received direct financial assistance by 1965. Since the government preferred to set up programs rather than to offer money to families with children the network of preschool establishments, extended school days, and Pioneer palaces was expanded so that working parents could leave their minors in some form of supervised care. By 1970 nearly 50 percent of Soviet children were in some form of day care, either in special preschool institutions or in schools with expanded hours; in the urbanized areas of the USSR fully 75 percent of children under the age of seven were so covered. Despite these efforts, a new problem emerged in the form of a significantly decreasing birthrate. In 1926 there were 159.1 births per thousand women in the USSR; by 1973 this had fallen to 66.8. The USSR thus had to start facing the issues of numerically fewer young people and the consequences of an aging population, questions that had received no answers by 1992.

During the 1970s and 1980s many Soviet authorities concluded that the system had "lost" its young people. Numerous newspaper editorials complained that young people were lazy and cared more for the latest material fads from the West than for participation in education and work for the good of society.

Once Gorbachev came to power and announced his goals of political reform, the numbers of young people enrolled as members of the Komsomol suffered a precipitous fall. Many Soviet leaders became convinced that the war in Afghanistan (1979-1989) not only exacerbated these tendencies but also introduced new problems such as illegal drug use, increasing incidence of sexually transmitted diseases, and widespread disdain among young people for anything political.

The accuracy of this belief in the political and social apathy of Soviet young people was revealed in the late 1980s and early 1990s when the USSR broke up into the Commonwealth of Independent States. The crowds attending demonstrations for the national independence of the various republics, the marches of support for various democratic leaders, and the protests over the ever higher costs of living were composed of older rather than younger people.

See Also: KOMSOMOL and ZALKIND, AARON BORISOVICH.

Bibliography: Urie Bronfenbrenner, *Two Worlds of Childhood. US and USSR* (New York, 1970); Walter D. Connor, *Deviance in Soviet Society. Crime, Delinquency, and Alchoholism* (New York, 1972); Ralph Talcott Fisher, *Pattern for Soviet Youth. A Study of the Congresses of the Komsomol, 1918-1954* (New York, 1959); Maurice Friedberg and Heyward Isham, eds., *Soviet Society Under Gorbachev. Current Trends and Prospects for Reform* (Armonk, NY, 1987); Peter H. Juviler, *Revolutionary Law and Order. Politics and Social Change in the USSR* (New York, 1976); Basile Kerblay, *Modern Soviet Society* (New York, 1983); William Medlin, et al., *Education and Development in Central Asia* (Leiden, 1971); Jaan Pennar, et al., *Modernization and Diversity in Soviet Education with Special Reference to Nationality Groups* (New York, 1971); Jim Riordan, *Soviet Youth Culture* (Bloomington, Ind., 1989); Margaret K. Stolee, "Homeless Children in the USSR 1917-1957," *Soviet Studies* (January, 1988); Cathy Young, *Growing up in Moscow. Memories of a Soviet Girlhood* (New York, 1989).

Margaret K. Stolee

YRJÖ-KOSKINEN, BARON YRJÖ SAKARI (Georg Zachris Forsman, 1830-1903). Finnish historian, nationalist, and political figure.

Yjrö-Koskinen was born in 10 December 1830. His father was a Swedish-speaking clergyman. As a youth he came under the influence of Johan Vilhelm Snellman, a journalist, educator, professor of philosophy at Helsinki University, and founder of the Finnish nationalist (Fennoman) movement.

Like Snellman, Yjrö-Koskinen viewed the issue of language and culture as primary. The historic mission of progressive nations was to enhance the attainments of civilization. For this a national language was essential. It was necessary that all the people became literate in the national language, including the small minority of Swedish speakers (Svecomans), Finland's traditional political and economic elite. Until Finnish displaced Swedish as the official language, he held, the alien Swedish culture would continue to dominate the Finns. Hence his slogan "Finland for the Finns."

Yrjö-Koskinen energetically promoted the idea that Finnish answered the demands of a language of culture. A professor of history at the University of Helsinki, he was one of the first to write his dissertation in Finnish. He later wrote the first major history of Finland (Suomen Kansan Historia, 1869-1873) in Finnish. He founded the newspaper Helsingin Uutiset in 1863 and the first important journal written in Finnish, The Literary Monthly (Kirjallinen Kuukauslehti) in 1866. He was the first important political figure to learn Finnish and to use it in public life.

These views had clear political consequences, challenging the leadership of the Svecoman aristocracy. This challenge was supplemented by the onset of industrialization in Finland after the 1850s. Modernization brought along with it demands for education among the Finnish-speakers, prosperity and claims to political power among an emergent Finnish middle class.

This internal development took place within a changing international context. Russia had taken Finland from Sweden in 1809. After the Crimean War many romantic nationalist Swedes longed to create a greater Scandinavian state, which would include a reconquered Finland. Tsar Alexander II (1855-1881) courted the loyalty of the Finns, going so far as to pass a Language Edict (1863) which made Finnish as well as Swedish an official language, to take full effect after twenty years. In the same year he summoned the Finnish Diet, which had not met for fifty-four years, and he confirmed its authority in local issues. His son Alexander III (1881-1894) also pledged to respect Finnish autonomy but grew suspicious of Finnish nationalism and began to ignore the Diet in important issues. Under Nicholas II (1894-1917) a consistent policy of Russification began, aimed at reducing the influence of the Diet and subjecting the Finnish army to direct Russian administration.

In these issues Yrjö-Koskinen, who began to assume the leadership of the Fennoman movement in the mid-1860s and who became a member of the Finnish Senate in 1882, took positions which gradually isolated him from many in the party. Conservative politically, he showed little interest in the liberal and democratic aspirations of the younger members. Regarding the Russian authorities he urged a conciliatory attitude. Although increasingly fearful of Russian attempts to restrict Finnish liberties, he argued that the Finns must cultivate the good will of the tsar. By 1891 Yrjö-Koskinen's almost exclusive concern with the language issue had become obsolete. His refusal to unite with the Svecomans to oppose Russification led to a split in the party. A group called Young Finns emerged, interested in issues of national independence and social justice.

On 15 February 1899 Nikolai Ivanovich Bobrikov, the Russifying governor-general of Finland, presented the so-called February Manifesto to the Finnish Senate for promulgation. This document threatened to reduce drastically Finland's autonomy within the Russian empire. As all members of the Senate agreed that the manifesto was unconstitutional and intended to petition the tsar to change it, the debate revolved around whether to petition before or after promulgation or whether to reject it under any circumstances. Ignoring petitions by mass meetings held in Helsinki, Yjrö-Koskinen, one of the most influential members of the Senate, voted for immediate promulgation and the acceptance of the Russian changes which that implied.

In the stormy aftermath of the vote on the February Manifesto Yjrö-Koskinen resigned his Senate scat. In the press he continued to express the opinion that conciliation of the Russians was the only way to preserve at least cultural autonomy for Finland. In this he continued to speak for an important segment of Finnish society. He died 13 November 1903.

See Also: FINLAND'S POSITION WITHIN THE RUSSIAN EMPIRE, 1809-1917 and ZILLIACUS, KONRAD (KONNI) VIKTOR.

Bibliography: Yjrö-Koskinen history of Finland has been translated into German, *Finnische Geschichte von den frühesten Zeiten bis auf die Gegenwart* (Leipzig, 1874). See also Steven Duncan Huxley, *Constitutional Insurgency in Finland. Finnish "Passive Resistance" against Russification as a Case of Nonmilitary Struggle in the European Resistance Tradition* (Helsinki, 1990); J. Hampden Jackson, *Finland* (New York, 1940); Eino Jutikkala and Kauko Pirinen, *A History of Finland*, trans. by Paul Sjöblom (London, 1979); David G. Kirby, ed. and trans., *Finland and Russia, 1808-1920. From Autonomy to Independence. A Selection of Documents* (London, 1975); C. Leonard Lundin, "Finland," in Edward C. Thaden, ed., *Russification in the Baltic Provinces and Finland* (Princeton, 1981); Fred Singleton, *A Short History of Finland* (New York, 1989); Anthony F. Upton, *The Finnish Revolution 1917-1918* (Minneapolis, 1980); John H. Wuorinen, *Nationalism in Modern Finland* (New York, 1931).

George N. Rhyne

YURENEV, KONSTANTIN KONSTANTINOVICH (1888-1938). Russian revolutionary, journalist, and diplomat. Born Konstantin Konstantinovich Krotovsky. In prerevolutionary days he adopted the pseudonym Ilya Yurenev.

Yurenev was born in Dünaburg (Dvinsk after 1893) in Vitebsk province. His father was a watchman at the railroad station. Despite his modest origins Yurenev received a secondary education. In 1904 he entered illegal student organizations and the next year joined the Russian Social Democratic Workers' Party (RSDRP), engaging in agitational work among students and workers. From the beginning he was a Bolshevik. He rose quickly in the local party organization, serving as delegate to the northwest regional party conference in March 1908 where he was elected a member of the regional party bureau. Arrested the next month, he served three years of exile in Archangel province.

Upon his liberation Yurenev returned to St. Petersburg where he immediately resumed party work, writing in the newspaper Zvezda (The Star) and Pravda (The Truth) and carrying on agitation among workers. In the next few years he was arrested three times. Apparently he became disillusioned with Bolshevism because in 1913, between arrests, he helped organize the famous "Interdistrict Group" (Mezhraiontsy). This group of brilliant men, which stood between the Mensheviks and Bolsheviks until the summer of 1917, included Anatoly Vasilievich Lunacharsky, Dmitry Zakharovich Manuilsky, Adolf Abramovich Ioffe, Mikhail Nikolaevich Pokrovsky, and others who had written for Leon Davidovich Trotsky's newspapers. They substantially raised the intellectual level of the Bolshevik party when they joined it in August 1917.

After the revolution of February 1917 Yurenev served as a member of the executive committee of the Petrograd Soviet. At the Sixth Congress of the RSDRP (26 July-3 August) he represented the Mezhraiontsy. At that time he joined the Bolshevik party along with them. In September he headed the Red

Guards in the capital. Early in 1918 Yurenev served on the committee that created the Red Army. He was among the leaders of the Revolutionary Military Committee (Revoliutsionno-voennyi soviet, or Revvoensoviet) which was formed on 6 September 1918. This institution directed the Red Army during the Civil War. As its representative, Yurenev served on the Eastern Front (April-August 1919) and Western Front (October 1919-January 1920).

During early 1920 he returned to party work as a member of the Moscow Committee of the Communist party and from the summer of 1920 to May 1921 as a member of the Kursk provincial party committee. This transfer might be seen as testimony to Yurenev's administrative skills as his job in Kursk was to build up the party organization there. More likely it was a demotion. At the Ninth Party Congress in 1920 Yurenev had criticized the growing bureaucratization of the party.

It was probably for the same reason that Yurenev was assigned to the diplomatic corps. For many in the party who came to criticize the new regime, service abroad represented honorable exile. In June 1921 Yurenev was appointed the Soviet representative to the Emirate of Bukhara. His task was "to establish a real Soviet regime" there (Barmine, 97). He bore the title of plenipotentiary (polnomochnyi predstavitel', or polpred). This title was used primarily for Soviet representatives to countries which had not yet granted the Soviet state de jure diplomatic recognition.

Yurenev served either as polpred or ambassador to a number of countries during his career: Latvia, 1922-1923; Czechoslovakia, 1923-1924; Italy, 1924-1925; Iran, 1925-1927; Austria, 1927-1933; Japan, 1933-1937; and Germany, 1937.

Soviet sources are notably reticent about the activities of Soviet diplomatic personnel. In part this reflects the subordination of the diplomatic establishment to the party. As Soviet leader Joseph Vissarionovich Stalin tightened his grip on power Soviet diplomats increasingly became mere mouthpieces of the government at home. Not only did they lose virtually all initiative in making policy, they also lost control of their own embassies, coming under the scrutiny of secret police agents assigned to their staffs. In part this reticence reflects the fate of the leading Soviet diplomats of the 1920s and 1930s who perished in Stalin's purges; their names were removed from the historical record until the 1960s, when they began to be rehabilitated.

Despite the paucity of detailed information about Yurenev's diplomatic work it seems clear that he was an important representative of the Soviet regime. He had demonstrated unusual administrative talents. His postings were increasingly significant. Many are associated with critical stages in Soviet relations with the host countries.

In Italy he worked to consolidate the good feelings stemming from fascist Italy's de jure recognition of Soviet Russia on 7 February 1924, despite premier Benito Mussolini's persecution of the Communist and Socialist parties there. For example, on 10 July 1924 the popular socialist parliamentarian Giacomo Matteoti, who had been seized by fascist thugs, was found murdered. The rest of the diplomatic community boycotted Mussolini for months. Yurenev, having invited Mussolini to dinner in the Soviet embassy the following evening, not only refused to cancel his invitation but received him with impressive cordiality. In doing so he ignored the vocal and public opposition of the head of the Italian Communist party, Antonio Gramsci. The ensuing scandal resulted in Yurenev's demotion to the ambassadorships in Iran and Austria.

Yurenev's service in Japan coincided with the growth of militarism there and the consolidation of Japan's hold on Manchuria. Yurenev played an active part in the negotiations to sell the Japanese the Chinese Eastern Railroad, the leg of the Trans-Siberian railroad which ran across Manchuria to Vladivostok on the Pacific. The final terms of this attempt to appease Japan were not formulated until 19 September 1935. By the time of conclusion of this deal relations had begun to worsen. As early as July Yurenev had begun to issue a series of protests to the Japanese about violations of the Russian-Manchurian border and Japanese ships on the Ussuri River.

Once it became clear that the Soviet policy of collective security had failed, Stalin sought to improve relations with Nazi Germany. Yurenev was ideal for the task and was appointed ambassador on 16 June 1937. His "teutonic" features recommended him to Chancellor Adolf Hitler at the outset. As a mark of special favor Hitler invited Yurenev to present his credentials at his mountain retreat at Berchtesgaden. Apparently they got along well because Hitler was furious when Yurenev was recalled to the Soviet Union in December 1937.

In the last of the public purge trials on 2-12 March 1938 one of the defendants, Christian Georgievich Rakovsky, implicated Yurenev in treasonous complicity in the alleged anti-Soviet schemes of Trotsky. Yurenev disappeared without trial and was shot on 1 August 1938. He has been rehabilitated posthumously.

Bibliography: Yurenev wrote a brief autobiographical entry in *Deiateli SSSR i revoliutsionnogo dvizheniia Rossii. Entsiklopedicheskii slovar' Granat* (M., 1989), 780-781. Even briefer sketches are E. Sultanov, "Iurenev, Il'ia," in G.I. Kopanov, ed., *Geroi oktiabria*, 2 vols., Vol. 2 (M., 1967), 621-622 and "Iurenev," *Sovietskaia istoricheskaia entsiklopediia*, Vol. 16 (M., 1976), col. 825. For brief references to Yurenev within the larger context of the other matters touched on here see Alexandre Barmine, *One Who Survived. The Life Story of a Russian under the Soviets* (New York, 1945); David J. Dallin, *Soviet Russia and the Far East* (New Haven, 1948); Louis Fischer, *Russia's Road from Peace to War. Soviet Foreign Relations, 1917-1941* (New York, 1969); Jiri Hochman, *The Soviet Union and the Failure of Collective Security, 1934-1938* (Itheca, 1984); Harriet Lucy Moore, *Soviet Far Eastern Policy, 1931-1945* (Princeton, 1945); Boris Souvarine, *Stalin. A Critical Survey of Bolshevism* (New York, 1939); Robert C. Tucker and Stephen F. Cohen, eds., *The Great Purge Trial* (New York, 1965); Teddy Uldricks, *Diplomacy and Ideology. The Origins of Soviet Foreign Relations, 1917-1930* (Beverly Hills, 1979).

George N. Rhyne

YURIEV-POLSKOY (1152-). Also Yuriev-Polsky. Town located about 75 miles (120 km) northeast of Moscow, noted especially for the unique architecture of its church, the Georgievsky Sobor (Cathedral of St. George). In 1970 it became part of the so-called "Golden Ring," a chain of ancient cities, including Suzdal and Vladimir, which are major tourist sites.

Yuriev-Polskoy lies some 30 miles (48 km) east of Suzdal and 37 miles (59.5 km) north northeast of Vladimir. It was founded in 1152 by Yury Dolgoruky (the Long Hand), who was also the reputed founder of Moscow. Dolgoruky was then prince of Rostov-Suzdal, a growing center of power which contested Kiev for leadership of the cities of ancient Russia. In this effort he consciously summoned settlers to these "new" lands to the north and built towns for them. Yuriev-Polskoy bears his name plus the adjective "Polskoy" (literally, "in the fields") to distinguish it from another Yuriev along the Dnieper River.

In 1212 Dolgoruky's youngest son, Vsevolod III, who had ruled as grand prince of Vladimir since 1176, died. As his sons fought over his inheritance the unity of the principality fragmented. Yuriev-Polskoy became a separate appanage (udel) controlled by one of Vsevolod's sons, Sviatoslav Vsevolodovich.

Yuriev-Polskoy is important for its Cathedral of St. George. Begun by Sviatoslav Vsevolodovich in 1230, this white limestone church replaced a simpler church built by Yury Dolgoruky. Completed in 1234, it is the last of the churches constructed in the Vladimir-Suzdal region before the Mongol invasion of 1237. This onslaught impoverished the area, drastically lowered its technical level, and consequently interrupted the highly original architectural traditions of the region. Thus the Georgievsky Sobor represents the culmination of Suzdalian stone construction.

The church collapsed in the mid-fifteenth century but on the order of Grand Prince Ivan III the Muscovite architect, Vasily D. Ermolin, rebuilt it in 1471. His reconstruction was clumsy. The building that emerged was lower and squatter than the original; its onion shaped dome seemed too large for the structure; and many of the stones were replaced haphazardly. This last flaw is especially unfortunate, as the original church was a marvel of stone carving.

Carved stone had become an important feature of Suzdalian churches, but the Georgievsky Sobor was unique in the abundance of its decoration. Most of the external surface as well as the Troitsky (Trinity) chapel inside was covered with images. Saints, animals, and mythological creatures were surrounded in a tapestry of garlands and other decorative motifs. The whole design involved interrelating and harmonizing two distinct types of stone carving, high and low relief. The planning and the technical abilities necessary to carry out such a project attest to the extremely high levels of skill reached in Vladimir-Suzdal. Some features, such as the first use of the ogee arch in Russia and the representation of the saints betray Western European influences. But the fantastic creatures and the overall pattern of the decoration is strikingly reminiscent of the decorations of Armenian and Georgian churches of the same period. This eastern influence on Suzdalian architecture was a natural development. The cities of the area traded in the east via the Volga River. Yury Dolgoruky and his sons Andrei Bogoliubsky and Vsevolod III married princesses from the east, and Bogoliubsky's youngest son married Queen Tamara of Georgia in 1184.

Judging by the hypothetical reconstructions of scholars such as Georgy Karlovich Vagner, the central space of the original church was small, roughly thirty-four feet (10.4 m) by thirty-five (10.7 m). Because the apses on the eastern side of the church and the vestibules on the other three sides opened directly into the center, and because the interior was uncluttered, the church nonetheless must have given the impression of roominess. Tall and graceful in the Suzdalian style, it possessed three tiers representing Earth, the Church, and Heaven. In its time it was justly considered a marvel of architecture. It served as a model for the Uspensky Sobor, the first stone church constructed in the Moscow Kremlin (1386).

Sviatoslav Vselodovich also began work on the Mikhailo-Archangelsky monastery in Yuriev-Polskoy, but that complex retains none of the original buildings. Most of its architecture dates from the seventeenth and eighteenth centuries. Except for the seventeenth-century belfry, none are of particular architectural note.

During the years of the Mongol occupation of Russia (1237-1480) the history of the town was uneventful. The line of the Yuriev princes died out in the middle of the fourteenth century and the town became a possession of Moscow. The Moscow grand princes gave the town as "feedings" (kormlenie), or subsistence, grants to foreign servitors. In the fifteenth century the Lithuanian prince Svidrigailo received its revenues as did Abdul-Letif, khan of Kazan, and Kaibul, son of the khan of Astrakhan, in the sixteenth century. Under these absentee rulers Yuriev-Polskoy declined. It has remained a small provincial town ever since. In 1708 it was included in Moscow province (guberniia), but in 1796 it was made part of Vladimir province. In 1970 its population was 22,000. In addition to its architectural monuments it possesses a museum of applied art of the fifteenth through the eighteenth centuries.

Bibliography: Brief descriptions of the Georgievsky Sobor are found in Robert Auty and Dimitri Obolensky, eds., *An Introduction to Russian Art and Architecture* (Cambridge, 1980); William Craft Brumfield, *Gold in Azure. One Thousand Years of Russian Architecture* (Boston, 1983); David Roden Buxton, *Russian Medieval Architecture. With an Account of the Transcaucasian Styles and Their Influence in the West* (New York, 1975), reprint of 1934 ed.; Hubert Faensen and Vladimir Ivanov, *Early Russian Architecture* (New York, 1975); George Heard Hamilton, *The Art and Architecture of Russia* (Baltimore, 1954); Kira V. Kornilovich and Abraam L. Kaganovich, *Arts of Russia. From the Origins to the End of the 18th Century*, trans. by James Hogarth (Geneva, 1976); Ksenia Sergeevna Polunina, *Architectural Monuments of Vladimir, Suzdal, Yuriev-Polskoi* (L., 1974); Tamara Talbot Rice, *A Concise History of Russian Art* (New York, 1963); and Arthur Voyce, *The Art and Architecture of Medieval Russia* (Norman, Okla., 1967). More substantive treatments are Nadezhda Nikolaevna Trofimova, ed., *Yur'ev-Pol'skoi. Pamiatniki arkhitektury i iskusstva. Al'bom*, with an afterword by Georgy Karlovich Vagner (M., 1985); Georgy Karlovich Vagner, *Skulptura Vladimiro-Suzdal'skoi Rusi, g. Iur'ev-Pol'skoi* (M., 1964) and *Mastera drevnerusskoi skul'ptury. Rel'efy Iur'eva-Pol'skogo* (M., 1966); and N.N. Voronin, *Vladimir. Bogoliubovo. Suzdal'. Iur'ev-Pol'skoi. Sputnik po drevnim gorodam Vladimirskoi zemli* (M., 1983).

George N. Rhyne

YUZOVKA (1870-). Industrial town on the Kalmius River in southeastern Ukraine, sixty-two miles (100 km) north of the Azov Sea port of Mariupol. It epitomized the rapid industrial growth of the late nineteenth century. First called "Yuzovsky zavod" (the Hughes factory), the settlement soon became known as Yuzovka.

Yuzovka was founded in August 1870 by the Welsh ironmaster John Hughes, who built the iron mill and coal mines of the New Russia Coal, Iron and Rail Producing Co. Officially a settlement in Bakhmut county (uezd) of Ekaterinoslav province (guberniia), Yuzovka quickly became the de facto capital of the Donbass industrial region. Since 1918 it has been the capital of Donetsk province. In 1924 its name was changed to Stalino and in 1962 to Donetsk. From its founding Yuzovka was a company town, owned and controlled by the New Russia Co. It gained municipal status in August 1917.

Yuzovka's population grew rapidly. In 1870 it numbered only 164 souls. In 1880 a population of 5,494 was counted and in 1892, some 20,000. The census of 1897 recorded 28,076 persons in the settlement. At the height of industrial activity during World War I Yuzovka reached a population of 70,000. After the revolution and civil war this dwindled to 54,701 in July 1917, and a low of 31,428 in 1923. The Soviet industrialization drive stimulated the city to grow once more and in 1989 it numbered 1.15 million.

From its beginning Russians were the dominant ethnic group in Yuzovka. Migrant peasants from Russian villages came south in the winter, seeking work, and in 1884 comprised 87 percent of the settlement's population. At this time Jews, who formed the commercial and service sector of the settlement, were 8 percent of the population; British and other Europeans made up the remainder. In July 1917 Russians constituted 58 percent of the population, Jews 18 percent, and Ukrainians, who because of the policies of the tsarist government did not previously appear separately, were recorded as 13 percent. Thirty-one other nationalities made up the remaining 11 percent of the population.

Ukrainian peasants maintained their traditional agricultural life as much as possible and resisted entering the mines and factories of Yuzovka and the Donbass that were foreign to their values. Only during the Soviet industrialization of the late 1920s was there a great influx of Ukrainian population into the city. Today close to half the population of Donetsk is of Ukrainian origin, although the culture and ambience remain largely Russified.

Yuzovka and Hughes' New Russia Co. were established on the basis of a concession from the Russian government, vitally interested in strengthening Russia's industrial potential. The availability of coking coal, iron ore, limestone, and water determined the site of Yuzovka. After an unsuccessful first attempt in April 1871 production of iron began in January 1872, and the first iron rails were produced in September 1873. Production of steel rails began in 1882. In 1873 the production of rails was 2,356 metric tons, increasing to 48,418 in 1890 and 84,756 metric tons in 1912. Production of coal, pig iron, and other iron products increased in similar fashion, although Russia's recurrent recessions brought temporary setbacks, particularly in 1899-1903. The labor force of the New Russia Co. grew commensurately, providing the impetus for the population growth of Yuzovka and the mining settlements around it.

Although the New Russia Co. remained the owner and dominant economic force in the settlement, the economy diversified. Yuzovka became the center for manufacture, maintenance, and distribution of mining equipment and related products. Lumber yards, leather tanning, clothing manufacture, and similar industries flourished. In the twentieth century five banks operated in Yuzovka. The settlement was the site of two annual fairs featuring sale of both manufactured and agricultural goods. In the years 1910-1913 the annual commercial turnover in the settlement averaged eight million rubles.

Distinctively urban in its structure, Yuzovka was served by the development of company-sponsored education and health facilities, as well as company housing. All of these enjoyed high priority in the values of John Hughes, who lived in Yuzovka and managed the New Russia Co. until his death in 1889. His four sons who succeeded him continued his social and managerial policies. These features of urban modernity were one source of the uniqueness that drew the attention of writers and social activists to Yuzovka. The other source was Yuzovka's rapid growth from the bare steppe, isolated from any moderating influence of established society. Hence the nicknames "Russia's California" and "Chicago of the steppes."

Despite the Hughes' good intentions urban facilities lagged constantly behind the needs of the rapidly growing settlement. Recurrent epidemics of cholera and typhus struck the crowded shacks and dugouts in which the transient population lived. In August 1892 "cholera riots" took place in which close to one hundred persons were killed and the commercial center of Yuzovka was burned.

The early strikes in Yuzovka and its surroundings, notably in 1887, often were accompanied by violence, sometimes involving factory workers against coal miners and frequently, as in the cholera riots, aimed at Jewish merchants and innkeepers. By 1898, when the factory labor force gained in stability and experience, labor disputes took on a more organized character, and whatever violence accompanied them most often was initiated by the tsarist regime.

As a center of industrial development Yuzovka drew the attention of the various revolutionary movements, beginning with the populists in the 1870s and 1880s. Until the turn of the century this was intermittent, and the revolutionaries were well controlled by the Okhrana, the tsarist political police. The factory workers, enjoying a rising standard of living, were not responsive to revolutionary agitation, but were conservative and patriotic in their outlook. In October 1905 an attempt to celebrate the tsar's manifesto of civil liberties gave rise to a three-day pogrom that resulted in at least twelve dead, one hundred injured and close to one million rubles property damage. Throughout December a soviet, elected from the New Russia factory and mines and surrounding mine settlements, functioned in Yuzovka, regulating supply and maintaining public order, but took no part in the armed conflict in the region.

In March 1917 a soviet formed, dominated first by Mensheviks, and then by Socialist Revolutionaries. In the beginning of November the Yuzovka Soviet twice condemned the Bolshevik seizure of power in Petrograd. A Bolshevik-Left SR coalition gained a majority on 17 November 1917, maintaining a tenuous existence until the spring. At the end of April 1918 the Germans captured Yuzovka. In November White forces under General Anton Ivanovich Denikin replaced them.

Bolshevik authority returned to Yuzovka on 1 January 1920. Reconstruction of the factory and mines began, hindered by inexperience, labor shortage, and famine. Yuzovka's real resurgence began only during the five-year plans, under its new name, Stalino. Both the name of Yuzovka and the attributes of a pioneering industrial town which it represented had passed into history.

Bibliography: Donetsk Oblast State Historical Archive; Donetsk Oblast Historical and Geographical Museum; Hughesovka Research Archive, Glamorgan County Record Office, Cardiff, Wales; Theodore H. Friedgut, *Iuzovka and Revolution*. Vol. 1, *Life and Work in Russia's Donbass, 1869-1924* (Princeton, 1989); Vol. 2, *Politics and Revolution in Russia's Donbass, 1869-1924* (Princeton, 1993); I.A. Gonimov, *Staraia Yuzovka* (M., 1967); S.I. Potolov, *Rabochie Donbassa v XIX veka* (M.-L., 1963); Emrys G. Bowen, *John Hughes (Yuzovka)* (Cardiff, 1978); Theodore H. Friedgut, "Labor Violence and Regime Brutality in Tsarist Russia. The Iuzovka Cholera Riots of 1892," *Slavic Review*, Vol. 46, No. 2, (Summer, 1987), 245-265; J.N. Westwood, "John Hughes and Russian Metallurgy," *Economic History Review*, Series 2, Vol. 17, (1965), 564-569. Also significant is the film "Hughesovka and the New Russia," (Cardiff: Teliesyn Productions, 1991).

Theodore H. Friedgut

Z

ZABAIKAL PROVINCE (1851-). Southeastern Siberian province extending eastward from Lake Baikal.

Zabaikal province was created in 1851 out of Irkutsk province. At that time it had two districts, Verkhneudinsk and Nerchinsk. By 1872 the number of districts had risen to seven. The governor-general of Eastern Siberia administered the area until 1884 when it was put under the Priamur governor-general. A military governor headed the province itself.

Cossacks first appeared in the area in 1639. With increasing Russian colonization, they became the frontier guards. Under a statute of 17 March 1851 the Zabaikal Cossack Host consisted of frontier cossacks, the city regiment, the station cossacks, the Tungus and Buriat regiments, and the civilian frontier population, a total of 52,350 males. In the early twentieth century cossacks made up about one-third of the population.

The chief highway from Siberia to the Pacific Ocean ran through Zabaikal province. From Lake Baikal it passed through Verkhneudinsk, Chita, Nerchinsk to Sretensk. There travelers transferred to boats on the Shilka River in summer or traveled on ice in the winter and continued their journey. Thawing and freezing interrupted travel on the river for six weeks in the spring and six weeks in the winter. A main road led south to Troitskosavsk and the Mongolian border, and further east roads connected the main highway with the mines at Nerchinsky Zavod and Petrovsky Zavod.

The Zabaikal Railroad opened for service in 1900, and the Circumbaikal section in 1905. Beginning at Innokentevskaia on the western side of Lake Baikal, the railroad runs for 1,344 miles (2,163 km) to Skovorodino. A branch from Karymskaia went southeast to the Chinese frontier, where it joined the Chinese Eastern Railroad. A telegraph line followed the main route and had branches to Kiakhta and Nerchinsky Zavod.

Gold was found in the Nerchinsk mountains between the Shilka and Gazimur rivers and also in the Chikoy and Tsipa river systems. Mining began in 1838. Production peaked in 1882 and then began to fall, although the number of mines increased. Mining began at the silver and tin deposits in Nerchinsk in 1704 but by the nineteenth century the yields of ore were falling. The same happened with lead. Mining began in 1811 and continued for thirty years, until the deposits were exhausted. Work began at the iron ore deposits between the Uda and Khilok rivers in 1789. The center was at Petrovsky Zavod (later, Petrovsk-Zabaikalsky).

Zabaikal province was well known in Russia as a place of forced labor. The Nerchinsk penal colony was divided into three regions: Zerentui, Algachinsk, and Kariisk. In 1891 Zerentui had four prisons, Algachinsk four, and Kariisk three, although later two were closed. At the end of 1891 there were 2,318 male and female prisoners. The prisoners worked in the mines, built prisons and other buildings, made clothing, baked bread, and performed other chores. In 1891 the government spent 30.1 kopecks to maintain one prisoner for one day.

According to the 1897 census the province had 676,407 permanent residents. Of the permanent residents 345,475 were male and 330,932 female. Broken down by language, Russians accounted for 444,900, Buriats 179,487, and Tungus 30,436.

In terms of religious belief the Russian Orthodox Church enrolled 443,009, Old Believers made up 36,623, and non-Christian native peoples (Buddhist, shamanists), 178,628. The Buriats and Tungus were mostly Buddhists, and by 1860 there were 157 Buddhist and shaman temples. By occupation 239,001 were peasants, 195,253 were military cossacks, and 184,046 were native peoples.

Chita, with a population of 11,511, was the largest town, followed by Troitskosavsk (8,788), Verkhneudinsk (8,086), Nerchinsk (6,639), and Nerchinsky Zavod (3,663).

Zabaikal province was bounded by Lake Baikal and Irkutsk province on the west, Yakutsk province on the north, Amur province on the east and China and Mongolia on the south. It lay between 102°37′ and 121°26′ east longitude and between 49°54′ and 57° north latitude. Its area was about 380, 894 square miles (613,000 sq. km).

Zabaikal's rivers belong to the Baikal, Lena, and Amur river systems. The major rivers of the Amur system include the Shilka and Argun, which flow together to form the Amur, the Onon, the Gazimur, and Ingoda. The Vitim is the chief river of the Lena system, but the Olekma and Bolshoy Patom are also significant tributaries. The Selenga, Chikoy, Uda, and Khilok all drain into Lake Baikal.

Several mountain systems cover the area. They generally run from southwest to northeast. The Yablonovy Mountains almost bisect the province. To the east, running along the Chinese frontier is the Borshchovochy range. The Stanovoy range blocks the north.

Winters are long and cold. The average air temperature in Chita is 23°F (-26.7°C) in January and 65.8°F (18.8°C) in July. For Sretensk, the corresponding temperatures are -26.6°F (-32.6°C) and 67.1°F (19.5°C). During the winter winds blow from the northwest to the southeast and bring clear, dry, cold weather. In the summer they blow in the opposite direction bringing rains from the Pacific Ocean.

Precipitation declines from north to south and from west to east as far as the Yablonovy range. It begins to increase further east. Flooding is common in the summer months. Chita averages 13.7 inches (348 mm) of precipitation a year, 66 percent of which falls in July, August, and September. Both Verkhneudinsk and Chita get about 7.9 inches (20 cm) of snow a year.

The chief original towns were Barguzin, founded in 1648 as a stockade (ostrog) to collect tribute from the Buriats and Tungus; Selenginsk, founded in 1840 as New Selenginsk on the left bank of Selenga River about 1.9 miles (3 km) from Old Selenginsk; Troitskosavsk, founded as Kiakhta trading post in 1743, named Troitskosavsk in 1851, renamed Kiakhta in 1934; Verkhneudinsk, founded in 1666 as a winter cabin (zimovie) and named Verkhneudinsk in 1783, later called Ulan-Ude; Chita, founded 1851; Nerchinsk founded as a stockade in 1654; and Aksha, founded in 1765 on the right bank of the Onon River.

In terms of area, the province covered what later became the Buriat ASSR (Autonomous Socialist Soviet Republic) and Chita province. It became the center of the Far Eastern Republic in 1921. The Mongols in the western part were organized into the Buriat Mongol Autonomous province in 1922, and in 1923 all Mongol administrative units in Zabaikal province and Irkutsk province were organized into the Buriat Mongol Republic. The eastern part, Chita, Aksha, Nerchinsk, and Nerchinsky Zavod districts, with the exception of the territory occupied by the Aginsk Buriats, became part of Far Eastern Territory. In 1930 these administrative units became subordinate to East Siberian Territory. They were included into Chita province when it was created on 26 September 1937.

Bibliography: A. Kremnev, *Chitinskaia oblast'* (Chita, 1959) is a short essay on natural resources, economics, and culture. *Predbaikal'e i Zabaikal'e* (M., 1965) is an economic geography of the region. See also *Pervaia vseobshchaia perepis' naseleniia Rossiiskoy imperii, 1897 g. v. 74, Zabaikal'skaia oblast* (SPb., 1904); *Istoriia Buriat-Mongol'skoi ASSR*. 2nd. ed., 2 vols. (Ulan-Ude, 1954-1959); *Entsiklopedicheskii slovar'*, Vol. 12, (SPb., 1894).

Robert B. Valliant

ZAGOSKIN, MIKHAIL NIKOLAEVICH (1789-1852). Historical novelist. The "father" of the Russian historical novel.

Zagoskin was born on 14 July 1789 on the family estate Ramzai near the city of Penza in Penza province. As was customary for the landed gentry of that time, he was taught a minimum of basic skills—reading, writing, and arithmetic—by tutors, and otherwise given complete freedom to do as he pleased. Zagoskin, a voracious reader, made good use of his father's library. Before he left for St. Petersburg to take a position in the civil service at age thirteen he had read the early fiction of Karamzin, the gothic novels of Anne Radcliffe, and the sentimental plays of the chauvinistic German playwright August Kotzebue (1761-1819) who was very popular in Russia at the end of the eighteenth century. All of these had considerable influence on his later life and especially on his writing.

Before he was eleven Zagoskin wrote a three-act play and at least one long tale. Once he was in St. Petersburg he did no writing, but instead concentrated on making up for deficiencies in his haphazard education. In 1812 he enrolled as an officer in the St. Petersburg volunteer corps. When the corps was disbanded he returned to the family estate. It was there that he wrote his first play, a one-act comedy The Rogue (Prokaznik), which survived only two performances in St. Petersburg. In 1815 his play A Comedy Versus Comedy (Komediia protiv komedii) was well received by the public and established Zagoskin's reputation as a dramatist. Between 1815 and 1823 Zagoskin published several plays, all of which were well received by the public at that time.

He held a variety of positions in the civil service. In 1820 he moved to Moscow where he was appointed to a position of theatrical management in the office of the Moscow governor. Between 1823 and 1828 he did not publish anything; instead he studied for civil service examinations in order to advance the rank of titular counselor. He passed brilliantly in 1828 and continued to rise in the civil service. In 1830 he was appointed director of Moscow theaters and elected to the Russian Academy. Zagoskin received many awards throughout his lifetime, including the coveted Cavalier of St. Anna first rank in 1851. He died in Moscow on 23 June 1852 after a long and painful illness.

Although Zagoskin began his literary career as a playwright, he also wrote short stories, ethnographic sketches, horror tales, novels in verse, and prose novels. He is remembered today primarily as a historical novelist. *Yury Miloslavsky or the Russians in 1612* (Yury Miloslavsky ili russkie v 1612 godu, 1829), his best known novel, generally is considered to be the first Russian prose novel and one that set the pattern for Russian historical fiction in the 1830s. It went through four editions in three years and more than twenty editions throughout the nineteenth century. Zagoskin became a literary hero overnight. Aleksandr Sergeevich Pushkin, Ivan Andreevich Krylov, Vasily Andreevich Zhukovsky, and others responded to the novel with exaggerated praise. Zagoskin was the first of a whole school of historical novelists who wrote in the 1830s, including Fadei Venediktovich Bulgarin, Ivan Ivanovich Lazhechnikov, Nikolai Alekseevich Polevoi, Aleksandr Fomich Veltman, and Rafael Mikhailovich Zotov. The war of 1812 and the emergence of a romantic ideology in the 1820s in Russia intensified the feeling of national self-awareness. This led to an interest in the national past, with the development of the historical fiction as a logical consequence.

Sir Walter Scott's novels, many of which had been translated into Russian, served as models for the developing Russian historical novel. In *Yury Miloslavsky* Zagoskin borrowed from Scott the techniques and devices of structure and development, motifs, the compositional function of characters, and the methodology of reconstructing historical time. Like Scott, Zagoskin combined the elements of a love story with an adventure story. The protagonist is an imaginary character who comes from a stratum of society which gives him access to characters at all social levels. A close comparison of *Yury Miloslavsky* and some of Scott's novels more than justifies the conclusion that in *Yury Miloslavsky* there is more of Scott than Zagoskin. One could even say that *Yury Miloslavsky* is a Russian adaptation of Scott's *Legend of Montrose*. *Yury Miloslavsky* is Zagoskin's expression of his patriotism and an affirmation of Russia's spiritual superiority over the West. He wanted to present the most glorious aspects of the Russian national spirit. Therefore he selected a historical period which was parallel in many respects to the recently experienced Napoleonic invasion, namely the Time of Troubles at the end of the sixteenth century. This was a period of interregnum, civil strife, and occupation and expulsion of an enemy, the Polish armies, lasting until 1613. It was this attention to the Russian national spirit that caused his contemporaries to greet his novel so enthusiastically.

His second novel, *Roslavlev or the Russians in 1812* (Roslavlev ili Russiye v 1812 godu, 1830), drew from his own experiences in 1812. It is probably the best treatment of 1812 prior to Leo Tolstoy's *War and Peace*, but the subject was still too close to those who had participated in it. For this reason it was too easily misinterpreted. The critics were not impressed. Even so, four editions appeared during the author's lifetime. The first of these was so large that it was the equivalent of seven normal editions.

Stung by criticism of this work, Zagoskin retreated to the distant past, to the prehistoric period of Prince Vladimir's Kiev and concentrated on the theme of Christianity versus paganism in *Askold's Grave* (Askol'dova mogila, 1833). Critics liked it even less than the second novel. Nonetheless it went through nineteen printings during the course of the nineteenth century.

The historical novels he wrote toward the end of his life, *Brynsky Forest* (Brynskii les, 1846) and *Russians at the Beginning of the Eighteenth Century* (Russkiye v nachale osemnadtsatago stoletiia, 1848), which encompass the period of Peter the Great, were not successful.

In the USSR Zagoskin was not published until 1956 when *Yury Miloslavsky* appeared, followed by *Roslavlev* in 1959, new editions of moderate size (100,000 copies) appearing every four or five years. In the 1980s all three of Zagoskin's first novels were published as well as some of his lesser known works and ethnographic sketches, especially a series entitled *Moscow and Muscovites* (Moskva i moskvichi, 1842). Zagoskin was one of the most widely read authors in nineteenth-century Russia, and it appears that this may also be true for the 1980s, when at least sixteen editions of his works were printed (four million copies) including nine editions of *Yury Miloslavsky* (1.35 million copies) and four editions of *Roslavlev* (1.2 million copies). Critical commentary was restricted to that in the introductions and notes accompanying the various editions.

Zagoskin was an excellent storyteller. What distinguishes him from most of the novelists of the early nineteenth century was his ability, which he learned as a playwright, to bring the past to life through use of dialogue. This readability and the fact that his novels emphasize Russian nationalism, patriotism, and Orthodoxy continued to ensure the popularity of his novels even in the 1990s.

Bibliography: Zagoskin's collected works are M.N. Zagoskin, *Polnoe sobranie sochinenii*, 10 vols., biographical essay by A.O. Kruglyi, Vol. 1 (Spb., 1898). An English translation is F. Chamier, ed., *The Young Muscovite* or *The Poles in Russia* (New York, 1834). The major secondary work in English is Miriam G. Schwartz, "M.N. Zagoskin as a Historical Novelist," (Ph.D. diss., The Ohio State University, 1978). See also A. Peskova, "Vstupitel'naia stat'ia," in M.N. Zagoskin, *Sochineniia v 2 t.* (M., 1988), 1, 5-32.

Leon I. Twarog

ZAGS. See ZAPIS' AKTOV GRAZHDANSKOGO SOSTOIANIIA

ZAIONCHKOVSKY, PETR ANDREEVICH (1904-1983). Russian historian. Professor of History at Moscow University, 1951-1983. Leading specialist on state politics of imperial Russia. Compiler of major historical reference works.

Zaionchkovsky was born on 5 September (18 September) 1904 in Uralsk. His father, Andrei Cheslavovich, was a military doctor from a west-Russian, middle-gentry family that took pride in its kinship with Admiral Pavel Stepanovich Nakhimov (1802-1855). His childhood was spent in various west-Russian towns, with summers on the family estate, Seltso Mikhailovskoe, Sychevsky district, Smolensk province. He enrolled in the First Moscow Cadet Corps in 1915, where he studied until April 1918. From September 1918 to mid-1919 he continued his studies in the Kiev Cadet Corps. In 1920 he went to work as a railway clerk and finished his secondary schooling. Excluded by his social origins from continuing his education, he worked at various jobs, including fireman and metalworker, from 1925 to 1936. In 1936 at the age of thirty-three Zaionchkovsky registered as an external or night-course student at the Moscow Institute of History, Philosophy, and Literature (MIFLI). His principal teacher there was Yury Vladimirovich Gote (1873-1943), himself a pupil of Vasily Osipovich Kliuchevsky (1841-1911) and an outstanding representative of the last prerevolutionary generation of Moscow historians. In 1936 Zaionchkovsky took his first teaching job as a history instructor at the Moscow Flour-Milling Technicum.

Graduating in 1937 from MIFLI, he entered graduate study in history at Moscow University, again as an external student. Between 1938 and 1940 he passed the candidate examinations and wrote his first candidate's dissertation, "The Cyrillo-Methodian Society." In 1940 he began teaching history at the Moscow Oblast Pedagogical Institute. Zaionchkovsky volunteered for the army in 1941 and served at the front—first Stalingrad, then the Kursk salient, and finally Right-Bank Ukraine—from September 1942 to December 1943. In December 1943 he suffered shell-shock near Elizavetgrad (Kirovograd) and was demobilized as a major in 1944. From December 1944 to October 1952 he was director of the Manuscript Collection of the Lenin Library. In 1944 he also returned to teaching at the pedagogical institute, where he remained until 1948, when he began his teaching career at Moscow University. In 1950 he defended his doctoral dissertation on the military reforms of the 1860s-1870s. The next year he received a professorship there and held that post the rest of his life.

Zaionchkovsky also served as director of the Moscow University (Gorky) Library from 1952 to 1954. Between 1958 and 1961 he was chief editor of the historical journal, Papers of the Higher Schools, The Historical Sciences. (Nauchnye doklady vysshei shkoly, Istoricheskie nauki.) He served as an adjunct professor at Gorky University (Nizhny Novgorod) from 1958 to 1972. Forty-eight candidates' dissertations were defended under his supervision, and by the time of his death nine of his students had defended doctoral dissertations. From the late 1950s onward Zaionchkovsky also served as advisor to a considerable number of exchange scholars, mostly graduate students from Western Europe, Britain, and North America.

Beginning with the work on his doctoral dissertation, Zaionchkovsky emerged as the pre-eminent historian of state politics of late imperial Russia, beginning with the reign of Alexander II (1855-1881). Indeed he almost single-handedly mapped out this field of study for historical scholarship with numerous works on the reforms of the 1860s-1870s, the "counterreforms" of the 1880s-1890s, and the social structure of the civilian and military bureaucracies. From the outset Zaionchkovsky's work was characterized by massive exploitation of archival sources, principally drafts of reform legislation and the personal papers—diaries, memoirs, and correspondence—of statesmen. It was his habit to combine work on a scholarly monograph with publication of principal sources for the subject, especially the diaries of the statesmen involved. Thus he accompanied his study of the military reforms with the publication of the diaries of Dmitry Alekseevich Miliutin, the war minister, the other reforms of the 1860s-1870s with the diaries of Petr Aleksandrovich Valuev during his tenure as interior minister under Alexander II, and his study of the "counterreforms" of Alexander III with the diaries of State Secretary Aleksandr Aleksandrovich Polovtsov for the years 1883-1892. Accompanied by biographies of these statesmen and extensive commentaries, these publications constitute major research projects in their own right and have become standard sources for the study of the political history of late imperial Russia.

The subject matter of Zaionchkovsky's work and his methodology, the construction of straightforward empirical narratives based on systematic exploitation of the papers of relevant government agencies, and the private papers of statesmen were new phenomena in Soviet historiography. Their impact on historical scholarship has been correspondingly great, giving rise to the term "the Zaionchkovsky school," whose membership includes not only his students, formally speaking, but a number of other younger scholars throughout Russia. One of Zaionchkovsky's students and an outstanding representative of his school, Larisa Georgievna Zakharova, succeeded to his chair at Moscow University.

Another favorite and closely related subject of Zaionchkovsky's scholarly interest was the social structure of the imperial bureaucracy, both civil and military. He devoted a monograph to each of these in the 1970s and was at work on a second volume on the army on the eve of World War I when he died. In this work Zaionchkovsky exploited to good advantage his characteristic fondness for statistical sources. Especially significant in this case were imperial service records (personnel files), a source that he was largely responsible for bringing into scholarly purview. This same attraction to statistical materials, or "mass sources" as they were known in Soviet scholarly jargon, can be seen in Zaionchkovsky's pioneering work of the 1950s *The Realization of the Peasant Reform of 1861* (Provedenie v zhizn' krest'ianskoi reformy 1861 g., 1958). He based this study of the related land and obligation settlements affected by the reform on wholesale analysis of the regulatory charters (ustavnye gramoty) drawn up between peasants and their former masters. In order to carry out this analysis on a country-wide basis Zaionchkovsky mobilized an entire generation of his graduate students, many of whom produced regional studies using the methods developed by their teacher. Their work was duly acknowledged by their teacher in his general study.

Zaionchkovsky's preoccupation with the history of the state and its bureaucracies, and with the institutional, personal, and statistical sources for its study led him into one other field of activity in which he made a lasting contribution to scholarship. Indeed it is almost certain that his work here, as he himself liked to predict, will prove the most enduring of all his many accomplishments. This is the field of historical reference works (spravochnye izdaniia), to which he turned with remarkable vigor in the late 1960s. In fact, Zaionchkovsky's first reference work had appeared as early as 1948, when he published with Elizaveta Nikolaevna Konshina (1890-) a short guide to the collections of the manuscript division of the Lenin Library, which he directed at that time. He also published a bibliography of Moscow University dissertations for the years 1934-1954 during his tenure as director of the university library. But his first great work as organizer and editor of reference materials was his *Guide to Reference Materials on the History of Prerevolutionary Russia* (Spravochniki po istorii dorevoliutsionnoi Rossii, 1971). This unique work lists and describes more than four thousand reference works of diverse kinds, from handbooks of government statistics to personnel lists and railroad timetables. A second edition in 1978 increased the number of listings by 25 percent.

Zaionchkovsky's greatest monument of this kind is *The History of Prerevolutionary Russia in Diaries and Memoirs* (Istoriia dorevoliutsionnoi Rossii v dnevnikakh i vospominaniiakh). This is a multivolume bibliography of Russian-language memoirs and diaries that he and a team of librarians from Moscow and Leningrad commenced in the early 1970s. The thirteenth, apparently final, volume (Vol. 5, pt. 2) of this enormous annotated bibliography appeared in 1989, six years after its creator's death. In the introductory articles to the volumes that appeared during his lifetime, Zaionchkovsky elaborated a classification of memoirs by their formal characteristics and a periodization of the development of the genre in Russia. Both of these publications were unprecedented in Russian national bibliography and have become standard tools for all scholars of the Russian cultural tradition.

Working in the near aftermath of the Stalin era, in a period in which dogmatism and enforced consensus still generally prevailed in matters of historical interpretation, Zaionchkovsky was cautious in interpretive matters, but his positivistic method of letting the documents speak for themselves carried a message of antidogmatism that was not lost on his contemporaries. On a variety of occasions he found his interpretation of tsarist politics, especially in matters of reform initiatives, challenged by the "class struggle" approach of Academician Militsa Nechkina and some of her followers. Their interpretation, following Lenin, treated the reform efforts of the tsar and his bureaucrats as the mere "by-product" of the "revolutionary situation" arising from the "class struggle" of the peasants. Zaionchkovsky implicitly challenged this interpretation in his general study of the emancipation, *The Abolition of Serfdom in Russia,* by discussing a variety of factors contributing to the reform, including the impact of the loss of the Crimean War and the initiative of the monarch and the reforming bureaucrats. In later editions he gradually put more emphasis on the initiative from above and eventually eliminated even the term "revolutionary situation" from his text.

His one outright polemic of historical interpretation was in his second major work on the politics of reform, *The Russian Autocracy in Crisis, 1878-1882,* where he directly challenged an attempt by Mikhail Isaevich Kheifets, in a book published the year before (*The Second Revolutionary Situation in Russia*), to carry the "peasant class-struggle" thesis of Nechkina over to the analysis of the crisis at the end of Alexander II's regime. Zaionchkovsky rejected this thesis by demonstrating that peasant disturbances at the time of the crisis were essentially insignificant and that the revolutionary terrorist movement was the direct cause of the governmental crisis.

In 1967 Zaionchkovsky was elected an honorary member of the American Historical Association. In 1972 he was awarded the McVane Prize at Harvard University. A year later he was elected an honorary member of the British Academy. It must be noted as a sign of the times that Zaionchkovsky was not permitted to travel abroad to receive these honors in person. Indeed the invitation to attend the award meeting of the British Academy was intercepted and concealed from Zaionchkovsky, possibly by the Moscow University faculty administration, and a reply declining the invitation on grounds of poor health was sent to the Academy over his name. In 1980 Zaionchkovsky was awarded the Russian order of merit in science (pochetnoe zvanie zasluzhennogo deiatelia nauki RSFSR).

Still teaching and in the full swing of his reference-work editing, Zaionchkovsky died of heart failure on 30 September 1983 while at work in the Lenin Library on a second volume about the Russian officers' corps on the eve of World War I. He was seventy-nine years old.

Bibliography: Petr Andreevich Zaionchkovskii. K semidesiatiletiiu so dnia rozhdeniia. Biobibliografiia (M., 1974).

Monographs by P.A. Zaionchkovsky are *Voennye reformy 1860-1870 godov v Rossii* (M., 1952); *The Abolition of Serfdom in Russia,* ed. and trans. by Susan Wobst (Gulf Breeze, Fla., Academic International Press, 1979) (Otmena krepostnogo prava v Rossii [three editions: M., 1954, 1960, 1968]); *Provedenie v zhizn' krest'ianskoi reformy 1861 g.* (M., 1958); *Kirillo-Mefodievskoe obshchestvo (1846-1847)* (M., 1959); *The Russia Autocracy in Crisis, 1878-1882,* ed. and trans. by Gary M. Hamburg (Gulf Breeze, Fla., Academic International

Press, 1980) (Krizis samoderzhaviia na rubezhe 1870-1880-kh godov [M., 1964]); *The Russian Autocracy under Alexander III*, ed. and trans. by David R. Jones (Gulf Breeze, Fla., Academic International Press, 1976) (Rossiiskoe samoderzhavie v kontse XIX stoletiia. Politicheskaia reaktsiia 80-kh-nachala 90-kh godov (M., 1970)); *Samoderzhavie i russkaia armiia na rubezhe XIX-XX stoletii. 1881-1903* (M., 1973); *Pravitel'stvennyi apparat samoderzhavnoi Rossii v XIX v.* (M., 1978).

Principal reference works edited by P.A. Zaionchkovsky are *Spravochniki po istorii dorevoliutsionnoi Rossii. Bibliograficheskii ukazatel'* (M., 1971; 2nd edition, revised and expanded, M., 1978); *Istoriia dorevoliutsionnoi Rossii v dnevnikakh i vospominaniiakh. Annotirovannyi ukazatel' knig i publikatsii v zhurnalakh. Nauchnoe rukovodstvo, redaktsiia i vvedenie professora P.A. Zaionchkovskogo*, 5 vols. in 13 parts (M., 1976-1989). A general index volume remains to be published.

Principal documentary publications edited by P.A. Zaionchkovsky are *Dnevnik D.A. Miliutina. 1873-1882. Redaktsiia, biograficheskii ocherk i primechaniia P.A. Zaionchkovskogo*, 4 vols. (M., 1947-1950); *Dnevnik P.A. Valueva, ministra vnutrennikh del. 1861-1876. Redaktsiia, vvedenie, biograficheskii ocherk i kommentarii Prof. P.A. Zaionchkovskogo*, 2 vols. (M., 1961); *Dnevnik gosudarstvennogo sekretaria A.A. Polovtsova. Redaktsiia, biograficheskii ocherk i kommentarii P.A. Zaionchkovskogo*, 2 vols. (M., 1966).

On Zaionchkovsky see Boris Vasil'evich Anan'ich, "Istoriia Rossii vtoroi poloviny XIX veka v trudakh P. Zaionchkovskogo (Ko 80-letiiu so dnia rozhdeniia)," *Istoriia SSSR*, No. 5 (1984), 80-88; Terence Emmons, "Petr Andreevich Zaionchkovskii (1904-1983)," *Slavic Review*, No. 4 (1984), 742-743; "Petr Andreevich Zaionchkovskii," *Voprosy istorii*, No. 11 (1983); Alfred J. Rieber, "Petr Andreevic Zajonckovskij † 1983," *Jahrbücher für Geschichte Osteuropas*, 33 (1985), H. 2, 313-316.   *Terence Emmons*

ZAIRE, SOVIET FOREIGN RELATIONS WITH (1960-). Zaire, known originally as the Republic of the Congo, received its independence from Belgium on 30 June 1960. The Congo's internal problems merged with cold war tensions and proved to be a major factor in Soviet-Zairian relations throughout most of the 1960s and 1970s.

Almost immediately the country was torn by mutiny in the armed forces and secessionist movements in several provinces. The major secessionist threat came from Katanga province led by the pro-Western leader Moise Tshombe. In Leopoldville a contest for power developed between the anti-Western premier, Patrice Lumumba and the moderate president, Joseph Kasavubu. Complicating internal problems was the presence of Belgian armed forces sent to protect Europeans in the country. The United Nations sent a peacekeeping force (ONUC) in July, but it was unable initially to restore order.

Lumumba, angered that the United Nations would confront neither the Belgian forces nor those of Tshombe, invited Soviet assistance. Moscow provided Lumumba with a small number of military vehicles and about two hundred technicians. This caused Kasavubu to dismiss Lumumba who in turn fired the president. The competing claims of the two leaders were resolved in September 1960. Joseph Mobuto, the chief of staff of the Congolese Army, threw his support behind Kasavubu and expelled all Soviet-bloc representatives. In February 1961 Lumumba was murdered under obscure circumstances, provoking Moscow's wrath toward United Nations Secretary-General Dag Hammerskjold, whom Soviet leader Nikita Sergeevich Khrushchev blamed for Lumumba's death. A Patrice Lumumba Afro-Asian Friendship University was established in Moscow as a symbol of the Soviet Union's commitment to African liberation from Western "imperialism."

Moscow made a limited and futile effort to support the Prague-trained Antoine Gizenga, Lumumba's successor as leader of the leftist forces in the Congo. Although the Soviet role was short-lived, these events in the early years of the country's independence had a long-term effect on relations between Zaire and the Soviet Union. In the autumn of 1963 Zaire expelled the Soviet diplomatic staff for their efforts to sponsor left-wing factions.

A major watershed in Congolese politics occurred in November 1965 when Joseph Mobuto—who later took the name Mobuto Sese Seko—seized power. Over time his rule became increasingly repressive and corrupt. In 1967 the Soviet Union and Zaire restored diplomatic ties after a five-year suspension, but relations remained tenuous. Mobuto relied increasingly on Western support and maintained a generally cool relationship with Moscow. Notwithstanding the exchange of parliamentary delegations in 1972, relations remained tense during much of the 1970s. Moscow accused Zaire of supporting insurgencies in neighboring Angola, a Marxist ally of the Soviet Union, while Mobuto suspected that the Soviet Union was aiding rebels fighting his government. Early in the 1970s the Kinshasa government expelled several Soviet diplomats for affiliating with leftist rebels.

In March 1977 and again in May 1978 Zaire's Shaba province was invaded by separatists who operated out of Angola apparently with Soviet and Cuban support, although Moscow and Havana both denied complicity in the Shaba incursions. Mobuto appealed to the West for help. The United States, France, and Belgium provided assistance, for which Moscow condemned them. Shortly after the Shaba events Soviet attention to Zaire receded and several of Moscow's allies, including Angola, East Germany, and Cuba, moved to normalize relations with the Mobuto regime. After 1982 the successors of Soviet leader Leonid Ilich Brezhnev substantially reduced Soviet commitments in Africa. During the 1980s relations with Zaire normalized as part of Mikhail Sergeevich Gorbachev's concerted effort to improve relations with the West by reducing points of conflict in the third world.

Bibliography: Stephen T. Hosmer and Thomas W. Wolfe, *Soviet Policy and Practice Toward Third World Conflicts* (Lexington, Mass., 1983); Charles B. McLane, "Soviet African Relations," *Soviet-Third World Relations*, Vol. 3 (London, 1974); Morris Rothenberg, *The USSR and Africa. New Dimensions of Soviet Global Power* (Miami, 1980); Carol R. Saivetz and Sylvia Woodby, *Soviet-Third World Relations* (Boulder, 1985); Christopher Stevens, *The Soviet Union and Black Africa* (London, 1976).

Joseph L. Nogee

ZAKAVKAZSKII KRAEVOI KOMITET (1922-1937). Abbreviated Zakkraikom. The Transcaucasian Regional Committee of the Russian Communist Party (bolshevik) (RCP[b]). Created in February 1922. Initially its main functions were to orchestrate the establishment of the Transcaucasian Federation (Zakavkaz'skaia Sotsialisticheskaia Federativnaia Sovetskaia Respublika, ZSFSR) and "to combat nationalist tendencies." It then acted as the governing body of the Federation until its dissolution in 1937. Zakkraikom was located in Tbilisi.

Zakkraikom superseded the Caucasian Bureau of the RCP(b) (Kavbiuro) which had coordinated the Bolshevik takeover of the independent Caucasian republics: Azerbaijan in the spring of 1920, Armenia in December 1920, and Georgia in spring 1921. At the First Congress of Communist Organizations of Transcaucasia (18-22 February 1922) Kavbiuro was criticized for "indecisiveness" in the battle against "nationalist tendencies." The Congress therefore established Zakkraikom to fight nationalist tendencies within the party and to speed the political unification of the Caucasian republics.

The membership of Zakkraikom was similar to that of Kavbiuro. Grigorii Konstantinovich ("Sergo") Ordzhonikidze and Sergei Mironovich Kirov, former chairman and assistant chairman of Kavbiuro respectively, were full members of Zakkraikom and its presidium. They were loyal to Joseph Vissarionovich Stalin. They had led the Soviet conquest of the Transcaucasian republics, and until their promotions to posts in Moscow and Leningrad in 1926 they remained leaders of the ZSFSR and Zakkraikom. Kirov became first secretary of the Azerbaijan party organization in July 1921. Among the other twelve members of the Zakkraikom in 1922 were two Armenians, two Azerbaijanis and four Georgians; the others were Russian. Like other all-Transcaucasian bodies, the Russians and Georgians dominated, although the latter did not necessarily reflect Georgian interests.

The two functions given Zakkraikom at its creation were closely related, for the Transcaucasian republics resisted "unification." The republics had been assured of their autonomy when the Bolsheviks took them over. In spring 1921 Lenin sent a telegram to Ordzhonikidze demanding "the creation of a regional economic organ for all Transcaucasia." The railroad, trade, and banking systems were merged first. Oil from Azerbaijan was distributed without charge. In November Kavbiuro declared the necessity for political union, a "Transcaucasian Federation."

Some republic leaders regarded this as the de facto recreation of the tsarist viceroyalty of Transcaucasia. Ordzhonikidze and Kirov branded as "nationalists" anyone who voiced opposition to federation. But the flurry of protest from high-ranking party members, mainly in Georgia and Azerbaijan, slowed the pace of the project. Lenin criticized Kavbiuro's tactless handling of the local party organizations and instructed Stalin, then Commissar of Nationalities Affairs, to initiate a campaign of "discussion, propaganda and soviets' action from below" to lay the ground for federation. Despite Kavbiuro's energetic propaganda efforts of 1921, native communist leaders in Transcaucasia continued to protest in early 1922. Kavbiuro was replaced by the newly formed Zakkraikom, staffed with the same leaders.

Zakkraikom promptly took control of the party organizations of each Caucasian republic. The Azerbaijani and Georgian leaders who had protested, Dr. Nariman Narimanov and Budu Mdivani, were sent to represent their republics at the Genoa Conference and were absent when the final vote on federation was taken.

Within a month of the creation of Zakkraikom representatives of each Caucasian republic accepted the plan for federation in March 1922. It called for the completion of integration by the end of the year. Zakkraikom guided each republican party and state apparatus in political and economic integration, including land use, the hated cotton cultivation, establishment of a Transcaucasian Communist University, the use of the press, and all foreign relations. Control was consolidated by subordinating of most republican commissariats to the corresponding ZSFSR commissariats.

The full Zakkraikom met eight times during 1922. Its presidium held sixty-two meetings on specific issues. Zakkraikom had the power to confirm or block appointments to republican parties, which were themselves only regional (oblast) level branches of RCP(b). Ordzhonikidze's political supremacy in Caucasia was not in doubt.

Zakkraikom began publishing its own newspaper in Tbilisi, Dawn of the East (Zaria Vostoka), in June 1922. The task of Dawn of the East was to explain the importance of the federation in terms of party affairs, cooperation among soviets, economic construction, and "worker and trade union life." It also discussed dangers to the regime from bourgeois and "White Guard" newspapers abroad. Its circulation grew from 2,500 in June 1922 to 13,500 by the end of the year. The newspaper long outlived Zakkraikom, and became the voice of the Georgian Communist Party.

Zakkraikom instituted commemorations of communist "martyrs" and substituted new holidays for national or religious ones. It sponsored a memorial in Turkmenistan on the site of the execution of the "twenty-six Baku commissars" who had controlled Baku briefly in the spring of 1918. In Tbilisi it erected a monument to the Armenian revolutionary, Kamo. Zakkraikom tried to substitute International Women's Day (8 March) for the 27 January celebration of Georgia's St. Nino, and a general "Youth Holiday" in place of Orthodox Christmas.

The culmination of the federation process coincided with the discussion of the first USSR constitution in December 1922. The federation, not the republics, was to be a constituent member of the USSR on a theoretically equal footing with Ukraine or Belorussia. To the resentment of the republican leaders, an extra layer of bureaucracy was interposed between the three Caucasian republics and the USSR government.

The federation and Zakkraikom survived until the "Stalin Constitution" of 1936 and the republican constitutions that copied it in 1937. The Transcaucasian republics then joined the USSR as individual soviet socialist republics. Having overseen collectivization and the first Five Year Plans, Zakkraikom and ZSFSR were said officially to have "fulfilled their historical missions" and were liquidated in February 1937.

Bibliography: Information on Zakkraikom must be taken from various works on Transcaucasian history, especially party history. There is not even an entry on Zakkraikom in the first edition of *Bol'shaia Sovetskaia Entsiklopediia*, nor is it mentioned in the long entry on the ZSFSR. On the formation and early activities of the Zakkraikom there is Segvard Vagarshakovich Kharmandarian, *Lenin i stanovlenie Zakavkaz'skoi federatsii* (Erevan, 1969). Events surrounding the formation of the Federation are described in Richard Pipes, *Formation of the Soviet Union, 1917-1923* (Cambridge, Mass., 1957), and description of its functioning during the full term of its existence is found in *Ocherki istorii kommunisticheskoi partii Gruzii* (Tbilisi, 1971). Its formation and impact on Azerbaijan are discussed in Audrey L. Altstadt, *Azerbaijani Turks. Power and Identity Under Russian Rule* (Stanford, 1992), Chapter 6.

Audrey L. Altstadt

ZAKHAROV, ANDREIAN DMITRIEVICH (1761-1811). Architect. Designer of the Main Admiralty in St. Petersburg.

Son of a minor official in the Admiralty, Zakharov was born in St. Petersburg on 8 (19) August 1761. In 1767 at the age of five he was accepted into the art school of the Imperial Academy of Arts in St. Petersburg. Having successfully completed nine years of general preparatory studies, he was admitted in 1776 to the Academy proper for six years of training in architecture. Little is known of Zakharov's studies and none of his student work has been preserved. In 1782 he won a gold medal for his graduation project, a suburban "Vauxhall" (public pavilion), and received a stipend to study in Europe for three years.

After arriving in Paris at the beginning of 1783 Zakharov spent much of the year sketching at the Royal Academy. His request to study at the studio of Charles de Wailly, whose work was much admired by Catherine II, was declined for lack of space. But by autumn Zakharov was accepted into the studio of the royal architect Jean François Thérèse Chalgrin (1739-1811), subsequently renowned for designing the Arc de triomphe in Paris. Chalgrin was a pupil of the French architectural theoretician Étienne-Louis Boullée, and from him derived a sense of monumentality based on massive, simplified geometric forms and large ensembles—qualities that in turn imbued Zakharov's design for the Admiralty.

Zakharov returned to St. Petersburg by the summer of 1786, and the following year he was appointed adjunct professor at the Academy of Arts, where he taught until the end of his life. He also engaged in design work and produced a number of finely drawn project sketches, such as festive decorations for a celebration of the Treaty of Jassy (December 1791). In 1794 he was appointed supervisory architect of construction at the academy, whose large building was completed only at the beginning of the next century. He was also responsible for building a number of ancillary structures, none of which remain. In the same year he achieved the rank of academician, and in 1797 he was promoted to professor.

Zakharov's dual position as professor and supervisory architect at the academy prevented him from undertaking original design work. But at the beginning of 1800 Emperor Paul (1796-1801) released him from the latter obligation and appointed him architect at the imperial estate of Gatchina. Zakharov began a number of projects there, including an Italianate monastery with a large church. But the assassination of Paul caused the cancellation of all but a few projects that were near completion, including park structures and a Finnish church.

In St. Petersburg at the beginning of the nineteenth century, Zakharov's professional critique of Thomas de Thomon's new design for the Bourse, or Stock Exchange, led to changes in the final design. In 1804 Zakharov submitted a proposal to link the buildings of the Academy of Sciences in a single complex that would have complemented the Bourse at the point of Vasilevsky Island. Although approved, the proposal was not adopted. For ten months in 1801-1802 Zakharov traveled through the provinces to establish sites and designs for military schools. After his return to St. Petersburg he continued to design "model" administrative buildings in a neoclassical style for provincial towns such as Chernigov, Kazan, Simbirsk, and Poltava, where he planned the central square and flanking administrative center (1803-1805).

Zakharov's major commissions in the last decade of his life came as a result of his appointment in 1805 as chief architect for the Main Admiralty, reorganized the same year as the Ministry of Naval Forces and Fleet Management. Within the ministry the admiralty department supported the construction of all naval structures, and Zakharov thus had a wide range of activity that included the design of port and navy facilities in Kazan, Astrakhan, Arkhangelsk, Kherson, Nikolaev, and other towns. None of these have survived. In St. Petersburg he undertook the reconstruction of the Galley Harbor, whose warehouses and other buildings had burned in 1796, as well as the Provisions Island. Preserved drawings of the latter's warehouse designs show some of the best examples of the laconic, monumental, late neoclassical style. Nothing remains of these projects, nor of the large naval hospital that he planned for the Vyborg Side. Indeed most of Zakharov's projects in St. Petersburg have been destroyed, such as a large church in the suburb of Aleksandrovskoe and the Cathedral of St. Andrew at Kronstadt, both demolished in the 1930s.

Zakharov's greatest work was the Main Admiralty building, located on the site of Peter's admiralty shipworks, which had been rebuilt by Ivan Korobov in the 1730s. A large fire in 1783 destroyed part of the structure and led Catherine to propose moving the shipworks to Kronstadt. Financial constraints dictated otherwise, and Charles Cameron and Zakharov later supervised repairs to the existing walls. The formation of the navy ministry in 1805 required a more imposing structure, and in 1806 Zakharov submitted plans for its reconstruction, which extended the length of the main facade to 1233.5 feet (376 m). At the center of this facade Zakharov retained the walls of Korobov's tower but expanded them and added an Ionic peristyle, allegorical statuary, and a gilded spire. The Doric order is used for the porticos that provide points of accent for the great extent of the structure. At each end of the main facade perpendicular wings, extending to monumental end blocks on the Neva River, enclosed the shipyards. In the course of construction Alexander I objected to the east wing, which obscured his view of the mouth of the Neva from the

Winter Palace. Zakharov razed part of that wing and redesigned the proportions in 1808. The tense situation in Europe accelerated construction; and by 1811 much of the building was in use, although it was not finished until 1819.

Zakharov never married. He died on 27 August 1811, apparently as a result of a heart condition, exacerbated by the strain of holding two demanding jobs, Admiralty architect and professor at the academy, with constantly inadequate staff. Although Zakharov did not live to see its completion, the Admiralty was greeted as one of the great ornaments of St. Petersburg and is now seen as a masterpiece of neoclassicism in European architecture.

Bibliography: V.K. Shuiskii, *Andreian Zakharov* (L., 1989), currently the standard monograph on Zakharov, with extensive use of archival sources. V.I. Piliavskii and N.Ia. Leiboshits, *Zodchii Zakharov* (L., 1963). Plans, photographic documentation, and commentary on the Admiralty are presented in English in W.C. Brumfield, *Gold in Azure. One Thousand Years of Russian Architecture* (Boston, 1983), 306-312.

William C. Brumfield

ZAKKRAIKOM. See ZAKAVKAZSKII KRAEVOI KOMITET

ZALKIND, AARON BORISOVICH (1889-1936). Early Soviet educator and psychologist. Leader of the school of "pedology," one of the major concepts of child development in the USSR in the 1920s and 1930s.

Zalkind was born in St. Petersburg to a middle-class, Jewish family. As a young man he was attracted both to political radicalism and to psychology, which then was emerging as a new discipline and field of study in imperial Russia. He studied at the Psychoneurological Institute founded in St. Petersburg in 1907 by Vladimir Mikhailovich Bekhterev (1857-1924). Zalkind eventually received his doctorate there. Some of his colleagues at the Psychoneurological Institute were Mikhail Yakovlevich Basov (1892-1931) and Lev Semenovich Vygotsky (1896-1934). They along with Zalkind became leaders of the Soviet science of pedology in the late 1920s and early 1930s. Zalkind's studies with Bekhterev and others taught him that the formation of the individual human personality came both from internal forces operating within the individual and from the process of the individual's conscious adaptation to and manipulation of the external environment. During his studies Zalkind came to the additional conviction that human society must be reconstructed along up-to-date scientific lines. He therefore embraced Marxism.

Zalkind's interest in the dynamic relationship between the internal drives of the individual and the individual's ability consciously to shape the external environment became the hallmark of his work after 1917. He himself claimed to be one of the premier warriors on the "psychoneurological front" during the 1920s. While a professor at Sverdlov University in the 1920s he advocated the scientific observation of young children to gain a better understanding of how the individual learns to use and adapt to these twin drives. As a consultant to the People's Commissariat of Enlightenment at the same time, he advised the Department of Pre-School Education on the appropriate teaching strategies to create emotionally healthy individuals capable of reordering their environment according to intellectualized rather than impulse-driven criteria. He also served as an advisor to the Experimental Schools Section of the Commissariat of Enlightenment and as a consultant to the adults who were establishing the Young Pioneers organization in 1923 and 1924.

His best-known works in the 1920s were his anthology *Revolution and Youth* (1925) and his monograph *Sexual Upbringing* (1928). In these works he presented his theory of "revolutionary sublimation." This stated that individuals should consciously channel their libidinal drives toward the reconstruction of society as a whole.

By the end of the 1920s Zalkind actively championed the new Soviet science of pedology as the most appropriate method to determine the guidelines for Soviet education. Pedology studied the tension between the two kinds of psychological adaptation that must take place to create individuals who can control their environment. Contemporary Soviet reflexologists and behaviorists described the first kind of adaptation as immediate or involuntary responses that nonetheless could be manipulated. The pioneering work of academician Ivan Petrovich Pavlov (1849-1936) had established the foundations of this view. The second form of adaptation was the willful or voluntary response of the individual to the surrounding environment as the individuals attempted to seize control of it in order to bend it to their needs. This second view had various origins ranging from the theories of Karl Marx to the ideas of social Darwinism.

Early pedologists advocated the observation of children and of native peoples within the new Soviet Union to determine the various ways humans learn to respond to their surroundings. Later pedologists concluded that some individuals were better than others at combining the two forms of adaptation. They therefore asserted that testing to find out which individuals were more able in this regard would best serve the modernizing needs of Soviet society. Those so identified would receive an education designed to enhance their abilities to control their environment so that they could emerge as catalysts for those who were less able. Zalkind's career as a pedologist spanned both stages. Between 1928 and 1931 he was the leading advocate of this approach in the Commissariat of Enlightenment.

By 1931 many opponents to pedology had emerged. Educators such as Aleksandr Samoilovich Zaluzhny objected that it was too rigid and deterministic, as it focused on testing to decide who would get what kind of education. In 1931 the Soviet government redefined the purpose of education. The emphasis of the 1920s on the creation of the "new Soviet Man" gave way to concentration on students' mastery of basic skills. With this change pedologists such as Zalkind lost their positions as advisors and consultants to the Commissariat of Enlightenment. Zalkind nevertheless continued a rearguard defense of pedology in a series of publications from 1931 to 1935.

In July 1936 the Central Committee of the Communist Party of the Soviet Union issued a decree which forbade the Commissariat of Enlightenment to use pedology in Soviet schools. The decree asserted that pedology was both anti-scientific and anti-Marxist and thus had no place in the Soviet system. The publication of this decree provoked a plethora of denunciations of this school of thought, including at least three articles in 1936 that attacked Zalkind personally. Zalkind's errors were also the primary subject of a book written by Zaluzhny in 1936. It was not published until 1937 so it is not clear whether Zalkind ever saw it. He died near the end of 1936; his death was apparently a suicide.

Of Zalkind's contemporaries, the ideas of Vygotsky alone have continued to play a role in the more recent years of Soviet history. The 1988 All-Union Congress of Soviet Teachers expressed an interest in dropping the emphasis on mastery of subject matter as the primary mission of education and in returning to the goal that was dominant in the 1920s when Zalkind was active, that of creating a whole person through education. The protocols of that meeting did not mention either Zalkind or pedology once.

See Also: YOUTH IN THE USSR

Bibliography: Aaron B. Zalkind, "The Pioneer Youth Movement as a Form of Cultural Work Among the Proletariat" (1924) in William G. Rosenberg, ed., *Bolshevik Visions*, Part 2 (Ann Arbor, Mich., 1990); Sheila Fitzpatrick, *Education and Social Mobility in the Soviet Union, 1921-1934* (New York, 1979); David Joravsky, *Russian Psychology. A Critical History* (Cambridge, Mass., 1989); Jann Valsiner, *Developmental Psychology in the Soviet Union* (Bloomington, 1988).

Margaret K. Stolee

ZAMIATNIN, DMITRY NIKOLAEVICH (1805-1881). Minister of Justice (1862-1867) and major figure in the court reform of 1864. Zamiatnin, a nobleman from Nizhnii Novgorod province, completed the elite lycée at Tsarskoe Selo in the first years of its existence. There he attended a course given by the jurist Aleksandr Petrovich Kunitsyn, who taught natural law theory and propounded principles of the liberty and equality of mankind. Zamiatnin also began governmental service under Kunitsyn in the Second (Codification) Section of the Imperial Chancellery. It is clear that his own liberal and westernizing attitudes toward the law owed much to his teacher. As an official in the Second Section Zamiatnin was responsible for gathering materials on civil law and on the history of Russian courts.

In the 1840s and 1850s Zamiatnin held important positions in the Ministry of Justice. He was a chief procurator (state attorney) of the Senate and a member of the ministry's Consultation, where Sergei Ivanovich Zarudny led discussions of difficult legal cases and legal issues under consideration in the courts. Zamiatnin was appointed senator in 1852. He was also a member of the court elite. In 1840 he received the court title of chamberlain and was appointed to the position of heraldry master of the Senate. Serving in this capacity he gained note by rooting out corruption in the Heraldry Department of the Senate and by eliminating the large backlog of cases. He also headed several ministerial investigations of provincial courts. Zamiatnin thus combined the finesse and personal loyalty to the tsar characteristic of a courtier with experience in legal administration and a sympathy with reform.

This combination of qualities served him well during the formulation and implementation of the court reform of 1864, the most consistent and successful of the Great Reforms. In 1858 Zamiatnin was appointed deputy minister of justice. He immediately introduced a kindly and accessible manner into the ministry, whose previous minister, Viktor Nikitich Panin, was a rigid and distant conservative. Zamiatnin showed his willingness to seek advice from officials more knowledgeable than himself and promoted educated officials to high positions in the ministry. Educational qualifications of provincial officials in the judicial administration also rose, largely at his initiative. Following the principles of "official openness" fostered by Grand Duke Constantine Nikolaevich, he established the Journal of the Ministry of Justice (Zhurnal ministerstva iustitsii) and succeeded in gaining permission to publish judicial decisions of the Senate for the first time in Russian history.

Zamiatnin was appointed acting minister of justice in 1862 and minister in 1864. He strongly supported the efforts of the jurists in the ministry to introduce radical changes in the court system. At his insistence the ministry solicited comments on the fundamental principles of reform from senators and officials in the judicial administration. Under the direction of his deputy minister, Nikolai I. Stoianovsky, a special commission used these comments to introduce more than a thousand corrections into the proposed judicial statutes.

Perhaps Zamiatnin's greatest contribution was his swift and effective organization of the new courts and recruitment of their staffs. A law he sponsored in 1865 immediately introduced public and oral procedure, which prepared the judges for the transition. Zamiatnin sent emissaries to the provinces to clear the backlog of cases in the old courts. He took a personal role in reviewing the qualifications and records of those considered for reappointment and in selecting those worthy of appointment to the new courts. The speeches he delivered on the opening of the new courts emphasized that they were independent institutions dedicated entirely to the protection of the law and the spread of respect for the law in Russia.

As minister, Zamiatnin also endeavored to extend the powers of the Senate to supervise the ministry's rulings on legal questions and to preempt the authority of the Committee of Ministers over questions of administrative law. These efforts met a strong rebuff from the other ministers and particularly from the minister of interior, Petr Aleksandrovich Valuev. After the attempt on the tsar's life by Dmitry Vladimirovich Karakazov in April 1866 Zamiatnin struggled to maintain the independence of the new courts against Valuev's attempts to extend the power of provincial governors to supervise the judiciary in matters connected with state order and security. Despite Zamiatnin's efforts the tsar approved a measure permitting governors to summon judicial officials and demand explanations from them on such matters.

Valuev's most serious attack on the independence of the courts came in the area of press violations. The courts dismissed charges against editors of Moskovskie Vedomosti and Sovremennik, who were accused of violating the press laws. Valuev responded by proposing that press violations be removed from the jurisdiction of the courts and placed under the jurisdiction of the Chief Bureau of the Press. Zamiatnin's memorandum of October 1866 stated eloquently the obligations of procurators to act as defenders of the law rather than of the state interest. Despite Zamiatnin's efforts and the pleas of Zarudny and several other senators, Valuev prevailed. The Chief Bureau of the Press received the right to formulate the briefs for cases to be tried in the courts and to close journals by administrative order.

Zamiatnin clashed personally with the tsar at the beginning of 1867 when Alexander tried to remove Senator Mark Nikolaevich Liuboshchinsky, who had taken part in a meeting of the St. Petersburg zemstvo that had called for a central zemstvo assembly. Zamiatnin pointed out that senators as judges enjoyed lifetime tenure, and Alexander relented. In April 1867 he was relieved as minister and replaced by Count Konstantin Ivanovich Pahlen. He continued to serve in the State Council, but his defense of the courts made him odious to those close to the tsar and he did not receive the customary signs of recognition for long service to the throne. His successors strove, not always successfully, to ensure that the courts help the administration in combating liberal and revolutionary challenges to the tsarist system of rule.

See Also: ZARUDNY, SERGEI IVANOVICH and ZHURNAL MINISTERSTVA IUSTITSII.

Bibliography: G.A. Dzhanshiev, *Stranitsa iz istorii sudebnoi reformy. D.N. Zamiatnin* (M., 1883); F.B. Kaiser, *Die russische Justizreform von 1864* (Leiden, 1972); A.M. Kulomzin, "Dmitry Nikolaevich Zamiatnin," *Zhurnal ministerstva iustitsii*, No. 9 (1914), 233-322; R.S. Wortman, *The Development of a Russian Legal Consciousness* (Chicago, 1976).

Richard S. Wortman

ZAMOYSKI, COUNT ANDRZEJ (1800-1874). Polish magnate, agricultural reformer, public figure.

The Zamoyskis had been one of Poland's leading aristocratic families since the early sixteenth century. Andrzej Zamoyski was heir to vast estates in Russian-controlled Poland (the Congress Kingdom), a grand name, and a tradition of public service. He was educated in Paris, Geneva, and Edinburgh.

In 1823 Zamoyski entered government service. In recognition of his knowledge of agriculture he was appointed head of the agriculture and trade section of the interior ministry. During the Polish revolution of 1830-1831 he served in a number of governmental positions before being sent to Vienna to seek Austria's help against Russia.

Upon his return to Poland after the revolution he became deeply involved in the so-called "organic work." This meant progressive reform, designed to appease social grievances and promote prosperity as a precondition to creating a nation capable of standing on its own. In this effort Zamoyski carried out extensive reforms on his estates, converting labor service to money rents and establishing schools. He was active in forming a shipping line on the Vistula River and ran an agricultural credit bank. In 1842 he began to publish an agricultural journal (Rocznik gospodarstwa wieskiego).

The most notable phase of Zamoyski's career began in 1857 and creation of the Agricultural Society (Towarzystwo Rolnicze). The Agricultural Society had branches in seventy-seven districts and soon had four thousand members. Representing the nobility throughout the Congress Kingdom, it resembled a parliament (Sejm); many viewed Zamoyski, its president, as the leader of the nation. The Agricultural Society gained even more prestige in 1859.

Alexander II, who had urged the Russian nobility to offer suggestions on serf reform there, invited the Agricultural Society to propose a land reform for the Congress Kingdom. The society debated the issue at its annual meeting in February 1861. Zamoyski, a conservative reformer, favored commuting service labor to rent. A more radical wing of the society led by Tomasz Potocki wanted land to go to the peasants outright. A compromise was reached, whereby labor was converted into rents. The peasants would become permanent tenants, who might then agree with the landowners to convert their tenancy into freeholds.

Meanwhile nationalist tensions in the kingdom had grown. The successes of nationalism in Italy and Rumania during 1860 gave hope to Polish nationalists. Dissatisfaction with the terms of the Russian decree on peasant emancipation, which was to be implemented in Russia's western provinces, which many Poles considered still to be part of the Polish nation, also played a part. At any rate demonstrations of the nationalistic forces, in which students played a major role, brought clashes with Russian troops in Warsaw. They appealed to the Agricultural Society to take up their cause. Zamoyski had opposed involving the Society in political issues. Hoping to avoid revolution and unwilling to serve as a tool of the Russians, he advocated moral resistance, while hoping for help from the West. This was an ineffective position.

The Russians turned to Margrave Alexander Wielopolski to pacify the kingdom through concessions and firmness. Even though he dissolved the Agricultural Society on 6 April 1861, Zamoyski continued to be influential. He was one of the leaders of the moderate "White" nationalists, who opposed the more revolutionary "Reds." Wielopolski failed to win over any significant section of Polish society but was confirmed as Russia's chief administrator there in May 1862. At the same time Alexander appointed his brother, Grand Duke Constantine Nikolaevich, viceroy in the kingdom with the mission of winning over the public. In September 1862 Constantine interviewed Zamoyski as a leader of the Whites. As the price for Polish collaboration with the tsar Zamoyski demanded full autonomy for all Poles in the Russian empire, including those in the Russian western provinces of Lithuania and Ruthenia. He called for a constitution and an independent Polish army. These demands were totally unrealistic.

Zamoyski was summoned to St. Petersburg for an interview with Alexander II. Confronted with Zamoyski's refusal to relent, the tsar exiled him. Zamoyski took up residence in Paris, never to return to Poland. In his last years he wrote on a number of topics, including prison reform.

See Also: POLISH REBELLION OF 1863-64, and POLISH-RUSSIAN RELATIONS 1795-1917.

Bibliography: Especially useful is Piotr S. Wandycz, The Lands of Partitioned Poland, 1795-1918 (Seattle, 1974), which has an extensive bibliography. See also "Zamoiskii, Andrei," in I.E. Andreev, ed., Entsiklopedicheskii slovar', 41 vols., Vol. 23, reprint of 1890 ed. (SPb., 1990-), 204-205; Norman Davies, God's Playground. A History of Poland, 2 vols., Vol. 2, (New York, 1982), 348-351; and William Fiddian Reddaway, et al., eds., The Cambridge History of Poland. From Augustus II to Pilsudski (1697-1935), 2 vols., Vol. 2, (Cambridge, England, 1951), 368-376.

George N. Rhyne

ZAPIS' AKTOV GRAZHDANSKOGO SOSTOIANIIA (1918). Registration of acts of civil status, or bureau of vital statistics. Most frequently referred to by its abbreviation ZAGS.

The keeping of vital statistics was introduced by Peter the Great in 1722. From that time until the Russian revolution such information was compiled by the Orthodox Church. In 1918 the Bolshevik regime introduced legislation about vital statistics for the Russian republic and in 1926 regulations went into force for the component republics of the USSR. In urban areas sections of ZAGS were established to register births, deaths, marriages and divorces. According to the rules, births had to be recorded within one month. Deaths had to be registered within three days except in the case of violent death, suicide, or accidental death when the limit was twenty-four hours. In villages or in workers' settlements in non-urban areas the local soviets assumed these functions.

George N. Rhyne

ZAPOROZHE. Also appears frequently as Zaporozhye in Western sources. City of 835,000 (1983). The administrative center of Zaporozhe Oblast of the Ukrainian Soviet Socialist Republic, located on the Dnieper River just below its former cataracts. It is forty-five miles (72 km) south of Dnepropetrovsk on the left bank before the river bends to the southwest. Zaporozhe, originally called Aleksandrovsk, is a river port, one of the largest industrial and energy centers of Ukraine and a major railway junction.

Poland and Lithuania conquered the western part of Ukraine in the fourteenth century. By the middle of the fifteenth century Lithuania controlled most of Ukraine. In 1569 the Lithuanian lands passed to Poland. This circumstance led to a religious and cultural struggle between the Ukrainian Orthodox Christians and the Polish Catholics. In an effort to escape Polish rule peasants moved into the unpopulated eastern steppes along the Dnieper River.

In the late sixteenth century militant Dnieper Cossacks established a center of power on Khortitsa Island beyond the Dnieper cataracts (Zaporozhe). They built a sech (fortress) guarded by wooden ramparts and defended with cannon captured in the wars with the Russians, Poles, and Tatars. The sech became the center for the "knighthood of the Zaporozhe host," which was a Cossack military and trading community. The militant Zaporozhian Cossacks had few democratic or patriotic values during their early uprisings.

Between 1591 and 1593 Krishtof Kosinskii (d. 1593) led an uprising of Zaporozhian Cossacks against the Polish and Ukrainian feudal lords. After several victories the rebels were routed at the village of Piatka and fell back to Zaporozhe. Failing in his negotiations with Moscow, the Crimean khan, and Turkey, Kosinskii and his rebels were routed at Cherkassy. Another rebellion over feudal and religious issues took place between 1594 and 1596 with similar results. Growing political pressure from Poland and Catholic persecution helped to unite the Zaporozhian Cossacks after 1596. In 1624 Metropolitan Iov of Kiev requested Muscovite protection of Ukrainian Orthodox Christians from the aggressive Poles. Finding Moscow too weak and preoccupied to respond, Iov appealed to the Zaporozhian Cossacks to aid Orthodoxy. This fighting between 1625 and 1630 also ended in a Polish victory over the Zaporozhians and virtually ended their autonomy.

In 1648 Bogdan Zinoviy Khmelnitsky roused the Zaporozhian Cossacks against Polish rule and won several victories with aid from the Crimean khan. After several negotiations, treaties, and renewed conflicts, Khmelnitsky obtained protection from Moscow, which led Ukraine and Zaporozhe to become a part of the Muscovite state in 1654. After the incorporation of Ukraine into Russia, the military and political importance of the Zaporozhe sech rapidly declined. During the Great Northern War (1700-1721) Zaporozhe and other parts of Ukraine supported the abortive effort of Hetman Ivan Mazepa to form an alliance with Sweden against Tsar Peter the Great. Zaporozhe continued to decline in population and influence during most of the eighteenth century.

In 1770 Zaporozhe was revitalized, or reestablished with the building of Aleksandrovsk Fortress as part of a defense line against the Crimean Tatars. By 1806 the settlement alongside the fortress also was called Aleksandrovsk and became the district city. Later, when the Russian border with Turkey expanded down to the Black Sea, the fortress of Aleksandrovsk lost its importance. Many demobilized soldiers settled in the town. Historical records show that the before 1917 there was only one three-story house in the town and only nine with two stories. Only about 120 structures were built of brick.

During the revolution of 1905-1907 the workers of Aleksandrovsk took an active part in the demonstrations and strikes. The revolution in Aleksandrovsk, like other parts of Russia, continued until the summer of 1907, when a series of reforms quieted the rebellious public. Soviet authority was established in the city on 2 January 1918. During World War I and the Russian civil war the city suffered extensive damage. As the city began to rebuild, the old name of Zaporozhe was restored to the city in 1921.

Industrialization came to Zaporozhe upon construction of the V.I. Lenin Dnieper Hydroelectric Power Station (Dneproges). The research and design work for this project had begun in tsarist times, but the construction did not commence until 1927. Many foreign firms were consulted and General Electric Company supplied most of the equipment to produce the 558,000-kilowatt capacity. Designed by I.G. Aleksandrov, the dam is 2493 feet (760 m) long and 203 feet (62 m) high. The opening of the station in 1932 was considered one of the initial triumphs of socialist construction. A second powerhouse built later on the left bank of the Dnieper doubled the output of the station.

During World War II the German army captured Zaporozhe and occupied it from October 1941 to October 1943. The occupation and fighting destroyed over 70 percent of the city. Over three-fourths of the hydroelectric plant was destroyed by the war; it took three years to repair and make it operational. Dneproges regained its former power capacity by 1950. Leonid Ilich Brezhnev, the party chief in Zaporozhe, credited with the rebuilding of the power station and the opening of a new steel plant, was rewarded with membership in the Ukrainian Politburo. The city had recovered from the war by 1949, but the introduction of new industry led to the foundation of a new town about 6.2 miles (10 km) away. Planned as a model socialist town, the plants and streets had been laid out in 1930 during the construction of the hydroelectric plant. I.I. Malozemov led the group of architects who drew up the plans for wide avenues, multistory houses, parks, gardens, and greenbelts. The old and new parts of the city are linked by a causeway known as Lenin Prospekt.

Industrial development was influenced by the available power from hydro-electric station. Additional power is derived from a newer thermal power plant. On this basis a large metallurgical industry developed, which included the Zaporozhstal Steel and Iron Plant. The largest factory is the Ordzhonikidze Metal Foundry. Other factories specialize in high quality steel, produced in electrical hearths (Dneprospetsstal Mills), ferro-alloys, aluminum, and titanium-smelting. The city had one of the largest strip-rolling mills in the former Soviet Union. Agricultural machinery, ball-bearings, motors, transformers, refracto-ries, tractors, and construction equipment are produced in the factories. The Zaporozhe Kommunar Automobile Plant manufactures passenger automobiles, spare parts, and malleable and gray-iron castings. The plant began as a farm machinery factory in 1863 and did not manufacture automobiles until 1960. The original "Zaporozhets" (ZAZ-965) was a compact car, but in 1971 the plant started manufacturing the ZAZ-966-V, ZAZ-966, and ZAZ-968 passenger cars.

Zaporozhe also has a wide range of engineering enterprises, light industries, food-processing, and electrical materials production. Coke by-products have stimulated an important chemical industry. Chemicals, paints, fertilizers, phar-maceuticals, and medical supplies are produced in large laboratories or facto-ries, like the Kremniipolimer Plants.

The V.I. Lenin Port is important as a transportation source for the industrial products of both the city and oblast of Zaporozhe. Navigation on the Dnieper River used to be impossible because of the Zaporozhe Cataracts. There were early attempts to avoid the rapids, and in the nineteenth century some by-pass channels were constructed. The construction of the hydroelectric dam in 1932 made complete navigation possible by submerging the rapids and raising the river by 121 feet (37 m).

Zaporozhe lies on the main railroad trunk line between Moscow and Sevastopol. The city also has rail connections with Donetsk and Krivoi Rog. It is also a junction on the Zaporozhe-Volnovakha and Zaporozhe-Berdiansk lines. Zaporozhe lies on the major highway systems that link the city to Mos-cow, Zhdanov, and Dnepropetrovsk. The city has an airport.

Zaporozhe has a moderate continental climate, with average July tempera-tures around 23°C (73.4°F) and a mild winter with little snow. The average January temperature is around -5°C (23°F).

The population of Zaporozhe was 51,000 in 1914; 282,000 in 1939; 435,000 in 1959; and 812,000 in 1981. The population is 68 percent Ukrainian and 25 percent Russian, the rest belonging to more than thirty nationalities, including Tatars, Greeks, Georgians, Bulgarians, Jews, and Poles.

Zaporozhe has over ninety ordinary schools, eight specialized secondary school, and fourteen trade and building schools, which provide intensive train-ing in electronics, metallurgy, and hydroenergy. There are higher educational institutions that specialize in medicine, engineering, education, and music. Zap-orozhe has divisions of the Dnepropetrovsk Institute of Metallurgy and the Donetsk Institute of Soviet Trade. The city had 126 libraries in 1973, as well as a museum of local history, the Glinka Concert Hall, the Philharmonic Society, a symphony orchestra, a drama theater, and a circus. There are three newspapers (Zaporozhe pravda, Industrialnoe Zaporozhe and Komsomolets

Zaporizhia) published in the city with regional circulations. There is a television center in Zaporozhe, and the city also has access to a radio station and two television stations in the oblast.

See Also: ZAPOROZHE COSSACKS.

Bibliography: Entries on Zaporozhe appear in the major Soviet encyclopedias, including the English translation of the third edition of the *Great Soviet Encyclopedia*. Books and monographs include *Zaporizhzh'iu 200 let, 1770-1970. Istoriia mist i sil Ukrains'koi RSR. Zaporiz'ka oblast* (K., 1970); *Narodne gospodarstvo Ukrains'koi RSR. Stat. zbirnyk* (K., 1970); and W.E.D. Allen, *The Ukraine. A History* (New York, 1941). For information on the role of Zaporozhe in the early wars of Ukrainian nationalism see V.A. Golobutskii, *Osvoboditel'naia voina ukrainskogo naroda pod rukovodstvom Khmel'nitskogo, 1648-1654* (M., 1954); V.A. Golobutskii, *Diplomaticheskaia istoriia osvobolditel'noi voiny ukrainskogo naroda, 1648-1654* (K., 1962); and G. Vernadsky, *Bogdan, Hetman of Ukraine* (New Haven, 1940). A useful reference work is Victor and Jennifer Louis, *The Complete Guide to the Soviet Union* (London, 1976).

Phillip E. Koerper

ZARIA VOSTOKA (1922-1990). In English, Dawn of the East. Official newspaper of the Communist party in the Caucasus.

Zaria Vostoka first was published on 20 June 1922 in Tbilisi, Georgia. Designed to reach the Russian-speaking population of Caucasia, it was the successor to the Bolshevik newspaper Pravda Zakavkazia, of which there were only twenty-four issues in 1922. Zaria Vostoka became the official voice of the Transcaucasian Regional Party Committee (Zakkraikom), which was created in February 1922. Its official founders according to Soviet sources were Grigory ("Sergo") Konstantinovich Ordzhonikidze and Sergei Mironovich Kirov, both of whom were leading members of Zakkraikom and the main organizers of the Transcaucasian Socialist Federative Soviet Republic (ZSFSR), set up in 1922. Ordzhonikidze and Kirov saw Zaria Vostoka as a central medium of Transcaucasian unity. The newspaper loyally supported their policy of Transcaucasian centralism, overruling the objections of the Georgian "national deviationists" who sought Georgia's separate entry into the Soviet Union. The first co-editors of the newspaper were Ivan ("Mamiia") Dmitrievich Orakhelashvili and Aleksandr Fedorovich Miasnikov. Orakhelashvili, a former chairman of the Georgian Revolutionary Committee (Revkom) and a secretary of the Central Committee of the Georgian Communist Party, subsequently was executed in 1937. Miasnikov, a leading light in the Armenian party organization and a first secretary of Zakkraikom, died in 1925.

In 1936 Georgia entered the USSR as a separate union republic. Upon abolition of the ZSFSR, Zaria Vostoka replaced Rabochaia pravda (formerly Pravda Gruzii) as the main Russian-language organ of the Georgian party. Its masthead described it as the newspaper of the Georgian Central Committee, the Georgian Supreme Soviet and Council of Ministers. Zaria Vostoka played a central role in the republic's propaganda network. It was the most authoritative of the twelve Russian-language newspapers produced in the republic in the

1970s. One source suggests that the newspaper employed forty "propagandists" at this time. From an initial circulation of four to five thousand copies in the 1920s, it reached 148,000 by 1978. This compared to 648,000 for Komunist'i, its Georgian-language equivalent. In October 1990 after the election of a new noncommunist Supreme Soviet, Zaria Vostoka was removed from Georgian party ownership and the following December it became the newspaper of the new parliament. As the official newspaper of the new Georgian nationalist government, in December 1990 it changed its name to Svobodnaia Gruziia (Free Georgia). Zaria Vostoka's last editor was V. Keshalava.

Bibliography: G. Zhvania, *Sakartvelos p'art'iuli da sabc'ota p'resa socialismis mshenoblobis p'eriodshi* (Tbilisi, 1975); P'aat'a Gugushvili, *Sakartvelos da amierk'avk'asiis ek'onomik'uri ganvit'areba XIX-XX ss*, Vol. 7 (Tbilisi, 1984).

Stephen F. Jones

ZARUDNY, SERGEI IVANOVICH (1821-1887). Official in the Ministry of Justice. Leading figure in the formulation of the court reform of 1864.

From an old but impoverished Ukrainian gentry family, Zarudny was graduated from the Mathematics Faculty of Kharkov University in 1842. There he read widely in literature and philosophy and became an enthusiast of idealistic and romantic doctrines current in the 1840s. He arrived in St. Petersburg hoping to secure a position at Pulkovo Observatory but was unsuccessful and instead began service in the Ministry of Justice. His skill at logical exposition and the protection of his relative Boris Karlovich Danzas, who served as head of the Department of the Ministry of Justice, allowed him to rise rapidly. He came to the attention of the minister, Viktor Nikitich Panin, who relied increasingly on Zarudny to write his reports. By the end of the 1840s he dominated the discussions in the ministry's consultation, where difficult cases came for recommendations. At this time Zarudny established his own informal weekly "school" where he analyzed cases under consideration in the consultation for young jurists in the ministry. He taught them how to develop and use legal norms in considering these cases and emphasized the importance of understanding legal issues in terms of general principles of law. Simultaneously Zarudny took part in the intellectual ferment occurring among the Petersburg intelligentsia and officialdom. He began to admire the democratic ideals of France. During his visit to France in 1847 he attended lectures on the law and came away impressed with the benefits of a system of public justice.

In 1856 Zarudny was appointed assistant state secretary in the State Chancellery, the chancellery of the State Council. The State Chancellery then was considering the initial, extremely moderate projects of judicial reform drafted by Dmitry Nikolaevich Bludov, head of Second Section of the Imperial Chancellery. In the State Chancellery, Zarudny showed the skill at intellectual leadership that he had exercised in the consultation of the ministry. He gathered around him the most knowledgeable legal experts in administration and guided and assisted them in the drafting of a reform that would secure genuine independence for the Russian courts. By quietly gathering criticisms of the Bludov projects, Zarudny exposed their fundamental deficiencies. He thus made clear the need to turn the drafting of a new reform over to officials with training and expertise in the law. In early 1860 he completed a digest of all the criticisms, which he had printed and circulated to each member of the State Council.

In January 1861 Zarudny was promoted to state secretary for the Department of Laws of the State Council. In October Petr Aleksandrovich Valuev convinced Alexander II of the need for radical reform of the court system, and the tsar officially transferred responsibility for the reform from the Second Section to the State Chancellery. This placed Zarudny and Nikolai I. Stoianovsky, acting state secretary in the Department of Laws, in key positions to direct the work on reform. Zarudny then arranged for the transfer of the most knowledgeable and talented legal officials to the State Chancellery: Dmitry Aleksandrovich Rovinsky, Konstantin Petrovich Pobedonostev, N.A. Butskovsky, A.M. Plavsky, A.P. Vilinbakhov, and Pii Nikodimovich Danevsky. They joined Zarudny, Stoianovsky, and Zarudny's protégé, S.P. Shubin-Pozdeev, and drafted fundamental principles for the court reform based on current European jurisprudence. These principles established the importance of an independent judiciary, verbal procedure, open courts, irremovability of judges, an independent bar, and jury trials for criminal cases. They were approved by the tsar and promulgated on 29 September 1862.

Once the State Council approved the principles Zarudny worked indefatigably on projects for the statutes themselves. He participated in the work of each of the sections of the commission preparing the statutes—the sections on judicial organization and criminal procedure and the section on civil procedure, which he chaired. After the completion of work on the reform statutes, which were promulgated on 14 November 1864, Zarudny continued to serve in the State Chancellery. He worked on projects for supplemental laws and served on a commission to formulate the rules for the implementation of the reform. Zarudny then compiled the seventy-six volumes of materials on the preparation of reforms (Delo o preobrazovanii sudebnoi chasti v Rossii). He also published an edition of the statutes including a discussion of the principles upon which they were based (Sudebnye ustavy, s razsuzhdeniami, na koikh oni osnovany).

The completion of the work on reform ended Zarudny's usefulness to the tsar and his advisors. Dmitry Vladimirovich Karakazov's attempt on the tsar's life in April 1866 and the appointment of Konstantin Ivanovich Pahlen as minister of justice in 1867 signaled the turn to more conservative policies and officials. Zarudny continued to work in the State Chancellery until 1869, when he was appointed senator. He was assigned to the vestigial Second Department of the Senate, which was part of the old system, rather than to one of the two new cassational departments of the Senate, which he had helped to create. He found himself isolated and prevented from working on behalf of the institutions he had helped to bring to life. Zarudny spent his last years translating Beccaria's *Crimes and Punishments* and Dante's *Inferno* into Russian.

See Also: ZAMIATNIN, DMITRY NIKOLAVEICH

Bibliography: G.A. Dzhanshiev, *Epokha velikikh reform* (M., 1896); G.A. Dzhanshiev, "S.I. Zarudny i sudebnaia reforma," in his *Sbornik statei* (M., 1914), 341-436; F.B. Kaiser, *Die russische Justizreform von 1864* (Leiden,

1972); R.S. Wortman, *The Development of a Russian Legal Consciousness* (Chicago, 1976).

Richard S. Wortman

ZAUMNYI YAZYK. Literally trans-mind language. Often shortened to zaum. A Russian Futurist term used to describe invented words or language whose sense is indefinite or indeterminate, although not necessarily totally lacking in meaning. Common English translations: transrational, trans-sense or metalogical language. The etymology of zaumnyi (adj.) and zaum (n.) (za = beyond; um = mind, intellect) suggests an idea, word or text that operates beyond the confines of logic and rationality and may combine mutually exclusive alternatives.

Zaumnyi yazyk was one of the most radical features of Russian Futurist poetry. It first appeared as a designation in Aleksei Eliseevich Kruchenykh's 1913 manifesto Declaration of the Word as Such. "THOUGHT AND SPEECH CANNOT KEEP UP WITH THE EMOTIONS OF SOMEONE IN A STATE OF INSPIRATION, therefore the artist is free to express himself not only in the common language (concepts), but also in a personal one (the creator is an individual), as well as in a language which does not have any definite meaning (not frozen), a transrational language" (Lawton, 67). Kruchenykh (1886-1968) is recognized as the originator and most active proponent and practitioner of zaumnyi yazyk. The initial works in this new language were three short poems which appeared in *Pomade* (Pomada, 1913) . The first of the three poems take its title from the first line, Dyr bul shchyl. The poem itself consists of five lines of what appear to be word fragments whose root meanings are obvious to varying degrees, but whose total significance remains unclear although a sexual subtext seems intended. Kruchenykh prefaced this work with a statement that he wrote it in his "own language different from others" and that the words "did not have a definite meaning."

Kruchenykh continued to experiment with and promote zaumnyi yazyk until the early 1920s, writing poems composed entirely of vowels or consonants, or coinages, or with syntax that was extensively dislocated. His most elaborate work, which combined all manner of zaum techniques, is the libretto to the opera Victory over the Sun (Pobeda nad solntsem) performed in Petersburg in December 1913. Most of Kruchenykh's zaum experiments predated comparable works by the Dadaists.

Although Viktor Vladimirovich Khlebnikov (1885-1922) may have contributed to the development of Kruchenykh's concept of zaumnyi yazyk and some of his quasi-zaum poems predated Kruchenykh's Dyr bul shchyl, Khlebnikov's own view of zaumnyi yazyk appears to be significantly different. His coinages usually are interpretable in context or are provided with commentaries by the author or a colleague as in his dramatic poem Zangezi (1922). Evidently they are intended to have clear meanings and to be usable to name phenomena that are perhaps still in the future. Few of his coinages are not interpretable, and it may be that we merely have lost the intended key to them. In the case of Khlebnikov the purpose of zaumnyi yazyk was expressly to be a language of the future, an improvement over existing languages. Its phonological and morphological structure was intended to be iconic in nature. That is, its sounds and shapes were designed to reflect the intended meaning more accurately than is the case with traditional languages, which in Khlebnikov's view, have lost this originally close relationship.

Other major practitioners of zaumnyi yazyk were Ilya M. Zdanevich (1894-1975), Igor G. Terentiev (1892-1941) and Aleksander V. Tufanov (1877-1942). In the period 1917-1919 Zdanevich, Terentiev, and Kruchenykh formed the core of a group of avant-garde poets in Tiflis, Georgia. Zdanevich's series of five absurdist one-act "dras" (plays) under the collective title of Dunkeeness, Donkeyness (aslaablIchie, 1918-1923) contain extensive passages of zaum, and the final play in the series, Le-Dantiu to Hedbeems (lidantIU fAram, 1923) uses over seventeen hundred zaum words elaborately composed into various speeches, choruses, and ensembles. Tufanov led a group of Petrograd avant-garde poets, several of whom formed the Obedinenie realnogo iskusstva (Oberiu, Society for Realistic Art) group which also experimented with some forms of zaumnyi yazyk. Tufanov's book *Toward Zaum* (K zaumi, 1924) is the last significant work of and about zaum in the pre-Stalin period.

A number of other avant-garde poets and artists, such as Nikolai N. Aseev, Konstantin A. Bolshakov (Anton Lotov), Vasily I. Gnedov, Kazimir S. Malevich, Olga V. Rozanova, and Varvara F. Stepanova wrote some poetry in zaumnyi yazyk. Others such as Vasily V. Kamensky, David D. Burliuk, and Aleksei N. Chicherin, often were termed practitioners by critics because they concocted unusual coinages or used exoticisms, although these were easily understood in most cases.

General critical and popular reaction to zaumnyi yazyk was always negative. It has been viewed as an excess of artistic freedom, if not a manifestation of outright insanity. Its scandalousness brought the Futurists a considerable portion of their notoriety. Moreover, zaumnyi yazyk was partly responsible for stimulating the development of Russian Formalist theories of language and art. The renowned linguist Roman Jakobson, who experimented with zaumnyi yazyk in his first major critical work, *The Latest Russian Poetry* (Noveishaia russkaia poeziia, 1921), dealt to some extent with zaumnyi yazyk in Khlebnikov. The Soviet government opposed such extremist poetry and by the mid-1920s writing in zaumnyi yazyk was a significant political liability.

Beginning in the 1960s there was renewed interest in zaumnyi yazyk among Russian avant-garde poets such as Sergei Sigei (Sergei V. Sigov), Ry Nikonova (Anna Aleksandrovna Tarshis), and Gleb Tsvel, who have extended its bounds.

See Also: MODERNISM IN RUSSIA and ZDANEVICH, ILYA MIKHAILOVICH.

Bibliography: Kornei Chukovsky, *Egofuturisty i kubofuturisty* (Letchworth, 1976); Vladimir Markov, *Russian Futurism. A History* (Berkeley, 1968); E. Beaujour, "Zaum" *Dada/Surrealism*, No. 2, 29-49; Roman Jakobson, *Noveishaia russkaia poeziia* (Prague, 1921); D. Mickiewicz, "Semantic Functions in Zaum'," *Russian Literature*, Vol. 15, 363-464; Gerald J. Janecek, "Zaum' as the Recollection of Primeval Oral Mimesis," *Wiener Slawistischer Almanach*, Vol. 16, 165-186; Gerald J. Janecek, "A Zaum Classification," *Canadian-American Slavic Studies*, Vol. 20, Nos. 1-2 (1986), 37-54; Aleksei Eliseevich

Kruchenykh, *Izbrannoe*, ed. by Vladimir Markov (Munich, 1973); V. Shklovsky, "On Poetry and Trans-Sense Language," *October*, No. 34 (1985), 2-24; Aleksandr V. Tufanov, *K zaumi* (Paris, 1924); Anna M. Lawton, ed., *Russian Futurism through Its Manifestoes, 1912-1928* (Ithaca, 1988).

Gerald J. Janecek

ZDANEVICH, ILIA MIKHAILOVICH (1894-1975). Russian avant-garde art critic, dramatist, poet, novelist, typographer, book designer, archeologist. Also known by the pseudonym Iliazd. Associate of artists Mikhail Fedorovich Larionov and Natalia Sergeevna Goncharova, founding member of Tiflis avant-garde literary group "41°". Later collaborated with Paris Dada and avant-garde artists, especially Picasso.

Born 21 April 1894 in Tiflis, Georgia, son of a lyceum professor of French, Zdanevich grew up in a cultured family. His older brother, Kirill, became a prominent artist. After graduating from the lyceum in 1911 he studied law at St. Petersburg University, where he became involved immediately in the activities of avant-garde and Futurist artists and poets, such as Larionov, Goncharova, Mikhail Vasilievich Le-Dantiu, Alexei Eliseevich Kruchenykh, and the Burliuk brothers, David, Nikolai, and Vladimir. In 1912 the Zdanevich brothers and Le-Dantiu discovered the Georgian primitive painter Niko Pirosmanashvili and were instrumental in bringing him to the attention of the public. Their efforts resulted in Pirosmanashvili's being considered today as one of Georgia's most important painters. In the summer of 1912 Zdanevich also began an archeological study of ancient Georgian churches and monasteries, which made him a leading expert on that subject. Under the pseudonym Eli Eganbiuri, in 1913 Zdanevich wrote the first serious catalog-monograph on the work of Larionov and Goncharova. Zdanevich paid particular attention to the activities of the Italian Futurists and was an exponent of their program. He gave a lecture in 1914 at the Wandering Dog Cabaret on Futurist face painting and with Larionov and Goncharova published a manifesto on this topic entitled "Why We Paint Ourselves." In 1915-1917 he served as Caucasus correspondent for the Petrograd newspaper Speech (Rech) and the Manchester Guardian. He received his law degree in February 1917 but, despite an offer of a position with the state duma, he decided to return home to Tiflis.

In Tiflis, which became especially lively at this time due to the influx of literary figures fleeing the war and revolution, Zdanevich was a focal point for avant-garde literary activities. With Kruchenykh and Igor Gerasimovich Terentiev he founded the Futurist "University 41°", apparently named after the latitude of the city. Under this label the group created a cabaret, "Fantasticheskii kabachok" (Fantastic Little Inn) in which they gave a series of lectures and presentations, produced a newspaper which had only one issue, and published a series of works which are noteworthy for their elaborate use of typographical resources and compare favorably with similar efforts by the Italian Futurists. Zdanevich was the key figure in this development. At this time he became a master typesetter and book designer, and applied his skills to setting not only his own works, but also those of his colleagues, Kruchenykh and Terentiev. Zdanevich's first major literary works were a series of five one-act plays (dras) to which he subsequently gave the collective title aslaabIchie (Donkeyness) because a donkey figures in them either explicitly or implicitly. Although Zdanevich used phonetic spelling in his Russian titles for these works, the English translations do not reflect this. The first is Yanko krul' albanskai (Yanko, King of Albania, written 1913-1916, published 1918) which has as its main character a donkey which is forced by a gang of Albanian bandits to become their king. In the second, Asel naprakat (Donkey for Rent, performed 1918, published 1918), the heroine, Zokhna, falls in love with a suitor who has been turned into a donkey. Ostraf Paskhi (Easter Island, performed 1918, published 1919) takes place in a shop of stone coffins as various characters proceed to kill others only to have everyone resurrected in the end. In Zga yakaby (As Though Zga, performed in 1918, published in 1920) the main character, Zga, awakes and looks in a mirror. The reflection comes alive, and then it generates other Zgas until the mirror is broken and Zga falls asleep again. In lidantIU fAram (Le-Dantiu to Headbeams, published Paris, 1923), Zdanevich's friend, the artist Le-Dantiu, who was killed during the war, defeats the evil forces of realist art and leads the forces of artistic freedom.

These plays have elements of folk drama and mythology, especially from Apuleius, but are most noteworthy for their extensive use of zaum (transrational language), or of invented words of indeterminate meaning, and for the system of phonetic transcription used to convey these words. The last of the series contains over 1700 such words and is the largest work of zaum created to date. The published versions of the dras are also noteworthy for their progressively more elaborate typography, needed to convey the many choruses and quasi-operatic ensembles of simultaneous speech, concluding in lidantIU with an ensemble of eleven separate voices. Other prominent features are their violence, eroticism, absurd plots, and somewhat disguised obscene language.

In 1921 Zdanevich emigrated to Paris, where he joined Larionov and Goncharova and immediately aligned himself with the Dadas, especially Tristan Tzara, lectured on the Russian avant-garde, and participated in and organized Dada activities. Excerpts from some of the dras were performed there in puppet theater or danced form. Zdanevich wrote several novels, one of which, *Voskhishchenie* (Rapture), about a mountain bandit, was published in 1930, causing a mild scandal in the Russian emigre community by its overt use of taboo words. He also authored a cycle of sonnets, Afet (1940). A number of his other literary and theoretical works remain unpublished.

The main focus of Zdanevich's later years, for which he is best known in France, was composition of a series of elegant, innovative, limited-edition bookworks under the pseudonym Iliazd. These involved the participation of prominent artists, such as Picasso, Survage, Braque, Chagall, Miro, Ernst, and others, sometimes with texts by Zdanevich, but more frequently with texts by other, sometimes forgotten authors. They immediately became collectors' items and in recent years have been the subject of exhibitions in Paris and North America.

Zdanevich was one of the most radical innovators in Russian avant-garde literature and his work is only beginning to be given detailed attention.

See Also: MODERNISM IN RUSSIA and ZAUMNYI YAZYK.

Bibliography: M. Larionov, I. Zdanevich, "Pochemu my raskrashivaemsia," *Argus* (1913), 112-118; V. Markov, *Russian Futurism. A History* (Berkeley, 1968), esp. 350-358; *Hommage a Iliazd, Bulletin du Bibliophile II* (1974); G. Janecek, "Il'ja Zdanvevic's 'aslaabllc'e' and the Transcription of 'zaum'" in Drama," *L'avanguardia a Tiflis*, L. Magarotto, et al., eds. (Venice, 1982); G. Janecek, *The Look of Russian Literature. Avant-Garde Visual Experiments, 1900-1930* (Princeton, 1984), Ch. 5; G. Janecek and G. Riggs, "Il'ja Zdanevic's Zaum'," *International Journal of Slavic Linguistics and Poetics*, 35-36 (1989), 217-237; *Iliazd* (Paris, Centre Georges Pompidou, 1978); F. Le Gris-Bergmann, ed., *Iliazd, Maitre d'oeuvre du livre moderne*, (Montreal, 1984); S. Sigov, "Onolatricheskaia misteriia Il'i Zdanevicha," *Zaumnyi futurizm i dadaizm v russkoi kul'ture*, L. Magarotto, M. Marzaduri and D. Ricci, eds. (New York, 1991) and other articles in this collection.

Gerald J. Janecek

ZENTRALE MOSKAU (1921-1933). Agency of the German army in Moscow. Entrusted with administration in the Soviet Union of all aspects of German-Soviet military cooperation.

In 1921 Soviet leaders and the leadership of the German army found it timely and convenient to enter into various forms of military collaboration. By that time the civil war in Russia was virtually over, and the regime could confront the necessity to restore the nation's ruined economy. The New Economic Policy and the associated policy of granting economic concessions to foreign interests reflected this urgent concern. One of the major Soviet goals was to gain access to western technology, both civil and military. The German army, held to Lilliputian dimensions by the armaments clauses of the Versailles treaty, sought ways to avoid these restrictions.

A Special Group R (Sondergruppe R) was formed within the German army to handle the collaboration with the Soviets. It gave the Junkers aircraft firm political and financial support, for example, enabling it to gain a concession to build aircraft engines at Fili, outside of Moscow. Other agreements led to production of poison gas and ammunition at various locations in Russia. Among the most successful were the training centers, one for tank warfare near Kazan and the other for pilots at Lipetsk in Tambov province. Hundreds of military personnel were sent to the Soviet Union in civilian guise to train at these institutes.

The role of Zentrale Moskau in this collaboration was to administer all aspects of this collaboration in Russia. It surreptitiously shuffled personnel in and out of Russia. It handled all fiscal and logistic matters concerned with them. At various times it conducted negotiations for the expansion of the on-going military collaboration. As it had regular contact with the highest officials of the Soviet military establishment and direct access to training facilities and other military bases, it was far better informed than the officially accredited military attaché. It submitted regular and detailed reports to the Ministry of War.

As the real functions of Zentrale Moskau were intended to be secret, many details of its operation are murky. It is unclear exactly when it was established, but was certainly functioning by the fall of 1923. All sources agree that the two directors of Zentrale Moskau were a Colonel von den Lieth-Thomsen and a Major Oskar Ritter von Niedermayer. The former had headed the German air force during World War I and began the flying school at Lipetsk; the latter served as an advisor in Turkey before World War I under General Hans von Seeckt, who became commander-in-chief of the German army in 1919. The sources disagree on which man was the first director. Perhaps they shared important roles. Both men arrived in Moscow during the fall of 1923, and the German ambassador to Moscow, Count Ulrich von Brockdorff-Rantzau, frequently complained that this cover organization needed a single leader. In any case the influential connections of the two testifies to the significance the German military leadership placed on Zentrale Moskau's operations.

In theory Zentrale Moskau was designed to function as totally independent of the German foreign ministry so as to avoid political problems if exposed. By 1926 Zentrale Moskau had begun to use the embassy's couriers, and the embassy and foreign office were aware of many of its activities. But it continued to operate independently for the most part, negotiating on its own. In 1928, perhaps to obscure further its real functions, Zentrale Moskau was renamed Heim Deutscher Angestellter Moskau (Club of German Civil Employees in Moscow); in this new guise it continued its former activities but cooperated more closely with the German embassy.

When Adolf Hitler became chancellor of Germany on 30 January 1933 the basis for Soviet-German military collaboration ended. Despite official German assurances of a desire to continue cooperation, a number of anti-Soviet acts convinced the Soviet government otherwise. In mid-May 1933 the Soviet government asked the Germans to liquidate their military enterprises in Russia. During the fall of 1933 the last of the German military officials left Russia, including those involved in Zentrale Moskau and its successor. This ended formally the military collaboration which had been so fruitful for both countries.

Bibliography: Francis Ludwig Carsten, "The Reichswehr and the Red Army," *Survey* (October, 1962), 114-132; Georges Castellan, "Reichswehr et Armée Rouge, 1920-1933," *Les relations Germano-Sovietiques de 1933 à 1939*, ed. by Jean-Baptiste Duroselle (Paris, 1954), 137-271; John Erickson, *The Soviet High Command. A Military-Political History, 1918-1941*. 2nd ed, (Boulder, Colo., 1984); Hans Gatzke, "Russo-German Military Collaboration During the Weimar Republic," *American Historical Review*, Vol. 63, No. 2 (April, 1958), 565-597; Gustav Hilger and Alfred G. Meyer, *The Incompatible Allies. A Memoir-History of German-Soviet Relations, 1918-1941* (New York, 1953); and Helm Speidel, "Reichswehr und rote Armee," *Vierteljahrhefte für Zeitgeschichte*, Vol. 1 (January, 1953), 9-45.

George N. Rhyne

ZERO OPTION (1981-). A United States negotiating position on intermediate nuclear forces (INF) in Europe put forward in late 1981 by the administration of President Ronald Reagan. It proposed the withdrawal of Soviet SS-20 missiles from Europe in return for an undertaking of the North Atlantic Treaty Organization (NATO) to refrain from deploying its cruise and Pershing II missiles. The Soviet Union declined the offer and American cruise and Pershing II missiles were deployed in Europe as planned in 1983. In December 1987 the United States and the Soviet Union signed an INF treaty which in essence produced the outcome envisaged by the original Zero Option proposal.

There are three perspectives through which the Zero Option can be viewed usefully, the first being the build-up of INF forces in Europe during the 1970s. The Soviet Union, which had deployed SS-20 missiles against China, decided in 1975 to install them in Europe as well. It did so as part of a general program of modernization but also in order to rectify what it regarded as an imbalance in intermediate range weapons in Europe. The Soviets claimed that American "forward base systems," chiefly manned bombers and submarine-based missiles, not only gave the United States an advantage in strike power from European air bases and from submarines, but also that British and French "independent" nuclear deterrents reinforced that advantage. Despite such arguments the West regarded SS-20 deployment as a destabilizing change in the status quo.

NATO's 1979 decision to deploy Pershing II and cruise missiles in Europe was in part a direct response to the Soviet SS-20s. It also reflected European anxieties about the potential nuclear "decoupling" of Europe from the United States. Effective superpower nuclear parity at the strategic level, codified in the SALT I and up-coming SALT II treaties, magnified, as West German Chancellor Helmut Schmidt put it, "the significance of the disparities between East and West in nuclear tactical and conventional weapons" in Europe (Garthoff, *Detente and Confrontation*, 855). The decision on cruise and Pershing missiles was intended to allay European fears on this score. Since the decision proved highly unpopular with the people of Europe, some European governments began to back away from the decision almost as soon as it was made.

The next stage of the process—and the second perspective on the Zero Option—was marked by the election in 1980 of Ronald Reagan as president of the United States. It created the irony of ever greater American pressure for INF deployment in the face of an ever more reluctant Europe, which originally had requested the missiles. Relations between the United States and the Soviet Union had worsened in President Jimmy Carter's last year in office, following the Soviet invasion of Afghanistan. In response Carter had withdrawn the SALT II treaty from ratification by the US Senate. Reagan came into office determined to rebuild America's military strength, which he regarded as having been woefully neglected during the period of detente with the Soviet Union. Detente, he was convinced, had been a one-way street.

Reagan's critics charge him with not being serious about arms control negotiations and of surrounding himself with advisors such as Richard Perle who held similar beliefs. However one interprets the Reagan administration's defense of its aggressive negotiating postures—a product, said Perle, not of cynicism about the possibility or desirability of success but simply of the fact that "we set a higher standard than our detractors"—there was a clear disposition to "negotiate from strength" (Talbott, *Deadly Gambits*, 18). The Zero Option was broadly in line with this attitude toward arms negotiations with the Soviet Union.

There was little chance of its succeeding. Not only did it require the removal of all SS-20s, including those deployed against China, but it left American forward base systems and British and French nuclear missiles intact. The Soviet leaders counted on public opinion in the West to embarrass NATO leaders and reinforce the Soviet Union's own justifications for rejecting American terms. This expectation relied on the unpopularity of the NATO INF decision in Europe, the Dutch Parliament's refusal to accept the missiles on Dutch soil, and the general resurgence of antinuclear protests in Europe and the United States. But these factors were not enough to stop deployment of cruise and Pershing, which went ahead in several countries as planned. When this took place in 1983 Soviet negotiators walked out of arms control talks and, "for the first time in nearly fifteen years, the Americans and the Soviets were no longer negotiating in any forum" (Talbott, *Deadly Gambits*, 4).

The sequel—and the third perspective on the Zero Option—is the INF treaty of December 1987, under which the Soviet Union undertook to remove its SS-20s and NATO its cruise and Pershing II missiles. The INF treaty was the first arms agreement between the United States and the Soviet Union which actually reduced arms. It must be understood in the light of the general change in the climate of US-Soviet relations following the advent of Soviet leader Mikhail Sergeevich Gorbachev to power in March 1985 and specific changes in Soviet negotiating positions. For the first time in INF negotiations the Soviet Union agreed to leave out of consideration the American forward base systems and the British and French nuclear deterrents.

The similarity between the original Zero Option and the provisions of the INF treaty raised the question, hotly debated among policy-makers and academic experts, of whether Reagan's "hardball" diplomacy paid off, and more generally whether the Reagan goal of "peace through strength" brought an end to the cold war. As of 1992 there were no clear answers to this question.

Bibliography: Strobe Talbott, *Deadly Gambits. The Reagan Administration and the Stalemate in Arms Control* (New York, 1984); Raymond L. Garthoff, *Detente and Confrontation. American Soviet Relations from Nixon to Reagan* (Washington, D.C., 1985); Gregory Treverton, "Intermediate-Nuclear-Force Negotiations: Issues and Alternatives," Marsha McGraw Olive and Jeffrey D. Porro, eds., *Nuclear Weapons in Europe. Modernization and Limitation* (Lexington, Mass., 1983), 81-102; Thomas Risse-Kappen, "Did 'Peace Through Strength' End the Cold War?" *International Security*, Vol. 16, No. 1 (Summer 1991), 162-188.

Richard D.G. Crockatt

ZEROV, MYKOLA (1890-1937). Ukrainian neoclassicist poet, translator, literary critic, and cultural activist.

The term neoclassicist has been applied to a loosely affiliated group of Ukrainian poets and critics that included, besides Zerov, Maksym Rylsky,

Pavlo Fylypovych, Mykhailo Drai-Khmara, and Yury Klen (pseudonym of Oswald Burghardt). The members of this "school" were well versed in the literature of antiquity and applied that expertise to their own works. Their writings fused a highly aesthetic vision of the poetic and literary text with a social as well as a national consciousness.

Zerov was born on 26 April 1890 in the town of Zinkiv in the Poltava region of Ukraine. His father Kostiantyn was a teacher and, later in his career, a school inspector. The rest of the family consisted of his mother Maria, five brothers, and two sisters. Three of his brothers became scholars, two in the sciences, and one in literature; the latter wrote under the pseudonym Mykhailo Orest. From 1900 to 1903 Zerov studied at the Okhtyr Gymnasium and from 1903 at the First Kiev Gymnasium, which he completed in 1908. In the gymnasium he learned Latin and ancient Greek and became acquainted with the literatures of those ancient cultures. He entered the University of Kiev in 1908 and actively participated in the Kiev Ukrainian student organization from 1908 to 1913. He received his degree in 1914 and began to work as a teacher in the provincial Zlatopil Gymnasium. In 1917 he took a position in the Kiev Second Gymnasium. He met his future wife Sophia Loboda in 1912 and married her in 1920.

Zerov began to publish in 1912 in the pedagogical journal The Light (Svitlo). Following the 1917 revolution Zerov became quite active in the teeming cultural revival in the Ukrainian capital. He penned literary criticism for the bibliographical journal The Bookseller (Knyhar) from 1919 to 1920, served as a member of the editorial board of The Voice of Printing (Holos druku) publishing house, and took an active role in the Academy of Sciences. He published extensively in the leading Soviet Ukrainian literary journals of the day, including Literary-Scientific Herald (Literaturno-naukovyi visnyk), The Red Path (Chervonyi shliakh), and Life and Revolution (Zhyttia i revoliutsiia), where he published his critical works, essays, poetry, and translations. In the "Literary Discussion" of the mid-1920's Zerov rejected the ideas of the Bolshevik party which called for a proletarian literature based on intrinsically provincial native and Russian models, and championed the side of Mykola Khvylovy, who advocated a European orientation for Ukranian literature. Stalin perceived this Western orientation as anticommunist and ultimately repressed all the intellectuals taking this posture.

Zerov quickly became the leading Ukrainian literary critic of his time and a remarkable polemicist. In 1920 he published an anthology of ancient Greek and Roman poetry in translation (Antolohiia antychnoi poezii). A single collection of his own poetry entitled Kamena appeared in Kiev in 1924. Besides these he published numerous individual articles and essays and several books of criticism. The latter included New Ukrainian Writing (Nove ukrains'ske pys'menstvo, 1924), his pathbreaking work in Ukrainian literary criticism To the Sources (Do dzherel, 1924; 2nd expanded ed., 1943); and From Kulish to Shevchenko (Vid Kulisha do Shevchenko, 1929). Zerov's work had an extraordinary impact on the Ukrainian cultural and literary renaissance of the 1920s. With great conviction and erudition he attacked the forces trying to swallow

Ukrainian culture. He hoped to bring the best of European culture into the Ukrainian with his classicist notion of literature as a high art form.

Attacks against Zerov from the Stalinist propaganda machine began in the mid-1920s and steadily increased in intensity. At the suicides in 1933 of leading Ukrainian cultural figures Mykola Khvylovy and Mykola Skrypnyk, the situation became extraordinarily bleak. Zerov was attacked both in party meetings and the press, first for his non-socialist vision, then as a Ukrainian nationalist. On 1 August 1934 Zerov was removed from his teaching position at Kiev State University, although he continued to work as a researcher until 1 November when he was summarily fired by the university rector without any explanation. In the spring of 1935 Zerov was arrested and falsely charged with terroristic activity. After a staged trial in February 1936 Zerov was exiled for a ten-year sentence to the infamous Solovki forced labor camp. Despite the harsh prison regime Zerov continued to write poetry and to translate. There he somehow managed to complete his translation of Virgil's *Aenead* into Ukrainian. He was executed on 3 November 1937 along with his colleagues Pavlo Fylypovych, Mykola Vorony, and Borys Pylypenko. Ironically this was the third anniversary of the death of his only son, Kostyk.

His brother Mykhailo Orest published Zerov's collected sonnets posthumously, both original works and translations, in Germany in 1948 under the title *Sonnetarium*. Most of Zerov's works were banned in Soviet Ukraine until Nikita Sergeevich Khrushchev's "thaw" of the late 1950s and early 1960s. Since the advent of Mikhail Sergeevich Gorbachev's reforms and Ukrainian independence, Zerov has taken his rightful public place as one of the leading Ukrainian literary historians and critics of the twentieth century.

Bibliography: For Zerov's works see his *Tvory v dvokh tomakh* (K., 1991); *Lektsii z istorii ukrainsʹkoi literatury* (Oakville, Ontario, 1977); and *Vybrane* (K., 1966). Works about Zerov include Viacheslav Briukhovetskyi, *Mykola Zerov* (K., 1990); C.H. Andrusyshen and Watson Kirkconnell, *The Ukrainian Poets, 1189-1962* (Toronto, 1963), 367-371; and George S.N. Luckyj, *Literary Politics in the Soviet Ukraine, 1917-1934* (Durham, N.C., 1990). Mikhailo Orest, ed., *Bezsmertni* (Munich, 1963) is a memoire about the neoclassicists.

Michael M. Naydan

ZHDANOV/MARIUPOL (Zhdanov, 1948-1989). A large port city located in the Donetsk Oblast of Ukraine, on the north shore of the Sea of Azov and at the mouth of the Kalmius River, at approximately 38° longitude and 47° latitude. It is not only the main port for the Don River Basin and the second largest port in Ukraine after Odessa, but it is also a center of iron and steel manufacturing.

Because of its favorable geographic location and relatively mild climate the area has been inhabited for a long time. The Mariupol burial ground, discovered in 1930, dates from the late neolithic era. Later the area was under the control of the early Eastern Slavs, then of the Khazars, then of the Mongols, during which time it became depopulated. Runaway serfs, later to develop into a group known as cossacks, repopulated the area after the fifteenth century; the Zaporozhe cossacks probably set up a fortress on the location of the current city.

The modern city was founded when the area became part of the Russian Empire during the reign of Catherine the Great, and in conjunction with the struggle between the Russian and Ottoman empires over the Crimea in the last decades of the 1700s. In 1779 Catherine gave some Crimean Greeks permission to reside in the area for trading purposes. They actually moved into the area in 1780. After the Crimea became Russian territory in 1783 some Greeks from the new town, called Mariupol, moved back to the Crimea.

Mariupol remained a small community for a century. One reason was that the Greeks apparently tried to keep other nationalities from settling in the town. Thus the first school, founded in 1820, was for Greeks. Only two years later did a section of the school open for Russians. Not until 1859 did a government decree permit all nationalities to reside in Mariupol. In addition to a rapid increase in Russians, Jews moved into Mariupol. Although 111 Jews had resided there by 1847, in the latter part of the century there was a rapid influx of Jews from Lithuania and White Russia; by 1897 the 5,013 Jews represented 16 percent of Mariupol's population.

Mariupol quickly developed into a trading and port town. By the beginning of the nineteenth century goods were being exported abroad. In 1800 the government opened a tariff office in Mariupol and in 1824 set up a port administration. The first ship was constructed in Mariupol in the 1820s, and the city also developed ship-repairing facilities. Non-maritime industrial development was much slower; what existed was light industry. A brick factory opened in 1820, a macaroni plant in the 1830s, and leather and candle plants in the 1850s. The use of Mariupol as a supply base during the Crimean War caused it to be attacked by an Anglo-French naval squadron which shelled the town and caused a good amount of destruction.

The period of reforms during the reign of Alexander II (1855-1881) brought some changes to Mariupol as well. Thus the Marinsky school opened in 1869, a school for Jewish children opened in 1870, and between 1870 and 1883 three elementary schools and two gymnasia (one for men and one for women) were established. In addition the first hospital, with thirty beds, opened in 1874.

The rapid development of the city came after the 1880s in conjunction with the development of the coal of the Don Basin, the use of steel for railroads, and the need of a convenient port facility for these in eastern Ukraine. One important factor was the building of the Ekaterinoslav Railroad and expansion of the port's capacity in the 1880s, both needed to handle the development of the coal fields and the export of wheat. Equally important was the building of two mills in the 1890s to use the resources of the Don area to manufacture iron and steel products close to the source of extraction and located near good transportation. The first mill was the Nikopol plant. The second, a Belgian-dominated plant, Providence, was fully operational by 1899. These came to play a major role in the city's economic life. By 1898 these two plants employed 6,000 people. On the eve of World War I the two plants accounted for six percent of the empire's steel production. War brought further expansion, and in 1916 there were 16,000 employees at the Nikopol plant alone.

The port also expanded rapidly. As with the railway, the major products were wheat and the production of the steel mills. By 1912 approximately 2,300 ships, about ten percent of foreign registry, entered and departed the port with a combined registered cargo of almost 2.2 million tons. This commerce justified the presence of the seven foreign consulates in Mariupol by the early 1900s.

Industrial development was accompanied by demographic expansion. Figures for earlier periods are sketchy but in 1892, before the steel mills were built, the town had 17,000 inhabitants. That shot up rapidly to 31,200 in 1897, 57,000 in 1900, and 97,000 by 1917.

The development of a proletariat accompanied industrial development. Not only were conditions of labor difficult and wages low, the periodic fluctuations of the world economy caused problems in Mariupol. In these circumstances a socialist movement developed. The first social democratic (SD) group, called the Mariupol Section of the Don Committee of the Russian Social Democratic Workers' Party (RSDRP), arose toward the end of 1898. But it was only in 1903 that a Mariupol Committee of the RSDRP came into being. From the beginning and until after the October revolution, the Mensheviks tended to dominate the local social democratic movement. Thus in early 1905 the local SD committee refused to participate in the (Bolshevik) Third Party Congress; instead it sent its delegate to the Menshevik Conference held in Geneva. During the 1905 revolution a Soviet of Workers Deputies arose in Mariupol. Social democrats dominated this body, which the authorities disbanded and arrested its members in January 1906, forcing the social democrats underground. The Mensheviks continued to control the local committee, which held its last large pre-1917 demonstration on May Day 1907.

In 1917 another Soviet arose in Mariupol. As before, the Mensheviks, now joined by the Socialist Revolutionary party (SRs), controlled it. The Bolsheviks were so weak that they did not even form a local committee until 1 July. The events of 1917 moved the masses away from the Mensheviks, although even here Mariupol trailed the country. Thus the Mariupol Soviet elected its first Bolshevik majority only at the end of September, and the Mensheviks and SRs continued to dominate the local duma administration until after the revolution, finally submitting to Bolshevik authority only at the end of December.

During the civil war years (1918-1921) Mariupol was alternately under the control of the Bolsheviks and their opponents. The Bolsheviks were pushed out of Mariupol in April 1918 by German-Austrian troops supporting the Ukrainian Rada (council) government. Anglo-French troops later occupied Mariupol. Even after the defeat of White General Anton Ivanovich Denikin in early 1920 the city again was attacked later that year when Baron Petr Nikolaevich Wrangel made a final effort to defeat the Bolsheviks. The result of this turmoil was that Mariupol's production fell disastrously. In 1920 iron and steel production was less than two percent of its 1913 level.

Restoration and expansion began during the period of the New Economic Policy (1921-1928) and expanded considerably during the period of the five-year plans of 1928-1940. The industrial establishments had been nationalized and combined before 1921. After the civil war the Nikopol plant was restored, but not all of the Providence plant. After Lenin's death in 1924 the plants were renamed Ilich and in 1927 the government decided to restore fully the former Providence plant. During the period of the five-year plans the major project was construction of another massive steel plant known as Azovstal. The population expanded rapidly, from 62,000 in 1926 (down from the 97,000 of 1917 because of the turmoil of subsequent years) to 190,000 in 1936 and 222,000 in 1939. Port facilities were expanded. An evening institute for metallurgical engineers was started at the Ilich Factory in 1929. In 1937 it became both a full-time day institute as well as a part-time, night institute.

Mariupol suffered greatly during World War II. It was occupied by fascist forces on 8 October 1941. The Jewish population, which numbered over 7,000 in 1926, was placed in a camp outside the city and shot to death on 18 October. Altogether over 50,000 of the citizens of Mariupol were killed. Another 70,000 were sent to Germany as slave laborers. Soviet troops began the liberation of Mariupol in September 1943. At war's end the population was only 85,000. One-third of the city's housing had been destroyed as were most of its schools, libraries, and industrial plants.

After the war it was once again necessary to rebuild Mariupol. As with the rest of the country, the restoration of the heavy industrial base upon which Mariupol rested was given top priority. In 1948, after the death of native son Andrei Aleksandrovich Zhdanov, the city was renamed in his honor. The population grew rapidly: to 284,000 in 1959, 446,000 in 1971, and 529,000 in 1987. In addition to the heavy industry previously mentioned, Mariupol has become a prominent health resort with numerous sanataria, rest homes, and facilities for mud baths and other cures. In addition to the port and steelworks, local enterprises manufacture medical technical equipment, home appliances, clothing, and nets, among others. There are several institutions of higher learning in the city.

In terms of personalities, the most eminent native sons are the well-known landscape painter Arkhip Ivanovich Kuindzhi (1841-1910) and Andrei Zhdanov (1896-1948). Grigorii Ivanovich Petrovsky, prominent revolutionary, head of Ukraine for almost two decades, and a Politburo member, worked in Mariupol between 1906 and 1912.

Bibliography: There are short entries on Mariupol/Zhdanov in all three editions of *Bol' shaia Sovetskaia entsiklopediia* (the third edition translated as The Great Soviet Encyclopedia), *Entsiklopedicheskii slovar' Granat*, and the *Encyclopaedia Judaica* (Vol. 16, col. 1008). Longer works include D.N. Grushevsky, *Zhdanov. Istoriko-ekonomicheskii ocherk* (Donetsk, 1971); *Mariupol i ego okrestnosti* (Mariupol, 1892); and V.K. Seleznev, *Zhdanov. Putevoditel'* (Donetsk, 1968).

Samuel A. Oppenheim

ZHELUDKOV, SERGEI ALEKSEEVICH (1909-1984). Russian Orthodox priest and human rights campaigner. Defended believers and nonbelievers within the dissident community.

Father Zheludkov was born in Pskov in 1909. He fought in the Red Army during World War II and then entered a Leningrad seminary at the close of the war in 1945, where he was ordained an Orthodox priest. For the next fifteen years Father Zheludkov served congregations in the Urals, Kirov, and his native Pskov, until he was barred from pastoral duties in 1960 because of his independent views about the church's role in Soviet society.

Father Zheludkov was among the first to protest the arrests and trials directed against human rights activists and the miserable conditions they faced in the prison camps. On 9 May 1968 he wrote a letter to leading Protestant figures in North America, and Western and Eastern Europe, calling to their attention the recently completed book of Anatoly Tikhonovich Marchenko *My Testimony* (Moi pakazanie), which was the first to describe the horrible treatment of political prisoners in the post-Stalin era. In this letter Zheludkov also appealed on behalf of Aleksander Ilich Ginzburg and Yury Timofeevich Galanskov, who had been convicted of "anti-Soviet agitation and propaganda" in a notorious trial in January 1968. Zheludkov concluded his letter with a typical challenge to their shared religious faith: "I am of the opinion that in our practical attitude to these facts today lies a test of the sincerity and spiritual strength of our Christianity" (Reddaway, 281).

He was even willing to disagree with Aleksander Isaevich Solzhenitsyn when the great writer criticized Patriarch Pimen, the official leader of the Russian Orthodox Church in 1972. Solzhenitsyn reminded Pimen of the lack of religious freedom and the demolition of churches in the Soviet Union. For Solzhenitsyn, instead of seeming to acquiesce to them, the church needed to challenge the regime's repressive policies.

In his open reply to Solzhenitsyn, Father Zheludkov accused him of telling a half truth and defended the church hierarchy which, as Father Zheludkov noted, was "known to be deprived of any opportunity of answering you." For Father Zheludkov the church faced the necessary and tragic decision to "join the system and use...all the opportunities which are allowed" under the rigid conditions enforced by the regime. The consequences of Solzhenitsyn's letter would "be the even greater discredit of the church hierarchy in the eyes of those who do not know the whole truth." (A Chronicle of Current Events, May 1972).

Over the following decade, writing and working from his home in Pskov, an ancient Russian town near the border with Estonia, Father Zheludkov provided a consistently eloquent voice in defense of spiritual values and freedom. He explored this theme with particular effectiveness in his uncensored, self-published book *Why I Am a Christian* (Pochemu i ya khristianin).

His activities were well-known to the Committee for State Security (KGB). In early 1973 Father Zheludkov was interrogated during investigations connected with the case of Viktor Aleksandrovich Krasin and Petr Ionovich Yakir. Krasin gave testimony that Father Zheludkov had given him philosophical and religious books published in the West. But Father Zheludkov refused to cooperate with the authorities "for professional reasons."

He continued his dissident activity. In 1973 he was among the founding members of Moscow's Amnesty International chapter. In 1974 he joined a collective appeal in defense of Solzhenitsyn on the day of Solzhenitsyn's expulsion from the Soviet Union for his book *The Gulag Archipelago*. That same month he appealed on behalf of the dissident Vladimir Konstantinovich Bukovsky, who was being threatened with transfer from Perm labor camp to the much harsher conditions of Vladimir prison. And in 1975 Father Zheludkov added his name to the friends and admirers of Andrei Dmitrievich Sakharov in congratulating him on receipt of the Nobel Peace Prize.

The activity of Father Zheludkov exemplified the tolerance and cooperation of believers and nonbelievers in defense of human rights in the Soviet Union. A deeply religious man, Father Zheludkov recognized the spiritual commitment of numerous activists who professed little or no religious faith. For him there existed not only Christianity of faith but also Christianity of conscience and will, which is confessed by "anonymous Christians," a term he used to describe people who do not believe in Christ but still live according to His precepts.

Father Sergei Zheludkov died in Moscow on 30 January 1984 after surgery for intestinal cancer. He was buried in Pskov.

Bibliography: *A Chronicle of Current Events*, No. 25 (May, 1972), 20; Peter Reddaway, ed., *The Trial of the Four*, trans. by Janis Sapiets (New York, 1972); Father Sergei Zheludkov, *Pochemu i ia khristianin* (Frankfurt, 1973); —, *Khristianstvo i ateizm* (Brussels, 1982).

Joshua Rubenstein

ZHEMCHUZHINA, POLINA SEMENOVNA (1894-1970). Bolshevik revolutionary, political leader, economic administrator, Stalinist, and wife of Viacheslav Mikhailovich Molotov.

Zhemchuzhina was born in Zaporozhe, Ukraine, in 1894. She was born into a Jewish family. As a child she spoke Yiddish and acquired deep feelings for her people and culture, but she was thoroughly Russified by the time she reached adulthood. Her sister, with whom she corresponded until 1939, and other family members fled Russia during the civil war period. After 1948 her sister joined other relatives in the newly-created state of Israel.

During her youth Zhemchuzhina was a factory worker, joined the Bolshevik party, wore a red kerchief, and became a party activist. She also became a great admirer of Aleksandra Mikhailovna Kollontai, the famous female revolutionary. In 1921 she worked in Podpole, Ukraine, where she headed the women's department in one of the party's provincial committees.

Zhemchuzhina attended an international conference of women in Petrograd in 1921. It was there that she met Molotov, who was conducting the conference. Molotov was already a secretary of the Central Committee of the Communist Party. They fell in love and were married that summer. Zhemchuzhina did not return to Ukraine, but went to Moscow where she managed her new husband's home.

Soon a daughter, Svetlana, was born and Zhemchuzhina, like the wives of the other leaders who lived in the Kremlin, dedicated herself to the child's care and upbringing. While rearing Svetlana she worked for the party and studied and read in her spare time. Sport had just become popular, and she became involved in playing tennis and croquet. More importantly in terms of her career, she became a close friend and confidant of Nadezhda Sergeevna Allilueva, the wife of Soviet leader Joseph Vissarionovich Stalin. On 8 November 1932 she attended the banquet celebrating the anniversary of the Russian revolution at which Stalin and Allilueva quarreled publicly. She accompanied Allilueva from the banquet and walked around the Kremlin Palace with her until she calmed down. She was one of the first people called in when Allilueva's suicide was discovered the next morning.

Zhemchuzhina was noted for her good taste. She was always the best dressed of the Kremlin wives. Her apartment in town and her country home (dacha) were luxuriously furnished and tastefully decorated. She visited Paris, Berlin, and New York. By the mid-1930s she had become Moscow's first lady, hosting diplomatic receptions in her own dacha and in other official residences. Zhemchuzhina managed everything with style.

During the 1930s she became an important figure in her own right. She was a member of the jury of the House of Models and she became a member of many different societies and institutions. Most importantly she attained a number of economically and politically significant posts, frequently with the support of Stalin. She was one of the first Bolshevik women to be assigned economic management responsibilities under the direct supervision of the Council of People's Commissars. In 1932 she was named head of the Perfume Trust which introduced lipstick and perfume to Soviet women. For some time she was deputy people's commissar of the food industry, and in 1939 she was appointed people's commissar of the fishing industry. On the political side she was a deputy to the Supreme Soviet and after the Eighteenth Party Congress held in March 1939 she became a candidate member of the Central Committee.

In February 1941 at the Eighteenth Party Conference Zhemchuzhina lost her candidate member status in the Central Committee to make way for military men such as Marshal Georgy Konstantinovich Zhukov as Stalin intensified the preparations for war. During the invasion of the Soviet Union on 22 June 1941 Zhemchuzhina was in the Crimea where she and her family frequently had vacationed with Stalin and other members of his leadership circle. After listening to Molotov's radio speech announcing the beginning of the war, she returned to Moscow by train before going on to Molotov's parental home in Viatka, and then on to Kuibishev, which had been chosen as temporary capital in the event of Moscow's fall. After the successful defense of Moscow in December 1941, she returned to the city. Between 1942 and 1945 she was active in defending the fatherland. Because of her political stature and her Jewish roots she became one of the leaders of the wartime Jewish Antifascist Committee, which had done much to mobilize world opinion against Nazism.

When the Jewish state of Israel was established in 1948 the Soviet Union was the first state to establish diplomatic relations with it. Golda Meir was sent to Moscow as Israel's first ambassador, and Zhemchuzhina as Molotov's wife and a leader of the Jewish Antifascist Committee had discussions with her on more than one occasion. The good relations with Israel proved to be short lived. Stalin began to fear the impact of Zionism on the loyalty of Soviet Jewry and unleashed a campaign to counter it by attacking so-called "rootless cosmopolitanism." The Jewish intelligentsia was punished harshly and Jewish social organizations were liquidated. The leading members of the Jewish Antifascist Defense Committee were arrested and charged with treason, among them Zhemchuzhina. She was charged specifically with spying for Israel and plotting an assassination attempt against Stalin. The case against her was presented to the Politburo and discussed. Molotov made no attempt to refute the evidence. Although he abstained in the voting that followed, he submitted to the Politburo's decision to remove her on grounds of his loyalty to party discipline. Zhemchuzhina was arrested in 1949 and spent more than a year in Lubianka prison in Moscow and more than three years in exile in Kazakhstan.

In January 1953 she, along with a group of Jewish doctors and others, was accused of participating in the so-called "Doctor's Plot," in which the conspirators were said to have hastened the death of highly placed officials, plotted Stalin's murder, and aimed at overturning the regime. There was no substance to these accusations; immediately after Stalin's death on 5 March 1953 these charges were dropped and the liberation and rehabilitation of the victims of his terror was begun. Two days after Stalin's funeral Zhemchuzhina was freed. At once she resumed her life with Molotov, blaming Lavrenty Pavlovich Beria, minister of internal affairs and minister of state security, for her imprisonment and exile. She was in good health and still firmly committed to achieving the radical goals of the revolution, and to Stalin, whom she described as a genius for having eliminated the fifth column and having united the party and the people before the war.

In her last years after Molotov's ouster from power she remained a party activist, attending meetings much as she had done in her youth. She bemoaned the decline of revolutionary spirit and was vehement in denouncing the new directions of Nikita Sergeevich Khrushchev, Stalin's successor. She was an energetic Stalinist and full of spirit to the last. She died in May 1970 and was buried in the Novodevichi cemetery in a place reserved for distinguished citizens of the Soviet Union. Molotov said: "It was my great good fortune that she was my wife. She was beautiful, intelligent, and most of all—a real Bolshevik, a real Soviet person" (Chuev, 473).

Explanations of Stalin's persecution of Zhemchuzhina are inconclusive but offer valuable insights about her career, her relationship to Stalin, and the times in which she lived. They start with the assertion that Stalin was naturally vengeful and suffered in his last years from acute paranoia. They then explore various scenarios which could have provoked him to unfounded fears and draconian countermeasures. Molotov stressed Stalin's "persecution mania" and Zhemchuzhina's contacts with Israeli ambassador Golda Meir and Zionist organizations. He also emphasized manipulation by Beria and others but he could find no fully satisfactory explanation. Svetlana Allilueva, Stalin's daughter, sought an explanation in her father's desperate search, which he mentioned frequently after 1948, for the reason of his wife's suicide. He felt betrayed and abandoned. He slowly grew convinced that Zhemchuzhina had a bad influence on her. Then there was Zhemchuzhina's Jewishness, her contact with the Zionists, and Stalin's fear that she was spying on Molotov. The historian Roy Aleksandrovich Medvedev emphasized Stalin's vengefulness in connection with Zhemchuzhina's deep friendship with his wife, her Jewishness, and her connections with international Zionism.

See Also: "DOCTOR'S PLOT" and MOLOTOV, VIACHESLAV KONSTANTINOVICH.

Bibliography: Svetlana Alliluyeva, *Twenty Letters to a Friend*, trans. by Priscilla Johnson (New York, 1967); Feliks Chuev, *Sto sorok besed s Molotovym. Iz devnika F. Chueva* (M., 1991); Mikhail L. Heller and Aleksandr M. Nekrich, *Utopia in Power. The History of the Soviet Union from 1917 to the Present* (New York, 1982); Nikita Sergeevich Khrushchev, *Khrushchev Remembers*, intro. by Edward Crankshaw, trans. by Strobe Talbott (Boston, 1970), 259-261; Roy A. Medvedev, *Khrushchev*, trans. by Brian Pearce, (New York, 1983); Roy A. Medvedev, *Oni okrushali Stalina* (M., 1990) is a slightly expanded edition of *All Stalin's Men*, trans. by Harold Shukman (New York, 1984); Golda Meir, *My Life*, (London, 1975); Dmitri M. Volkogonov, *Stalin. Triumph and Tragedy*, ed. and trans. by Harold Shukman (London, 1991).

Loren D. Calder

ZHITOMIR. See ZHYTOMYR

ZHIVOPISETS (1772-1773). In English, The Portrait Painter. A weekly satirical journal published by Nikolai Ivanovich Novikov (1744-1818) between April 1772 and June 1773. Zhivopisets was the third of four successive satirical journals brought out by Novikov within a five-year period. The first two were Truten' (The Drone, May 1769-April 1770) and Pustomelia (The Tattler, June-July 1770). The last was entitled Koshelek (variously translated as the Money Bag or Hair Net, July-September 1774). All four have attracted great attention, especially from Soviet scholars, who tended to read them as evidence of ideological struggle in eighteenth-century Russia.

The brief era of the Russian satirical journal began with Vsiakaia vsiachina (All Sorts of Things), which made its appearance in early January 1769 and to which Catherine II was known to be an active contributor. It was followed by well over a dozen imitators, the best and most interesting of which were associated with the name of Novikov. The avowed intent of all his journals was to poke fun at and, by doing so, repair errant social behavior. To this extent they, together with all their Russian counterparts, adhered consciously to the tradition of the British satirical journals of the early part of the century, especially Addison and Steele's Spectator.

Like his previous two journals and like their English ancestor, Novikov's Zhivopisets employed the literary device of a fictitious editor with his own editorial persona, created by the real editor who remained anonymous. In Zhivopisets the editor purported to be an artisan painter, someone from the middle stratum of society. This fictitious editor allegedly stood aloof from the world, and looked down upon its many parts, gathering material from all corners and offering wide-ranging observations on human behavior. As in the case of the other journals, no one has yet succeeded in identifying to any great extent just which entries Novikov himself wrote, which he translated or adapted from foreign sources, and which were submitted by other contributors.

Zhivopisets contains two contributions in particular that Soviet scholars were prone to elevate above all others. The first, "Fragment of a Journey to *** by I*** T***," appearing in issues number five and fourteen of Part I, pilloried the mistreatment by some landlords of their serfs. In the mid-nineteenth century Nikolai Aleksandrovich Dobroliubov identified it as perhaps the harshest condemnation of the excesses of serfdom in the Russian press of the time. Some scholars think it was written by Novikov himself. Others attributed it to Aleksandr Nikolaevich Radishchev, who recently had returned from Germany. The second contribution, published in issues number fifteen, twenty-three, and twenty-four of Part I and number five of Part II, consists of a series of six "Letters to Falalei," purporting to be an exchange of correspondence among coarse, bigoted, and ignorant members of a noble family. Because they satirized the mores of the old nobility in terms reminiscent of Denis Ivanovich Fonvizin's classic satires, some suggest that the dramatist himself may have written them. Others attribute them to Novikov. Given the total absence of evidence, as in the case of the "Fragment of a Journey," identification must rely on thematic concurrence alone and therefore remain highly speculative at best.

While the problem of authorship has garnered its share of attention from scholars, the larger issue of the political orientation of Novikov's journals in general, and of Zhivopisets in particular, remains paramount. Opinion tends to divide into two distinct schools: the Soviet and Soviet-influenced on one hand, and the non-Soviet on the other. The former takes as its point of departure Lenin's two-cultures thesis, which holds that in every property-owning society two opposing cultures exist in a state of tension. It sees the culture of the ruling class in the second half of the eighteenth century as reactionary, since it sought to sustain the outdated status quo by whatever means necessary. It views the culture of the non-noble or "democratic" element, on the other hand, as progressive, expressing as it did the interests of the exploited masses. Intellectual life allegedly mirrored this class conflict. According to the practitioners of the two-cultures thesis, who frequently resort to military terminology, journalism became a major battlefield, as the two camps faced off in an attempt to sway public opinion.

The first of the schools placed Novikov in the vanguard of the struggle against the Empress Catherine II, nobiliary privilege, and serfdom: in sum, against the feudal order. In his attempt to "unmask" the reactionary nature of Catherine II's reign, he appeared as a paragon of the Russian Enlightenment. As such he suffered the enlightener's fate. Despite his use of Aesopian language to confound the censorship, he fell afoul of autocracy. When it became clear to the empress that she was losing the struggle for public opinion, according to this class interpretation, she responded by closing down Zhivopisets, just as she earlier had closed down Truten' and Pustomelia. Harsher still was the punishment visited upon the publisher in 1792, when he suffered arrest and imprisonment, presumably a victim of Catherine's fear of radical political thought.

The second school refused to recognize in the journalism of the late 1760s and early seventies a serious confrontation between conflicting world views. Instead, its members saw Novikov as simply another entrant, albeit a very talented one, in a literary game with well-established rules. Novikov's objective, as Addison and Steele's, was to improve the nation's moral level and, not incidentally, to sell copies of journals. The adherents of this school espied dialogue rather than polemics. Whatever debate took place between Novikov and the empress did so within a generally-accepted framework. It concerned the nature of satire and whether or not it was proper to direct it at identifiable people. The debate threatened no one, least of all the empress, who had initiated it in the first place. The adherents of this school dismissed references to Aesopian language as anachronistic, the product of transposing back to the eighteenth century the nineteenth-century intelligentsia's confrontation with Nicholas I's gendarmes. To see in Zhivopisets' articles attacks on serfdom and autocracy, they argued, is to read into the writing what was not intended.

The available evidence does not substantiate the thesis of a struggle between the empress and Novikov. The exchanges between Novikov's journals and those of the empress represented, in Gareth Jones' words, collaboration rather than defiance. The empress approved of Novikov's literary endeavors, and even contributed to Zhivopisets, along with Pavel Sergeevich Potemkin, Princess Ekaterina Romanovna Dashkova, and other prominent court and church figures. Like the other satirical journals, Zhivopisets was published on the Academy of Sciences press, which the government controlled. For that matter, not only was the journal full of praise for the empress, but Novikov dedicated it to her. As to censorship, no evidence exists to support its application, nor is there a shred of evidence to suggest that Catherine II had Zhivopisets, or any of Novikov's journals, closed down. Declining circulation and exhaustion of suitable material and reader interest alone suffice to account for its demise, as they do for Catherine's own Vsiakaia vsiachina. By the time Zhivopisets ceased publication in June 1773, after the appearance of fifty-two issues, or exactly one year's worth, its maximum press run was no more than 750, little more than half of Truten's at its peak. Moreover it seems highly implausible that the empress, having closed down one Novikov journal, would then permit another to spring up immediately thereafter, and so on through the publication of four journals. Finally Zhivopisets was republished four times in the course of Catherine's reign, the last time in 1793, after Novikov's arrest and in the heat of the French Revolution.

As to Novikov's arrest, it should probably be attributed not to his political views or journalistic activities but to his membership in a secret society, the Moscow Freemasons, and to Catherine II's fear that the Masons had established ties with the Old Believers, with her own son Grand Duke Paul, and with her enemy Prussia. Since they dealt with his religious rather than his more secular publications, the questions posed to him at his interrogation would seem to confirm this interpretation. Finally if Catherine II truly feared Novikov's satirical writings, it seems logical to assume that she would have had the publisher arrested in the early 1770s, when these writings were appearing, rather than two decades later. The publication of Novikov's complete correspondence would go far toward resolving the problem of his political outlook. His collected letters were prepared for press in the 1920s and again in the 1930s, under the title "The Correspondence of Nikolai Ivanovich Novikov," and still again in 1949. In all three instances publication was halted at the last moment, presumably because the letters evinced a concern with religious matters that the prevailing Soviet interpretation deemed incompatible with Novikov. As a leading figure of the Russian Enlightenment, and hence by definition, in the tortuous logic that Soviet scholarship had to employ, he should have been hostile to religion. As of May 1992 at least fifty-one of his letters remain unpublished.

See Also: NOVIKOV, NIKOLAI IVANOVICH.

Bibliography: The standard Soviet biography of Novikov, which leaves much to be desired, is G.P. Makogonenko, ed., *Nikolai Novikov i russkoe prosveshchenie XVIII veka* (M., 1952). Hardly more satisfactory are Aleksandr Vasil'evich Zapadov's *Novikov* (M., 1968), Grigorii Aleksandrovich Likhotkin's *Oklevetannyi Kolovion* (L., 1972), or Leonard Adamovich Derbov's *Obshchestvenno-politicheskie i istoricheskie vzgliady N.I. Novikova* (1974). Far more reliable is Welsh scholar W. Gareth Jones' *Nikolay Novikov. Enlightener of Russia* (Cambridge, 1984). For a brief but well-balanced discussion of Novikov see Michael A. von Herzen, "Novikov, Nikolai Ivanovich," in *The Modern Encyclopedia of Russian and Soviet History, Vol. 25* (Gulf Breeze, Fla., Academic International Press, 1981), 98-104. The most accessible collection of Novikov's satirical journals is found in Pavel Naumovich Berkov, ed., *Satiricheskie zhurnaly N.I. Novikova. Triuten' 1769-1770. Pustomelia 1770. Zhivopisets 1772-1773. Koshelek 1774* (M., 1951). Useful also is Igor Vasilievich Malyshev and Leonid Borisovich Svetlov, eds., *N.I. Novikov i ego sovremenniki. Izbrannye sochineniia* (M., 1961). A convenient English-language translation of selections from the Drone is contained in the appropriate section of Volume 1 of Harold B. Segel's *The Literature of Eighteenth-Century Russia* (New York, 1976), although the accompanying commentary bears the heavy marks of reliance on simplistic Marxist-Leninist literature, as does that in William Edward Brown's *A History of Eighteenth Century Russian Literature* (Ann Arbor, 1980) and André Monnier's *Un publiciste frondeur sous Catherine II. Nicolas Novikov* (Paris, 1981). For the Soviet historiographic context see David M. Griffiths "In Search of Enlightenment. Recent Soviet Interpretation of Eighteenth-Century Russian Intellectual History," in *Canadian-American Slavic Studies*, Vol. 16, Nos. 3-4 (1982), 317-356. The standard Soviet accounts of Novikov's journalistic activity are Pavel Naumovich Berkov, *Istoriia russkoi zhurnalistiki XVIII veka* (1952), Aleksandr Vasil'evich Zapadov, *Istoriia russkoi zhurnalistiki XVIII-XIX vekov* (1963), and Ivan Fedorovich Martynov, *Knigoizdatel' Nikolai Novikov* (1981). Still, despite their age, those presented in the pre-Soviet studies of A.I. Nezelenev, *N.I. Novikov, izdatel' zhurnalov 1769-1785 godov* (SPb., 1875), V.P. Semennikov, *Russkie satiricheskie zhurnaly 1769-1774 gg.* (SPb., 1914), and A.N. Afanas'ev, *Russkie satiricheskie zhurnaly 1769-1774 godov*, 2nd ed. (Kazan, 1921), tend to be more satisfying. Insightful commentaries are to be found in a number of W. Gareth Jones' articles, two of which are his "The Polemics of the 1769 Journals. A Reappraisal," *Canadian-American Slavic Studies*, Vol. 16, Nos. 3-4 (1982), 432-443, and "The Eighteenth Century View of English Moral Satire.

Palliative or Purgative?" A.G. Cross, ed., *Great Britain and Russia in the Eighteenth Century. Contrasts and Comparisons* (Newtonville, Mass., 1979), 75-83. Volume 11 (Leningrad, 1976) of the serial publication *XVIII vek*, subtitled *N.I. Novikov i obshchestveno-literaturnoe dvizhenie ego vremeni*, marked a brave attempt to break new ground in Soviet literature, although the papers from the conference from which it originated experienced difficulty in seeing the light of day, and the introduction by I.Z. Serman, the organizer of the conference, was eliminated altogether. Still, especially insightful are the contributions by L.I. Kulakova, V.P. Stepanov, and Aleksandr Vasil'evich Zapadov. With the collapse of Marxism-Leninism more profound Novikov scholarship emanating from the former Soviet Union can be anticipated.

David M. Griffiths

ZHOLTOVSKY, IVAN VLADISLAVOVICH (1867-1959). Architect and urban designer. Scholar and promoter of the Italian Renaissance in Moscow who received the Stalin Award (1950) for his contributions to socialist realism.

Born in Pinsk, Brestsky province in Belorussia, Zholtovsky studied architecture at the St. Petersburg Academy of Art (1887-1898). He supplemented his education by traveling abroad and gained practical experience by working in architectural firms. In 1900 Zholtovsky settled in Moscow and began teaching at the Stroganov School of Art and Applied Art. This school, reorganized in 1918 and renamed Vkhutemas/Vkhutein (Vysshie khudozhestvenno-tekhnicheskie masterskie [Higher Artistic and Technical Studios]/Vysshii khudozhestvenno-tekhnicheskii institut [Higher Artistic and Technical Institute]), was renowned during the 1920s as the leader in avant-garde art and architectural education. Yet Zholtovsky continued to promote Italian Renaissance and Baroque as the universal symbols of eternal beauty. A consistent and charismatic educator, he insisted that only classical proportions and composition could train an architect's eye and provide him with the foundations of aesthetic experience. His method endured social and political changes, and he continued to teach through the 1940s.

Two of Zholtovsky's prerevolutionary buildings in Moscow demonstrate the evolution of his architectural style. He designed the Equestrian Society Headquarters (1905) in the prevailing style of Russian neoclassicism. But in the Gavril Tarasov mansion (1909-1912) he followed Italian precedents, the Palazzo Thiene in Vicenza and the Palazzo Ducale in Venice. After the revolution Zholtovsky headed the architectural division of the Commissariat of Enlightenment (Narkompros) and, with Aleksei Viktorovich Shchusev, the MosSoviet Design Studio. From 1922 to 1923 he prepared the master plan for the First All-Russian Agricultural and Handicraft Industries Exhibition and designed its entrance gate and the pavilions for machine-building industries. Since all exhibition buildings were constructed in wood, Zholtovsky imitated classical forms, such as stone arches, columns, and masonry in painted wood, as if they were theatrical props. This pretentious and contrived manner of design became the hallmark of socialist realism.

In 1926 Zholtovsky won a competition for the design of the House of the Soviets of Dagestan Autonomous Socialist Soviet Republic (ASSR). Built in

Makhachkala, the capital city of Dagestan, this government edifice combined elements of traditional Muslim architecture with the symbols of Soviet power. It demonstrated the direction Soviet architecture would take in the ethnic republics in order to comply with the definition of socialist realism: socialist in form and national in character.

In 1933 private architectural practice was banned and state design organizations were formed. Zholtovsky was appointed to head Architectural Studio No. 1 of MosSoviet. His most important buildings of this period are the apartment house (later the Intourist Agency) on Mokhovaia (later Marx) Street in Moscow (1933-1934) and his City Hall (later the Art Exhibitions Building) in Sochi on the Black Sea shore (1934-1936). The facade of the Moscow housing block was a reproduction of the sixteenth-century Loggia del Capitano in Vicenza by Andrea Palladio. The magnificent, yet only decorative, colonnade dictated the interior arrangement of the apartments, where some windows are at floor level in order to comply with the pattern of the facade. The City Hall in Sochi reiterated a Palladian villa in its plan, colonnaded porticoes, and detailing. Both buildings were clear statements of Zholtovsky's commitment to the timeless value of classical harmony. They became suitable and convincing models for the architects of the 1930s and 1940s. Zholtovsky translated Palladio's *Four Books on Architecture* (1939) as an authoritative guide for future architecture developments.

World War II interrupted all construction activities. Zholtovsky's housing complex on Bolshaia Kaluzhskaia (later Lenin) Boulevard in Moscow, although designed in 1940 was not completed until 1949. For this adaptation of Renaissance motives to a multistoried apartment house, Zholtovsky received the Stalin Award (1950). He was favored with privileges for his subsequent contributions to socialist realism: the main building of Moscow's Hippodrome (1951-1955, with V. Voskresensky and P. Skokan), the housing on Smolensk Square (1952-1955, designed in 1941), the huge cold storage building in Sokolniki outside Moscow, and many unexecuted projects.

During the 1920s Zholtovsky was the target of attack and criticism by the Russian Constructivists. Although he prevailed, at the end of his life he saw his work discredited when socialist realism was rejected after Stalin's death. Zholtovsky died in Moscow at the age of ninety-two.

Bibliography: Mikhail Grigorievich Barkhin, ed., *Mastera sovetskoi arkhitektury ob arkhitekture*, Vol. 1 (M., 1975), 23-55; Andrei Ikonnikov, *Russian Architecture of the Soviet Period* (M., 1988), 67-69, 90-91, 221-223, 243-244, 262-263; Anatole Kopp, *L'architecture de la période Stalinienne* (Grenoble, France, 1978); Grigori D. Oshchepkov, *I.V. Zholtovskii. Proekty i postroiki* (M., 1955); Anatole Senkevitch, Jr., *Soviet Architecture, 1917-1962. A Bibliographical Guide to Source Material* (Charlottesville, Virginia, 1974), 256-259; Aleksandr V. Vlasov, "Zodchii, uchenyi, pedagog (k vosmidesiatipiatiletiiu akademika arkhitektury I.V. Zholtovskogo)," *Sovetskaia arkhitektura*, No.4 (1953), 46-69.   *Milka T. Bliznakov*

ZHUCHENKO-GERNGROSS, ZINAIDA FEDOROVNA (187?-19??). Tsarist police agent who successfully infiltrated Russian revolutionary organizations, 1893-1909.

Little personal information is available about Zhuchenko, who was born into the gentile Gerngross family in the 1870s. She was educated at a prestigious institute for noble girls and subsequently enrolled in a course of higher education for women in Moscow. Her life and early political loyalties remain largely obscure until 1893 when she offered her services to the Moscow section of the Russian security police, the Okhrana, then headed by Sergei Vasilievich Zubatov. In 1895, as a member of a Moscow terrorist group led by student Ivan Rasputin, she assisted the authorities in uncovering the revolutionaries' plan to assassinate Tsar Nicholas II during his coronation ceremonies. Because of her actual participation in the conspiracy she was arrested, spent eleven months in prison and was sentenced to five years of exile in the city of Kutais. There she married a medical student by the name of Zhuchenko in 1897 and later that year moved to the town of Yurev (Derpt, Dorpat) in the Baltics. In April 1898 she left her husband and went abroad with her young son.

Zhuchenko dedicated herself to raising her beloved child and did not return to political activity until 1903. At that time, outraged by the rise of the revolutionary movement in Russia, she considered it her duty as a convinced monarchist to assist the Russian government in its struggle against the radicals. In the spring of 1903, concluding that the most effective method of disorganizing the revolutionary ranks would be to provide the security police with inside information about the extremists, Zhuchenko resumed her activities as a police agent. She joined the Socialist Revolutionary Party (PSR) and began to supply information on the organization's activities to her new police superior, Arkady Mikhailovich Garting (Harting), one of the Okhrana's top officers.

In September 1905 Zhuchenko was instructed by the government to return to Moscow, where she became a member of the PSR Regional Committee. Around the end of 1907 she was elected secretary of the organization and held that position until 1909. She was involved in planning terrorist operations and took part in a number of party conferences. Simultaneously she continued to provide the authorities information on the internal operations of local PSR groups. Largely because of Zhuchenko's reports, the authorities were able to arrest a number of leading revolutionaries, including the notorious Fruma Frumkina, and to prevent a series of political assassinations, including an attack planned against Governor Reinbot of Moscow. She occasionally chose not to reveal to the authorities all she knew about the radical's plans in order to protect her own position in their ranks. This was apparently the case when she failed to inform the Okhrana about a planned attempt on the life of Admiral Fedor Vasilievich Dubasov, governor-general of Moscow, in 1906. Despite such lapses, Zhuchenko's police superiors considered her an outstanding and dedicated agent.

In the summer of 1909 Leonid Petrovich Menshchikov, a former high-ranking police officer who had defected to the revolutionary camp, provided revolutionary Vladimir Lvovich Burtsev with definitive proof of Zhuchenko's connections with the Russian secret police. On 14 August of the same year the

PSR Central Committee declared Zhuchenko an "agent provocateur." She protested this label, which indeed in its traditional sense does not bear scrutiny, for there is little evidence suggesting that Zhuchenko provoked or instigated any revolutionary combat operations.

Far from denying her role as a police informer following her exposure in 1909, Zhuchenko declared that she was proud to have served her motherland by betraying the radicals to tsarist justice. She claimed to have been driven by ideological convictions rather than material interests and expressed no misgivings or regrets about her past. Convinced of the sincerity of her motives, Burtsev could not help but recognize the strength of Zhuchenko's moral stand. As they parted after a brief meeting in Charlottenburg, Germany, where she was residing with her son, he acknowledged, "I shake the hand of an honest person" (Spiridovich, 47). Similarly, the PSR Central Committee, regardless of its public stand, seemed to treat her as a political enemy rather than a traitor. Because she no longer could harm the party following her exposure, her life was spared and the PSR leaders refrained from taking any punitive steps against her.

The Russian government expressed its appreciation for Zhuchenko's services by granting her a permanent annual pension of 3,600 rubles in response to a request on 12 October 1909 to Nicholas II from Prime Minister Petr Arkadievich Stolypin. She remained under Russian protection while living abroad, and when police authorities in Berlin, reacting to pressure from local socialists, sought to expel her from Germany in 1910, the St. Petersburg Police Department intervened and secured permission for her to remain in the country. In August 1914, a few days after the outbreak of the World War I, she was arrested in Germany and imprisoned on charges of espionage; she is known to have remained in custody until 1917. Her subsequent life and activities remain as obscure as the years preceding her work as the most successful female spy in the history of the Russian revolutionary movement.

Bibliography: A.V. Gerasimov, *Na lezvii s terroristami* (Paris, 1985); L.P. Men'shchikov, *Okhrana i revoliutsiia* (M., 1925); P. Pavlov, *Agenty, zhandarmy, palachi* (Pg., 1922); Nurit Schleifman, *Undercover Agents in the Russian Revolutionary Movement. The SR Party, 1902-1914* (New York, 1988); A.V. Pribylev-Korba, *Zinaida Zhuchenko. Iz vospominanii* (n.p., 1919); A. Spiridovich, *Zapiski zhandarma* (M., 1991).

Anna Geifman

ZHUKOV, GEORGY KONSTANTINOVICH (1896-1974). Soviet military commander, Marshal of the Soviet Union (18 January 1943), four times Hero of the Soviet Union (29 August 1939, 29 July 1944, 1 June 1945, 1 December 1956), Hero of the Mongolian People's Republic (1969), member of the Communist Party of the Soviet Union since March 1919.

Zhukov was born 19 November (1 December) 1896 to a peasant family (Konstantin and Ustina Zhukov) in the village of Strelkovka in the Kaluga Region. His father was a cobbler, his mother a farm girl. From 1903 to 1906 he studied in a parish school and received an award for good conduct and progress. In the summer of 1908 he left his village to go to Moscow as an apprentice in a furrier shop owned by a relative. In 1910 he enrolled in evening courses and the next year successfully completed the examination for the full course of the city's academy. From the end of 1912 to 1915 he continued to learn the fur trade and was soon a master furrier.

World War I broke out and in August 1915 the young man was called to the army as a private in the Fifth Reserve Cavalry Regiment. In the spring of 1916 he was sent to a training command and graduated as a "vice noncommissioned officer." He saw service with the Tenth Dragoon Novgorod Regiment on the Southeastern Front in the summer of 1916. In October of the same year Zhukov participated in battles as a reconnaissance soldier in the Bystritsk region. He captured a German officer, which earned him his first St. George Cross. Soon afterward he was wounded in action and awarded another St. George Cross. Upon recovery he was assigned at the end of 1916 to a training command as a noncommissioned officer. In February 1917 as revolutionary fervor swept the country, Zhukov was voted chairman of his squadron's soldiers' committee and chosen as one of three delegates to the regimental soviet, which supported the Bolsheviks. In December 1917 his squadron was disbanded and Zhukov returned to his village.

He decided to join the new Red Guards, but a serious bout with typhus and relapsing fever delayed his enlistment for half a year. Finally in August 1918 he volunteered for the Red Army and was assigned to the Fourth Cavalry Regiment, First Moscow Cavalry Division. On 1 March 1919 Zhukov became a member of the Russian Communist Party (Bolsheviks). Civil war had broken out in Russia, and in May 1919 Zhukov's division was ordered to the Urals to fight the White cossacks. From June to August 1919 Zhukov participated in battles for Uralsk on the Ural River. He served under the talented Mikhail Vasilievich Frunze, the army group (front) commander. In September 1919 he fought on the approaches to Tsaritsyn (later Stalingrad and Volgograd). In close combat with White cossacks he was wounded and hospitalized. In January 1920 Zhukov attended cavalry courses, where he was assigned to teach other cadets the use of "cold" weapons: the pike, sword, and bayonet. Between April and August 1920 Zhukov, as a member of the composite cadet regiment, trained in Moscow. The regiment became part of the Second Moscow Brigade, which was sent to fight General Petr Nikolaevich Wrangel. Soon thereafter he was promoted to platoon leader in the First Cavalry Regiment, then to squadron commander. At the end of December 1920 Zhukov's brigade engaged bands in Voronezh province. In exceptionally hard hand-to-hand fighting in March 1921 Zhukov's squadron performed well, and he was awarded the Order of the Red Banner. The next month, under the command of Mikhail Nikolaevich Tukhachevsky, Zhukov's cavalrymen fought Aleksandr Stepanovich Antonov's anti-Bolshevik guerrillas. In a single day in May 1921 Zhukov lost two horses in close combat and narrowly escaped death. At the end of the summer he participated in the final defeat of Antonov's forces.

After the civil war Zhukov decided to remain in the army. From June 1922 to March 1923 he served as squadron commander in the Thirty-eighth Cavalry Regiment and deputy commander of the Fortieth Cavalry Regiment, Seventh Samara Division. At the end of May 1923 he became commander of the Thirty-ninth Buzuluk Cavalry Regiment of the Seventh Samara Cavalry Division. In the autumn of 1924 he attended the year-long Higher Cavalry School in

Leningrad, where his fellow officers included future wartime commanders Konstantin Konstantinovich Rokossovsky, Ivan Khristoforovich Bagramian, and Andrei Ivanovich Eremenko. Upon completion of the course Zhukov resumed command of the Thirty-ninth Cavalry Regiment. He would serve almost seven years with this regiment, which was located in the important Belorussian Military District (MD).

In the winter of 1926 Zhukov was designated one-man commander (edinonachalnik), a significant step in his career. Until 1925 military commanders and political commissars comprised a dual command of units, and all commands and orders had to bear the signature of both the commander and the commissar. Throughout his career Zhukov strongly believed that the civil authorities should trust a commander to run his unit without the constant interference of the party representative, the commissar. The principle of one-man command (edinonachalie) was introduced into the Soviet armed forces in 1925 and combined in the person of the commander all the rights and privileges connected with the military, political, administrative, and logistical control of a unit. The Soviets introduced the commissar system, or dual command, three times, in 1918, 1937, and 1941. Three times they instituted the principle of one-man command, in 1925, 1940, and 1942. Usually the commissar system coincided with a period of instability and revealed internal weaknesses of the regime.

In May 1930 Zhukov became commander of the Second Cavalry Brigade, part of Rokossovsky's Seventh Samara Division. In his efficiency report on Zhukov, Rokossovsky described him as "a commander of strong will and decisiveness," possessing "a wealth of initiative." He noted that Zhukov was disciplined, exacting, and persistent in his demands. "He loves military matters and constantly improves himself" (Svetlishin, 32).

From February 1931 to March 1933 Zhukov served in the People's Defense Commissariat as deputy inspector of cavalry. Because of a decline in the division's combat and political training, Zhukov was sent to command the Fourth Cavalry Division in the Belorussian MD. By July 1935 it ranked among the best, earning for Zhukov the prestigious Order of Lenin. While commanding this division Zhukov studied the employment of tanks on the future battlefield, especially their coordination with other arms such as aviation. He believed that the tank could play an independent role in combat operations and that this new powerful weapon must not be spread out with slower moving infantry units, dissipating its strength. From July 1937 until March 1938 he commanded the Third Cavalry Corps, headquartered in Minsk, and was promoted to corps commander (komkor) on 31 July 1937. In March 1938 he took command of the Sixth Cavalry Corps, and at the end of the year became deputy commander for cavalry of the Belorussian MD.

In the meantime Soviet leader Joseph Vissarionovich Stalin, having purged the party, lashed out against perceived threats among the military leadership. In the period from 1937 until October 1941 he liquidated more than forty thousand Red Army officers on trumped-up charges and forced confessions. Three of the five Marshals of the Soviet Union (the gifted Tukhachevsky, Egorov, Vasily Konstantinovich Bliukher) were killed, as were most army, corps, and division commanders. The surviving marshals, Semen Mikhailovich Budenny and Kliment Efremovich Voroshilov, friends of Stalin, would prove their total incompetence in the early months of World War II and be replaced in their commands. Zhukov, who had been brought before a party commission and dealt with rather harshly, may have been a candidate for arrest, but suddenly he was summoned to Moscow on 1 June 1939 and ordered to proceed immediately to the Mongolian People's Republic. With the Soviets preoccupied with events in Europe—the Munich crisis and Germany's preparations for war—the Japanese decided to stage a test of the Soviet Union's military might on the Manchurian and Mongolian frontiers. In 1938 the Soviets and Japanese had clashed near Lake Khasan, and both sides had suffered heavy casualties. In May 1939 hostilities again broke out and several hundred Japanese cavalrymen moved up to the Khalkhin-Gol River. Mongolian troops sent to restore the frontier were scattered by enemy fire. The Soviet government, fulfilling its mutual assistance pact with the Mongolian People's Republic, ordered its troops to defend the borders of the two countries.

Placed in command of the combined Soviet-Mongolian forces, Zhukov began planning the defeat of the Japanese in the area of Khalkhin-Gol (Nomonhan). Tough fighting took place in June and July, especially around Bain-Tsagan. In the first days of July the Japanese began concentrating troops for a fresh offensive; their numbers reached about thirty thousand. Soviet and Mongolian troops were fewer, but they had considerably more tanks and armored cars, providing Zhukov an excellent opportunity to test the effectiveness of Soviet tanks and tactics. In early July as the Japanese prepared to attack, Zhukov guessed their plan and decided on a bold preemptive strike. His attack was so sudden that the Japanese ranks were thrown into disorder.

Zhukov's bold leadership style was revealed in this campaign: clever use of deception; close coordination of tanks, artillery, and air; and willingness to take large casualties to achieve critical objectives. For example, Zhukov carried out elaborate deception measures designed to create the impression that the Soviet-Mongolian forces were only building up defenses and nothing else. He even had a booklet printed on the Soviet soldier in the defense, which was allowed to fall into the hands of the Japanese. Radio messages which could be deciphered easily mentioned defensive works and an autumn and winter campaign. The deception worked. The Japanese command, confident that the Soviet-Mongolian forces would not attack, allowed its senior officers to take off Sunday, 20 August. Suddenly, at 5:45 A.M., 150 bombers sent by Zhukov carried out a massive raid on the Japanese positions, while simultaneously his artillery pounded the enemy. Then Zhukov ordered his soldiers into the assault along the whole front.

When things slowed down on the third day of the offensive, Zhukov had a conversation with the commander of the Transbaikal Army Group, Grigorii Mikhailovich Shtern, who was responsible for supplying Zhukov's forces. Shtern recommended that Zhukov spend the next two or three days to build up for subsequent strikes and warned of great losses. Zhukov replied that "war is war and it is impossible not to have losses." And he reminded Shtern that high losses were acceptable "especially when we are faced with such a serious and cruel enemy as the Japanese." Then Zhukov told him that he rejected his recommendations: "I am in command here. And you are charged with supporting me and providing for my rear. And I ask that you not exceed the limits of your authority" ("Marshal Zhukov," *Ogonek*, No. 48, 8).

Zhukov carried out the encirclement of the enemy; then he methodically set about destroying them. By the end of the month he had cleared the Japanese from Mongolian territory, for which he was awarded the title Hero of the Soviet Union. In April 1941 a Soviet-Japanese nonaggression pact was signed, and the two nations refrained from attacking each other until the Soviet Union broke the agreement in 1945. This pact allowed the Soviets to fight on only one front and shift vital Siberian forces to the west.

When Zhukov returned to the Soviet capital in May 1940 events in Europe had taken an ominous turn. Hitler had sent his troops into Vienna, and had declared Austria part of the German Reich. In mid-March 1939 the Germans invaded Czechoslovakia, completing the dismemberment of that tragic country. On 23 August 1939 German Foreign Minister Joachim von Ribbentrop arrived in Moscow to sign the infamous nonaggression pact between Germany and the Soviet Union. In the "Secret Additional Protocol" the Germans and Soviets divided Eastern Europe into spheres of influence. In Poland these spheres were to be bounded by the line of the Narew, Vistula, and San rivers. The Soviets expressed an interest in Bessarabia. Eight days later the German armies attacked Poland and World War II began. Stalin sent Soviet forces into eastern Poland, "liberating" more than twelve million people occupying 190 thousand square miles (300 sq. km) of territory.

Arriving in Moscow Zhukov was chosen personally by Stalin to command a key district, the Kiev Special MD. In June 1940 he was promoted to General of the Army. In the same month Stalin decided to incorporate the Baltic states into the Soviet Union. At the same time he presented an ultimatum to Rumania, forcing it to cede to the USSR the province of Bessarabia, as well as Northern Bukovina, about which nothing had been said in the agreement with Hitler. On 28 June Soviet troops under Zhukov's command moved into Bessarabia and Northern Bukovina in two echelons. On 30 June Red Army troops arrived on the Prut River, and soon the territories were under Soviet control.

In December 1940 and early January 1941 the Soviet High Command held an important conference in Moscow, followed by war games executed on maps. The meeting drew the attention of Stalin and the entire defense establishment. Zhukov, who played the "blue" (western) side in the first game, recalled with pride his successful performance. Using realistic data on German forces, he developed "blue" operations exactly along those lines which the Germans later used. The main strikes were delivered against the "red" (eastern) side where later they were delivered. And the concentration of forces took shape about how they did during the war. "The border configuration, the terrain, the situation—all prompted me to make just those decisions which later, in 1941, the Germans made," he said ("Marshal Zhukov," *Ogonek*, No. 49, 6-13 December 1986, 6-7). Zhukov's performance so impressed Stalin that he was designated Chief of the General Staff of the Red Army and deputy defense commissar.

His political role was also growing. From 15 to 20 February 1941 he participated in the work of the Eighteenth Party Congress and was chosen candidate member of the Central Committee. Zhukov urgently began to prepare the Soviet armed forces for a possible war with Germany. His work was greatly hampered by Stalin, who was determined not to provoke Hitler in any way. With time running out, he continued to ignore warnings from sincere individuals such as British Prime Minister Winston Churchill, insisting that these warnings were attempts by Western leaders to set the Germans and Soviets against each other.

Occupying newly-annexed lands—much of Poland, for example—resulted in new challenges for Zhukov and his General Staff. These territories had to be included in the Soviet defensive arrangements, and the task of fortifying them was far from complete when the Germans struck. Also complicating Zhukov's job was Stalin's belief that any future aggression against the USSR would be directed primarily against the Ukraine and that all troop redeployments should be concentrated there.

In May 1941 Zhukov submitted to Stalin a plan which proposed a strong preemptive strike against German forces massing in Poland. The idea was rejected for good reason, since the Soviets were just beginning to mobilize and they did not yet have sufficient forces for such a daring strike. Possibly Zhukov was trying to draw Stalin's attention to the ominous German buildup in neighboring Poland.

On 14 July 1941 Zhukov and Defense Commissar Semen Konstantinovich Timoshenko urged that troops of the border MDs be brought to full combat readiness, but again Stalin feared Hitler's reaction. On the evening of 21 June an urgent meeting of the Politburo was held. Defense Commissar Timoshenko told the group that a directive must be issued to all border troops bringing them to combat readiness. Zhukov read the directive, but Stalin still feared provocation. Zhukov and his first deputy, General Nikolai Fedorovich Vatutin, went into the next room and quickly drafted a fresh directive which Stalin approved. It warned the border districts that a sudden German attack was possible during the period 22-23 June; warned of provocative actions; and ordered firing positions to be occupied secretly, aircraft dispersed, cities blacked out, and all units brought to combat readiness. Signed by Timoshenko and Zhukov, the directive was transmitted at 12:30 A.M. on June 22. It would never arrive in time.

In the early hours of June 22 some 140 Axis divisions in three strike groups poured across the Soviet border. Shortly before the attack Zhukov had called up five armies from the hinterland to form a general reserve, intended for a counter-offensive, but they were still 250 to 310 miles (400-500 km) from the scene of action.

Zhukov and all personnel of the General Staff and Defense Commissariat remained overnight in their offices. Near dawn he was called by the commander of the Black Sea Fleet, who declared that a large number of unidentified aircraft were approaching his base. A few minutes later other commanders reported air raids in Belorussia, Ukraine, and in the Baltic area. Zhukov phoned Stalin, who after some minutes picked up the receiver. He ordered that

Timoshenko and Zhukov come immediately to the Kremlin. Arriving at 4:30 A.M. the men found a pale Stalin and all members of the Politburo. Told of the situation Stalin agreed with Zhukov that all available Soviet forces strike the Germans and halt their advance. The Soviet leader insisted that except for aviation no Red Army units violate the border. Even at this extremely tense hour Stalin "still hoped to escape war," Zhukov wrote. Although Soviet cities were under air attack, Stalin still asked, "Is this not a provocation of the German generals?" Timoshenko tried to change his mind, but Stalin resisted: "If it is necessary to organize a provocation, then the German generals would even bomb their own cities...." Then thinking a little, he continued: "For sure Hitler did not know about this" (Zhukov, 2, 9).

Faced with the stark reality of Germans sweeping over their borders, the Soviets took desperate measures to tighten control and revitalize the entire defense establishment. One of their first steps was instituted on 23 June with creation of General Headquarters (Stavka) of the High Command. Timoshenko was appointed chairman, with Stalin, Zhukov, Viacheslav Mikhailovich Molotov, Voroshilov, Budenny, and Admiral Nikolai Gerasimovich Kuznetsov as members. The body was entrusted with the leadership of all military activities of the armed forces. The General Staff was subordinated to Stavka and served as a source of planning and information upon which Stavka could draw. Despite these measures Zhukov recalled that Timoshenko could make no decision without Stalin. Thus there were two commanders in chief, Timoshenko, de jure, and Stalin, de facto. Zhukov wrote that this arrangement complicated the job of troop control and wasted time in making decisions and issuing orders.

Complicating matters was the fact that the German attack left Stalin catatonic—in Nikita Sergeevich Khrushchev's words, "paralyzed by his fear of Hitler, like a rabbit in front of a boa constrictor. For a long time, Stalin actually did not direct military operations and ceased to do anything whatever." A few days into the war Stalin told his secret police chief Lavrenty Pavlovich Beria that "everything is lost. I give up. Lenin left us a proletarian state, and now we've been caught with our pants down and let the whole thing go to ____." (Khrushchev, 169-170.)

As German units raced across the Soviet border, Stalin ordered Zhukov to fly to the headquarters of the Southwestern Army Group to coordinate defensive actions. For most of the war Zhukov served as Stavka representative, traveling from one critical sector of the front to another. Often accompanied by General Aleksandr Mikhailovich Vasilievsky, his mission was to exercise firm control over the planning of military campaigns and the direction of operations. The Stavka representatives decided how to use reserves, and very little escaped their attention. They made sure that the Supreme Commander's directives and orders were carried out; Zhukov was even empowered to make on-the-spot decisions in Stalin's name.

Back in Moscow after a few days with the Southwestern Army Group, Zhukov coordinated the combat actions of the various army groups which were engaged. But the German forces pushed deeper into the USSR, encircling entire Soviet armies. On 29 July 1941 Zhukov recommended that Stalin abandon Kiev, the Ukrainian capital, and that the entire Southwestern Army Group be pulled back beyond the Dnieper River. Stalin snapped at him, accusing Zhukov of talking nonsense. Zhukov angrily replied: "If you think that the Chief of the General Staff is only able to talk nonsense, then he has no business here. I ask to be relieved from my duties and sent to the front. There maybe I shall be of more use to the Motherland." After an oppressive silence, Stalin spoke: "We managed without Lenin, and we can all the better manage without you." (Zhukov, 2, 121-122). A few hours later, after a cooling off period, it was agreed that Zhukov would take command of the reserve army group operating along the approaches to Moscow.

Zhukov's troops were largely responsible for taking much of the shock out of Hitler's blitzkrieg and allowing the Soviets to regroup and bring up reserves. Stalin, pleased with Zhukov, summoned him to Moscow on 8 September 1941 and told him that he had performed very well in the fighting at the Elnia salient. Referring to their July confrontation over abandoning Kiev, Stalin told Zhukov that he had been right. Stalin then told him that the situation around Leningrad was extremely difficult and that he needed Zhukov to rush there to take charge of the city's defenses. The Germans had just completed surrounding Leningrad, which was cut off from the rest of the Soviet Union. The incompetent Voroshilov, commanding the Leningrad Army Group, had disappointed and embarrassed Stalin, and Zhukov was to replace him. Arriving in the blockaded city on 10 September Zhukov informed Voroshilov that he was to depart immediately for Moscow. He then immediately began a hectic work schedule, overseeing the preparation of new defensive positions around the city and drafting detailed plans for breaking the German stranglehold.

While commanding the Leningrad Army Group, Zhukov, as a member of Stavka, received continuous reports from the General Staff about the combat situation in other areas. In the early days of October he followed the progress of the German forces as they advanced toward the Mozhaisk fortified line some fifty miles (80 km) west of Moscow. At this critical juncture Stalin once again turned to Zhukov, ordering him to take command of the Western Army Group fighting on the approaches to Moscow. As Alan Clark observed, it was Zhukov who was sent here and there throughout the war, the "fireman" who in his day was to visit and stabilize every dangerous sector of the eastern front (Clark, 119).

For the next two months Zhukov organized the defenses before Moscow and began planning a massive counteroffensive. On 20 October a state of siege was declared in Moscow and many government functions were transferred to Kuibyshev, although Stalin remained in the city. As the fighting grew more critical, Stalin phoned Zhukov, asking, "Are you sure we can hold Moscow? I say this to you with a heavy heart. Speak honestly, as a Communist." "There is no doubt we can hold Moscow," Zhukov replied. "But we still need no less than two armies and at least 200 tanks" (Zhukov, 233-234). Stalin promised him the armies by the end of November. By this time Zhukov's army group had received large numbers of reinforcements and consisted of six armies.

The German offensive ran out of steam in late November, and a retreat began in the early days of December. At this moment Zhukov ordered his counteroffensive against the exhausted and half-frozen enemy. On 6 December after concentrated air strikes and artillery preparation, troops of Zhukov's army group began their attack north and south of Moscow. The initiative proved to be in the hands of the now high-spirited Red Army men. By Christmas Day the Germans had lost more than a thousand tanks and fourteen hundred guns, together with large quantities of other equipment. The threat which had hung over Moscow had been dispelled. Never again would the Wehrmacht get as close to Moscow as it had in the early days of December 1941.

On 1 February 1942 Stavka, recognizing the need for closer cooperation between the Kalinin and Western army groups, reestablished the position of commander-in-chief of the Western Direction and assigned Zhukov to the post. He set about applying renewed pressure to the Germans, pushing them back, and improving the operational situation.

At the coming of spring Hitler issued a new directive that when weather conditions were favorable his troops were to break through into the Caucasus, capture its oil fields, and push on to Stalingrad (now Volgograd). As the Germans moved toward the city Stavka sent Zhukov and Chief of the General Staff Vasilievsky to the area to organize defenses and plan a counteroffensive. During the next several months Zhukov often traveled between Moscow and Stalingrad and briefed Stalin on the counteroffensive plan that was unfolding. On the morning of 19 November 1942 the thunder of artillery heralded the start of the Soviet counteroffensive. Four days later the Soviets had closed the ring around the Axis armies, numbering twenty-two divisions and about 330,000 men, and their slow strangulation began. By 1 February 1943 the remnants of General Friedrich von Paulus's Sixth Army began to surrender en masse, and the battle of Stalingrad was over. Zhukov was awarded the Order of Suvorov First Class, and was promoted to Marshal of the Soviet Union, the first commander of the Second World War so honored. Earlier on 22 August 1942 Stalin had appointed Zhukov his deputy.

Stalin then sent his busy deputy to Leningrad to assist in operations to lift the siege of that tragic city. In December Zhukov worked out a plan for converging strikes by two army groups, and two weeks later reinforced Red Army troops began to move. On 18 January 1943 the forces of the Leningrad and Volkhov army groups linked up and the blockade of Leningrad was broken.

Many miles to the south another critical situation was unfolding. A large bulge had developed in the Russian line, the Kursk salient. To the German high command this broad salient posed a serious threat, in that it could serve as a jumping-off point for attacks against the flanks of the two German army groups in this sector. The Germans therefore decided to pinch off this salient, believing if the attack was launched early enough the Red Army would be caught unprepared. While "Operation Citadel" (the German code name) was still in the planning stage, Zhukov flew to the Kursk area to study the situation. Later the same day Zhukov phoned Stalin to urge his chief to rush everything possible from Stavka reserves and neighboring army groups to prevent the Germans from developing a strike along the Kursk axis. Zhukov and Vasilievsky spent much of the next six months in the area, closely supervising operations and planning the counteroffensive.

In early July when the Germans finally launched their attack Zhukov's counteroffensive checked it in the largest tank battle in history. Both sides suffered immense losses, but a few days later the Germans were forced to withdraw to the defensive positions they had prepared before the offensive began. As Stalin put it: "If the battle of Stalingrad foreshadowed the decline of the German army, the battle of Kursk confronted it with disaster" (Stalin, 114).

In February 1944 Zhukov was sent to the Ukraine to coordinate actions of Vatutin's First Ukrainian and Ivan Stepanovich Konev's Second Ukrainian army groups. When Vatutin was mortally wounded on 1 March, Zhukov was appointed commander in his place, a post he held until early May. From June to November 1944 he coordinated the actions of the First and Second Belorussian army groups in the liberation of Belorussia.

Zhukov's forces liberated what was left of Warsaw in January 1945 and pushed on toward the Oder River, halting there in February. Zhukov later was criticized for stopping at the Oder rather than driving on toward Berlin. He defended himself, claiming that his troops had advanced more than three hundred miles (480 km) in twenty days, and naturally supplies had lagged behind. His units were in need of combat material, especially fuel. Similarly the aviation units had been unable to shift their bases forward to support front operations. Another danger to Zhukov's forces was the German units on their flanks in East Pomerania.

During planning for the final offensive against Germany Zhukov commanded the First Belorussian Army Group, which with Konev's First Ukrainian Army Group made the main assault on Berlin. In a meeting in early April Stalin played one commander against the other. He listened as Konev and Zhukov briefed their plans for taking Berlin and then went to the map and drew boundaries for the army groups. With his own hand he drew the northern dividing line from the Neisse River through Berlin to Potsdam. Then he drew a line running only to Lubben, about thirty-seven miles (59 km) southeast of Berlin. The message was clear. Both commanders were being told that what happened after they reached the Lubben area would be decided largely by the actions of the individual army groups up to that point. In the event Zhukov's army group met stiff resistance, Konev's forces would swing north and move against Berlin. After the massive offensive began on 16 April, with more than one and a half million Soviet soldiers advancing toward the German capital, Zhukov's First Belorussian troops were delayed temporarily by General Gotthard Heinrici's defenders. Konev received permission to move against Berlin. Extremely worked up, Zhukov ordered his troops forward. As both army groups entered Berlin, Stalin issued new boundaries for the final assault. Konev was crestfallen. The boundary line placed his forces about 150 yards short of the Reichstag, the symbol of final victory over Germany's capital, where the Red flag was to be planted.

Zhukov's forces entered Berlin in late April, and on 30 April they poured through the holes in the walls of the Reichstag building and raised the Red flag over the ruined edifice. At the same time Hitler and his new bride committed suicide. "The bodies were burned in the courtyard," wrote Churchill, "and Hitler's funeral pyre, with the din of Russian guns growing ever louder, made a lurid end to the Third Reich" (Churchill, 533).

The capture of Berlin was costly. In a rare admission Soviet historians wrote that "from 16 April until 8 May our forces lost 2,156 tanks, 1,220 guns and mortars, 527 planes. The First and Second Belorussian and First Ukrainian Army Groups lost about 300,000 men killed and wounded" ("Marshal Zhukov," *Ogonek*, No. 50, 8).

Zhukov accepted the German surrender in the suburb of Karlshorst on 8 May 1945. On 24 June 1945 he participated in the victory parade in Moscow, and in July attended the Potsdam Conference. Appointed Soviet member of the Allied Control Council, he helped supervise the occupation of postwar Germany. On 10 April 1946 he left Berlin to become commander of all Soviet ground forces but occupied that post only briefly. A jealous Stalin, who wanted no other popular figure to eclipse his image, banished Zhukov to the Odessa MD and subsequently (1948) to the Ural MD.

After Stalin's death in March 1953 Zhukov was appointed first deputy minister of defense. When Beria attempted to seize power in June 1953, Zhukov personally arrested him, and Beria was later shot. Zhukov became minister of defense in February 1955 and immediately set about rehabilitating the memories of Red Army officers purged by Stalin. In June 1957 when Soviet leader Khrushchev was fighting for his political life against the "anti-Party group," Zhukov threw his support behind the premier by rushing central committee members to Moscow on military aircraft. Khrushchev survived the power struggle but began to worry about Zhukov's new political and military power. Khrushchev believed that Zhukov displayed certain "Bonapartist" tendencies. He sent him on a good-will trip to Yugoslavia and Albania and during his absence decided to relieve him as defense minister in October 1957. His retirement was announced in March 1958.

After his departure from government Zhukov found that he had joined the ranks of the Soviet "unpersons." Having received the highest honors his country could bestow, he watched helplessly as one colleague after another denounced him. His name again was removed from wartime histories, even though he was the country's greatest military hero. His periods of disgrace or partial disgrace covered almost twenty-five years of the postwar period: 1946-1953, 1957-1965, and the partial disgrace, from 1965 to 1974. Only after he passed away was the process of his rehabilitation completed. In 1990 some 125 pages of his memoirs censored in 1969 were reinserted in the tenth edition. Busts of the marshal, a commemorative coin, new statues, and even a comic book, reminiscent of the old "Classic Comics," recently made their appearance.

After the ouster of Khrushchev in 1964 Zhukov was invited to participate in the parade marking the twentieth anniversary of victory in Europe. In 1966 his serialized memoirs began appearing, and in 1969 his book *Memoirs and Reflections* was published in Moscow. Translated into many foreign languages, the book tantalizingly ends in 1946, when a fascinating new chapter of Zhukov's life was beginning. Zhukov died on 18 June 1974 and was buried in the Kremlin Wall. His three daughters—Era, Ella, and Maria—still lived in Moscow as of 1992.

Zhukov was a candidate member of the Central Committee of the CPSU from 1941 to 1946 and from 1952 to 1953, and a full member from 1953 to

1956. From 1956 to 1957 he was a candidate member and member of the Presidium of the Central Committee and a deputy at convocations of the Supreme Soviet of the USSR.

His decorations include six Orders of Lenin, the Order of the October Revolution, two Orders of Victory, three Orders of the Red Banner, two Orders of Suvorov First Class, and other awards, including twenty foreign decorations.

Bibliography: Georgy K. Zhukov, *Vospominaniia i razmyshleniia*, 3 vols., 10th ed. (M., 1969-1990); I.G. Aleksandrov, ed., *Marshal Zhukov. Polkovodets i chelovek* (M., 1988); Winston S. Churchill, *Triumph and Tragedy* (Boston, 1953); Alan Clark, *Barbarossa. The Russian-German Conflict, 1941-1945* (New York, 1965); John Erickson, *The Soviet High Command. A Military-Political History, 1918-1941* (London, 1962); David Glantz, *Soviet Military Deception in the Second World War* (London, 1989); Nikita Sergeevich Khrushchev, *Khrushchev Remembers* (Boston, 1970); A.E. Porozhniakov, ed., *G.K. Zhukov. Fotoalbom* (M., 1984); Konstantin K. Rokossovsky, *A Soldier's Duty* (M., 1970); Harrison E. Salisbury, *Marshal Zhukov's Greatest Battles* (New York, 1969); Sergei M. Shtemenko, *The Soviet General Staff at War, 1941-1945* (M., 1981); S.S. Smirnov, ed., *Marshal Zhukov. Kakim my ego pomnim* (M., 1988); Iosef V. Stalin, *O Velikoi Otechestvennoi Voine Sovetskogo Soiuza* (M., 1947); N. Svetlishin, "Ot Soldata do Marshala," *Voenno-istoricheskii zhurnal* (November, 1966), 31-40; Aleksandr Mikhailovich Vasilievsky, *Delo vsei zhizni* (M., 1975); Alexander Werth, *Russia at War, 1941-1945* (New York, 1964); "Marshal Zhukov," *Ogonek*, No. 48 (November 1986), 5-8; "Marshal Zhukov," *Ogonek*, No. 49 (November, 1986), 6-9; Otto Preston Chaney, *Zhukov* (Norman, 1971) and *Zhukov. Marshal of the Soviet Union* (New York, 1974). Given the political changes in Russia after 1991, much more information has become known about this remarkable Russian patriot. An eleventh edition of his memoirs, delivered to the press in early 1992, probably will include approximately eighty-five pages which were not included in earlier editions.

Otto Preston Chaney

ZHUKOV, PAVEL SEMENOVICH (1870-1942). Russian and Soviet photographer. His portraits and pictures taken during the 1920s and 1930s constitute an important historical record of this period of dramatic change.

Zhukov was born in Simbirsk. After finishing the gymnasium there he moved to St. Petersburg, where he studied photography at the studio of the noted photographer Konstantin Shapiro. Under the patronage of the St. Petersburg Academy of Arts Zhukov attended the St. Petersburg College of Arts and the Academy of Arts in Rome. During his studies he specialized in the techniques of portraiture. He developed his own style with a narrow depth of field. That is, he focused on the chief features of the face, especially the eyes, throwing the rest of the face, body, and background out of focus. The result was an intensely personal interpretation, which sought to capture the character behind the image.

In the years before the October revolution Zhukov developed a reputation as a portraitist and a genre photographer. He executed portraits of such cultural luminaries as Leo Nikolaevich Tolstoy, Anton Pavlovich Chekhov, Petr Ilich Chaikovsky, and Anton Grigorevich Rubinstein. His photographs of pre-revolutionary St. Petersburg are important documents of the life of that city.

After the revolution of October 1917 Zhukov became the official photographer of the political administration of the Petrograd military district. In this capacity he documented military activity on a number of fronts during the Civil War and captured the likenesses of commanders and political figures of the Red Army. In 1920 he was sent to Moscow. There he photographed major figures of the regime including Mikhail Ivanovich Kalinin, Georgy Vasilievich Chicherin, and Anatoly Vasilievich Lunacharsky. While in Moscow he also executed a portrait of Vladimir Ilich Lenin. This portrait, which has become famous, is considered one of the best likenesses of the founder of the Soviet state.

During the 1930s Zhukov served as a photojournalist recording the achievements of the five-year plans. He photographed the construction of the first Soviet hydroelectrical project, the Volkhovstroi, as well as metallurgical plants, factories, the reconstruction of the wharves in Leningrad, and other industrial projects.

Zhukov was killed during the siege of Leningrad during World War II when an artillery shell destroyed his apartment house. Although many valuable negatives were lost, much of his best work has been preserved in the Leningrad State Archive of Film and Photo Documents.

George N. Rhyne

ZHURNAL MINISTERSTVA YUSTITSII (1859-1917). The Journal of the Ministry of Justice was published in 1859-1868, 1869-1870, and 1894-1917. From 1873 to 1876 it appeared under the titles Court Journal (Sudebnyi zhurnal), a supplement to Court Herald (Sudebnyi vestnik). The official organ of the ministry of justice, it was the first journal devoted to problems of Russian legal theory and practice.

Founded by the assistant minister of interior, Dmitry Nikolaevich Zamiatnin, the journal reflected the new policy of "official glasnost" or openness of the era of reforms in the reign of Alexander II. Zamiatnin, an ally of Grand Duke Constantine Nikolaevich, used the journal to stimulate discussion of reforms within the administration. The journal became a forum for the exchange of ideas on legal theory and reform and an important means to introduce the notion of professional competence and expertise in the operation of the court system. It inspired the publications of other legal journals, such as Juridical Herald (Yuridicheskii vestnik) and Juridical Journal (Yuridicheskii zhurnal), the beginnings of a Russian legal press.

The "official section" of the journal included resolutions and rulings of the ministry and notice of personnel changes. Zamiatnin succeeded, for the first time, in obtaining the right to publish legal decisions of the Senate. The unofficial section included scholarly articles on the law and legal principles. Articles appeared on specific questions of the law regarding such matters as debts and mortgages. Among the journal's contributors were Ya.G. Esipovich, I.I. Ivanov and Professor Vladimir Danilovich Spasovich. Excerpts from D.I. Meier's pioneering lectures on Russian civil law and translations from the works of European scholars such as C.F. Mittermaier also appeared in its pages.

Perhaps the journal's most significant contribution to the work on the court reform was the publication of articles on Western court systems and procedural reforms. Sergei Ivanovich Zarudny wrote a series of articles on common law courts and the jury system in Great Britain. Articles by F. Korzon and P. Khovansky gave comparative analyses of the French and English system. Other studies dealt with American and French penal law. Aleksandr Knirim, an assistant editor of the journal, contributed an influential study of the reforms of the Hanoverian court system, which showed the possibility of a rapid transition to oral procedure and public courts. After the implementation of the court reform in the late 1860s the journal lost its purpose and was published fitfully as a supplement to the legal newspaper, The Court Herald (Sudebnyi vestnik). This publication took a critical, liberal approach to the new institutions and was closed in 1877. It was revived in 1894 and continued publication until the October revolution.

See Also: ZAMIATNIN, DMITRY NIKOLAEVICH and ZARUDNY, SERGEI IVANOVICH.

Bibliography: N.M. Lisovskii, *Russkaia periodicheskaia pechat', 1703-1900 gg.* (Pg., 1915); *Russkaia periodicheskaia pechat' (1702-1894 gg.)* (M., 1959); Richard Wortman, *The Development of a Russian Legal Consciousness* (Chicago, 1976).

Richard S. Wortman

ZHYTOMYR. In Russian, Zhitomir. Ukrainian city with a population of 264,000 as of 1983, located approximately eighty-four miles (135 km) west of Kiev. Located on the banks of the Teterev River, a tributary of the Dnieper. It is a crossroads for highway and rail traffic, as well as the administrative center of Zhytomyr province.

Traces of ancient settlements and burial mounds dating from 2000 B.C. are found in the area around Zhytomyr. Although most scholars indicate that the city was founded in the second half of the ninth century, the first mention of the city in the chronicle *Tale of Bygone Years* (Povest vremmenykh let) dates from 1240, when Zhytomyr was ravaged by the Tatars.

Zhytomyr remained part of Kievan Rus until 1320, when the troops of Lithuanian Grand Prince Gedymin (r. 1316-1341) occupied it. By the end of the fourteenth century the Lithuanian princes had succeeded, by marriage and conquest, in placing their own rulers on the thrones of key Ukrainian cities. In 1385 Lithuanian Grand Prince Jagiello (c. 1350-1434) was baptized a Catholic and married the Polish queen Jadwiga (1374-1399). This "Krewo Union" created a dynastic tie between the two states. The other Lithuanian princes subsequently converted to Roman Catholicism, and the principalities of Kiev, Volhynia (to which Zhytomyr belonged) and Podolia were absorbed in the centralized Lithuanian administrative system. The Lithuanians constructed a fortified castle to protect Zhytomyr from Tatar incursions into the area, which continued until the beginning of the seventeenth century. The Magdeburg Law, a German code of municipal self-government which had been established in Poland, was introduced into Zhytomyr in 1444.

Certain factions of the Ukrainian nobility, hoping to receive full Polish political rights, including the right to retain their own (Orthodox) faith and still remain members of the nobility (szlachta), pleaded for secession from the Grand Duchy of Lithuania and for direct incorporation into the Kingdom of Poland. By the terms of the Union of Lublin (1569) Poland and Lithuania were merged politically, concluding the process begun with the Krewo Union. As a consequence Ukraine was ceded directly to Poland. In 1596 the Union of Brest created the Uniate Church, which retained the Orthodox rite but recognized the authority of the Pope, in the newly annexed lands. These events threw Ukraine into turmoil as the Orthodox faithful and cossacks strove to preserve their ancient liberties.

Residents of Zhytomyr participated in the cossack revolts of 1592-1596 and in the revolt against the Polish landlords led by Bohdan Khmelnitsky in 1648. His successful appeal to Russian Tsar Alexis to take Ukraine under his protection led to war between Russia and Poland (1654-1667). By the terms of the Andrusovo Armistice of 1667, Zhytomyr, as part of "right-bank Ukraine," once again was ceded to Poland. In 1668 it became the principal city of the Kiev military governorship (voevodstvo) as well as the center of Zhytomyr district.

A Carmelite monastery was founded in Zhytomyr in 1634-1636 by the Zhytomyr headman (starosta) as part of the Polish effort to increase Roman Catholic influence in Ukraine. During the Counter-Reformation a Jesuit college (1720), monastery (1724), and church (1737) were established in Zhytomyr. In 1761 a Bernardine monastery was founded and in 1766 a women's monastery was founded by the Order of St. Vincent.

After the second partition of Poland between Prussia and Russia in 1793 right-bank Ukraine was ceded to the Russian Empire. Under Russian administration Zhytomyr became an important center for trade and the administrative center of Volhynia province, although it also figured prominently in various movements directed against tsarist authority. In 1823-1825 many prominent members of the Society of United Slavs and of the Southern Society of the Decembrist movement—including Sergei Ivanovich Muraviev-Apostol, Pavel Ivanovich Pestel and Ilia Ivanovich Ivanov—conducted activities in the Zhytomyr area. According to a plan drawn up on 30 December 1825, the southern wing of the Decembrists intended to secure the garrison in Zhytomyr as a key step before seizing Kiev. The Decembrist movement was crushed before any of these plans could be implemented.

Although the vast majority of the population of right-bank Ukraine was Ukrainian, Poles retained important posts in local government and the court system, and Poles or polonized Ukrainian gentry constituted the vast majority of large landowners. Polish cultural influence remained strong. Following the unsuccessful Polish uprising against the tsarist government in 1830-1831, a Polish revolutionary group founded in Switzerland in 1834, Young Poland, sent Szymon Konarski, one of its most prominent members, to Ukraine to try to establish contacts between the lesser Polish nobility and the Ukrainian peasantry. Konarski and his followers centered their activity in Kiev, Zhytomyr, Berdychiv, and Kremianets. After Konarski's execution in 1839 all of the centers were destroyed, and an intense campaign of russification of right-bank Ukraine began.

Throughout the remainder of the nineteenth century Zhytomyr continued to develop as an administrative, industrial, and trade center of the Russian Empire. Elementary and secondary schools were established, a municipal hospital (in addition to the monastery and military hospitals which had existed since the end of the eighteenth century), theaters, and a public library were opened. In 1896 the Zhytomyr-Berdychiv railroad line was opened, linking the city and the region around it to the main railroad lines in the rest of Ukraine and the empire. By 1897 Zhytomyr was the sixth largest city in Ukraine, with a population of 65,895, and boasted a literacy rate of 45 percent. As in the rest of Ukraine the Russian administration banned publications in Ukrainian until 1905 and forbade instruction in Ukrainian in schools until 1917.

During World War I the tsarist government subjected the residents of Volhynia to repressive measures directed against budding Ukrainian nationalism. It suspended Ukrainian language publications and deported inhabitants of some areas to Russia. Upon the collapse of the Romanov dynasty in the revolution of February 1917 Ukrainian nationalists succeeded in organizing the Ukrainian Central Council (Ukrainska Centralna Rada). This assembly of representatives of various social classes and political persuasions united in working for Ukrainian autonomy within the framework of a Russian federation. Provincial councils, which recognized the Central Rada as the supreme Ukrainian national government, were organized also. On 7 (20) November 1917 the Rada declared the formation of a Ukrainian National Republic. Fearing that it would harbor enemies of Bolshevism, the government in Petrograd formally declared war on Ukraine three weeks later. Russian troops were sent to Ukraine, and on 11 (24) December 1917 a rival Bolshevik government was set up in Kharkiv (Kharkov). Civil war ensued. Bolshevik forces besieged Kiev throughout January 1918; the Central Rada moved the seat of government to Zhytomyr on 25 January (7 February). It passed legislation regarding the boundaries, flag, and currency of the new Ukrainian republic during this time and adopted the Gregorian calendar. As a consequence of the intervention of the Central Powers into the conflict 26 January (8 February 1918), a joint German-Ukrainian force retook Kiev on 1 March, and the government followed it there a few days later.

These developments did not bring peace. The collapse of the Austro-Hungarian Empire in October 1918 stimulated new conflicts. A reconstituted Poland claimed former Austro-Hungarian territories in Galicia, and a Polish-Ukrainian war broke out. A Directory under the leadership of Semen Petliura had been set up in Eastern Ukraine, and a union of the West and East Ukrainian states was proclaimed in January of 1919. Both sides allied to fight the Bolsheviks. Divided by political loyalties and in their attitudes toward the

Whites, these Ukrainian factions were unable to coordinate their military activity. By fall of 1919 they found themselves fighting the Whites, Bolsheviks, Poles, and Rumanians simultaneously. On 21 April 1920 Petliura, after renouncing all claims to Eastern Galicia, concluded an alliance with Poland and established his headquarters at Zhytomyr, from where he hoped to mobilize all Ukrainian forces against the Bolsheviks. The allied forces took Kiev on 6 May, but by June they were forced to retreat from Volhynia. Petliura and members of his Directory took refuge in Poland. Bolshevik troops occupied Zhytomyr on 7 June 1920 and most of Eastern Ukraine by November, although Bolshevik power was not consolidated in the area until the following year.

Under Soviet rule Zhytomyr became a regional center of Kiev province, and on 22 September 1937 it became the center of its own province. During the period of the five-year plans which began in 1929, industrial development proceeded apace, the city growing correspondingly. From 1926 to 1939 the population increased from 76,678 to 95,090. During the same period the surrounding region suffered desperately from the effects of the policies of forced collectivization. According to a noted Western specialist, Robert Conquest, Zhytomyr province lost 15 to 20 percent of its population to starvation during the government-inspired "terror-famine" in the years 1932-1934. During World War II it was occupied twice by Nazi forces, 9 July 1941—13 November 1943 and 20 November—31 December 1943. Zhytomyr suffered tremendous losses during the war. A considerable portion of the city was destroyed, then rebuilt after the war.

Present day Zhytomyr boasts pedagogical and agricultural institutes, the general technical department of Kiev Polytechnic Institute, and ten specialized secondary educational institutions. Cultural attractions include the Zhytomyr Regional Studies Museum, founded in 1864 as the Volhynian Scholarly Museum. It contains archaeological collections from the surrounding area. The Zhytomyr State Museum initiated postgraduate courses in 1917 for young people who had completed higher education in fields such as archaeology, art criticism, ethnography, and the natural sciences. Zhytomyr has a library, musical drama and puppet theaters, a printing shop, and bookstores dating from the nineteenth century. In addition to the historic Zhytomyr Castle, built in the fourteenth century, there are numerous examples of fine baroque and neoclassical architecture in the city. A philharmonic society and an art gallery are additional attractions.

Zhytomyr is a center of light industry of various kinds. A flax combine, hosiery, clothing, and shoe factories are located in the city, as are flour mills, and meat and cannery combines. The wood products industry holds a significant place in Zhytomyr's economy; furniture, musical instruments, and building materials are all produced there. Metallurgy and machine building are also important.

Many distinguished Russians, Poles, and Ukrainians have lived and worked in Zhytomyr. Among its notable natives are Viktor Galaktionovich Korolenko (1853-1921), a Russian writer, publicist and social activist. He participated in the movement "To the people" (v narod) in the 1870s and later became editor of the journal Russian Wealth (Russkoe bogatstvo) in St. Petersburg. Another important figure born in Zhytomyr was Jaroslaw Dąbrowski (1836-1871), a Polish general in the Russian army and revolutionary, a leader and commandant of the city of Warsaw during the Polish insurrection of 1862. After the uprising was crushed he emigrated to Paris, where he was active in emigre circles. He became a leader of the Paris Commune and died on the barricades.

In the twentieth century one of the distinguished natives of Zhytomyr was Sergei Pavlovich Korolev (1906-1966), a Soviet scientist and academician who helped design the Soviet space-rocket system. The space ships Vostok and Voskhod, used in the first manned space flights, were built under his direction. His research also contributed to the construction of space stations, surveillance, and communications satellites, and to technology used in the exploration of the moon, Venus, and Mars.

Tadeusz Borowski (1922-1951), an outstanding Polish poet and prose writer, was born in Zhytomyr to Polish parents who subsequently were exiled to the White Sea area and to Siberia. He was active in the Polish political and literary underground during the Nazi occupation, for which he was arrested by the Gestapo and sent to Auschwitz. After his liberation he returned to Poland and resumed his literary activity, writing one of the most wrenching and memorable accounts of life in the Nazi concentration camps. It was published in English under the title *This Way for the Gas, Ladies and Gentlemen*. He committed suicide before his thirtieth birthday.

Among prominent Soviet cultural figures who worked in Zhytomyr were the film makers Aleksandr Petrovich Dovzhenko and Sergei Fedorovich Bondarchuk.

Bibliography: William E.D. Allen, *The Ukraine. A History* (New York, 1963); Yaroslav Bilinsky, *The Second Soviet Republic. The Ukraine after World War II* (New Brunswick, 1964); *Bolshaia sovetskaia entsiklopediia*, 3rd ed., 30 vols., Vol. 9 (M., 1970-1978), 226-229 and Vol. 12, 196-199; G.P. Bulkin, Z.D. Vakhbreit, O.M. Ivashchenko, O.O. Pavlov, *Istoriia mist i sil ukrainskoi RSR. Zhytomyrska oblast* (K., 1973), 86-120; Robert Conquest, *Harvest of Sorrow* (New York, 1986); Michael Hrushevsky, *A History of Ukraine* (Hamden, Conn., 1970); *Great Soviet Encyclopedia*. (New York, 1981), Vols. 7, 9; Orest Subtelny, *Ukraine. A History* (Toronto, 1988); Volodymyr Kubijovyc, *Ukraine. A Concise Encyclopedia* (Buffalo, 1984—), Vols. 1, 2; *Wielka Encyklopedia Powszechna PWN*, 13 vols. (Warsaw, 1962-1970).

Barbara A. Niemczyk

ZILLIACUS, KONRAD (KONNI) VIKTOR (1855-1924). Leader of the Finnish opposition to Russification before 1905, subsequently an advocate of complete Finnish separation from the Russian Empire.

Exceptional historical circumstances sometimes make it possible for charismatic persons to step onto the historical stage and play major roles even if for only fleeting moments. Zilliacus was such a man in the history of modern Finland. Born into an upper middle-class Swedish-Finnish family in 1855, he was not psychologically disposed to conforming to the social role expected of him.

Early in life Zilliacus showed that he felt constrained by the mores of his conservative, bourgeois social environment. From his early teenage years he exhibited a keen, inquiring mind more interested in pursuing ideas than social conventions. His curiosity led him eventually to master eight languages, including Japanese; he corresponded regularly in six languages.

Although a nonconformist, he submitted during the early years of his life to his family's considerable pressure to follow the appropriate path of the son of a bourgeois family. He completed a degree in law at the University of Helsinki and attempted to settle into the role of a government official. Unable to conform completely Zilliacus scandalized his relatives in 1878 by marrying a widow who was eleven years his senior and the mother of seven children.

To escape what he considered confining circumstances, he left Finland and his wife and children in 1889. For the next ten years he traveled in Central America, the United States, the Far East, and other places. During that time he lived in Japan for almost three years. Zilliacus described in vivid literary style his adventures and experiences abroad in some one dozen books and hundreds of newspaper articles published by Swedish-language newspapers in the United States, Sweden, and Finland. Zilliacus's first-hand observations of political and social conditions made a deep, permanent impression; he grew convinced that Finnish society needed political and social reforms. In Tokyo, Paris, and London he came into contact with other advocates of social reform and with radical intellectuals, including a few Russian publicists such as Feliks Volkhovsky (1846-1914).

In late 1898 Zilliacus returned to Finland with a well-established reputation as a world traveler and illustrious writer. The timing of his return could not have been more propitious. Political passions were overflowing as Finns confronted the reality that Russia intended to destroy the autonomous status that Finland possessed in the Russian Empire for nearly a century. At the time of his return the country's intelligentsia had launched an impressive although futile effort to rally West European political opinion in support of Finland's cause.

The failure of passive means to halt Russification gave rise to demands for more radical resistance measures. Finnish resistance leaders were pleased to have the service of Zilliacus, who was passionately devoted to Finnish separatism. At this point, when national minorities as well as Russian political parties were creating their own opposition groups, Zilliacus played an important role in the history of Finland's struggle against Russification. Virtually singlehandedly he articulated the rationale for uniting the various segments of the Russian antigovernment movement to achieve reform in the empire. Particularly unifying among segments of the Finnish opposition was his explanation, produced by the knowledge and vision he had acquired through his travels, that Finland's struggle was not a separate effort but was part of a broader attempt to reform the Russian state and society. Most Finnish resistance leaders were willing to collaborate with Russian liberal groups but vehemently opposed the notion that they also collaborate with Russian revolutionaries.

With a small group of Finnish resistance "activists" Zilliacus tried to inform the passive Finnish resistance movement about the history of the struggle in Russia for political and social justice. The activists undertook to transport underground literature for various Russian opposition groups and to run safe houses for Russian revolutionaries passing through or hiding in Finland. When Zilliacus and the most important Finnish resistance leaders were exiled to Sweden in 1903, and especially after the Russo-Japanese War began in early 1904, Zilliacus's effort to create a common opposition front began to produce results.

In September-October 1904 eight Russian resistance groups sent observers or delegates to a meeting which Zilliacus organized in Paris. The main purpose of this historical conclave was to consider the possibility of cooperation among Russian antigovernment groups. The most radical groups—organizations representing the Poles, some Finns, and the Russian Socialist-Revolutionaries, among others—already were negotiating in late 1904 with the Japanese government, asking for support of the revolutionaries' plans to weaken tsarist Russia further. More fundamental historical forces decided the outcome of the Russo-Japanese War and the course of the 1905 revolution in Russia. But the growing threat of a unified antigovernment movement supported by Japan—the tsarist secret police were aware of the contacts between the Finnish opposition and the Japanese ambassador to Sweden—played a role in prompting the Russian government to abandon the war effort and to grant some concessions to the opposition. When Nicholas II again sought to tighten his grip on Russia in 1906, a tradition of cooperation was well established between Finnish nationalists and the Russian underground.

Zilliacus is assured a place in Finnish history not only because of his vision of a unified front against the Russian autocracy, but also by the fact that he was one of the first Finns to articulate the revolutionary idea that Finland should seek total separation—independence—from Russia. A number of Finnish political leaders secretly had harbored such an ideal, but it was Zilliacus who dared to articulate such a bold plan openly, as he did from 1902 onward in Free Word (Fria Ord), an underground newspaper which he and his followers published.

It was not Zilliacus but other equally bold and farsighted Finnish resistance leaders who a decade later implemented Zilliacus' dream when they declared Finland independent from Russia on 6 December 1917.

See Also: FINLAND'S POSITION WITHIN THE RUSSIAN EMPIRE, 1809-1917 and YRJÖ-KOSKINEN, BARON YRJÖ SAKARI.

Bibliography: For a list of archival sources on the general topic of Finnish-Russian revolutionary collaboration from 1899-1904, many of which include accounts of Zilliacus's activities, see William R. Copeland, The Uneasy Alliance. Collaboration Between the Finnish Opposition and the Russian Underground, 1899-1904 (Helsinki, 1973). The most useful printed sources for Zilliacus's contacts with Russian revolutionaries are Mikhail Borodkin, Finlandiia v Russkoi pechati Materialy dlia bibliografii, 1901-1913 (Pg., 1915); F. Dan, Vsenarodnoe uchreditelnoe sobranie (Geneva, 1905). Zilliacus's own publications on the revolutionary movement in Russia and the resistance movement in Finland are Finlands senat förr och nu (Stockholm, 1903);

Suomen uusimmasta historiasta, I-II (Stockholm, 1900-1901); *The Russian Revolutionary Movement* (New York, 1905); *Supplement till Det Revolutionära Ryssland* (Helsingfors, 1906); and *Revolution och Kontrarevolution i Ryssland och Finland* (Stockholm, 1912). Virtually nothing has been written on Zilliacus in English. In addition to the bibliography in *Uneasy Alliance* of secondary works in other languages, see Olavi K. Fält, "Collaboration Between Japanese Intelligence and the Finnish Underground During the Russo-Japanese War," *Asian Profile*, Vol. 4 (1976), 216-222, and Richard Pipes, *Struve, Liberal on the Left, 1870-1905* (Cambridge, 1970), passim.

William R. Copeland

ZIMBABWE, SOVIET RELATIONS WITH. The support given by the Soviet Union to opposition groups in Rhodesia and its successor state Zimbabwe were important elements in its search for political influence in sub-Saharan Africa during the 1970s and 1980s.

On 11 November 1965 the British colony of Southern Rhodesia under the leadership of Ian Smith declared itself independent and assumed the name Rhodesia. Throughout the late 1960s and the 1970s the country, whose independence the international community did not recognize, was torn by a struggle for political power between the white minority and the black African majority. The fight for majority rule was led principally by two liberation groups, the Zimbabwe African People's Union (ZAPU) whose leader was Joshua Nkomo and the Zimbabwe African National Union (ZANU) led by Robert Mugabe. Both groups found support along tribal lines; Nkomo's base was the Ndebele people and Mugabe's the Shona. Each developed different foreign affiliations. Although both leaders declared themselves to be Marxists, Moscow opted in the 1970s to support Nkomo who traveled to the Soviet Union in 1976, 1977, and 1978. Nkomo was more receptive to Soviet and Cuban advisers than was Mugabe who maintained strict control over his forces and their deployment. Another factor in Moscow's unwillingness to support Mugabe was the close ties between ZANU and China. In 1976 ZANU and ZAPU formed a Patriotic Front to coordinate their activities, but relations between the two were tenuous. In March 1977 Soviet Premier Aleksei Nikolaevich Kosygin traveled to Africa visiting the leaders of Africa's front-line states hostile to the Smith regime. He pledged Soviet assistance to the armed struggle against it. During the late 1970s the Soviet Union sent military assistance to Nkomo's forces in Zambia. Moscow strongly encouraged the strategy of armed struggle in preference to negotiations as the avenue to black majority rule.

Against Soviet advice Nkomo agreed to negotiate with Mugabe and the Smith government. In September 1979 talks began under British mediation. Within three months the parties agreed to a draft constitution, a transition government in which blacks and whites would share power, and a cease fire which ended the civil war. Zimbabwe celebrated its statehood on 18 April 1980.

Meanwhile, elections held in February 1980 resulted in an overwhelming victory by Mugabe's ZANU which gained 63 percent of the total vote. Mugabe became prime minister and later president, and although Nkomo participated for a while in the government he was forced eventually into the opposition.

Moscow's support for the losing side among the black groups was a setback for Soviet influence in Southern Africa. Mugabe limited his ties to the USSR, refusing to permit the establishment of a Soviet embassy until the mid-1980s. Mugabe meanwhile moved to improve relations with Great Britain. Notwithstanding his commitment to Marxist ideology, Mugabe encouraged the country's white farmers to remain in Zimbabwe and help restore the country's devastated economy.

The accession of Mikhail Sergeevich Gorbachev to power in the USSR led to an improvement in Soviet-Zimbabwe relations. President Mugabe paid his first visit to the Soviet Union in December 1985. His distrust of Moscow was overcome to some degree by threats from South Africa as well as Zimbabwe's growing military involvement in Mozambique. Mugabe signed a party-to-party accord with Moscow and an air transport agreement.

During the late 1980s Soviet foreign policy increasingly focused on improving relations with the West. As this policy change included reducing points of conflict in the third world, Soviet support for Marxist and anti-Western regimes declined. For their part many African states, acknowledging the loss of Soviet support and the failure of socialism in the USSR, gave up their commitment to Marxism. In June 1991 Zimbabwe's ruling party, ZANU, abandoned Marxist-Leninist ideology and removed from its constitution the phrases "Marxism-Leninism" and "scientific socialism."

Bibliography: Edmund J. Keller and Donald Rothchild, eds., *Afro-Marxist Regimes, Ideology and Public Policy* (Boulder, 1987); R. Craig Nation and Mark V. Kauppi, eds., *The Soviet Impact in Africa* (Lexington, Mass., 1984); Morris Rothenberg, *The USSR and Africa. New Dimensions of Soviet Global Power* (Miami, 1980); Alvin Z. Rubenstein, *Moscow's Third Strategy* (Princeton, 1990); Carol R. Saivetz., ed., *The Soviet Union in the Third World* (Boulder, 1989).

Joseph L. Nogee

ZIMIN, ALEKSANDR ALEKSANDROVICH (1920-1980). Historian of ancient and medieval Russia. Zimin was one of the most important Soviet historians of medieval Muscovy. He belonged to a group of intrepid scholars who sought to illuminate this seminal period of Russian history, the womb of institutions and practices that affected much of Russia's future economic, social, political, and religious developments.

Zimin was born on 20 February 1920. After finishing his secondary education he attended the University of Central Asia in Tashkent, from which he graduated in 1942. Zimin then entered the Institute of History at the USSR Academy of Sciences. While there he studied under a number of luminaries of Soviet historiography: Boris Dmitrievich Grekov, Aleksandr Ignatievich Andreev, Sergei Danilovich Skazkin, Nikolai Mikhailovich Druzhinin, and Anna Mikhailovna Pankratova. He received his doctoral degree in 1959. From 1947 he taught at the Historical-Archival institute in Moscow, receiving the rank of professor in 1971.

Nineteenth-century historians favored large overviews of the histories of various countries. This penchant was exemplified in Russia by the works of

Sergei Mikhailovich Soloviev and Vasily Osipovich Kliuchevsky. These multi-volume compendia unrolled themes based on schema conceived in the minds of the authors. Twentieth-century historians approached their problems more inductively, as they sought to move from detailed source investigations to challenge and revise many of the nineteenth-century dicta. Among the foremost practitioners in this group concerned with the mainstream of Muscovite political development were Aleksandr Evgenievich Presniakov, Stepan Borisovich Veselovsky, and Zimin. In a magisterial source-based study *The Formation of the Great Russian State*, Presniakov sought to explain how and why the Muscovite state evolved between the thirteenth and fifteenth century. Veselovsky published documentary sources when the political climate prevented the publication of his manuscript studies. These appeared after his death in the post-Stalin era. They include monographs on landholding, the evolution of the service class in the fourteenth and fifteenth centuries, and a collection of seminal articles on the oprichnina period (during the reign of Ivan IV, "The Terrible") in the sixteenth century.

Zimin's publishing career began immediately after the end of World War II. Between 1946 and 1968 his output was enormous. In the two decades he produced eighty-three articles, forty-seven reviews, a host of encyclopedia items of various size, and contributed chapters or sections to a number of books. He edited alone or with others eleven major sources. These included chronicles, monastic cartularies and registers, documents related to Russian law, and the letters of Abbot Joseph of the Volok monastery. His interest in Kliuchevsky prompted him to turn out an eight-volume set of Kliuchevsky's selected works that included a newly annotated edition of the ever-popular *Course on Russian History*. He later followed this with an edition of the master's diary and letters. Despite the heavy demands on his time he also produced three monographs on sixteenth-century Muscovy, all of them published in Moscow: *I.S. Peresvetov and His Contemporaries* (I.S. Peresvetov i ego sovremenniki, 1958), *The Reforms of Ivan the Terrible* (Reformy Ivana Groznogo, 1960), and *The Oprichnina of Ivan the Terrible* (Oprichnina Ivana Groznogo, 1964). As of early 1992 none of these or other major works have been translated into English.

The general quality and quantity of Zimin's publications, along with his other contributions in the Institute of History, earned him the respect of his peers. Many began to speak of a "Zimin chair" which he would receive when the next vacancy occurred in the ranks of the corresponding members (the second level of members behind the academics) of the Academy of Sciences. At the moment when this seemed about to happen, disaster struck.

Among the many projects Zimin had in process was a full-blown attack on the authenticity of Russia's celebrated twelfth-century épopée, *The Song of Igor's Campaign*. His manuscript ran to 661 typewritten pages and was submitted for publication. He claimed, after a study of the language and forms, that the work was actually an eighteenth-century fabrication, and one that relied on earlier tales of valor. It appeared only in an in-house edition mimeographed at the Institute for purposes of discussion. The full weight of authority was leveled against him. He outraged both communists and nationalists with the thesis that Russia's finest piece of medieval literature was a hoax. Without that masterpiece the level of Russia's medieval culture would be debased.

His opponents, who included specialists in literature, pointed out errors on various levels. Zimin's few proponents vainly argued that publication should be allowed before attacking him in print. His friends and family hoped he would give up the quest in order to safeguard his future, but Zimin was obstinate. He revised his manuscript even as articles appeared denouncing his thesis. Even scholars in the West, with vested interests in their work on the *Slovo* (Song), joined in the opposition. His stiff-necked persistence cost Zimin appointment to the Academy's second highest tier, a position which then went to Valentin Lavrentovich Yanin, the talented archaeologist and historian of medieval Novgorod. Yanin, who admired Zimin, admitted that he held the "Zimin chair."

Zimin had paid a heavy price, for his fair-weather friends abandoned him rather than imperil their own advancement. The Zimin circle contracted to a few loyal friends and students. But the consequences only convinced Zimin to bolster his reputation with further publications, even as a debilitating progressive respiratory disease decreased his energy. In his later years he spent part of the winters in the Crimea to guard his health and to recoup his strength. He wrote a number of articles on the medieval Russian epic, the *Zadonshchina*, which he considered to have preceded the *Slovo*. At the same time he turned from his earlier concentration on Ivan IV's reign to the antecedents of monarchical government and power. Tied to this was his growing recognition of the need to examine the impact of the elite servitor structure on government. He moved in the direction of a synthesis of the middle period of Muscovite history.

Part of the impetus for this last interest arose from his methodological study of the membership of the boyar ranks from 1462 to 1584, which appeared in article form in *Archeographical Yearbook for 1957* (Arkheograficheskii ezhegodnik za 1957). He had suggested a method for determining the members of the duma (council), the gathering of the boyars, by utilizing only information from documentary sources. The resulting list suggested that the evidence used for 150 years for evaluation and generalizations was faulty. Others employed the revised membership list to examine other aspects of the elite presence via the prosopographic approach, which concentrates on relations between family, economic, social, and political relationships. These efforts in turn prompted Zimin to expand his own investigations, which helped to push his interest back to the late fifteenth and early sixteenth centuries. The fruits of his labors appeared largely after he passed away.

Between 1968 and his death on 25 February 1980 three of his monographs appeared. He also published at least forty-seven articles and a valuable documentary publication and commentary on *The State Archive of Russia. XVI Century* (Gosudarstvennyi arkhiv Rossii XVI v., 1978). Unhappily, this three-volume edition appeared only in a bound mimeographed issue of 350 sets. His books continued to appear after his death. Among them were *Russia in the Time of Ivan the Terrible* (Rossiia vremeni Ivana Groznogo, 1982) and *Russia at the Turn of the XV and XVI Centuries* (Rossiia na rubezhe XV-XVI stoletii, 1982). His wife and close colleagues persevered to see some of his unfinished manuscripts into print: *The Formation of the Boyar Aristocracy in Russia* (Formirovanie boiarskoi aristokratii v Rossii, 1988) and most recently *Hero at the Crossroads. Feudal War in Russia in the XV Century* (Vitiaz' na rasput'e. Feodal'naia voina v Rossii XV v., 1991). Had he lived longer, they would have undergone revisions.

The most striking of these volumes is *Formation*, which contains the genealogies of the important service families of the fourteenth and fifteenth centuries. In essence it is a revision of the information found in the *Sovereign's Genealogical Book* (Gosudarev rodoslovets, compiled 1555). It constitutes a useful aid in the further investigation of the important service families in the formation of the Muscovite monarchy and their relationship to the crown.

Zimin's achievements rank him with the best masters of earlier Russian history, past and present. Anyone who traverses this field will find his deep footsteps in the sands of time.

Bibliography: Aleksandr Evgenievich Presniakov, *The Formation of the Great Russian State* (Chicago, 1970). Chief among the works of Stepan Borisovich Veselovsky are *Feodal'noe zemlevladenie v severo-vostochnoi Rusi* (M., 1947), *Issledovaniia po istorii klassa sluzhilykh zemlevladel'tsev* (M., 1969), and *Issledovanie po istorii oprichniny* (M., 1963). Vasily O. Kliuchevsky, *Course on Russian History*. 5 vols., trans. by C. Hogarth (New York, 1960), is an English version of the great historian's major work. Zimin's major works have been mentioned in the text. An abbreviated bibliography of Zimin's work edited by A. L. Khoroshkevich can be found in *Arkheograficheskii ezhegodnik za 1980 god* (M., 1981), 274-284. A more complete and updated one is found in Daniel C. Waugh, ed., *Essays in Honor of A. A. Zimin* (Cleveland, 1985). This volume also includes an extensive evaluation of Zimin's work.

Gustave Alef

ZIONISM IN RUSSIA. Zionism is the term for a variety of ideological orientations and political movements sharing the common assumption that in order to live a secure, healthy, and normal life in the modern world the Jewish people require a territorial base in their ancient homeland. The word itself focuses attention on Zion, which in classical Hebrew literature is synonymous with Jerusalem. While the earliest texts in the history of Zionism can be traced to Central Europe in the middle of the nineteenth century, the first concerted effort on behalf of a Jewish return to Zion surfaced in the immediate aftermath of the 1881 pogroms that raged through the Russian Pale of Settlement.

The principal Jewish response to the assaults of 1881 was flight. In the main, Jewish emigration from Russia went to the West. A number of secular-minded Russian Jews were influenced sufficiently by the nationalist ideologies of the day to call for a Jewish, territorially-based nationalism too. Some of these young people fixed on the ancient homeland as the location for the new Jewish land upon which a revived and regenerated modern Jewish community could be built. Accordingly they initiated a move in that direction. Simultaneously Dr. Leon Pinsker (1821-1891) of Odessa, heretofore active in a number of liberal-minded efforts aimed at facilitating the legal and cultural integration of the Jewish people into Russian life, came to believe that such acceptance was not only impossible but that efforts to that end were misguided.

Instead, he argued that Jews could gain true security and acceptance only after they settled a territory recognized as their very own.

Pinsker concluded that antisemitism was an incurable disease to be endured rather than eradicated once and for all. He explained that even though they had no territorial home of their own and presented themselves everywhere as a group tied together by their religious traditions, Jews continued to be viewed as a distinct people who moved from place to place without ever becoming one with the native population. Hence they continually generated feelings of unease and even hostility against themselves. Pinsker asserted that Jews fooled themselves when they believed that, through legal emancipation, they would gain true acceptance and equality in their places of residence. In his pamphlet *Autoemancipation* (1882) he argued that the Jewish nation must be normalized and that this was possible only by acknowledging the reality of antisemitism and developing a home territory in response. Such a home would serve two purposes. First, it would be readily available to all those who felt threatened in either physical, economic, or even psychological ways, and second; the existence of such a home would dignify and stabilize the lives of those Jews who continued to reside outside of that territory. In effect, Jews who chose not to live in the Jewish land would become "passport-carrying" Jews; that is, individuals who were perceived as living away from their home rather than as perpetual guests in someone else's land.

These first efforts and ideas were given both structure and organization in 1884 upon the formation of a group known as the Lovers of Zion. Under the leadership of Dr. Pinsker and Moshe Leib Lilienblum (1843-1910) that group committed itself to a three-point program: to promote migration to the ancient homeland, to raise funds in order to facilitate that emigration, and to lay the base for the new Jewish community in Palestine by establishing self-sustaining settlements there. In fact twenty-two new Jewish settlements were founded in Palestine between the early 1880s and 1898. In all, nearly 25,000 Jews, most of them from the Russian Empire, chose to settle in Palestine in that period. Of that number, just over 20 percent moved to the new settlements, and others took up residence in urban locations which already had existing Jewish communities.

Completely independent of these efforts, the Viennese journalist Theodor Herzl (1860-1904) took the idea of Jewish nationalism into the world arena by publishing his pamphlet *The Jewish State* in 1896, by convening the first Zionist World Congress in Basle, Switzerland in 1897, and by undertaking a diplomatic effort to secure a publicly recognized home for the Jewish people in Palestine. Motivated by stimuli similar to those that had moved Pinsker, Herzl came to recognize antisemitism as the principal dilemma of modern Jewish life. For Herzl though, the precipitating factor was the Dreyfus case in France. In that instance a French military officer, a Jew, was accused and found guilty of treason against his native land. Herzl was convinced of Dreyfus' innocence even before others raised questions about the propriety of those proceedings. Herzl surmised that it was Dreyfus' Jewish origins which made him vulnerable to those charges. The Dreyfus case in all its ramifications made clear to Herzl that a century after the emancipation of Jews in France the question of their full acceptance as French citizens was still at issue there. Those events convinced him that emancipation, legal equality, and political rights were insufficient and that only the relocation of world Jewry to its own nation-state would eradicate the various forms of antisemitism which continued to beset Jewish life in modern Europe.

Herzl's presentation and views differed from those offered by Pinsker. For Herzl the move to a Jewish land would not be restricted to those facing immediate difficulties but would be incumbent upon all. True, those in jeopardy would go first in order to lay the groundwork. They would be followed by wave upon wave of Jewish immigrants until the diaspora itself would be liquidated. Herzl contended that those Jews who chose not to settle in the Jewish state once it was founded and fully established lost the right to identify themselves as Jews. For him the Jewish state was intended to be the national home for all of world Jewry since the continuation of Jewish life outside that state served to perpetuate antisemitism. Because the repercussions of antisemitism not only haunted Jews but also created considerable social unrest, Herzl believed it was in everyone's interest to solve the problem. Hence he addressed himself directly to political leaders and heads of state in order to gain their support for his views and proposed plan of action. Herzl believed that once a particular location was designated as the future Jewish state, emigration to that land could proceed on the basis of right and not sufferance. Jews would not be going to yet another refuge but to their own place, and the problem of antisemitism would be solved forever. Herzl quickly became convinced that the only place to which Jews had any claim and to which they could be relocated was Zion. Therefore Herzl created a structure, the World Zionist Organization, which gave him the mandate to negotiate for Zion and to embark on a diplomatic offensive to that end.

Pinsker and Herzl represented one aspect of the Zionist ideology. Their approach reflected a political orientation intended to address what they identified as the key threat facing modern Jewry: victimization as a consequence of homelessness in an age of nationalism. Their remedy was a simple one—to find a place that Jews could call their own, a place so recognized not only by Jews but by all others. Herzl and Pinsker were not the only ones to see the return to Zion as the key to the resolution of the particular dilemma of modern Jewry. Prominent in the formulation of such programs were the Russian Jews, Asher Ginsberg, who wrote under the pen name of Ahad Ha'am, Aaron David Gordon, and Ber Borochov.

Asher Ginsberg (1856-1927) was raised in a traditional Russian-Jewish milieu. While he was extremely well-read in Judaica, he began to explore the wider world of learning only in his teenage years. That encounter not only estranged him from the world of his fathers but also became his point of departure for assessing the condition of modern Jewry. In a series of essays which he published in Hebrew from 1889 through the first decade of the twentieth century under the pen name Ahad Ha'am ("One of the People"), Ginsberg delineated his views on that dilemma and the means by which it could be resolved. In brief he argued that the religion of the Jews fashioned by its rabbinic leaders in the aftermath of the destruction of Jerusalem in 70 A.D. was intended to preserve Jewish life at a time when Jews had neither a religious nor a political center and were dispersed physically over the whole of the known world. While this religious culture kept the Jewish community together and enabled it to resist both the Christian and Moslem worlds for more than seventeen hundred years, it was not able to withstand the powerful forces of modernity, especially the emerging modern, secular, national cultures. Ahad Ha'am saw the younger generation of Jews, including himself, rapidly abandoning Jewish life everywhere, even in those locations where Jews had not been emancipated legally. In short, Ahad Ha'am preached that the critical dilemma of modern Jewish life was not antisemitism, but rather Jewish assimilation, a problem that could not be resolved by any of the means that contemporary Jewish life had at its disposal.

Accordingly, Ahad Ha'am proposed that the immediate need was to develop a modern national Jewish culture which could channel the creative energies of contemporary Jews into Jewish life. In this way Jewish life throughout the diaspora would be sustained and could offer Jewish options to the young people of the present and future. He concluded that the Judaism of the past was no longer meaningful and that a new Jewish culture was needed. While he was unable to describe the exact character of this new culture, Ahad Ha'am was certain that it would be Hebrew-based and that it would emanate from Zion, the one and only true home for all authentic Jewish expressions.

Ahad Ha'am saw the spontaneous move to Zion in 1881 and the formation of the Lovers of Zion as an instinctive and correct Jewish response to the danger then threatening Jewish life. The return to Zion indicated the centrality of that location for Jews as they considered their future in those troubled times. For him, what was called for in Zion was not an independent nation-state, but the settlement of a Jewish vanguard committed to fashioning the framework of that modern Jewish culture which would spread to all corners of the Jewish world. While that settlement eventually could evolve politically into a state, that process was not one which either concerned him or even appealed to him. Ahad Ha'am thought that the Jewish diaspora would continue but worried as to what would be Jewish about it. For him Zionism was the means by which that dispersion could be infused with Jewish content so that Jews could live both comfortably and creatively away from their ancient homeland as they had been doing for nearly two thousand years.

Aaron David Gordon (1856-1922) was also a Russian-born Jew who offered yet another perspective on the Jewish question and its resolution. When Gordon lost his office job in 1904 he decided to go to Palestine where, at the age of forty-six, he became a migrant field worker, moving from one Jewish settlement to another. At the same time he formulated an altogether different Zionist ideology which fused Jewish mystical strains with elements that he borrowed from contemporary Russian populism.

Gordon asserted that the crisis of modern life arose out of the separation of mankind from the natural landscape in which that life had originated. In Gordon's view this separation led to the estrangement of humanity from its true self, thereby leading to a state of alienation. Gordon believed that a "cosmic" element linked every human soul with the particular soil where it first was nurtured. The severing of that relationship through modernization with its attendant increase in urbanization was, in his view, the chief contributing factor to human alienation in the modern period. In opposition to those who identified alienation with the forces of industrialization, Gordon considered it inherent in the essence of modernity, which had the effect of removing man from direct interaction with that soil from which he had emerged. Therefore Gordon declared that a return to nature was the necessary first step in the regeneration of modern humanity.

Since this condition of alienation was the general condition of modern man, Jews also were its victims. Jewish suffering was even greater since as a people they had been estranged from active interaction with the soil for nearly two thousand years; that is, since they were expelled from their ancient homeland and became an urban mercantile people. In applying his general insight to the Jewish condition Gordon called upon Jews everywhere to abandon their diaspora existence in order to be born again through a return to their own origins, that soil upon which they initially became a human organism. For Gordon the return to Zion was not just the physical relocation as it was for Herzl, but truly a spiritual and regenerative act. He called upon Jews to abandon not only the physical aspects of the diaspora, but also the values and mores of middle class life. In Gordon's presentation Zionism marked a new beginning for Jews in the ancient homeland. By draining the swamps, reclaiming the land, and making it productive, they were regaining their own humanity while also building a new community based upon the principles of justice and equality. Gordon's personal example and his teachings were especially influential. His views are reflected in the formation of the kibbutz, that experiment in communal agricultural land tenure which dated to 1909 and remains to this day one of the more successful Zionist enterprises.

While A.D. Gordon intertwined strains of Russian populism with Jewish nationalism, Ber Borochov (1881-1917) fused a Marxist perspective with his Jewish nationalist commitments. To do so in a convincing manner, Borochov first had to prove that the factor of nationality was an important one currently missing in the overall Marxist analysis of society and economy. Then he had to convince his audience that Jewish identity also should be understood as a national one, a position which was rejected both historically and theoretically by contemporary Marxists.

Borochov asserted that the classical Marxist analysis had overlooked the important variable of geographical differentiation. He argued that this one factor, so significant in the shaping of both the cultural and economic structure of particular societies, had to be incorporated in any scientific reconstruction of the development of modern economic life. In Borochov's view, the external and internal differences across societies were not to be dismissed as trivial or irrelevant, but were indeed fundamental to the character of those societies. The availability of mineral resources, the fertility of the soil, and the quantity and quality of fresh water in different parts of the world were not uniform. Similarly the cultural and economic evolution of the peoples of the world did not conform to one particular pattern but were tied instead to the character of the location in which they came into existence as a people. In this way Borochov offered a materialist explanation of national culture in order to account for those differentiations which he, as a resident of the multinational Russian Empire, perceived so sharply.

Having established geographical terrain as a significant variable, Borochov went on to claim that the first objective in the unfolding of the revolution should be the conquest of the territorial base upon which the whole of the society stood. Rather than calling for a coalition of workers across national borders, Borochov's revolutionary effort would have workers seize power over their own lands in order to bring those vital resources under their control in the interests of the future workers' revolution. Only after the triumph of these nationalist revolutions could the internationalist dimension of the revolution be implemented.

In dealing with the issue of Jewish identity Borochov approached his topic more obliquely. Here he undertook a series of linguistic and philological studies of Yiddish and its development. These enabled him to document a vibrant and living culture that was centuries old. Hence his assertion of a Jewish nationality rested upon these cultural rather than geographic or anthropological bases. His analyses led Borochov to conclude that even though Jews were a national community they constituted an abnormal and unhealthy one. Geographically they were dispersed across the face of the earth and so had been and continued to be subject to a variety of disparate forces. Economically Jewish society had not developed across a broad base; rather it was nearly entirely middle class and commercial in character. Borochov attributed these conditions of Jewish life to the impact of the diaspora. Hence his first priority was for the complete liquidation of that diaspora and for the full reconstitution of Jewish life in the ancient homeland. There he believed a Jewish working class would be able to revolutionize the structure of Jewish life, creating a normal and healthy society upon a solid foundation. Then it could be in position to assert authority over the geographical domain which eventually would become the modern state of the Jews. Clearly Borochov's Zionism was the expression of an ideology intended to create a Jewish workers' movement in Palestine, which would establish a Jewish proletarian-based society there before participating in the world-wide workers' movement committed to the liberation of mankind.

Beyond these secular presentations of Zionism, a number of religiously-based formulations began to appear at the beginning of the twentieth century. In their initial reactions many traditional Jewish leaders rejected projects promoting a Jewish return to what they termed the Holy Land. They saw these both as reflecting a false messianism and as advocating a human intrusion into the divinely ordained historical process. By the twentieth century sufficient numbers of traditional Jews found themselves captivated by the bold new spirit of Jewish life articulated by Zionists. The most interesting of these formulations was developed by Rabbi Abraham Isaac Kook.

Rabbi Kook (1865-1935), a religious mystic from a small town in what later became Latvia, saw in the return of Jews to the ancient Holy Land the beginnings of the messianic age foretold in traditional sources. Even though they were secularists acting in accord with their own understanding of contemporary Jewish needs, the Zionists, in Kook's presentation, were guided by the hidden hand of Providence. They were engaged in an enterprise which would result not only in the restoration of Israel but also the redemption of all of mankind. For this reason Kook took a positive approach to all contemporary Zionist efforts, seeing them as a first step in that larger process. Kook came to these conclusions on the basis of his understanding of World War I and its aftermath. He believed that the war not only had devastated European life but was indeed the death knell of European, Western, Christian civilization. Visions of the future must come from other sources.

Curiously, two such messianic heralds were sounded in November 1917. On 2 November the British cabinet issued the Balfour Declaration announcing the government's commitment to support the return of Jews to their ancient homeland in order to create a Jewish national home in Palestine. On 7 November the Bolsheviks stormed the Winter Palace, overthrew the Provisional government in the name of the councils of workers and soldiers, and stood ready to proclaim the International Revolution. In Kook's view these two messianic projections coming together at the close of the terrible war were not coincidental but were instead two alternate paths open to mankind to attain future salvation. He concluded that only the path of Jewish messianism was the authentic one and so invested the Zionist movement with a mission far greater than that imposed upon it by any previous ideological formulation. Kook now urged full support for the Zionist effort, seeing it as the first stage in that ultimate redemption referred to in the prophetic passages found in Scripture.

In his own day Kook's views did not attract a mass audience. In recent years first after 1948 and especially after 1967 the idea that the Zionist movement and its product, the state of Israel, was indeed the living incarnation of the divine promise has attracted the support of more and more Jews who invested the state of Israel with a meaning far beyond what any of the secular ideologists envisioned. In the 1990s the Zionist views of Rabbi Kook and Aaron David Gordon have been welded together by groups that have formed both political and settlement programs aimed at reclaiming territories captured by Israel in the 1967 war, especially those lands identified as the West Bank, the Biblical Judea, and Samaria.

In addition to producing a diverse and at times self-contradictory ideology, Zionism also generated a political action program for modern Jewry. At first all Zionist efforts were directed toward the goal of ending the Jewish diaspora through the systematic transfer of world Jewry to Zion. To that end Zionist groups established themselves in most European countries as legal entities to promote Jewish emigration to Palestine. Those groups organized educational and cultural activities to stimulate Jewish self-awareness and initiated active campaigns intended to facilitate Jewish colonization of Palestine. Simultaneously, acting on behalf of the movement as a whole, Herzl undertook an extensive diplomatic campaign to secure Palestine as the future national home of the Jewish people. The renewal of violence against the Jewish people in the Russian Empire in 1903, and the eruption of a new wave of pogroms even more injurious than was the first wave twenty years earlier, forced a reorientation in Zionist activities.

Herzl visited Russia in the summer of 1903 and met with Minister of the Interior Viacheslav Konstantinovich von Plehve as well as Minister of Finance Sergei Yulievich Witte. He did so in order to gain legal recognition for the Zionist effort toward bringing about the emigration of the Russian Jews to Zion. In addition he hoped to secure Russian diplomatic support in Constantinople for the concept of a Jewish charter for Palestine. Finally, he wished to visit and to familiarize himself with the conditions of Jewish life in the empire. In the meantime, some Zionist leaders, especially those on the left, such as Borochov, outraged by the new wave of violence directed at the community, undertook to organize Zionist-based self-defense groups to defend the community. With this step Zionist political activities in diaspora settings moved beyond propaganda and fund-raising to active defense of diaspora Jewish interests.

When it became clear that some form of political process was going to be introduced in Russia in 1905 another group of Zionists joined Jewish intellectuals and other Jewish activists to create a political organization to lobby for Jewish rights in the proposed new order. These efforts proved to be successful when Jews secured the franchise in 1905 and then proceeded to elect to the first state duma (parliament) twelve Jewish deputies, five of whom were Zionists. Failure to fashion a united Jewish delegation of this contingent and misgivings about acting in concert with non-Zionists led Russian Zionists in December 1906 to announce an independent political action program for diaspora Jewry. Russian Zionists reached the conclusion that unless they took an active role in representing what they determined to be the true interests of diaspora Jews there would be no community to transport to Zion in the future. Hence the immediate difficulties of the period 1903-1906 served as the catalyst for the delineation of a Zionist diaspora political program. That program became the cornerstone of Zionist political efforts in the subsequent interwar period, especially so in those countries, such as Poland, where a Zionist political party was active in both Jewish and national politics.

The Balfour Declaration was an important milestone for the movement. Upon official recognition from Britain and with the imminent collapse of the Ottoman Empire, colonization efforts sponsored by the movement increased in both scope and importance. The visibility and the stature of Zionist organizations around the world increased dramatically as they began to work actively to promote the interests of Jewish settlement in Palestine. In Russia, Zionist ascendancy among Jews was reflected in a variety of electoral results. For instance, in the elections to the All-Russian Jewish Congress held in the spring of 1917 Zionist candidates received the majority of the votes. Subsequently, at a conference of 149 delegates representing 40 Jewish communities held in Moscow in 1918, Zionist representatives held the majority. Finally, in elections to the Jewish community councils in Ukraine, Zionists received over 50 percent of the vote and over 54 percent of the vote for the Jewish National Council in Ukraine elected in November 1918.

The new Soviet government declared the Zionist party illegal in 1921 when it outlawed all non-Bolshevik political parties. Furthermore, it suppressed all Zionist educational and cultural programs at that time, and the communist leaders declared Zionism itself a reactionary movement. Even though the Soviet leadership worked actively for the partition of Palestine and the formation of a Jewish state there in 1947, the campaign against Zionism in the USSR intensified after World War II. Zionism was identified as an agent of Western imperialism. The accusations against the head of the Czechoslovak Communist Party, Rudolf Slansky, and his "co-conspirators" in 1952 included acting on behalf of international Zionism. The charges in the Doctors' Plot in the USSR in January 1953 claimed that Zionist agents conspired with Jewish doctors to poison Soviet leaders.

Within the Jewish community the emigrationist movement to Israel was intensified sharply by a variety of factors including even the circulation of banned literature such as Leon Uris' popular novel, *Exodus*. The Six Day War of 1967 further encouraged Jewish identity among Soviet Jews, and the ensuing Soviet effort to repress emigration stimulated even greater interest in Israel and Jewish life there. Activists arrested for their public efforts on behalf of the right to emigrate or to disseminate Jewish culture, especially the right to teach Hebrew, referred to themselves as "prisoners of Zion."

After the introduction of new policies in the Gorbachev era, Jewish cultural efforts in the USSR, including the study of Hebrew and emigration of Jews from the Union to Israel, increased dramatically. Between 1989 and 1992 over 300,000 Jews left the Soviet Union for the state of Israel, continuing a movement that began one hundred years earlier.

See Also: YIDDISH LANGUAGE and YIDDISH LITERATURE.

Bibliography: Shlomo Avineri, *The Making of Modern Zionism. Intellectual Origins of the Jewish State* (New York, 1981); Adolf Boehm, *Die Zionistische Bewegung*, 2 vols. (Berlin, 1935); Mitchell Cohen, *Zion and State. Nation, Class and the Shaping of Modern Israel* (New York, 1987); Ben Halpern, *The Idea of the Jewish State* (Cambridge, 1961); Walter Laqueur, *A History of Zionism* (New York, 1972); Ehud Luz, *Parallels Meet. Religion and Nationalism in the Early Zionist Movement, 1882-1904* (Philadelphia, 1988); Yitzhak Maor, *Sionistskoe dvizhenie v Rossii* (Jerusalem, 1977); David Vital, *The Origins of Zionism* (Oxford, 1975); David Vital, *Zionism. The Formative Years* (Oxford, 1982); David Vital, *Zionism. The Crucial Phase* (Oxford, 1987).

Alexander Orbach

ZIZANY, LAVRENTY (1555?-1634?). Also Kukil Tustanovsky. Ruthenian (Ukrainian-Belorussian) writer, philologist, translator, pedagogue, and ecclesiastical figure. Brother of Stephen Zizany, a noted opponent of Catholicism and the Uniat Church. Author of the first original grammar of the Church Slavonic language in the Eastern Slavic area and compiler of the first printed dictionary of East Slavic.

Zizany was born into a burgher family in Galicia in the Polish-Lithuanian Commonwealth. After receiving his education he taught at various orthodox brotherhood schools: in Lviv (Lvov) until 1592, in Brest until 1595, and in Vilnius up to 1597. Subsequently he was employed as a private tutor in the houses of the princes B. Solomeretsky (1597-1600) in Barkulab (Belorussia) and O. Ostrozky (1600-1602) in the city of Yaroslavl. From 1612 he served as a tutor in the house of the wealthy and influential Prince Yakym Koretsky in Korets

(Volhynia). There he became archpriest and was given a parish. It was during this time that he became an active participant in the anti-Catholic movement.

In the sixteenth and seventeenth centuries Church Slavonic continued to play a major role in the written culture and ideology of the Eastern Slavs. Zizany participated in the movement to revive and purify Church Slavonic texts so that these might better accomplish their religious and cultural ends. Central to the movement was the desire to counteract the inroads made not only by Catholicism and Polish culture but to meet head-on the rising wave of Protestantism with its insistence on the use of the vernacular.

To counterbalance these threats from without and preserve their own form of religious and national culture, Orthodox brotherhoods, which established schools and printing houses, began to form at the end of the sixteenth century. Church Slavonic at this time still lacked grammars and dictionaries. If the brotherhood schools were to carry out their mission of elevating the status of Church Slavonic, these two serious gaps had to be filled. Zizany helped to do this.

In his *Lexicon* (Leksys, 1596), a fairly short Slavonic-Ruthenian dictionary in octavo, Zizany provided 1,061 Slavonic head words arranged alphabetically and supplied with stress marks. Occasionally, in the interests of space, the Slavonic entries are clustered according to root stems. Where in Ruthenian direct synonymic or near-synonymic equivalents were lacking, he betrayed his bent as a polymath by furnishing explanatory definitions that sometimes verge on the encyclopedic. The work, published by the Vilnius Brotherhood, appeared as an addendum attached to his primer, *Instruction for Reading and Understanding Slavonic Writing* (Nauka ku chitaniu i rozumieniu pisma slovenskago, 1596) and marks a pioneering effort in Church Slavonic lexicology. Its methodology became a model for succeeding lexicographers who applied and further developed it.

In the same year under the same auspices he assembled another important work, his *Slavonic Grammar* (Hrammatika slovenska). Here for the first time Zizany presented systematically the morphology of the Church Slavonic language, assisting its normalization and codification.

In 1619 Archimandrite Yelisei Pletenetsky (1550-1624), who had set up a printing press, invited Zizany to the Kievan Cave Monastery to join a group of scholars working there. Here Zizany taught and also worked for the press as a translator and proofreader. He compared the Church Slavonic text of John Chrysostom's *Discourse on the Fourteen Epistles* (Ioanna Zlatousta besiedy na 14 poslany, 1623) with the Greek original and translated into Church Slavonic Andrew Caesarea's *Exegesis of the Apocalypse* (Andrea arkhiepiskopa Kesaria Kappadokiiskia tlkovanie na apokalipsii, 1625).

Zizany spent the years 1620 through 1623 in compiling a *Catechism* (Katekhizis) in which he sought to present a more rational view of church doctrines and included in it information taken from the fields of history, natural sciences, and other branches of knowledge. With the aim of publishing his *Catechism* he traveled to Moscow where he was well received by the tsar and Patriarch Filaret. While there he held debates with workers of the Muscow Printing House.

Although Zizany's *Catechism* was printed in edited form in 1627, it was deemed heretical and not distributed. The extant copies lack a title page. The work nevertheless was circulated in printed copies and came to be highly regarded by the Old Believers who later published it in Grodno (1783, 1787, 1788).

Zizany returned to Korets where he died not later than 1634.

Bibliography: Zizany's major works are *Nauka ku chitaniu i rozumieniu pisma slovenskago: tu tyzh o sviatoi Troitsi i o v"chloviechenii Gospodni* printed together with *Leksis, siriech recheniia v"krat"stie s"branny i iz slovenskago iazyka na prostoi ruskii diialekt: istolkovany L.Z.* (Vilno, 1596) and *Grammatika slovenska s'vershennago iskustva osmi chastii slova i inykh nuzhdnyk* (Vilno, 1596). The *Leksis* has been reprinted in V. Sakharov, *Skazaniia russkogo naroda*, Vol. 11 (SPb., 1849); *Zapysky Naukovoho Tovarystva im. Shevchenka* (henceforth cited ZNTSH), Vol. 102 (1911); *Kryvich*, No. 2 (1924), 8; and V.V. Nimchuk, *Leksys Lavrentiia Zyzaniia. Synonima slavianorosskaia* (K., 1964). The *Grammatika* was reprinted in M. Vozniiak, "Hramatyka Lavrentiia Zyzaniia z 1596 r.," *ZNTSH* (1911), vyp. 1, Vol. 101, 5-35; vyp. 2 Vol. 102, 11-87. This latter edition was reprinted in *Specimina philologiae Slavica*, Vol. 88 (1990); G. Freidhof, "Hrammatika slovenska," *Specimina philologiae Slavica*, 2nd ed., Vol. 1 (1972), Vol. 26 (1980); V.V. Nimchuk, *Hramatyka slovens'ka* (K., 1980). The following two works remain basic studies: K. Kharlampovich, *Zapadnorusskie pravoslavnye shkoly XVII veka* (Kazan, 1898); M. Vozniak, "Prychynky do studii nad pysanniamy Lavrentiia Zyzaniia," ZNTSH (1911), Vol. 101. See also V.V. Anichienka, "Hramatyka L. Zizzniia," *Vestsi* AN BSSR. Ser. hramad, navuk, No. 4 (1957), 93-105; *Ukrains'ki pys'mennyky. Bio-bibliohrafichnyi slovnyk* 5 vols. (K., 1960-1965), Vol. 1, 347-349; V.V. Nimchuk, *Leksys Lavrentiia Zyzaniia. Synonima slavenorosskaia* (K., 1964); Ya.D. Isaevych, *Preemniki pervopechatnika* (M., 1981); N. Mechovskaia, *Rannie vostochnoslavianskie grammatiki* (Minsk, 1984). M. Votvinnik, *Lavrentii Zizanii* (Minsk, 1973) contains a good overview of sources.

Natalia K. Zitzelsberger

ZLATOVRATSKY, NIKOLAI NIKOLAEVICH (1845-1911). Populist writer, journalist.

Zlatovratsky was born in Vladimir into a clerical family. His father, at one time a priest, became secretary to the Vladimir province marshal of nobility during the later 1850s when proposals and statistics relating to the impending serf reform were being gathered. When the marshal was not reelected to this post, Zlatovratsky's father lost his job and lived in poverty thereafter.

Zlatovratsky attended the high school (gymnazium) in Vladimir until 1864. Because of his straightened circumstances, he could not enroll in the University of Moscow, but he audited classes during the fall of 1864. In 1865 he attended the Technological Institute in St. Petersburg. In the capital Zlatovratsky worked as a typesetter. The damp climate, his frail constitution, and his excessive drinking undermined his health and forced him to return to his native Vladimir.

Here he began to write, concentrating on the social changes then underway in Russia. Rejecting urban society, he concentrated on describing country life, which he thought preserved Russia's inner strength and vital heritage. His chief work was the long novel *The Foundations* (Ustoi), which appeared in serial form in the journal Notes of the Fatherland (Otechestvennye zapiski). In this work he extolled the enduring values of Russia's peasantry born of the traditional commune. He assured his readers that, despite the already discernible impact of industry and urbanization on the village, these values would endure.

Zlatovratsky was not important as a theoretician; he purposely avoided involvement in contemporary politics. Although his clear sympathy with a form of life that already was undergoing irrevocable changes endeared him to many followers of Leo Nikolaevich Tolstoy, his failure to draw political conclusions from his knowledge of rural conditions frustrated many of his fellow populists. His fiction had little literary merit. His characters, bearing the noble and generous traits which he ascribed to the traditional communal environment, were often idealized. The plot of *The Foundations* became badly confused toward the end.

Despite these flaws, Zlatovratsky was important for his portrayal of village life. In *The Foundations* and in his articles for a number of the populist journals he provided urban readers with a more accurate portrayal of peasant life than any previous writer. His reproduction of the details of village life, mores, and speech created for urban readers a vivid and complex world.

Bibliography: The major writings of Zlatovratskii are *Ustoi. Istoriia odnoi derevni* (M., 1951); *Vospominaniia* (M., 1956); and *Sobranie sochinenii*, 3 vols. (M., 1897). In English see Richard Wortman, *The Crisis of Russian Populism* (Cambridge, England, 1967), especially ch. 4.

George N. Rhyne

ZOLOTOE RUNO (1906-1910). In English, The Golden Fleece. A monthly literature and art journal financed and published by the Moscow millionaire Nikolai Petrovich Riabushinsky. The journal brought together the symbolists in literature and all varieties of modernism in the fine arts. It also intended to show the distinctive character of the Russian "fin de siècle" and its closeness to national traditions.

Zolotoe Runo appeared shortly after the first Russian revolution of 1905 and reflected the contradictions and frustrations of that time. It conveyed the aspirations of the artists and writers to escape from political and social problems and to create art as an expression of the spirit and an appreciation of beauty in a world of bloody conflicts. In contrast to the journals of the nineteenth century which preached social ideas, Zolotoe Runo expressed the idea of art not only as art but also as a way to change life through beauty. It encouraged its readers to treasure pure aesthetic values, and its articles tended toward the mystical and spiritual, lacking the analytical and scholarly emphasis of its predecessors.

Riabushinsky, a man of extravagance and admiration for beauty, published the journal in the most fashionable way. Even the publishing house, situated in an old wooden building on Novinsky Boulevard, was strikingly elegant. One of the concerns of the editors was the strict relevance of illustration to text. The visual appearance of every issue of Zolotoe Runo was designed by the most innovative artistry and was richly decorated. Its printing and layout, its unusual paper and fine reproductions, the decorative graphic images of garlands, acacia leaves and spouting fountains, infants and female forms, the title pages, and the vignettes—all these made the journal especially expressive. Thus the first issue appeared in a large square format with parallel texts in Russian and French with vignettes made by Riabushinsky himself, who often contributed to the journal as both an artist and a poet under the pseudonym N. Shinsky.

Zolotoe Runo did not have a clear program and did not openly oppose other artistic magazines. Its credo was tolerance and the free expression of different points of view. Unlike the many publications that clearly favored literature, Zolotoe Runo gave its main attention to the fine arts. Many of the most brilliant artists of the time contributed to the journal at different periods. The new magazine employed the talent of many members of the St. Petersburg World of Art group, artists such as Aleksandr Nikolaevich Benois, Konstantin Andreevich Somov and Lev Samoilovich Bakst along with such Moscow artists as Mikhail Aleksandrovich Vrubel and Ivan Yakovlevich Bilibin. The followers of Viktor Borisov-Musatov, the young symbolists of the Blue Rose (Golubaia Roza) group—Pavel Varfolomeevich Kuznetsov, Martiros Sergeevich Sarian and others—also were represented. The artists Nikolai Konstantinovich Roerich and Mikalous Chiurlionis and such popular art critics as Sergei Konstantinovich Makovsky and Nikolai Vrangel were contributors to the journal as well. The literary section featured the writings of Aleksandr Aleksandrovich Blok, Valerii Yakovlevich Briusov, Konstantin Dmitrievich Balmont, Andrei Bely, Dmitry Sergeevich Merezhkovski, Viacheslav Ivanovich Ivanov, Aleksei Mikhailovich Remizov, Fedor Kuzmich Sologub and others. Great attention was paid to modern music, including the works of such composers as Aleksandr Nikolaevich Scriabin. In addition to its interest in fine arts, the magazine published materials about decorative art and industrial design.

Zolotoe Runo supported everything innovative in Russian and foreign contemporary art and presented it in an original way. Monographic issues dedicated to the most distinctive artists and groups of the time became a tradition. Special editions were devoted to Vrubel and Borisov-Musatov, the leaders of symbolism. Other issues of the journal introduced to the public the world of allusions and presentiments of the Blue Rose group—the romantic fantasies of Roerich and the tender emotionality of Sergei Yurievich Sudeikin. A great many artistic works were created especially for the journal under the influence of Riabushinsky himself. He commissioned portraits of symbolist writers from various artists, including Valentin Aleksandrovich Serov, Somov, Boris Mikhailovich Kustodiev, and others. The most striking of these portraits were those of the poets Andrei Bely by Bakst (1906) and Valerii Briusov by Vrubel (1907).

It would be difficult to overestimate the role of Zolotoe Runo in popularizing all kinds of past and contemporary Russian and foreign art. For example, in 1907 it published thirty-nine works of the nineteenth-century artist Aleksei

Gavrilovich Venetsianov and pictures of his followers accompanied by articles about the Venetsianov school. Pictures of French artists and writers were featured also, including translations of Vincent Van Gogh's letters, fragments from Paul Gauguin's "Noa" and critical articles about them.

The exhibitions of modern art organized by the journal were extremely popular—Blue Rose in 1907, Wreath (Venok) in 1908, the famous Salon of the Zolotoe Runo in 1908. The exhibitions in January and December of 1909 displayed the stylized and vivid works of the neoprimitivists Mikhail Fedorovich Larionov and Natalia Sergeevna Goncharova and 197 modern French paintings, including works by Van Gogh, Paul Cèzanne, Henri Matisse and Gauguin.

Long-smoldering differences among contributors to the journal eventually reached the point where in mid-1907 many of them left and moved to the magazine Vesy (Scales), an old rival of Zolotoe Runo. The main point of contention between the two journals concerned their different understanding of symbolism. Vesy understood symbolism to be purely an artistic method, while to Zolotoe Runo it was a total philosophy which included even religious aspects. The leaders of the new Zolotoe Runo group were Blok, Ivanov, and Georgii Ivanovich Chulkov, but it was the mystical-anarchist philosophy of Chulkov, who became the literary editor, which came to be associated with the journal in the public mind.

Over its lifetime Zolotoe Runo played an important role as a catalyst in Russian cultural life and a champion of innovation in the arts.

See Also: MODERNISM IN RUSSIA.

Bibliography: William Richardson, *"Zolotoe Runo" and Russian Modernism* (Ann Arbor, 1986); V. Lobanov, *Kanuny* (M., 1968); A. Rusakova, *Pavel Kuznetsov* (L., 1977); M. Kiselev, "Graphic Design and Russian Art Journals of the Early Twentieth Century," *The Journal of Decorative and Propaganda Arts*, Vol. 11 (Winter 1989); B. Rozenthal, "'Zolotoe Runo' and Russian Modernism," *American Historical Review*, Vol. 93, No. 3 (1988); D.M. Bethea, "'Zolotoe Runo' and Russian Modernism," *Slavic and East European Journal*, Vol. 33, No. 1 (Spring 1989), 5.

Musya M. Glants

ZUSKIN, VENIAMIN (BENJAMIN) LVOVICH (1899-1952). Jewish Soviet actor and director. Leading member of the Jewish intellectual and cultural community and member of the internationally known State Jewish Theater (GOSET).

Zuskin was born in a small Lithuanian town where he was influenced by the local community of actors during his childhood. In 1921 he enrolled in the theater school of the State Jewish Theater, then called the State Jewish Chamber Theater (GOSEKT). After only a few months the talented Zuskin became a member of the theater's troupe and made his theatrical debut in a production of Sholem Aleichem's classic Salience. His first starring role was in Abraham Goldfaden's musical The Sorceress (1922). Noted for his musical talent and improvisational skill, Zuskin played numerous parts in dramas, plays, musical productions, and revues on the stage of GOSET. Many of these displayed the wide range of Zuskin's particular talents since they employed elements of pantomime and dance.

As a dramatic actor Zuskin extensively researched his roles, sketching pictures of his impressions and often searching for live models on which to base his portrayals. Despite his capacity for humor and lyricism, he was also a master of transformation. He displayed this talent in a 1930 production of David Bergelson's The Deaf Man, in which he played the role of Iosele Bobtses, an imperious sponger.

Beginning in 1929 and for most of the rest of his career Zuskin was the theatrical partner of Solomon Mikhailovich Mikhoels (1890-1948), who was by then chief director of GOSET, as well as a celebrated actor. It is important to note the significance of GOSET. While it was indeed a theater devoted to Jewish cultural traditions, its artistic achievements extended well beyond ethnic priorities, and it occupied an important place within the context of world theater. For example, one of the most famous and successful collaborations of Mikhoels and Zuskin took place in 1935 when GOSET staged a performance of Shakespeare's King Lear, directed by Mikhoels who played Lear to Zuskin's Fool. This production, at the time highly acclaimed and credited as a new reading of Shakespeare, continues to be noteworthy in the curriculum of modern theater studies.

In 1945 Zuskin and Mikhoels received the Stalin prize as actor and director, respectively, in a play based on Jewish folklore entitled Freilechs. Zuskin accepted the award on behalf of all Soviet Jewish people.

Both Zuskin and Mikhoels fell victims to Stalin's terror during the 1940s. In January 1948 Mikhoels was reported to have been killed in a traffic accident in Minsk. After Mikhoels's death Zuskin took over as head of a weakened GOSET. Its subsidies were reduced substantially and it was not permitted to stage as many performances as previously. The members of the Jewish intellectual and cultural community regarded Mikhoels's death with suspicion, especially after Zuskin, too, "disappeared."

In September 1948 Zuskin was forced to sign a document in which he promised not to leave Moscow. Shortly afterwards he was hospitalized under a pretext and moved to Lubianka prison while in a drug-induced sleep. By April 1949 the State Jewish Theater had been dissolved.

Zuskin, along with other Jewish literary figures who were arrested falsely for an alleged plot to separate Crimea from the rest of the Soviet Union, remained in Lubianka prison for several years. They were tried fraudulently between 11 and 18 July 1952, and executed the following month.

Bibliography: A.N. Anastafiev, et al. eds., Istoriia sovetskogo dramaticheskogo teatra v shesti tomakh, 6 vols. (M., 1971); P.A. Markov, et al. eds., Teatral'naia entsiklopediia, Vol. 2 (M., 1963); Solomon Mikhailovich Mikhoels, Stat'i, besedy, rechi (M., 1964); Yehoshua A. Gilboa, The Black Years of Soviet Jewry, 1939-1953, trans. by Yosef Shachter and Dov Ben-Abba (Boston, 1971); Louis Rapoport, Stalin's War Against the Jews (New York, 1990).

Therese M. Malhame

ZVENIGOROD. City located on the banks of the Moscow River, 37 miles (60 km) east of Moscow. It lies on the old road to Smolensk, Lithuania, and Poland. In medieval times it was a major appanage (udel) of the grand princes of Moscow. It was important both for trade and as an outpost defending Moscow.

Zvenigorod is the second oldest town in the Moscow area. Archeological excavations suggest that it was populated as early as the eleventh century, but the first written record of it dates from 1339 (Tikhomirov, p. 5, says 1328) in the testament of Grand Prince Ivan I (Kalita) of Moscow (1328-1341).

The early history of Zvenigorod illustrates the change in political concepts which occurred during the so-called appanage period of Russian history, during which Moscow became the dominant power in Russia. For roughly a century Zvenigorod was used as an appanage territory. It was given, along with other territories, including at times parts of Moscow itself, to the junior sons of the grand princes of Moscow. This practice harked back to the older Kievan tradition of viewing territory as property of the clan, rather than of a single individual. For example Kalita left Zvenigorod, parts of Moscow and its customs revenues, as well as assorted villages to his second son, also named Ivan. Zvenigorod was reunited with the rest of Moscow's territory in 1353, when upon the death of his elder brother Semen "The Proud" (1341-1353), Ivan succeeded him as prince of Moscow.

This prince, Ivan II of Moscow, died in 1359. He left the major share of his property to his ten-year-old son Dmitry "Donskoy" (1359-1389). Ivan II bequeathed Zvenigorod to Dmitry's younger brother, who also was named Ivan. When he died childless it reverted to Dmitry Donskoy. It is possible that Donskoy considered his deceased brother Ivan's lands to constitute an integral territory, because in his own testament he left them to his own second son, Yury Dmitrievich, who ruled it from 1389 to 1434.

During the fourteenth century Zvenigorod became one of the most thickly populated towns of Muscovy, as people fled there from areas ravaged by the raids of the Tatars. Despite the fact that it too was devastated by the Tatars under Tokhtamysh in 1382 and under Edigei in 1408, Zvenigorod continued to grow. It became a center for production of pottery and metal-working, and it was noted for its bonecarving and leather handicrafts.

It is likely that this growing wealth and influence inspired Yury Dmitrievich to make Zvenigorod his residence, unlike his predecessors, who preferred to remain in Moscow. Zvenigorod flourished under Yury Dmitrievich, who built churches there and surrounded the city with stone walls.

This same Yury Dmitrievich set off a major civil conflict, which raged for a quarter century and for a time drastically weakened the power of the Muscovite grand princes. When his elder brother, Vasily I of Moscow, died in 1425, Yury Dmitrievich contested his will, which left Moscow and the princely title to Vasily's son, Vasily II (1425-1462). Yury Dmitrievich based his claims on the older tradition, begun three centuries earlier in Kiev, according to which the surviving senior brother inherited the lands and titles of the deceased. That Yury Dmitrievich failed to dispossess his nephew is held by most historians to indicate that the idea of property as patrimony, handed down from father to son, had won out over the older clan-based concept. His pretensions were rejected by the boyars of Moscow, the Church, and by the khan of the Golden Horde, who still claimed dominion over Russia and held the right to invest the grand princes in office. The Golden Horde was riven by factionalism at this time, and its voice did not command obedience as it had in the previous century. Yury Dmitrievich refused to accept the verdict and began a contest for Moscow. Upon his death in 1434 his sons, Vasily the Squint (Kosoy) and Dmitry Sheimiaka, continued the struggle until the death of the latter in 1453. In this epic conflict Vasily II lost Moscow twice and was captured and blinded before eventually emerging the victor.

In the meantime Zvenigorod, won by Vasily II in this struggle, was given to his ally Vasily of Serpukhov. In 1456 Vasily II quarreled with him and seized his lands, including Zvenigorod.

When Vasily II's violent reign ended with his death in 1462, his eldest son Ivan III (1462-1505) inherited the largest share of his lands. Zvenigorod along with other lands went to the third son of Vasily II, Andrei the Elder. Andrei and his three other brothers resented the growing power of Ivan III as he successfully "gathered in" the Russian lands. They supported him in some of his campaigns, particularly the conquest of Novgorod, but they received little reward for their services. In 1491 Andrei the Elder refused to aid Ivan against the Tatars, for which Ivan imprisoned him in Moscow. When Andrei died in 1494 Ivan seized his lands, and Zvenigorod reverted again to Moscow.

Zvenigorod passed out of the direct line of succession of the Muscovite princes for the last time when Ivan III willed it to his second surviving son, Yury, in 1505. Because he died without children, it reverted to Vasily III (1505-1533).

Like many cities in the Moscow area Zvenigorod was affected by the Time of Troubles (1598-1612). The rebel forces of Ivan Isaevich Bolotnikov passed through on their way to Moscow in 1606, inciting peasant rebellions as they went. The troops of the First and Second False Dmitry passed through the region. The city was captured by the Poles, and the Polish pretender Wladyslaw resided there for a time. Zvenigorod suffered enormous damage from these events; in the 1620s only twenty houses remained standing.

Zvenigorod never recovered its political significance, but in the 1650s it gained new importance as a religious center. The Savvino-Storozhevsky Monastery, founded in 1398 at a distance of .9 miles (1.5 km) from Zvenigorod, was a favorite retreat of Tsar Alexis (1645-1676). In the 1650s the monastery was greatly expanded and embellished on his orders through construction of the tsar's palace (1650-1654), the tsarina's palace (1650-1652), the refectory (1652-1654), and the Trinity Church (1652), as well as the Preobrazhensky Church and a bell tower, both constructed during the 1650s. Between 1650 and 1654 a new, powerful set of walls and towers was built, so that the monastery could serve as a fortress protecting Moscow. Under Alexis' patronage Savvino-Storozhevsky became one of the richest monasteries in the country. A complete restoration of this striking architectural ensemble was still going on in mid-1992.

In 1708 Zvenigorod was included in Moscow province (guberniia) and in 1781 it became a county seat (uezdnyi gorod). Aside from its function as a religious center, it became a typical rustic town. Its population in 1787 was 970 and in 1860, 1720. Although some local handicrafts developed, the economy of the town and surrounding region remained predominantly agricultural during the nineteenth century.

During the Soviet period the town grew substantially; in 1923 its population was 2,693 and in 1970, about ten thousand. It also received many modern facilities: running water, electricity, schools, a stadium, and a hospital. Its economy is based on agriculture, especially dairy farming and chicken breeding; the area is one of the most important sources of supply for Moscow. Some light industries exist, which produce furniture, clothing, school and office supplies, sports equipment, and toys.

Zvenigorod was most noted in the late twentieth century as a health resort. The absence of heavy industry and the fact that much of the area is forested combine to provide fresh air and a picturesque rustic setting. Sanatoria and other tourist facilities in the area around Zvenigorod, most controlled by official institutions, can serve up to 200,000 vacationers.

Aside from the Savvino-Storozhevsky Monastery, the most impressive of the ancient architectural sites is the Uspensky Cathedral, located on the "Gorodok" (little town), the site of the ancient fortress (kreml) 1.9 miles (3 km) from the present city. Constructed between 1396 and 1399 by Yury Dmitrievich, it retains its original external appearance. It is built of white stone. Its dome, columns, apses, and facades with portals and carved bands are a rare surviving example of early Muscovite architecture.

See Also: APPANAGE PERIOD OF RUSSIAN HISTORY.

Bibliography: Robert Craig Howes, trans. and ed., *The Testaments of the Grand Princes of Moscow* (Ithaca, N.Y., 1967); Aleksandr Evgenievich Presniakov, *The Formation of the Great Russian State* (Chicago, 1970); John L.I. Fennell, *The Emergence of Moscow, 1304-1359* (Berkeley, 1968); George Vernadsky, *A History of Russia*. 5 vols. in 6, Vol. 3, *The Mongols and Russia* (1953) and Vol. 4, *Russia at the Dawn of the Modern Age* (1959); N. Tikhomirov, *Zvenigorod* (M., 1948); A.F. Kruglov, *Zvenigorod. Turbaza marshruty turisticheskikh pokhodov i ekskursii* (M., 1963); S. Borovka, *Zvenigorod i okrestnosti*, 2nd ed. (M., 1970); O. Boiar, et al., *Zvenigorod. Istoriko-kul'turnye pamiatniki Zvenigorodskogo kraia. Putivoditel'* (M., 1974); T.V. Nikolaeva, *Drevnii Zvenigorod. Arkhitektura. Iskusstvo* (M., 1978). Brief surveys can be found in *Bolshaia Sovietskaia Entsyclopediia* and *Entsiklopedicheskii slovar'*, ed. by Ivan E. Andreevsky, et al. 43 vols. in 86 parts (SPb., 1890-1907).

George N. Rhyne

CONTENTS

FROM ACADEMIC INTERNATIONAL PRESS*

*Request catalogs **OP—out of print